GENDER, POWER, LAW & LEADERSHIP

■ ■ ■

Hannah Brenner

Vice Dean for Academic and Student Affairs
Associate Professor of Law
California Western School of Law

Renee Knake

Joanne & Larry Doherty Chair in Legal Ethics
Professor of Law
University of Houston Law Center

AMERICAN CASEBOOK SERIES®

WEST
ACADEMIC
PUBLISHING

American Casebook Series is a trademark registered in the U.S. Patent and Trademark Office.

© 2020 LEG, Inc. d/b/a West Academic
　　　444 Cedar Street, Suite 700
　　　St. Paul, MN 55101
　　　1-877-888-1330

West, West Academic Publishing, and West Academic are trademarks of West Publishing Corporation, used under license.

Printed in the United States of America

ISBN: 978-1-64242-843-8

This book is dedicated to
the women who led before us
and
to our students who will lead on.

ACKNOWLEDGMENTS

A project like this would be impossible without contributions from other authors sharing their writing and images. We thank the following individuals (or their representatives) for granting and securing permission to reprint portions of their work as well as their photographs: Ori Aronson, Julie Ashby, Theresa Beiner, Douglas Branson, Erin Buzuvis, Pat Chew, Kimberle Crenshaw, Denise Cuthbert, Leslie Culver, Elyssa Darling, Richard Delgado, Rangita de Silva de Alwis, Virginia Drachman, Terry Dworkin, Elizabeth Emens, Jessica Fink, Amanda Fricke, MaryAnn Grover, Alex Haslam, Tonja Jacobi, Anthony Kreis, Rebecca K. Lee, Christy Harris Lemak, Justin Levinson, Nancy Levit, Melinda Molina, Paula Monopoli, Elie Mystal, Alexander Nourafshan, Angela Onwuachi-Willig, Abigail Perdue, Dominique Potvin, Carla Pratt, Aarti Ramaswami, Deborah Rhode, Laura Rosenbury, Allen Rostron, Michelle Ryan, Paula Schaeffer, Cindy Schipani, Dylan Schweers, Carrie Sharlow, J. Clay Smith, Janet Stanton, Jonathan Stubbs, Jennifer Thorpe-Moscon, Dnika Travis, Saurabh Vishnubhakat, Alice Wooley, Robert Yablon, Danielle Young, and Fiona Zammit. All other images in this book are either part of the public domain or used with credit noted as appropriate. Footnotes originally appearing in excerpted material have been omitted to aid in readability, but can be easily located via the citation to the original publication appearing at the beginning of each excerpt. When other material is omitted from the original publication, it is indicated with * * *.

We offer special thanks to the wonderful people at West Academic for their support of this project: Pam Chandler, Staci Herr, Louis Higgins, Laura Holle, and Megan Putler. Exceptional research assistance was provided by Kirby Swartz and Melia Thompson-Dudiak, and Donna Kelley was instrumental in helping us finalize the text for publication. Thanks also to our respective law schools, California Western School of Law and the University of Houston Law Center, for supporting both this project and our teaching of seminars on gender, power, law, and leadership. We are especially grateful to our students over the years for their feedback on portions of material and their enthusiasm for learning about these issues.

Neither of us could do what we do without the support of wonderful life partners—thanks for joining us on this ride, Wallace Jefferson and Mark Johnson. Most important, we thank our children for making the world a better place every day as they each lead in their own unique ways. Aidan, Grace, Isaac, James, and Willow—you've got this!

HANNAH BRENNER
RENEE KNAKE

INTRODUCTION

Welcome

In addition to co-authoring this casebook, we have been friends and colleagues for more than a decade. Our professional collaborations include different articles, books, events, presentations, and projects that all address gender inequality in the legal profession. Our first article, *Rethinking Gender Equality in the Legal Profession's Pipeline to Power: A Study on Media Coverage of Supreme Court Nominees*, was a winner of the 2012 Association of American Law Schools New Voices in Gender Paper Competition. Following the publication of this article, we hosted a symposium with the Michigan State Law Review, *Gender and the Legal Profession's Pipeline to Power,* which engaged scholars and others to contemplate the ongoing inequality among lawyers. Many of the participants are featured in this book, several of whom have gone on to achieve significant leadership roles including becoming law school deans. Our collaboration continued as we wrote an essay about women who were shortlisted—but not selected—to the United States Supreme Court, which we subsequently developed into a book, SHORTLISTED: WOMEN IN THE SHADOWS OF THE SUPREME COURT (NYU Press 2020). And most recently, we are thrilled to welcome you to the inaugural edition of our casebook, Gender, Power, Law & Leadership, which brings our scholarly work back into higher education, appealing directly to students just like you who are in the midst of their studies to become lawyers or pursue other professional paths.

Hannah is the Vice Dean for Academic and Student Affairs and Associate Professor of Law at California Western School of Law in San Diego. She received her JD from the University of Iowa College of Law. Renee is a Professor of Law and the holds the Joanne and Larry Doherty Chair in Legal Ethics at the University of Houston Law Center. She received her JD from the University of Chicago Law School.

We invite you to join us on the journey to learn about leadership in law and beyond, and to help change the landscape to be one more inclusive of diverse experiences and perspectives. We hope you find this work as inspiring to read and engage with as we did in writing it.

—Hannah Brenner and Renee Knake

Goals

Women enter professional life in relatively equal numbers to men, but they remain outside of the structures of power—in fields like the corporate world, higher education, the judiciary, law firms, and politics—in the United States and beyond. This reality is even worse for women of color. Despite attempts to change the landscape, progress has stalled. Our overarching goal in this book is to expose this inequality through telling the stories of women leaders and curating in one central place significant excerpts of the rich scholarly literature that exists in this field.

When Hannah first created the Gender, Power, Law, and Leadership seminar in 2010, it came to fruition in large part due to the observation that law school, as the place where new lawyers are trained and educated, did not address the rampant inequality that plagued the profession's leadership. It seemed intuitive that law schools should be educating students about these realities.

It is important to make clear that this book is NOT about *how* to lead. You can find dozens if not hundreds of books to help you cultivate leadership skills, and there are an abundance of leadership courses, continuing education programs, and even certificate and degree programs at many universities that focus on developing these competencies. Instead, we seek to inspire you and impart numerous important leadership lessons through nine carefully curated chapters. Each has a very intentional focus, all featuring the stories of women leaders in highlight boxes, along with excerpts of case opinions, articles, and other materials. This book is about the historical and institutional barriers that prevent women, and especially minority women, from ascending into leadership roles in the legal profession and how we can best work to transcend these barriers.

How to Use This Book

There are several ways this book might be used. We primarily envision adoption in its entirely in upper-level law school seminars that address issues of gender and law. There is an abundance of material that can easily fill an entire semester's worth of reading. Faculty can also select one or more chapters to incorporate into other specialty courses, or single chapters could be assigned outside of the classroom during events like law school orientation. Although the focus of the text is on lawyers and the legal profession, much of the content has applicability beyond this context including corporate settings, politics, and many other fields. The book is also relevant in courses that are a part of other undergraduate and advanced degree programs in a wide range of disciplines.

How We Designed the Book

Collectively, we have taught courses on gender, law, and leadership over a dozen times spanning the last ten-plus years at three different law schools, in an undergraduate honors college, and an undergraduate women's studies and political science department. We have also advised student organizations, facilitated extra-curricular women's leadership workshops, and spoken at dozens of professional and academic conferences and student events. We know from first-hand experience the stark void that exists among undergraduate, graduate, and legal academic offerings for a book like this, which is why we devoted our time and energy to write it. Each semester teaching our seminars in the past, we painstakingly pieced together articles, cases, and our own original analysis to provide students with necessary reading and discussion guides. We frequently field questions from other faculty and scholars assigned to teach gender courses seeking relevant materials. Our students repeatedly validate the importance of this curricular offering, some citing it as the most important course they have taken in law school. We are thrilled that a handful of our students have taken the ideas from our courses seriously and have published their scholarly work.[1] Some have even pursued academic paths themselves.

A number of casebooks cover traditional material on women, gender, and feminism, but none embrace the focus described here. The earliest courses on women and the law date back to the 1970s,[2] but after the initial creation of casebooks for these courses, teaching materials have not kept pace with the pedagogical needs that appropriately facilitate student preparation and classroom discussion for modern leadership. Traditional

---

[1] *See, e.g.*, Janee T. Prince, *"Can I Touch Your Hair?" Exploring Double Binds and the Black Tax in Law School*, 20 UNIV. OF PENN. J. OF L. AND SOCIAL CHANGE 29 (2017); Abigail A. Rury, *The Pipeline to the Legal Profession: Perspectives from Michigan State University College of Law*, 2012 MICH. ST. L. REV. 1717 (2012).

[2] For a comprehensive and historical discussion of women's entrance into the legal profession, see Robin West, *Women in the Legal Academy,* 87 FORDHAM L. REV. 977 (2018).

casebooks on feminism and gender introduce students to a range of topics and perspectives, and identify the most important arguments and cases that support them.

Our book, by contrast, is written in direct response to the glaring omission of women from positions of power and leadership. The book is intentional and comprehensive in its coverage; it begins in the past with a historical overview of early organizing for women's rights, before offering an overview of gender and leadership generally, and exploring many of the ways that inequality, discrimination, and bias manifest. It then shifts focus to cover different professional sectors and concludes with strategies and solutions for change, ultimately equipping the reader to develop future reforms. The book contains excerpts of legal cases and scholarly articles designed to facilitate discussion based upon carefully crafted questions. We expose readers to various theories of leadership and law, and pursue an ongoing exploration of intersections of gender, race, class, power, and law throughout all of the chapters. We also identify post-feminism discrimination that the legal system does not yet address, including emotional taxation, gender sidelining, the glass cliff, imposter syndrome, life admin, shortlisting, work wives, and other gender-based barriers. As one way to educate, inspire, and even mentor readers, we rely on the use of narrative; to this end, the stories of transformative leaders in the profession are woven throughout the text. The casebook concludes with concrete guidance for individual readers in their navigation of professional lives, pursuit of leadership paths, as well as policy reform proposals to create a world of leaders who most accurately reflect the public they serve.

Why All the Photographs?

As Sandra Day O'Connor explained in a 1990 speech, "The first step to getting power is to become visible to others."[3] Following her sage advice, and as a nod to her, we endeavored to make the authors of the works excerpted here visible by including their photographs. We believe that the identity of the authors is as important as—and in some instances *more* important than—the substance of their writing. Accordingly, we prefaced each excerpt with a brief description about the author and/or context of the writing along with a photograph, to the extent we could. (Some authors declined permission to reproduce their image here.) Understanding and practicing this technique, discerning the author in addition to distilling the message, is one we believe will serve you well as you navigate various leadership roles. There are a few important caveats, however. First, space constraints led us to be faced with very difficult decisions about *which* women to feature in the highlight boxes, especially given the growing number of women who have achieved significant accomplishments.

---

[3] Ruth Bader Ginsburg, Associate Justice, Supreme Court of the United States, American Sociological Association Annual Meeting Montreal (Aug. 11, 2006) (quoting Justice O'Connor).

Assuredly, for every woman we profile, there are dozens more we could have easily selected. To address this shortcoming, you will find in the very last pages a long list of autobiographies and biographies about transformative female leaders in the law. This bibliography is primarily made up of books that our students have read and written about over the past ten years. Second, our selection of the women throughout the pages that follow is informed by our desire to make their identities known in large part because they have blazed paths once thought impossible. This does not mean, however, that their inclusion in this book means that they are perfect people or that we agree with every decision they have made or every position they take. Third, we faced a similar dilemma in selecting articles and cases. We have done our best to include a diverse sampling, and welcome feedback about what to include (or not include) in future editions.

A Roadmap for Reading this Casebook

Chapter 1 (Defining the Leadership Landscape) investigates diversity in leadership and examines the implications of gender and gender roles, schemas, and stereotyping of "traditional" leaders. Rather than proceeding with the automatic assumption that gender does indeed matter in leadership, the chapter explores the myriad reasons why diversity in leadership is a critical goal. In doing so, it looks to Supreme Court decisions in the affirmative action context, and also includes excerpts from a range of scholarly works that wrestle with this all-important question.

Chapter 2 (Historical Perspectives on Women Leaders) offers important background surrounding the dismantling of separate spheres that for so long kept some women relegated to the home, outside of professional life, and without access to power structures. Beginning with the critical drafting of the Declaration of Sentiments in 1848 as the first official document that addressed women's rights in this country, the chapter focuses on the suffrage movement and the passage of the 19th amendment, and the Equal Rights Amendment. The chapter explores the emergence of women into professional life and leadership roles in a variety of contexts, and acknowledges the racial tensions involved in this history, which continue today. Relying to some extent on biographies of early women leaders, including the women who formed the first international women lawyer's organization (The Equity Club), the chapter helps readers understand how women have emerged as leaders today and highlights some of the tools and strategies they used to navigate their way into positions previously unavailable to them.

Chapter 3 (Intersectionality in Leadership) explores the intersection of multiple parts of our identity like ability, class, ethnicity, gender, geography, race, religion, sexual orientation, socio-economic status, and more that are part of systemic bias and discrimination. Scholars over the past several decades have developed new genres of study like critical race theory, and this chapter explores their work relying on an expansive framework.

Chapter 4 (The Glass Cliff, Emotional Tax, Shortlisting, Life Admin, #MeToo and Other Post-Feminism Discrimination) identifies many forms of bias and discrimination that are not readily apparent as impediments to advancement. It has long been understood that many women work full-time jobs both in and outside the home, documented as "the second shift" or "double-binds." But recent scholarship identifies new impediments, including the administrative burdens placed on women and the selection of women for advancement only when organizations are already in trouble. For example, this latter phenomenon, termed the "glass cliff," played out with Carly Fiorina's stint at Hewlett Packard and Marissa Mayer at Yahoo. It is also not well known that while women are indeed being selected for corporate leadership roles more than before, they are also being forced out of these roles at higher rates than men. Finally, the #MeToo movement has brought to the forefront of our collective public consciousness the reality of workplace sexual harassment and violence that many women have lived with for years.

Chapter 5 (Leadership in the Legal Profession) considers how the legal profession is the gatekeeper of equality, yet it has not achieved this equality internally for its own members. The upper echelons of law practice are still dominated by white men who retain power and control. This chapter explores the historical entrance of women into the profession and considers their contemporary existence as they have navigated the pipeline to power across sectors.

Chapter 6 (Political Leadership) contemplates how while the United States has never had a female president—other nations have more longstanding traditions of female leaders in their top political positions. The Prime Minister of New Zealand, Jacinda Ardern, recently shocked the world with her revelation that she was pregnant . . . and planned to stay in office! The field of women and politics has been the subject of study by political scientists who explore questions like why women don't run for office and the impact of women on committees, lawmaking, etc. This chapter explores the history of women's political leadership from past to present, while considering the impact of women in political leadership roles.

Chapter 7 (Corporate Leadership) explores the conundrum that despite research supporting the idea that the presence of women in corporate leadership roles can increase the financial performance of corporations, women remain under-represented in corporate leadership roles. This chapter also examines gender disparity both in the boardroom and at the helm of corporate life, whether as CEO or in the general counsel's office.

Chapter 8 (Leadership in Other Contexts: Athletics, Higher Education, Medicine, Military, Science and More) recognizes that although some differences exist, many of the gendered leadership dynamics that exist in the legal profession are also present in other professional contexts. This chapter focuses on the ways in which gender and leadership intersect in other fields and draws out lessons to apply to the legal profession specifically.

Finally, **Chapter 9 (A Guide for Restructuring the Pipeline to Power)** challenges some of the common solutions that have been promulgated over the past decades and offers new ideas to break through barriers and transcend the pervasive inequality that persists across professions. This chapter urges a restructuring of the pipeline to power, rather than an assimilation to the dominant culture. More than mere recitation of the common advice, we push you to critically analyze and evaluate reforms as well as formulate your own solutions.

Please share your experiences with us. We welcome your thoughts and feedback—Hannah Brenner hbrenner@cwsl.edu or Renee Knake rknake@uh.edu.

TABLE OF CONTENTS

TABLE OF CASES

GENDER, POWER, LAW & LEADERSHIP

CHAPTER 1

DEFINING THE LEADERSHIP LANDSCAPE

■ ■ ■

INTRODUCTION

As the Introduction to this casebook observed, there is no doubt that the legal profession lacks diversity in its most prestigious positions of power. This phenomenon is not unique to law, however, and is in fact present across professional sectors. We begin here by highlighting a few examples of this lack of diversity, and then the chapters that follow will dive into greater detail. In the nation's tripartite federal governmental structure, women's representation is dismal across all three branches. As of 2019, in the Executive Branch, the United States has never had a female president or vice-president. In Congress, 23.7 percent of the 535 members are women.[1] And on the Supreme Court, while one-third of justices during this same time period are women,[2] less than one percent of all the justices have been female since the Court's inception. At the state level, across the country, women comprise only 28.7 percent of legislatures.[3] A recent study by Catalyst, the *Missing Pieces Report*, demonstrates how the make-up of corporate boards of directors in the Fortune 500 are still dominated by men. As but one example, in 2018, 4.6 percent of Fortune 500 corporate board seats were held by minority women, with white women occupying more than four times this number of seats, at 17.9 percent.[4] The legal academy has recently seen an increase in the number of women serving as law school deans, with the number hovering around thirty-two percent, though this is a rapidly changing landscape.[5] Other professional sectors look very similar. Comprehensive research reports like the American Association of

---

[1] *Women in the U.S. Congress: 2019*, CTR. FOR AM. WOMEN AND POLITICS, https://www.cawp.rutgers.edu/women-us-congress-2019.

[2] Sital Kalantry, *Women in Robes*, AM. QUARTERLY (2012), https://www.americasquarterly.org/women-in-robes.

[3] *Women in State Legislatures for 2019*, NATIONAL CONF. OF STATE LEGISLATORS, www.ncsl.org/legislators-staff/legislators/womens-legislative-network/women-instate-legislatures-for-2019.aspx.

[4] *Missing Pieces Report: The 2018 Board Diversity Census of Women and Minorities on Fortune 500 Boards,* https://www.catalyst.org/wp-content/uploads/2019/01/missing_pieces_report_01152019_final.pdf.

[5] Laura Padilla, *Women Law Deans, Gender Sidelining and Presumptions of Incompetence*, 34 BERKELEY J. GENDER, LAW & JUSTICE ___ (forthcoming, 2020).

University Women report, *Barriers and Bias: The Status of Women in Leadership*, provide extensive data supporting this reality.[6]

All of these examples illustrate what is known as "positional" leadership. In other words, what constitutes leadership is defined by the people who occupy roles at the top of the professional hierarchy. In focusing on these kinds of leaders, we do not imply that leaders cannot be found elsewhere.

To be sure, there are many ways to exhibit leadership informally, within groups, and even without a formal title. These discussions, however, are outside the parameters of this book, because we are not attempting to advise you on *how* to lead. There are many books and courses and professionals who can provide that kind of guidance. (The biography of transformational female leaders included in the Appendix of this book is an excellent resource.)

One of the primary goals in this chapter is to help you develop a sense of whether having diverse representation in positions of power matters. To begin, we urge you to consider one of the fundamental 'so what' questions. What difference does it make if the upper echelons of power in a given organization or social structure are dominated predominately by white men, or expressed differently, if these leadership roles exclude women and minorities? We think it is imperative to give you the opportunity to consider the question for yourself. Assuming that it is an inquiry you answer in the affirmative, and we speculate that for many if not all of you this is the case, we next urge you to consider the more difficult question: *why* does diversity in leadership matter? And what are the problems and pitfalls that arise when women and minorities are kept from accessing educational opportunities or attaining these coveted and highly valued positional leadership posts?

To aid in your exploration of these questions, we begin with an excerpt from *Fisher v. University of Texas at Austin,* a Supreme Court opinion that considered the constitutionality of the way admissions decisions were made at the University of Texas. While this is an opinion typically studied as an affirmative action case in a Constitutional Law course, we include it here not to debate that specific issue, but instead to illustrate the importance of diversity as opined by members of the nation's highest court. After reading the *Fisher* case, we invite you to read several of the amicus briefs written in support of the University of Texas and its desire to create a diverse student body. The chapter also considers whether more diversity in leadership impacts the public good and explores some of the barriers that impede women's progress. In the second part of this chapter we present the idea of learning through stories. We are inspired by the use of narrative and storytelling as a way to learn about the women who have forged paths

---

[6]   *Barriers and Bias: The Status of Women in Leadership*, AAUW (2016).

and trailblazed their way into leadership roles. Their lives, which are often overlooked in historical accountings, can help guide and inspire you in navigating your own professional paths.

Credit: University of Chicago Photographic Archive, [apf1-04392], Special Collections Research Center, University of Chicago Library

After several years of law practice, **Soia Mentschikoff** devoted herself to leadership in legal education. In 1947, she became the first female professor at Harvard Law School before women were even admitted as students. In 1951, the University of Chicago Law School hired her as its first female professor. She became the first permanent woman Dean of Miami Law School in 1974. (Minnette Massey was technically the first as an interim dean). During that time, Mentschikoff was named President of the Association of American Law Schools, the first woman to hold the role. While she was not particularly known as an activist in women's causes, under her leadership changes were made to better accommodate women, for example modifying the timing of the AALS annual meeting to the week after winter holidays instead of between them. She also mentored future female leaders. As one example, included in her archives are letters exchanged with former student Carol Mosely Braun, who would go on to become the first African American female U.S. Senator in 1993. Mentschikoff was also an elected member of the prestigious American Law Institute (ALI) and was instrumental in drafting the Uniform Commercial Code (UCC).

THOUGHT QUESTIONS

As you read the articles excerpted below, consider the following questions:

1. What is diversity? Why might diversity be an important component of leadership?

2. Take some time to read through the amicus curiae briefs submitted on behalf of the University of Texas in the *Fisher* case, available here: https://tarlton.law.utexas.edu/c.php?g=457795&p=3128940. How do these various interest groups express the value of diversity?

3.   Generate a list of people who you consider to be leaders. Who are they and how do they lead? Is your list inclusive of gender, racial, and ethnic diversity? What are other forms of diversity that might make a difference in leadership?

4.   What does a leader look like to you? What are some of the qualities that define a leader? How do gender stereotypes inform your perspective or the perspective of others?

5.   Describe some of the barriers that prevent women's advancement into leadership roles. Have you encountered or observed any of these barriers yourself?

6.   How can narrative be used as a tool to inspire and inform leadership? How might narrative help address concerns regarding essentialism? Do you have ideas about how to address competing narratives?

FISHER V. UNIVERSITY OF TEXAS AT AUSTIN

Supreme Court of the United States
136 S.Ct. 2198 (2016)

Abigail Fisher, a white student, applied for college admission to the University of Texas and was not accepted. She sued the university, alleging its consideration of race as a factor in its admissions decisions was unconstitutional under the Equal Protection Clause of the 14th Amendment. The Supreme Court ruled in favor of the University of Texas in a 4–3 opinion written by Justice Kennedy (pictured left).

Opinion

KENNEDY, J.

The Court is asked once again to consider whether the race-conscious admissions program at the University of Texas is lawful under the Equal Protection Clause.

I

The University of Texas at Austin (or University) relies upon a complex system of admissions that has undergone significant evolution over the past two decades. Until 1996, the University made its admissions decisions primarily based on a measure called "Academic Index" (or AI), which it calculated by combining an applicant's SAT score and academic performance in high school. In assessing applicants, preference was given to racial minorities.

In 1996, the Court of Appeals for the Fifth Circuit invalidated this admissions system, holding that any consideration of race in college admissions violates the Equal Protection Clause. See Hopwood v. Texas, 78 F. 3d 932, 934–935, 948.

One year later the University adopted a new admissions policy. Instead of considering race, the University began making admissions decisions based on an applicant's AI and his or her "Personal Achievement Index" (PAI). The PAI was a numerical score based on a holistic review of an application. Included in the number were the applicant's essays, leadership and work experience, extracurricular activities, community service, and other "special characteristics" that might give the admissions committee insight into a student's background. Consistent with Hopwood, race was not a consideration in calculating an applicant's AI or PAI.

The Texas Legislature responded to Hopwood as well. It enacted H. B. 588, commonly known as the Top Ten Percent Law. Tex. Educ. Code Ann. § 51.803 (West Cum. Supp. 2015). As its name suggests, the Top Ten Percent Law guarantees college admission to students who graduate from a Texas high school in the top 10 percent of their class. Those students may choose to attend any of the public universities in the State.

The University implemented the Top Ten Percent Law in 1998. After first admitting any student who qualified for admission under that law, the University filled the remainder of its incoming freshman class using a combination of an applicant's AI and PAI scores—again, without considering race.

The University used this admissions system until 2003, when this Court decided the companion cases of Grutter v. Bollinger, 539 U.S. 306, and Gratz v. Bollinger, 539 U.S. 244. In Gratz, this Court struck down the University of Michigan's undergraduate system of admissions, which at the time allocated predetermined points to racial minority candidates. See 539 U.S., at 255, 275–276. In Grutter, however, the Court upheld the University of Michigan Law School's system of holistic review—a system that did not mechanically assign points but rather treated race as a relevant feature within the broader context of a candidate's application. See 539 U.S., at 337, 343–344, 123 S.Ct. 2325. In upholding this nuanced use of race, Grutter implicitly overruled Hopwood's categorical prohibition.

In the wake of Grutter, the University embarked upon a year-long study seeking to ascertain whether its admissions policy was allowing it to provide "the educational benefits of a diverse student body . . . to all of the University's undergraduate students." App. 481a–482a (affidavit of N. Bruce Walker ¶ 11 (Walker Aff.)); see also id., at 445a–447a. The University concluded that its admissions policy was not providing these benefits. Supp. App. 24a–25a.

To change its system, the University submitted a proposal to the Board of Regents that requested permission to begin taking race into consideration as one of "the many ways in which [an] academically qualified individual might contribute to, and benefit from, the rich, diverse, and challenging educational environment of the University." Id., at 23a. After the board approved the proposal, the University adopted a new admissions policy to implement it. The University has continued to use that admissions policy to this day.

Although the University's new admissions policy was a direct result of Grutter, it is not identical to the policy this Court approved in that case. Instead, consistent with the State's legislative directive, the University continues to fill a significant majority of its class through the Top Ten Percent Plan (or Plan). Today, up to 75 percent of the places in the freshman class are filled through the Plan. As a practical matter, this 75 percent cap, which has now been fixed by statute, means that, while the Plan continues to be referenced as a "Top Ten Percent Plan," a student actually needs to finish in the top seven or eight percent of his or her class in order to be admitted under this category.

The University did adopt an approach similar to the one in Grutter for the remaining 25 percent or so of the incoming class. This portion of the class continues to be admitted based on a combination of their AI and PAI scores. Now, however, race is given weight as a subfactor within the PAI. The PAI is a number from 1 to 6 (6 is the best) that is based on two primary components. The first component is the average score a reader gives the applicant on two required essays. The second component is a full-file review that results in another 1-to-6 score, the "Personal Achievement Score" or PAS. The PAS is determined by a separate reader, who (1) rereads the applicant's required essays, (2) reviews any supplemental information the applicant submits (letters of recommendation, resumes, an additional optional essay, writing samples, artwork, etc.), and (3) evaluates the applicant's potential contributions to the University's student body based on the applicant's leadership experience, extracurricular activities, awards/honors, community service, and other "special circumstances."

"Special circumstances" include the socioeconomic status of the applicant's family, the socioeconomic status of the applicant's school, the applicant's family responsibilities, whether the applicant lives in a single-parent home, the applicant's SAT score in relation to the average SAT score at the applicant's school, the language spoken at the applicant's home, and, finally, the applicant's race. See App. 218a–220a, 430a.

* * *

Petitioner Abigail Fisher applied for admission to the University's 2008 freshman class. She was not in the top 10 percent of her high school class, so she was evaluated for admission through holistic, full-file review. Petitioner's application was rejected.

Petitioner then filed suit alleging that the University's consideration of race as part of its holistic-review process disadvantaged her and other Caucasian applicants, in violation of the Equal Protection Clause. See U.S. Const., Amdt. 14, § 1 (no State shall "deny to any person within its jurisdiction the equal protection of the laws"). The District Court entered summary judgment in the University's favor, and the Court of Appeals affirmed.

This Court granted certiorari and vacated the judgment of the Court of Appeals, Fisher v. University of Tex. at Austin, 570 U.S. ___ (2013) (Fisher I), because it had applied an overly deferential "good-faith" standard in assessing the constitutionality of the University's program. The Court remanded the case for the Court of Appeals to assess the parties' claims under the correct legal standard.

Without further remanding to the District Court, the Court of Appeals again affirmed the entry of summary judgment in the University's favor. 758 F. 3d 633 (CA5 2014). This Court granted certiorari for a second time, 576 U.S. ___ (2015), and now affirms.

* * *

IV

In seeking to reverse the judgment of the Court of Appeals, petitioner makes four arguments. First, she argues that the University has not articulated its compelling interest with sufficient clarity. According to petitioner, the University must set forth more precisely the level of minority enrollment that would constitute a "critical mass." Without a clearer sense of what the University's ultimate goal is, petitioner argues, a reviewing court cannot assess whether the University's admissions program is narrowly tailored to that goal.

As this Court's cases have made clear, however, the compelling interest that justifies consideration of race in college admissions is not an interest in enrolling a certain number of minority students. Rather, a university may institute a race-conscious admissions program as a means of obtaining "the educational benefits that flow from student body diversity." Fisher I, 570 U.S., at ___ (internal quotation marks omitted); see also Grutter, 539 U.S., at 328. As this Court has said, enrolling a diverse student body "promotes cross-racial understanding, helps to break down racial stereotypes, and enables students to better understand persons of different races." Id., at 330 (internal quotation marks and alteration omitted). Equally important, "student body diversity promotes learning outcomes, and better prepares students for an increasingly diverse workforce and society." Ibid. (internal quotation marks omitted).

* * *

On the other hand, asserting an interest in the educational benefits of diversity writ large is insufficient. A university's goals cannot be elusory or amorphous—they must be sufficiently measurable to permit judicial scrutiny of the policies adopted to reach them.

The record reveals that in first setting forth its current admissions policy, the University articulated concrete and precise goals. On the first page of its 2004 "Proposal to Consider Race and Ethnicity in Admissions," the University identifies the educational values it seeks to realize through its admissions process: the destruction of stereotypes, the " 'promot[ion of] cross-racial understanding,' " the preparation of a student body " 'for an increasingly diverse workforce and society,' " and the " 'cultivat[ion of] a set of leaders with legitimacy in the eyes of the citizenry.' " Supp. App. 1a; see also id., at 69a; App. 314a–315a (deposition of N. Bruce Walker (Walker Dep.)), 478a–479a (Walker Aff. ¶ 4) (setting forth the same goals). Later in Court the proposal, the University explains that it strives to provide an "academic environment" that offers a "robust exchange of ideas, exposure to differing cultures, preparation for the challenges of an increasingly diverse workforce, and acquisition of competencies required of future leaders." Supp. App. 23a. All of these objectives, as a general matter, mirror the "compelling interest" this Court has approved in its prior cases.

The University has provided in addition a "reasoned, principled explanation" for its decision to pursue these goals. Fisher I, *supra*, at ___ (slip op., at 9). The University's 39-page proposal was written following a year-long study, which concluded that "[t]he use of race-neutral policies and programs ha[d] not been successful" in "provid[ing] an educational setting that fosters cross-racial understanding, provid[ing] enlightened discussion and learning, [or] prepar[ing] students to function in an increasingly diverse workforce and society." Supp. App. 25a; see also App. 481a–482a (Walker Aff. ¶¶ 8–12) (describing the "thoughtful review" the University undertook when it faced the "important decision . . . whether or not to use race in its admissions process"). Further support for the University's conclusion can be found in the depositions and affidavits from various admissions officers, all of whom articulate the same, consistent "reasoned, principled explanation." See, e.g., id., at 253a (Ishop Dep.), 314a–318a, 359a (Walker Dep.), 415a–416a (Defendant's Statement of Facts), 478a–479a, 481a–482a (Walker Aff. ¶¶ 4, 10–13). Petitioner's contention that the University's goal was insufficiently concrete is rebutted by the record.

* * *

In addition to this broad demographic data, the University put forward evidence that minority students admitted under the Hopwood regime experienced feelings of loneliness and isolation.

This anecdotal evidence is, in turn, bolstered by further, more nuanced quantitative data. In 2002, 52 percent of undergraduate classes with at least five students had no African-American students enrolled in them, and 27 percent had only one African-American student. Supp. App. 140a. In other words, only 21 percent of undergraduate classes with five or more students in them had more than one African-American student enrolled. Twelve percent of these classes had no Hispanic students, as compared to 10 percent in 1996. Id., at 74a, 140a. Though a college must continually reassess its need for race-conscious review, here that assessment appears to have been done with care, and a reasonable determination was made that the University had not yet attained its goals.

* * *

In short, none of petitioner's suggested alternatives—nor other proposals considered or discussed in the course of this litigation—have been shown to be "available" and "workable" means through which the University could have met its educational goals, as it understood and defined them in 2008. Fisher I, *supra*, at ___ (slip op., at 11). The University has thus met its burden of showing that the admissions policy it used at the time it rejected petitioner's application was narrowly tailored.

* * *

A university is in large part defined by those intangible "qualities which are incapable of objective measurement but which make for greatness." Sweatt v. Painter, 339 U.S. 629, 634 (1950). Considerable deference is owed to a university in defining those intangible characteristics, like student body diversity, that are central to its identity and educational mission. But still, it remains an enduring challenge to our Nation's education system to reconcile the pursuit of diversity with the constitutional promise of equal treatment and dignity. In striking this sensitive balance, public universities, like the States themselves, can serve as "laboratories for experimentation." United States v. Lopez, 514 U.S. 549, 581 (1995) (KENNEDY, J., concurring); see also New State Ice Co. v. Liebmann, 285 U.S. 262, 311 (1932) (Brandeis, J., dissenting). The University of Texas at Austin has a special opportunity to learn and to teach. The University now has at its disposal valuable data about the manner in which different approaches to admissions may foster diversity or instead dilute it. The University must continue to use this data to scrutinize the fairness of its admissions program; to assess whether changing demographics have undermined the need for a race-conscious policy; and to identify the effects, both positive and negative, of the affirmative-action measures it deems necessary. The Court's affirmance of the University's admissions policy today does not necessarily mean the University may rely on that same policy without refinement. It is the

University's ongoing obligation to engage in constant deliberation and continued reflection regarding its admissions policies.

REBECCA K. LEE, *IMPLEMENTING GRUTTER'S DIVERSITY RATIONALE: DIVERSITY AND EMPATHY IN LEADERSHIP*

19 DUKE JOURNAL OF GENDER LAW & POLICY 133 (2011)

Lee is an expert in the areas of employment discrimination, employment law, affirmative action, and leadership. She is an Associate Professor of Law at Thomas Jefferson School of Law.

I.   INTRODUCTION

The United States Supreme Court has recognized that our country's leaders must know how to operate in our diverse society, identifying an important link between leadership and diversity.' In Grutter v. Bollinger, the Court held that the University of Michigan Law School's use of race in selecting students for admission did not violate the Fourteenth Amendment's Equal Protection Clause. In reaching this holding, the Court affirmed Justice Powell's diversity rationale as expressed in an earlier case, Regents of University of California v. Bakke, in which he noted that " 'the nation's future depends upon leaders trained through wide exposure' to the ideas and mores of students as diverse as this Nation of many peoples." The Supreme Court highlighted the importance of leadership and leadership preparation when it endorsed Justice Powell's justification. But the Court did not elaborate on the interdependent relationship between diversity and leadership and how leadership skills in a diverse setting may be developed and learned at school and afterward in the workplace. Yet it seems clear that diversity matters for leadership training, as a number of businesses and other amici curiae reiterated Justice Powell's reasoning in their amicus briefs supporting the Law School in Grutter. Like the Grutter Court, however, these amici also neglected to discuss the process by which leadership skills would be acquired and implemented in a diverse environment.

To address this missing piece of the analysis, we must examine the role of leadership and think about how to diversify our leadership ranks as well as ensure that our present, as well as future, leaders are indeed exposed to diverse perspectives. This is necessary to fulfill the promise of better leadership in a diverse context, as argued and acknowledged in Grutter. This Article asserts that more diversity is needed in leadership and that all leaders must draw out diverse viewpoints using a process of empathetic learning in guiding their institutions. By infusing organizational leadership with greater diversity and empathy, organizations will be better able to achieve substantive diversity and, in turn, be better able to achieve substantive equality. Although research on leadership is an integral part of the diversity discourse, only brief attention has been paid to leadership issues in antidiscrimination literature and in legal literature more broadly.

* * *

This Article contends that organizations must diversify their leadership ranks and that organizational leaders ought to develop their capacity for empathy in order to effectively lead in diverse settings. Women and minority groups continue to face challenges in ascending to leadership posts, and in particular elite leadership posts, due to conventional expectations regarding leadership and the ways in which leaders tend to emerge and succeed. Opportunities for formal leadership must be strengthened to allow for better representation of diverse individuals at the leadership level, and any differences in the leadership styles of diverse leaders should be studied to discern how these differences influence organizational culture and habits. To support a culture of core diversity and substantive equality, this Article further maintains that the act of leading must include an empathetic aspect, which requires both a focused effort on the part of organizational leaders and a collective effort on the part of organizational members in modeling and reinforcing certain behavior. Finally, the practice of leadership should be broadened to include both formal and informal leadership, to recognize that leadership can occur both with and without authority, and to treat the work of leading as a shared responsibility.

* * *

Leaders must challenge institutional norms that suppress equality and diversity in order to enhance the participation and success of diverse members at all levels, including at the formal leadership levels. If, as Grutter reaffirms, we want to build a nation with leaders broadly exposed to ideas as diverse as our nation's population, then we must tailor the purpose and practice of leadership toward the realization of this goal.

II. UNDERSTANDING DIVERSITY AND LEADERSHIP IN GRUTTER

In Grutter v. Bollinger, the U.S. Supreme Court held that the University of Michigan Law School ("the Law School") did not violate the Constitution's Equal Protection Clause by considering race as a factor in admissions decisions. Petitioner Barbara Grutter, a white Michigan resident and unsuccessful applicant to the Law School, sued the school in addition to the Regents of the University of Michigan and several

University officials and administrators, alleging race discrimination in violation of the Constitution's Fourteenth Amendment, Title VI of the Civil Rights Act of 1964, and § 1981. She alleged that the Law School improperly factored in race during the admissions process, giving an advantage to particular minority students while disadvantaging students from other racial groups with comparable qualifications. The Law School had a formal policy on student admissions which was devised with the aim of admitting a diverse student body while complying with the Supreme Court's decision in Bakke's concerning whether race may be considered in higher education admissions. The Law School's policy required a broad evaluation of each applicant using the information in the applicant's file, including the applicant's personal statement, recommendation letters, an essay about how the applicant would enrich the Law School community and add to the school's diversity, the applicant's college grade point average, and the applicant's Law School Admission Test score.' Under this policy, the Law School took into account many kinds of diversity that could help an applicant's chance for admission and, as part of its assessment, maintained a "longstanding commitment to. . . 'racial and ethnic diversity with special reference to the inclusion of students from groups which have been historically discriminated against, like African-Americans, Hispanics and Native Americans, who without this commitment might not be represented in our student body in meaningful numbers.'" The diversity factors considered by the school, however, were not limited to racial and ethnic diversity.

During a bench trial in federal district court, the Law School's then Director of Admissions, Dennis Shields, explained that he and his staff were not trying to meet a numeric or percentage goal in admitting applicants from underrepresented minority groups but took into account the race of the applicant, in addition to all other relevant considerations, to recruit a "critical mass of underrepresented minority students . . . so as to realize the educational benefits of a diverse student body." Shields' successor, Erica Munzel, also testified, stating that a "critical mass" was needed so that underrepresented minority students could engage in the classroom without feeling surrounded by only non-minority classmates, but that attaining a critical mass does not require having a certain number or percentage of minorities.' The testimony by Law School Dean Jeffrey Lehman explained critical mass in the same terms. Law School faculty members supplied additional testimony, and experts for both sides presented evidence.

The district court, using a strict scrutiny standard, held that the Law School's use of race in student admissions violated the Equal Protection Clause because diversifying the student population was not deemed a compelling interest under Bakke; moreover, even if it was a compelling interest, the Law School's use of race did not meet the narrowly-tailored requirement. As a result, the district court granted the petitioner's request for declaratory relief and her request for an injunction to bar the Law School from considering race in its admissions process.? The Sixth Circuit, in an en banc ruling, reversed the district court's decision and vacated the order of injunction, explaining that diversity had been found to be a compelling interest under Justice Powell's opinion in Bakke, the controlling precedent. The Sixth Circuit further held that the Law School narrowly tailored its. use of race by regarding this use of race as a possible "plus factor," and that its admissions policy closely resembled the admissions policy used at Harvard, which was upheld by Justice Powell in Bakke.

Bakke addressed the issue of whether race may be considered in medical school admissions by reserving a number of seats in the entering class to be filled by minority students from particular groups. This highly divided case produced no majority opinion, but Justice Powell cast the fifth vote that struck down the racial set-aside policy while also lifting the state court's injunction prohibiting all use of race in university admissions. Justice Powell's opinion, which provided the Court's judgment, validated the medical school's use of race to promote the specific interest of achieving a diverse student body. Bakke thus held that a "State has a substantial interest that legitimately may be served by a properly devised admissions program involving the competitive consideration of race and ethnic origin." In recognizing diversity as a substantial interest, Justice Powell stressed that the "'nation's future depends upon leaders trained through wide exposure' to the ideas and mores of students as diverse as this Nation of many peoples." He added that race or ethnicity is just one of many significant factors that a school may take into account to achieve a diversified class of students.

Referring to the Bakke decision, the Supreme Court in Grutter supported Justice Powell's position that diversity constitutes a compelling interest; thus, universities may use race in selecting students for admission. The Court accordingly held that the Law School's interest in diversifying its student population was compelling, deferring in some measure to the Law School's assertion that having a critical mass of underrepresented students is necessary to further its pedagogical goals while also taking into account materials submitted by amici in support of the Law School's policy. The Court further determined that the policy met the narrow-tailoring requirement in achieving its stated purpose, as required by the Equal Protection Clause's strict scrutiny analysis, because the Law School's program used race or ethnic background as a "plus" factor in considering each applicant on an individualized basis within the context of the entire admissions pool and did not adhere to any quota or set numbers in admitting students from a particular background. The Court, therefore, held that the Law School's admissions program did not violate the Equal Protection Clause and, accordingly, did not run afoul of either Title VI or § 1981.

Justice Powell expressly made a connection between leadership and diversity by stating in Bakke that the country's leadership must be grounded in familiarity with different people and differing viewpoints. In Grutter, the Supreme Court further noted that universities and law schools produce many of our country's leaders and, hence, must help prepare them for future leadership responsibilities. The Grutter Court stated that universities play a critical role in equipping students for the workforce and civic involvement and that the hope of a unified nation requires civic engagement by individuals from various racial and ethnic groups. Indisputably, attaining a racially and ethnically diverse environment is a necessary precondition to reaping the benefits that diversity has to offer. But neither the Bakke nor the Grutter decision explained exactly how such leadership skills would be developed and utilized in a diverse environment, whether at school, afterward at work, or in broader society. This Article argues that diversity's full benefits must be actively reaped-that is, active engagement with diversity must be encouraged and, moreover, cultivating leadership skills with respect to diversity-related issues is needed. Although bringing diverse groups together naturally increases opportunities for inter-group interaction and discussion, studies have shown that a real sharing of ideas and viewpoints may require guidance and thus should not be left to occur by chance.

* * *

B.   The Diversity Justification and Core Diversity

Due to dominant norms embedded in organizational cultures, members of historically subordinated groups may feel they have to align their views with the majority or worry their differing views will be neither welcome nor understood. They may then refrain from fully contributing to the conversation, either in the classroom or in a work meeting, and attempt to blend in by not bringing attention to their differences. This is the model of surface diversity pursued by many employers. Under the surface diversity approach, organizations aim for demographic diversity but expect all of their members to conform to the organization's long-standing norms regarding how to act and interact and how the organization carries out its work. Adhering to a model of surface diversity in the law school setting, for instance, would have law faculty using traditional teaching methods and materials and relying on dominant assumptions in discussing issues instead of eliciting varying student viewpoints.

Other organizations follow the marginal diversity approach. This approach values diverse perspectives only as supplemental niche areas rather than as something that could influence an organization's core functions Looking again at the law classroom as an example, law professors follow a marginal diversity model if they bring up non-mainstream perspectives only when discussing a non-mainstream subject-such as raising feminist issues while studying feminist legal theory, or raising racial issues while learning critical race studies and omit covering a broad set of views when teaching central legal doctrines.

Both the surface diversity and marginal diversity models are limiting in that they view diversity and its value in narrow terms. Organizations, hence, should adopt the core diversity model, which aims to promote the sharing of information by drawing upon the experiences and ideas of diverse members; this approach values diversity in the ways recognized by the Grutter majority. The core diversity model understands that organizations need to actively promote inclusive cultures in places where diversity is present. Individuals whose voices are typically not heard-meaning members of socially subordinated groups must know that it is safe to convey views that do not conform to the majority perspective. Individuals belonging to groups historically excluded from membership when the organization was first formed should be seen as new sources of ideas about how the organization should function in order to achieve maximum inclusivity and performance. But organizations cannot function at the highest levels if members are not given the opportunity to contribute at or near their full capacity, and organizations commonly utilize only a small portion of their members' abilities. Institutional leaders are starting to recognize that rather than simply pressure members to fit into a certain institutional construct, organizations should better incorporate and demonstrate the varied knowledge and skills their members have to offer.

Under the core diversity approach, institutions would learn to question the traditions and institutional dynamics that tend to have exclusionary and discriminatory effects and learn to elicit and incorporate different members' various ideas concerning the organization's central work. Educational and work institutions must tap into the full reservoir of student or employee knowledge, experiences, and skills that relate to their studies or work and to the organization's primary goals. The core diversity model does more than simply advance demographic diversity as seen with surface diversity or view people's differences only for specialized purposes as seen with marginal diversity. The core diversity approach values diverse members in a more substantive way, understanding that their full range of knowledge and viewpoints can better inform the organization's main practices. Research has shown that groups comprised of people with varied backgrounds and perspectives are more likely to come up with novel ways of thinking and doing, avoiding the common trap of groupthink.

To seize diversity's full value, organizational leaders must reconsider their own assumptions and perspectives by actively listening to the views of others within their organizations who can offer new ways of moving the organization forward. An inclusive process of actively seeking broad input does not mean, however, that everyone's proposals will be implemented, and this may lead some to feel a sense of deprivation if their suggestions are not adopted. As a practical matter, people's ideas on how to address a given issue will diverge to varying extents, and leaders will need to examine their own beliefs, as well as others' assumptions, in sorting through the competing views. Nonetheless, inclusion requires that diverse voices be heard and considered. Leaders who make wise decisions know the importance of listening to others beyond those in their inner circles, and they constantly seek broad input, particularly from individuals who may view the problem or situation differently. Wise leaders understand that information from diverse sources provides a larger base of knowledge from which to make better-considered decisions.

III. WHY LEADERSHIP MATTERS IN DIVERSE SETTINGS

Toni Riccardi, former partner and chief diversity officer of PricewaterhouseCoopers, once stated: "We need to recognize that diversity-managing and leading across differences-is not an initiative or a program; it should be a competency that anyone who manages people must learn if he or she is to be an effective leader." In any institutional setting where people work together, if people's different views and feelings are not acknowledged and taken into account, employees (or other categories of organizational members) will often feel invisible, ignored, and undervalued. Consequently, their morale and productivity can fall, and their interactions with others in the organization may become uncomfortable.? Further, in organizations where workers' roles and actions are strictly regulated by upper-level management to maintain employee control and conformity, workers will not only suffer from a lack of learning and motivation in their work but in extreme cases may even channel their silent frustrations toward impairing the organization's success. This trajectory of events, predictable but far from inevitable, harms the functioning and output of both individual employees and the organization as a whole.

Leaders must seek to hear and learn from the diverse population in their organizations in a way that is comfortable and sincere so as to elicit the most feedback, especially from those with less power. Individuals belonging to traditionally subordinated groups often do not have their perspectives heard as fully or as often as those of the majority group, allowing the organization to continue enforcing biased norms and continue relying on incomplete input that leads to poor decisions. Knowing how to effectively draw out and learn from individuals' different experiences and ideas then becomes critically important. While anyone can initiate the discussions needed to encourage equal information-sharing, institutional leaders have a special responsibility, by virtue of their recognized leadership roles, to ensure that a range of voices is included when discussing and deciding organizational matters.

Leaders must be carefully attuned to issues of communication and inclusion to address embedded inequality and foster a culture of core diversity, but the topic of leadership has garnered little discussion in the legal scholarship concerning antidiscrimination efforts and reform. In fact, leadership in general has not been extensively examined in legal literature. Moreover, unlike in other professional schools, the study of leadership is not typically offered as part of the law school curriculum and thus is rarely explored in law school classrooms. And yet law schools-as asserted in Grutter-clearly seek to admit students with leadership capability and produce graduates who reach for, and step into, leadership roles. Law school graduates indeed heavily occupy leadership positions in a range of fields, whether in the government, private, or public sectors. Thus, both law schools and other institutions need to explore what leadership entails and how it can serve to either advance or undermine socio-legal objectives.

Promoting diversity in institutions requires institutional leadership. To cultivate the next generation of leaders who will be "wide[ly] exposed to ideas as diverse as this Nation of many peoples," current institutional leaders must help ensure that future leaders will not only be exposed to different ideas but also know how to elicit and incorporate the different visions that those ideas convey. Communication is necessary for ideas to be shared, but effective communication between individuals from diverse backgrounds or with different outlooks may not flow easily. Effective communication also involves both speaking up and listening; for broad perspectives to be shared, members of subordinated groups must be encouraged to share what they know with an understanding that others will listen. Because speaking up can be difficult, particularly if one's viewpoint differs from mainstream accounts, institutional leaders must help create safe spaces and opportunities for such exchanges of ideas to occur.

For the diversity effort to be prioritized, the organization's top leadership must make it a clear goal and be involved in its implementation. As a starting point, leaders can use organizational re-signaling to publicly and firmly indicate the organization's diversity-related goals and direction. This re-signaling can be especially helpful if the organization is seeking to change course with respect to its traditions or past events and reestablish itself as being committed to diversity and inclusion in a meaningful way. A re-signaling campaign would need to be supported by improved internal practices and processes to encourage information-sharing that could influence the institution's core work.

In pursuing core diversity, leaders must increase diversity at the leadership levels and establish a culture of learning in their organizations. In order for people's differences to actually inform the organization's work and practices, leaders must diligently draw out these differences and use them to advance the organization's central goals. It is additionally vital that minorities and women step into positions of formal leadership for their perspectives to have sway at the highest levels.

* * *

IV. CHALLENGES TO DIVERSITY IN LEADERSHIP

Women and racial and ethnic minorities who aspire to hold formal positions of leadership continue to face difficulties in obtaining such positions, particularly given that our perception of leaders has been largely shaped by those in the majority who have long occupied the leadership role. Leaders typically have been white and male, rendering it more difficult for women and people of color to be perceived as potential leaders. Yet leaders from diverse backgrounds offer different experiences and points of view that can help avoid organizational blind spots and contribute to organizational change and advancement. Having more members of historically subordinated groups in recognized positions of leadership will also lessen the force of stereotypes. Interaction with minority and female leaders, or even simple exposure to them, can decrease the magnitude of implicit or unconscious biases by familiarizing others with diverse individuals in leadership roles. Diversity in leadership alone, however, may not necessarily kindle reform in the way an organization operates unless diverse leaders are in fact interested in changing the organization's norms and use their influence to do so.

* * *

B.   Opportunities for Formal Leadership

* * *

A number of factors contribute to this leadership disparity in terms of gender. Although women reach educational levels at the same or higher rate than men and share the same level of commitment to work, women spend more time away from the workforce-mostly due to family and domestic obligations that unequally fall on women's shoulders-and therefore have fewer opportunities to make significant accomplishments in the work arena and obtain the typically needed seniority to be considered "eligible" for many leadership roles. Women with children, if they engage in paid employment, often work fewer hours compared with women without children, and mothers who leave their jobs find it challenging to rejoin the full-time workforce at the same level and pay they previously enjoyed. On the whole, women contribute more time to childrearing and home duties than men do-even women with careers as equally demanding as their husbands' careers assume more of these responsibilities, and they still tend to be hard on themselves when it comes to their household performance. Men tend to spend less time on such duties, even when they do share some of the chores. Also, men with children often are employed and work more hours than men without children, indicating that fathers do not suffer the same career setbacks as mothers in terms of work experience gained when also raising a family. Moreover, mothers are seen by employers as less competent and less committed to paid work as compared to fathers, even when there is no difference in education levels or qualifications between job applicants, contributing to indirect discrimination against women with children at the hiring and, also likely, at the promotion stages.'

To bring about balance in the distribution of work and domestic obligations and better allow women to fill leadership roles, there needs to be a reordering of duties both at home and at work. Women can push for this "structural role redefinition" by negotiating expectations with family and employers-such as negotiating the division of childcare and household work with one's spouse and negotiating with one's employer for work policies that facilitate meeting one's responsibilities both inside and outside the workplace. There is an added benefit to doing this: by practicing their negotiation skills, women will improve their chances of advancing to higher leadership posts; men more frequently rise to the highest leadership levels in part because they are more comfortable with the negotiating process. It is also less common for women to self-nominate and purposefully position themselves for formal leadership openings.' One reason for this is that women generally are less well-received than men when they advocate on behalf of themselves due to social norms that discourage women from displaying ambition. When women do accept leadership responsibility, they tend to assume such duties informally, without the full recognition that comes with official leadership, referring to their role as "facilitator or organizer instead of leaders." Even prominent female leaders may downplay their pioneering status in heading major organizations, preferring to shift the attention away from themselves and instead direct it toward their organizations and the goals achieved or yet to be accomplished. But this does not mean that women do not want to lead in a formal capacity; in fact, when presented with the chance to take on leadership roles, women agree to undertake such positions as often as men do. To provide women with more opportunities to serve in formally appointed positions, current leaders ought to support greater diversity in their leadership ranks, including at the highest levels, and provide better work-life schedules and positive leadership-oriented mentoring.

While it is clear that increased diversity in leadership is needed, it is less clear how often women and minorities have the opportunity to ascend to positions of recognized leadership. Some argue that women are more likely to be selected for leadership positions when the institution is facing a crisis or has recently undergone an upheaval, but this can be both a liability and an asset for women who step into leadership roles. The instability and uncertainty inherent in this type of leadership situation mean there is a greater likelihood for disapproval and failure. At the same time, women usually are seen as agents of change, giving them leeway to try a new or different leadership approach, particularly if they are the first women to occupy their roles. In any event, the leadership challenges are not small.

* * *

C.   Leadership Styles

More minorities and women should engage in formal leadership to advance core diversity, but will diversifying the face of leadership introduce fresh thinking regarding the leadership role itself? While many female and minority leaders follow traditional leadership behavior due to the pressure to conform to the leader prototype, some have nonetheless exhibited a different kind of leadership style. Women who lead often adopt a mix of masculine and feminine styles and try to involve others in the decision-making process. Female and feminist leaders have reconsidered the way power is exercised in light of their different experiences from men in their own paths to leadership and access to power. Women tend to be more keenly aware that domineering power-wielding by a few can be disempowering for the remaining many. Thus, female leaders may opt to interact with their employees and consult them more frequently when making decisions, while male leaders may prefer to rely on a limited circle of people in management when deciding important matters.

Leaders who emphasize the personal element in leading by being approachable and welcoming are more likely to be effective, as female leaders have demonstrated. Being an open leader includes being receptive to input by soliciting feedback on an informal basis, for example, and chatting with employees about what is on their minds. Linda Hudson, president of the Land and Armaments Group for the large defense contractor BAE Systems, described her method for obtaining broad input in the following way: I look for every opportunity, when I'm out visiting locations, just to sit down informally with a cross section of employees, from hourly workers to others, and say: "Anything's on the table. What do you want to talk about?" I do that as frequently as I can find an opportunity to do it. I find that it's extremely well received.

Female leaders may be more likely to adopt inclusive styles, with a focus on hearing what others have to say, not because of any inborn differences in leadership style but due to differences in the way women's lives are shaped and experienced. To the extent that female leaders use a more collaborative and open approach, their preferred styles are supported by the recent general trend in leadership that places less emphasis on hierarchy and more attention to relationship-building in leading. Company leaders, male or female, who rely less on control from the top have found that supporting the creativity and entrepreneurial leadership of their employees can lead to innovative products and services that reap big gains in a constantly evolving market and world.

Whether in the business or political realm, newer directions in the leadership literature recognize that successful leadership needs to incorporate both masculine and feminine aspects, something that observers say President Obama has succeeded in doing with respect to his self-presentation. His 2008 presidential campaign notably reflected traditionally feminine qualities with its focus on people and emotion. It is possible that Obama displayed his feminine side to a greater degree than other male candidates to offset the stereotype of the threatening black male, as one commentator has argued. At the same time, appearing fit for the presidency meant that Obama could not appear overly feminine, although as a male leader he could embrace more femininity in his style than could female candidates and still be a viable presidential candidate. Ultimately, however, Obama exemplified a gender-balanced or "unisex" approach, modifying his style according to the particular setting or circumstance and thereby providing an example for other male leaders to do the same. Male leaders who demonstrate an emotional side tend to be received well; femininity in female leaders, on the other hand, may be viewed less positively. Yet there exists a catch-22: if female leaders use a masculine style while occupying or seeking a traditionally masculine role (such as the role of President), they are judged more poorly than their male counterparts. Obama's rival in the presidential primaries, Hillary Clinton, faced this double-bind. Her campaign made a significant effort to showcase Clinton as an assertive candidate competent for the role of commander-in-chief, but she was criticized for appearing too tough and likely was more severely judged as a woman. As seen in her case, evaluating women unfavorably for being either too feminine or too masculine can hinder their ascendance to elite leadership roles and render it challenging for women to be considered successful leaders.

Notably, diverse leaders may feel accountable to more than just their organizational members; they may also view as their constituents individuals in society outside of the specific organization they lead-such as external supporters who helped them along their path to leadership and who remind them about their larger responsibility to the community. As a result, diverse leaders may feel additional pressures if they are expected to push for socio-political change early on as public figures representing not just their particular organization but also the larger community. Indeed, leaders who are elected have a clear responsibility to represent the interests of constituents whose views may differ from those of their elected officials. To represent their constituents' interests, executive and legislative leaders must try to understand the range of perspectives that exist. In this respect, lawmaking in a truly representative democracy requires empathic skills.

* * *

V. THE IMPORTANCE OF LEADING WITH EMPATHY

In rethinking the work of leadership to support substantive equality and core diversity, it is imperative that leaders try to elicit and better understand the different perspectives of others by leading with empathy. This is not to say that demonstrating empathy is the sole criterion for good leadership, but a focus on strong empathetic ability in leadership is needed to promote a vision of substantive equality in our progressively diverse workplaces, schools, organizations, and society.

What exactly is empathy? Empathy has been defined in a number of ways, most systematically in psychology literature. An examination of law and the emotions, including the study of empathy, has emerged in recent decades, contributing to our understanding of emotions as they relate to the law. Challenging the long-held conception of law and legal reasoning as purely rational processes, scholars have argued that emotions inevitably influence legal players and the decisions they produce, even if legal players choose not to acknowledge the relationship between emotions and the thought process, and moreover, that emotions should be incorporated to improve legal decision-making. In this sense, emotional and rational responses are not separate forces but in fact represent largely overlapping spheres of ways to process information.

Situated within the broader realm of emotions, empathy consists of both affective and cognitive components and contributes to emotional intelligence, which as noted earlier may be to some extent more important than mental intelligence in determining whether individuals become leaders and succeed as leaders. To be clear, in this work the term "empathy" is used to refer to our capacity to better comprehend-through both knowledge and feeling-another's perspective by trying to view the world from that person's position rather than simply observing another's position from where we stand. Displaying empathy requires that individuals be more cognizant of their own predisposed positions, taking into account their race, gender, class, and all other relevant considerations that have contributed to their particular life and career opportunities. Because people in general tend to view others and the world, consciously and unconsciously, from a certain vantage point depending on what they are accustomed to and how they are situated in society, it is crucial that leaders try to step outside of their own worlds in order to be open to different forms of thinking and experience. Especially since individuals tend to empathize more easily, even reflexively, with others like themselves, leaders routinely make decisions that disproportionately benefit similarly-situated individuals within their organizations. Therefore, it is incumbent upon leaders to put effort and thought into broadening their abilities to empathize with different organizational members in order to avoid further embedding dominant norms that produce inequality.

To give an example of empathy at work, a chief operating officer at a major global company displayed empathetic leadership when, during a time of restrictions on firm-wide costs, he nonetheless agreed to still fund an internally organized women's conference for the firm's female employees. Despite the need to reduce expenses throughout the company, the COO made an exception because he understood the significance of the annual conference to the women who had worked hard to organize it and the conference's special function in bringing together the company's female workers who worked in a mostly male work environment. The COO further agreed to address the female crowd at the start of the conference, and he began by remarking, "This must be how you feel"-noting the experience of being the only man in the room and acknowledging the everyday feeling of the female employees at the company.

Consistent with this understanding of empathy, our nation's top leader has remarked on the need for each of us to "stand in someone else's shoes" when addressing issues of discrimination and inequity. In commenting on Shirley Sherrod's termination from her job at the U.S. Department of Agriculture after a speech she gave was taken out of context, President Obama stated: When it comes to race, let's acknowledge that of course there is still tension out there. There is still discrimination. There is still inequality. But we've made progress and if each of us takes it upon ourselves to treat people with fairness and stand in someone else's shoes . . . then we can make more progress. Obama's own diverse background and status as a racial and ethnic minority may have helped him see that it takes standing in another person's place to reduce instances of inequality. Individuals who have experienced discrimination, or who have felt excluded or overlooked, are likely to be more mindful of adopting an empathetic leadership approach that seeks to include others. In this regard, diversifying our leadership ranks would help install leaders who, by virtue of their different backgrounds and experiences, would prioritize the exercise of empathy in working with others and may be better attuned to noticing and correcting various forms of subordination.

Ironically, however, Obama has been criticized for neglecting to display empathy himself when making public appearances as President-a seeming departure from the way he was portrayed during his hope-inspiring presidential campaign. The view from observers in Washington is that Obama, with his calm and even-keeled demeanor, lacks the kind of empathetic touch for which former President Bill Clinton was known. Clinton had a talent for relating to his audience and used this skill to his advantage during his 1992 presidential campaign against then-President George Bush. As this shows, there is an expectation that our modem leaders must be capable of showing some feeling, while also demonstrating toughness, if they want to be seen as both likable and competent.

In fact, evidence shows that people evaluate others largely based on whether a person seems warm (versus cold), relying at least in part on stereotypes associated with race and gender. When assessing a person, how warm the person appears to be is actually more important than the person's competence. At the same time, people also consider competence when categorizing and evaluating others, and a person's competence is usually based on whether a person demonstrates dominance and power. Leaders who possess power while in formal positions of authority may likely exhibit dominance and thus be viewed as highly competent, but their effectiveness may be determined to a larger extent by their demonstrations of warmth.

The perception of a leader's warmth may further be affected by whether the person is genuinely caring and shows interest in and concern for others. While being seen as competent is important for leadership, leaders will be less effective if they are focused on being the most dominant or competent person in the group because such self-aggrandizing activity inhibits receptivity to others and their suggestions. Over-dominant leaders may be seen as insecure and will be less efficacious than leaders who strive to learn from their members. Steady self confidence allows one to respond more empathetically toward others, and self security is also correlated with leadership potential. Moreover, leaders who pay careful attention to how they present themselves and engage interpersonally will tend to engender positive feelings in organizational members who, as a result, are likely to work better together, come up with better ideas, better absorb information, and feel more capable of individual and group accomplishments. Building and demonstrating one's self-confidence (but not becoming or appearing over-confident), then, is important for empathetic leadership.

Individuals are innately endowed with some level of empathetic ability (save for people suffering from certain psychological conditions), and although this capability may differ in extent from person to person, it nonetheless can be cultivated from an early or later age and encouraged through one's environment and interactions. Furthermore, although empathy, due to its association with care and attentiveness toward others, tends to be viewed as a female trait, research fails to demonstrate clear differences in empathic behavior between females and males, either in childhood or adulthood. While girls may be socialized to think more about others or to engage in more caretaking than boys, studies indicate that sex or gender is largely irrelevant in determining one's ability to empathize.

* * *

VII. CONCLUSION

The diversity justification affirmed by the Supreme Court in Grutter and echoed by many major businesses and employers as amici in the case makes clear that access to diverse perspectives is needed for leadership in our heterogeneous society and institutions. While recognizing the importance of diversity for leadership, the Court and amici nonetheless left unfinished the task of explaining how to ensure that this access to diversity translates into an exchange of views that actually inform what leaders do. Diverse settings create opportunities for information sharing and learning, but such opportunities may not be maximized without effective facilitation and careful understanding. To benefit from the views of diverse organizational members, especially the views of those belonging to historically non-dominant groups, such views have to be actively elicited. Leaders, thus, have a crucial role to play in facilitating the exchange of perspectives in diverse environments, and they must do so to concretely implement Grutter's diversity rationale in everyday behavior and in everyday conversation. Encouraging diverse leadership would also help ensure that a range of perspectives are shared at the upper-most levels.

* * *

It is vital that our leaders learn to develop competency on issues of diversity because, as understood in Grutter, the nation's future depends on it.

RANGITA DE SILVA DE ALWIS, *WHY WOMEN'S LEADERSHIP IS THE CAUSE OF OUR TIME*

18 U.C.L.A. JOURNAL OF INTERNATIONAL LAW & FOREIGN AFFAIRS 87 (2013)

Rangita de Silva de Alwis is a globally recognized international women's rights expert. She serves as the Associate Dean of International Affairs at the University of Pennsylvania Law School where she teaches international women's rights.

Introduction

Historically, women have lagged behind in the fields of politics and public policy across the world. Even when women have headed social movements and civil society organizations that have shaped social change, there has been a marked gender gap in the political and decision-making spheres in public administration, arenas that usually hold the most sway. As Zainab Bangura, the current Special Representative for Violence against Women in Armed Conflict and former Sierra Leone Minister has said, "[t]he real power isn't in civil society; it's in policymaking."

Revolutions have been waged across the world in recent years, but the ongoing struggle for women's rights remains unfinished. Although uprisings brought women to the forefront of change, protests alone were not enough to open the political sphere to women, and transitional governments have even threatened to roll back prior gains. The possibility of backsliding makes it all the more crucial that women have a seat at the table during this critical time.

The cost of women's exclusion from the political and public service sphere is a heavy one, impacting not just women but their communities and countries.

* * *

This Article outlines the way in which greater representation of women in leadership impacts the public good. It also examines the barriers that keep women from participating in the public sphere and the mechanisms that are used to mitigate these challenges.

Women's leadership in politics has been pivotal in developing laws on healthcare, childcare, and violence against women that have bolstered human security. In the economic sphere, increased women's participation is paramount to growth and development at all levels, from agriculture to the top of the corporate ladder. The inclusion of women in conflict resolution development at all levels, from agriculture to the top of the corporate ladder. The inclusion of women in conflict resolution can have a powerful impact on conflict transformation and can bring a more holistic response to constitution-making and law-drafting that advance issues such as post-conflict access to land, water, and education. In all areas, the presence of women in leadership roles serves as a powerful model to girls and has been shown to change societal views of gender roles. More women in leadership positions will not only break the glass ceiling but open wide the pipeline for other women to follow in their footsteps.

This Article explores some of the barriers to women's leadership across the world that harm both women and men and their communities' social and economic progress. The masculinization of political and corporate culture often overtly and insidiously discourages women from seeking leadership positions. Gender-based violence also deters women from entering the public sphere. From Afghanistan to Zimbabwe, women political candidates face threats of violence and sexual abuse. Moreover, women's disproportionate caregiving responsibilities are often some of the greatest impediments to women's equal public sphere participation, and the nexus between gender discrimination in the home and subordination in the political sphere will require significant changes to policy and culture that facilitate greater male engagement in family care.

* * *

I.   Addressing the Problem

In one of her first appearances after stepping down as Secretary of State, Hillary Clinton called women's empowerment the unfinished business of the twenty-first century. Her powerful reminder that empowering women is not only a moral imperative, but a prerequisite for economic development, echoed her 1995 call that "[w]omen's rights are human rights." At the UN World Conference on Women in Beijing fifteen years ago, she revitalized a new movement to amplify women's voices on all urgent causes of our times, but the work begun there is far from over.

During her time as Secretary of State, Secretary Clinton established women's leadership as not only a critical cornerstone of foreign policy but as the continuum of women's rights as human rights. In December 2011, furthering the agenda she had outlined in Beijing, Secretary Clinton launched the Women in Public Service Project in partnership with the Seven Sisters Colleges to inspire a new generation of women to leadership in public service. The first of its kind, this initiative has now grown to include over one hundred partners, including universities, women's colleges, ministries, agencies, and embassies around the world. The Women in Public Service Project (WPSP) is housed at the Global Women's Leadership Initiative at the Woodrow Wilson International Center for Scholars. By 2050, the WPSP hopes that its efforts will catalyze a more equal world where women will constitute at least fifty percent of decision-makers in public sector jobs.

However, fifty percent is still an aspirational target for most of the world. Globally, women are vastly under-represented in leadership positions across all sectors and regions. At the 1995 Fourth World Conference in Beijing, governments undertook to work to raise women's representation to a critical mass of thirty percent. To date, only 37 countries have reached the thirty percent mark recognized as the critical mass of change. Women are the majority of parliament in only two small countries, Rwanda and Andorra. Nine still have no women members at all. However, progress has been made: in 2013, the world average of women in parliament stands at 20.8 percent. In 1995, it was only 11.3 percent.

David Rothkopf, editor of Foreign Policy, writes, "the underrepresentation of women in positions of power is proof not so much that men still dominate the top of the pyramid as it is of a system of the most egregious, widespread, pernicious, destructive pattern of human rights abuses in the history of civilization." He argues that more women have lost their lives to discrimination and violence than any genocide in the world. Whether it be the "missing women" caused by male-biased sex ratios, inadequate healthcare and reproductive care for women that results in preventable death, or the countless number of women who are raped, beaten, and murdered because of honor crimes—these human rights violations have cost more lives of women than any casualty in war. He further points out that, of the most important persons in foreign policy identified in Foreign Policy's "Power Issue," only ten percent are women. Rothkopf is right when he says, "[t]he systematic, persistent acceptance of women's second-class status is history's greatest shame."

We live in a world where injustices against women remain endemic in all countries, even though there is evidence that women's empowerment leads to higher development. The absence of women in positions of power continues to minimize, marginalize, and ignore women's interests. This not only holds back women but entire communities and countries.

Despite an increase in the number of women in decision-making positions, there is still a persistent and glaring disparity in the number of women who hold decision-making positions at various levels worldwide. Deeply embedded gender roles—including customs and traditions which confine women's roles to the private sphere and exclude them from male-dominated traditional political systems—have been largely responsible for women's underrepresentation in political processes. Without women present at the negotiating table, urgent concerns affecting half of the world often remain silenced.

The most effective way to get attention and action on the very same human rights abuses that hold women back is to get more women into public office. Women's leadership has never been more significant than at this particular time in history, during an era of revolution, post-revolution, and transitional justice.

Of the almost two hundred national constitutions, over fifty percent have been drafted and revised since 1974, often as part of post-conflict and transitional justice. States emerging from conflict or authoritarian rule have the opportunity to recast constitutions as well as the process of forming new constitutions. Political transitions such as the Arab Spring provide a window of opportunity to recast constitutions and legal systems. During transitions—perhaps the most vital time when the future course of the country is designed—women must be at the table. Democratic change calls for close examination of the causes and consequences of women's marginalization in high-level political decision-making. This is pivotal to the negotiations of constitutions and other legal system reforms as well as in peace-building. Today, the Middle East and North Africa (MENA) region is home to some of the most critical transitional justice processes in the world. It is important to ensure transitional justice measures do not further entrench the invisibility of gender-based abuses.

In Egypt, although women were at the forefront of the revolutions, they were marginalized soon thereafter by transitional processes and were shamelessly beaten back and subject to virginity testing when they reassembled on Tahrir Square on International Women's Day on March 9, 2011. The percentage of women in the Egyptian legislature fell to only two percent following the revolution. Tunisia has one of the highest percentages of women in the region, but women still make up only 27 percent of parliamentarians despite a parity law. In Libya, though women lobbied for a thirty percent quota in the election law, women only comprise 17 percent of the General National Congress.

When women are not represented in transitional justice mechanisms, their experiences are often ignored in the new narratives of nation-building. New constitutions must serve to rectify, not replicate, patterns of discrimination against women. For example, it was only because of women's mass mobilizing that the second draft of the Tunisian Constitution dropped language stating that women, rather than being equal to men, were "complementary." The Jordanian women's movement is building on the new awakenings in the Arab region to include gender as a prohibited category of discrimination.

Women's representation in these processes of transitional justice has been unusually low in the MENA region. But even outside the MENA region, a review of the 24 peace processes taking place between 1992 and 2010 shows that female representation was as low as 2.5 percent of signatories to peace treaties and 7.6 percent of negotiating parties.

Women's participation in decision-making processes is critical to moving toward more gender-equal societies. For women to inform reform and for their voices to be transformative, their voices need to be heard. They need to serve in parliaments, village councils, and school boards. They need to serve as judges and police officers. Kim Campbell, the former Prime Minister of Canada, argues that when women lead, men can be more of the things they want to be. She points out that when more women began to be elected to the House of Commons, the House stopped night sittings, and most men relished the opportunity to spend more time with their families. She writes: "It was the presence of women that began to push against the way the institution was created. Institutions are created by the people who inhabit them and have a voice in creating their structure." Women cannot shy away from power, however much it has been defined in male terms or tarnished. As Campbell contends, "[p]ower is essential. Women cannot afford to shy away from the leverage that will change society."

II. Why is Women's Leadership Transformative?

* * *

Increasing women's participation in politics and the public sphere is not only an issue of justice; it also makes economic sense, and the plurality of perspectives strengthens national security, efficiency, and transparency in government. Moreover, women in policymaking have an intergenerational impact on societies' attitudes towards women and girls.

* * *

a.   Women and Policy-Making

Across the world, when women are at the table, legislatures enact policies and measures that advance the development of women, their families, and their countries. Rwanda boasts the highest proportion of women parliamentarians in the world. Working across party lines, Rwanda's Forum of Women Parliamentarians helped pass a law combating violence against women. When the number of women in the Costa Rican parliament reached a critical mass of over thirty percent, a General Law on the Protection of Adolescent Mothers was promulgated to provide free health services and education to young women. In Tanzania, a gender quota was enacted to ensure that women held no less than twenty percent of the seats in parliament. Because of their presence, an amendment to the Land Act grants women equal access to land, loans, and credit.

In the United States, women leaders have helped pass bills that make women and families more secure. This legislation has included the Violence Against Women Act of 1994 and the Family and Medical Leave Act of 1993. Other measures have increased assistance for survivors of domestic violence, increased penalties for batterers, supported federal rape-shield laws to protect rape victims, and furthered policies on payment of child support by non-custodial parents. In many cases, it was only after women took their place in Congress that critical issues such as healthcare, childcare and support, sexual harassment, domestic violence, and gender-based wage differentials were given priority.

Because women were present at the process of negotiating the new constitution in South Africa, its preamble contains a clause explaining gender oppression and its impact on society, in addition to an equality clause, a provision to protect women from cultural practices that discriminate against them, and a recognition of reproductive rights.

In India, gender quotas at the local government level increased the percentage of women elected leaders from less than five percent in 1992 to over forty percent by 2000. Evidence shows that women in elected office in India are more likely to invest in public infrastructure—particularly safe drinking water—and are less likely to feed into corruption than their male counterparts. At the local level, women-led village councils approved sixty percent more drinking water projects than those led by men. The correlation between women's leadership and development outcomes is made clear by Esther Duflo's research, which shows that there was less corruption and more access to public goods in India's villages where council head positions were reserved for women.

b.   Women and Economic Empowerment

* * *

The World Development Report 2012: Gender Equality and Development argues that closing gender gaps is both a core development objective in its own right as well as smart economics. Greater gender equality can enhance productivity, improve development outcomes for the next generation, and make institutions more representative. The report argues that productivity gains will increase if women's skills and talents are used more fully. For example, maize yields in Malawi and Ghana will improve by one-sixth if women have the same access as men to fertilizers and other inputs.

Most importantly, barriers, such as violence and bias against women, impede access to resources. Eliminating these discriminatory barriers will raise labor productivity by 25 percent. Women's empowerment also has an important intergenerational effect. Greater control and input over household decisions can amplify a nation's growth prospects by affecting positive outcomes for children. Improvements in women's education have led to better outcomes for children in countries from Brazil to Senegal.

* * *

c.   Women, Peace, and Security

War and peace have historically been defined in terms of men who waged wars, signed peace treaties, and drafted constitutions, while women's varied roles, from victims to peacemakers, still remain largely invisible in history. Women's role in peacemaking has been largely ignored, and war's effects on women have not been acknowledged in peace treaties, post-conflict resolutions, resource allocation, or law enforcement. Through international tribunals and Security Council resolutions, acknowledgements of rape as a tool of war have helped to unmask the silence on gender violence in war and have pierced the veil of silence and impunity that shroud these crimes.

Even though evidence shows that critical security issues are often highlighted when women are at the peace-negotiating table, women have been continuously underrepresented as mediators and negotiators to major peace processes. The absence of women in negotiation processes and post-conflict reconstruction efforts threatens the possibility of sustainable peace. Rule of law processes must be shaped by and responsive to both women and men.

* * *

d.   The Intergenerational Impact of Women in Leadership

Having a woman in a seat of power can be transformative and can help inspire peers and a future generation of women. Studies show the positive effect of exposure to a female leader. In communities where women leaders are more visible, fathers tend to send their daughters to school and to keep them in school. In short, fathers have greater aspirations for their daughters in communities where women leaders are more visible, and female role models also impact fathers' attitudes towards their girls.

Research on the Panchayat Raj in India has shown that the role model effect reaches beyond the realm of aspirations into real educational impacts. Role models can challenge prevalent stereotypes. Studies show that girls may be less likely to aspire to become scientists because there are few female scientists. Exposure to women leaders can provide such role models, break stereotypes regarding gender roles, and improve individual women's aspirations and propensity to enter traditionally male-dominated arenas.

President Ellen Johnson-Sirleaf, President of Liberia and Nobelist, is an example of a woman in leadership making a big impact. On the first day of her first term as President, she discussed the taboo issue of rape in her inauguration speech, placing women and the issue of violence against women at the forefront of her presidency and thus creating a new discourse on leadership. Swanee Hunt quotes Bertha Amanor, a Liberian women working in a women's NGO, saying of Johnson-Sirleaf: "If you look today where the big house is, a woman is sitting there. And if she is there, we can be leaders here! Men—listen up—we no longer walk behind you."

In a poem dedicated to Shirin Ebadi in celebration of Ebadi's Nobel Prize for Peace, Paulo Coelho writes that women's leadership today is "so that the next generation will not have to strive for what has already been accomplished." More recently, in 2011 when Dilma Rousseff was inaugurated as Brazil's first woman president, she said: "I am here to open doors so that in the future many other women can also be President. . . ."

* * *

Women in power can create a new discourse that can make gender matter in political discourse. President Sirleaf transformed and feminized the discourse of leadership when she referred to herself as "Ma Sirleaf" as a positive reference to power. President Sirleaf stated, "[y]ou . . . are the midwives." She has drawn on maternity as a label of power when inspiring leadership. "As a mother, I understand what is needed," she asserted. "As a grandmother, I'm thinking about our future." Rather than avoiding metaphors of gender, Sirleaf was unafraid to create a brand of leadership that is determinedly feminine.

* * *

IV. Barriers to Women's Leadership

Despite strong international conventions that are ostensibly agreed upon by most UN member states, low levels of women's participation remain the norm around the world. Structural and cultural barriers keep women from fully participating in the public sphere, and widespread social and political changes are necessary in order to eliminate them.

* * *

a. The Masculinization of Politics

Deep-seated patriarchy in politics is one of the core barriers to women's leadership. Myriaum Aucar writes that patriarchy in the family is often replicated in political parties. Men who drive political parties often determine the outcomes of the elections.

Even when electoral laws call for quotas or targets for women in political parties, parties led by male hierarchies are reluctant to place women on top of their lists, thus limiting women's chances of getting elected. Cultural norms preserve and perpetuate a male-dominated political scene. Thus, even in countries emerging from conflict, where civil society is looking for a new type of political arrangement women continue to be excluded from politics.

* * *

Hayat Arslan of Lebanon, who declared proudly that women have both a right and a duty to run for office and that women must seize their natural position beside men in politics, was forced by familial and tribal pressure to withdraw her candidacy during Lebanon's last election. Her story underscores the difficulties women face when breaking into male-dominated politics. When she ran as a candidate for the 2005 elections, Arslan's challenge at a personal level was her family. Along her sociopolitical march, she worked on awareness programs for both men and women to show that national roles complement rather than conflict with family. Although Arslan withdrew her candidacy in favor of her brother-in-law, she blazed a trail and opened doors for women in politics. She argues passionately that patriarchal forces are born in the family and are reinforced by social concepts and the law. Challenging patriarchal forces is not an end in itself but a means to achieving equality.

Male leaders can transform patriarchy by championing women in leadership as a public good. Strategic alliances with men are key to unleashing the potential of men as champions of women's empowerment.

b.   Reconciling Work/Family Balance

Historically, male hierarchies drafted laws. During this time, work/family reconciliation and childcare issues were considered outside the ambit of lawmaking. With more and more women at the drafting table, laws are being created in the image of women, men, and children. Work/family reconciliation is now becoming a pivotal policy issue at the heart of gender equality in private and public life.

Frances Raday has argued that one of the most globally pervasive harmful cultural practices "is the stereotyping of women exclusively as mothers and housewives in a way that limits their opportunity to participate in public life, whether political or economic." As Raday rightly stated, the assumption that women are the primary or sole caregivers of children is often used to exclude women from the public sphere, especially with regard to political life, promotions, and high-profile employment opportunities.

The paucity of women in leadership positions in corporations, politics, the arts, health care, education, academia, and human rights work is mainly due to the disproportionate share of caregiving responsibilities women often carry. Women leaders across the world have identified their dual responsibilities in the public sphere and the family life as being one of the impediments in their advancement in public life. In a study done in Kenya by the Heinrich Boll Stiftung Foundation, support or lack of support by family played a major role in women's ascendancy in politics. This explained why a majority of the women in politics in Kenya were widowed, divorced, or never married. The married ones had to get the full support of their husbands before joining politics. On the other hand, male politicians had the full, unstinted support of their wives, and wives were expected both to support them and also to continue looking after the children. Nviya Mwendwa, an MP in the 9th Parliament, talks about the difficulties of balancing young children and a political career. As to how she managed with young children (aged eight and six when she joined politics), she notes, "[i]t was quite trying. Whenever I would leave they would say: 'Mummy are you going again?' but with a supportive husband, who could spend time with them, it was easier." Dr. Ruth Oniang'o, a former member of the Kenyan parliament, said, "I waited until my last born was a little bigger. I held back my career . . . ." The biggest gender inequality gap is in access to inputs, with the largest input gap being time, because women carry a disproportionate household workload.

The 2012 World Bank Development Report bears witness that women's decision-making, both in the home and in public, impacts development outcomes. The construct of the male head of household is often carried over and replicated in politics. When women are still legally disenfranchised as heads of household, how can they be heads of state?

When women are shut out of equal ownership of property and land, inheritance and credit, how can the playing field be made equal for them? Women's disproportionate share of family and caretaking responsibilities directly relates to the discrimination they face in the labor market and subsequent inequalities in their political, social, and economic progress.

Workplace regulations that support both fathers and mothers in taking more responsibility for caring for children are a key pre-determinant of gender equality in the public sphere. These family reconciliation policies are in fact the most critical determinant of gender equality. Both women and men should be able to advance in the public sphere and undertake traditional caregiving roles. Women long ago entered the job market, and men are increasingly playing an equal role in caregiving. Translating these realities into the language of law means to challenge the patriarchal and masculinized norms that frame the market. The provision of parental care is not only about equal opportunities in the workplace but also about equal caregiving opportunities for both men and women.

If men are given the opportunity and are required to carry an equal share of caregiving work, caregiving will be privileged and acknowledged in high-level careers. Sheila Wellington writes, "[h]alf of women in both law firms and in-house legal departments want reduced hour schedules, but fewer than 20 percent of men indicate that interest." When women in leadership are not invested in childcare, it affects the child, the father, and the long-term career prospects of the mother.

The question of the head of the household is also pivotal to employment benefits. The denial of agency, full citizenship, and decision-making powers in the home is considered one of the four major barriers to women's empowerment by the World Development Report of 2012. Because in many parts of the world men are considered head of household, women have no access to land. Often, the government's land tenure, credit, and employment benefits are given to male heads of household. The notion of a male as head of household is no longer consistent with rapidly shifting economic and social change.

Because of the male head of household construct, in many countries women face unequal workplace benefits that are provided to dependent spouses of male heads of household but not to the spouses of female heads of households. Even when women participate in public life, laws fail to recognize them in leadership positions in the domestic sphere. Subordination in the private sector is directly linked to women's inferior position in the public sphere.

c.   Violence Against Women

Women's access to leadership cannot take place in an environment that subordinates and disempowers women. Women's leadership cannot be isolated from the general status of women in society. Violence against women both in the home and in public is one of the biggest impediments to women's agency and has enormous social, political, and economic ramifications on women and society. In 2005, the World Health Organization (WHO) established that violence against women caused more death and disabilities among women aged 15 to 44 than cancer, malaria, traffic accidents, and war.

The threat of violence against women who run for elected office is used to subordinate women as well as to prevent them from running. Okiyah Omtatah notes that the threat of violence is often insidiously used by men who pretend to be advocating against it, as a way of discouraging women from participating in the electoral process. Likewise, Deborah Okumu asserts that violence or the threat of violence has traditionally been used during electioneering periods to silence aspiring women leaders and women's activism in general. Okumu attributes gender-based violence to the patriarchy that is a large part of society. She notes, "it appears that the patriarchal hegemony provides dense institutional supports that socialize men for violence while also obscuring it from public scrutiny." Although electoral violence in Kenya in the past has targeted both male and female politicians, the threat is particularly ominous to women, who often have less protection and tend to be smaller and more vulnerable to assailants, a fact that seems to further embolden political goons to attack them. Violence against women in politics is a horrific act of violence aimed at controlling the power and agency of women.

* * *

NANCY LEVIT AND ALLEN ROSTRON, *CALLING FOR STORIES*
75 UMKC LAW REVIEW 1127 (2007)

Levit (above) is Associate Dean for Faculty and Curators' Professor and Edward D. Ellison Professor of Law at the University of Missouri-Kansas City School of Law. Her scholarship is principally in the areas of employment discrimination, legal pedagogy, constitutional law, jurisprudence, torts, and feminist legal theory. Rostron (below) is the Associate Dean of Students and the William R. Jacques Constitutional Law Scholar and Professor of Law. His research focuses on constitutional law, tort law, products liability, and conflict of laws.

Storytelling is a fundamental part of legal practice, teaching, and thought. Telling stories as a method of practicing law reaches back to the days of the classical Greek orators who were lawyers. Before legal education became an academic matter, the apprenticeship system for training lawyers consisted of mentoring and telling "war stories." As the law and literature movement evolved, it sorted itself into three strands: law in literature, law as literature, and storytelling. The storytelling branch blossomed.

Over the last few decades, storytelling became a subject of enormous interest and controversy within the world of legal scholarship. Law review articles appeared in the form of stories. Law professors pointed out that legal decisions were really stories that told a dominant narrative. Critical theorists began to tell counter stories to challenge or critique the traditional canon. Some used fictional stories as a method of analytical critique; others told accounts of actual events in ways that gave voice to the experiences of outsiders.

Storytelling began to make its way into legal education in new ways. For instance, a major textbook publisher developed a new series of books that recount the stories behind landmark cases in specific subject areas, such as Torts or Employment Discrimination, to help students appreciate not only the players in major cases, but also the social context in which cases arise. Meanwhile, Scott Turow, John Grisham, and a legion of other lawyers invaded the realm of popular fiction and conquered the bestseller lists.

Legal theorists began to recognize what historians and practicing lawyers had long known and what cognitive psychologists were just discovering-the extraordinary power of stories. Stories are the way people, including judges and jurors, understand situations. People recall events in story form. Stories are educative; they illuminate different perspectives and evoke empathy. Stories create bonds; their evocative details engage people in ways that sterile legal arguments do not.

RICHARD DELGADO, *LEGAL STORYTELLING: STORYTELLING FOR OPPOSITIONISTS AND OTHERS: A PLEA FOR NARRATIVE*

87 MICHIGAN LAW REVIEW 2411 (1989)

Delgado is the John J. Sparkman Chair of Law at the University of Alabama School of Law. His scholarship focuses on race, the legal profession, and social change. His books have won numerous national book prizes, including six Gustavus Myers awards for outstanding book on human rights in North America, the American Library Association's Outstanding Academic Book, and a Pulitzer Prize nomination.

Everyone has been writing stories these days. And I don't just mean writing *about* stories or narrative theory, important as those are. I mean actual stories, as in "once-upon-a-time" type stories. Derrick Bell has been writing "Chronicles," and in the *Harvard Law Review* at that. Others have been writing dialogues, stories, and metastories. Many others have been daring to become more personal in their writing, to inject narrative, perspective, and feeling—how it was for me—into their otherwise scholarly, footnoted articles and, in the case of the truly brave, into their teaching.

Many, but by no means all, who have been telling legal stories are members of what could be loosely described as outgroups, groups whose marginality defines the boundaries of the mainstream, whose voice and perspective—whose consciousness—has been suppressed, devalued, and abnormalized. The attraction of stories for these groups should come as no surprise. For stories create their own bonds, represent cohesion, shared understandings, and meanings. The cohesiveness that stories bring is part of the strength of the outgroup. An outgroup creates its own stories, which circulate within the group as a kind of counter-reality.

The dominant group creates its own stories, as well. The stories or narratives told by the ingroup remind it of its identity in relation to outgroups, and provide it with a form of shared reality in which its own superior position is seen as natural.

The stories of outgroups aim to subvert that ingroup reality. In civil rights, for example, many in the majority hold that any inequality between blacks and whites is due either to cultural lag, or inadequate enforcement of currently existing beneficial laws—both of which are easily correctable. For many minority persons, the principal instrument of their subordination is neither of these. Rather, it is the prevailing *mindset* by means of which members of the dominant group justify the world as it is, that is, with whites on top and browns and blacks at the bottom.

Stories, parables, chronicles, and narratives are powerful means for destroying mindset—the bundle of presuppositions, received wisdoms, and shared understandings against a background of which legal and political discourse takes place. These matters are rarely focused on. They are like eyeglasses we have worn a long time. They are nearly invisible; we use them to scan and interpret the world and only rarely examine them for themselves. Ideology—the received wisdom—makes current social arrangements seem fair and natural. Those in power sleep well at night—their conduct does not seem to them like oppression.

The cure is storytelling (or as I shall sometimes call it, counterstorytelling). As Derrick Bell, Bruno Bettelheim, and others show, stories can shatter complacency and challenge the status quo. Stories told by underdogs are frequently ironic or satiric; a root word for "humor" is humus—bringing low, down to earth. Along with the tradition of storytelling in black culture there exists the Spanish tradition of the picaresque novel or story, which tells of humble folk piquing the pompous or powerful and bringing them down to more human levels.

Most who write about storytelling focus on its community-building functions: stories build consensus, a common culture of shared understandings, and deeper, more vital ethics. Counterstories, which challenge the received wisdom, do that as well. They can open new windows into reality, showing us that there are possibilities for life other than the ones we live. They enrich imagination and teach that by combining elements from the story and current reality, we may construct a new world richer than either alone. Counterstories can quicken and engage conscience. Their graphic quality can stir imagination in ways in which more conventional discourse cannot.

But stories and counterstories can serve an equally important destructive function. They can show that what we believe is ridiculous, self-serving, or cruel. They can show us the way out of the trap of unjustified exclusion. They can help us understand when it is time to reallocate power. They are the other half—the destructive half—of the creative dialectic.

Stories and counterstories, to be effective, must be or must appear to be noncoercive. They invite the reader to suspend judgment, listen for their point or message, and then decide what measure of truth they contain. They are insinuative, not frontal; they offer a respite from the linear, coercive discourse that characterizes much legal writing.

This essay examines the use of stories in the struggle for racial reform.

* * *

I.   STORYTELLING AND COUNTER-STORYTELLING

The same object, as everyone knows, can be described in many ways. A rectangular red object on my living room floor may be a nuisance if I stub my toe on it in the dark, a doorstop if I use it for that purpose, further evidence of my lackadaisical housekeeping to my visiting mother, a toy to my young daughter, or simply a brick left over from my patio restoration project. There is no single true, or all-encompassing description. The same holds true of events. Watching an individual perform strenuous repetitive movements, we might say that he or she is exercising, discharging nervous energy, seeing to his or her health under doctor's orders, or suffering a seizure or convulsion. Often, we will not be able to ascertain the single best description or interpretation of what we have seen. We participate in creating what we see in the very act of describing it.

Social and moral realities, the subject of this essay, are just as indeterminate and subject to interpretation as single objects or events, if not more so. For example, what is the "correct" answer to the question, The American Indians are—(A) a colonized people; (B) tragic victims of technological progress; (C) subjects of a suffocating, misdirected federal beneficence; (D) a minority stubbornly resistant to assimilation; or (E); or (F)?

My premise is that much of social reality is constructed. We decide what is, and, almost simultaneously, what ought to be. Narrative habits, patterns of seeing, shape what we see and that to which we aspire. These patterns of perception become habitual, tempting us to believe that the way things are is inevitable, or the best that can be in an imperfect world. Alternative visions of reality are not explored, or, if they are, rejected as extreme or implausible.

In the area of racial reform the majority story would go something like this:

> Early in our history there was slavery, which was a terrible thing. Blacks were brought to this country from Africa in chains and made to work in the fields. Some were viciously mistreated, which was, of course, an unforgivable wrong; others were treated kindly. Slavery ended with the Civil War, although many blacks remained poor, uneducated, and outside the cultural mainstream. As the country's racial sensitivity to blacks' plight increased, the vestiges of slavery were gradually eliminated by federal statutes and case law. Today, blacks have many civil rights and are protected from discrimination in such areas as housing, public education, employment, and voting. The gap between blacks and whites is steadily closing, although it may take some time for it to close completely. At the same time, it is important not to go too far in providing special benefits for blacks. Doing so induces dependency and welfare mentality. It can also cause a backlash among innocent white victims of reverse discrimination. Most Americans are fair-minded individuals who harbor little racial

prejudice. The few who do can be punished when they act on those beliefs.

Yet, coexisting with that rather comforting tale is another story of black subordination in America, a history "gory, brutal, filled with more murder, mutilation, rape, and brutality than most of us can imagine or easily comprehend." This other history continues into the present, implicating individuals still alive. It includes infant death rates among blacks nearly double those of whites, unemployment rates among black males nearly triple those of whites, and a gap between the races in income, wealth, and life expectancy that is the same as it was fifteen years ago, if not greater. It includes despair, crime, and drug addiction in black neighborhoods, and college and university enrollment figures for blacks that are dropping for the first time in decades. It dares to call our most prized legal doctrines and protections shams—devices enacted with great fanfare, only to be ignored, obstructed, or cut back as soon as the celebrations die down.

How can there be such divergent stories? Why do they not combine? Is it simply that members of the dominant group see the same glass as half full, blacks as half empty? I believe there is more than this at work; there is a war between stories. They contend for, tug at, our minds. To see how the dialectic of competition and rejection works—to see the reality-creating potential of stories and the normative implications of adopting one story rather than another—consider the following series of accounts, each describing the same event.

A.   *A Standard Event and a Stock Story That Explains It*

The following series of stories revolves around the same event: A black lawyer interviews for a teaching position at a major law school (school *X*), and is rejected. Any other race-tinged event could have served equally well for purposes of illustration. This particular event was chosen because it occurs on familiar ground—most readers of this essay are past or present members of a law school community who have heard about or participated in events like the one described.

The Stock Story

Setting. A professor and student are talking in the professor's office. Both are white. The professor, Blas Vernier, is tenured, in mid-career, and well regarded by his colleagues and students. The student, Judith Rogers, is a member of the student advisory appointments committee.

Rogers: Professor Vernier, what happened with the black candidate, John Henry? I heard he was voted down at the faculty meeting yesterday. The students on my committee liked him a lot.

Vernier: It was a difficult decision, Judith. We discussed him for over two hours. I can't tell you the final vote, of course, but it wasn't particularly close. Even some of my colleagues who were initially for his appointment voted against him when the full record came out.

Rogers: But we have no minority professors at all, except for Professor Chen, who is untenured, and Professor Tompkins, who teaches Trial Practice on loan from the district attorney's office once a year.

Vernier: Don't forget Mary Foster, the Assistant Dean.

Rogers: But she doesn't teach, just handles admissions and the placement office.

Vernier: And does those things very well. But back to John Henry. I understand your disappointment. Henry was a strong candidate, one of the stronger blacks we've interviewed recently. But ultimately he didn't measure up. We didn't think he wanted to teach for the right reasons. He was vague and diffuse about his research interests. All he could say was that he wanted to write about equality and civil rights, but so far as we could tell, he had nothing new to say about those areas. What's more, we had some problems with his teaching interests. He wanted to teach peripheral courses, in areas where we already have enough people. And we had the sense that he wouldn't be really rigorous in those areas, either.

Rogers: But we need courses in employment discrimination and civil rights. And he's had a long career with the NAACP Legal Defense Fund and really seemed to know his stuff.

Vernier: It's true we could stand to add a course or two of that nature, although as you know our main needs are in Commercial Law and Corporations, and Henry doesn't teach either. But I think our need is not as acute as you say. Many of the topics you're interested in are covered in the second half of the Constitutional Law course taught by Professor White, who has a national reputation for his work in civil liberties and freedom of speech.

Rogers: But Henry could have taught those topics from a black perspective. And he would have been a wonderful role model for our minority students.

Vernier: Those things are true, and we gave them considerable weight. But when it came right down to it, we felt we couldn't take that great a risk. Henry wasn't on the law review at school, as you are, Judith, and has never written a line in a legal journal. Some of us doubted he ever would. And then, what would happen five years from now when he came up for tenure? It wouldn't be fair to place him in an environment like this. He'd just have to pick up his career and start over if he didn't produce.

Rogers: With all due respect, Professor, that's paternalistic. I think Henry should have been given the chance. He might have surprised us.

Vernier: So I thought, too, until I heard my colleagues' discussion, which I'm afraid, given the demands of confidentiality, I can't share with you. Just let me say that we examined his case long and hard and I am convinced, fairly. The decision, while painful, was correct.

Rogers: So another year is going to go by without a minority candidate or professor?

Vernier: These things take time. I was on the appointments committee last year, chaired it in fact. And I can tell you we would love nothing better than to find a qualified black. Every year, we call the Supreme Court to check on current clerks, telephone our colleagues at other leading law schools, and place ads in black newspapers and journals. But the pool is so small. And the few good ones have many opportunities. We can't pay nearly as much as private practice, you know.

[*Rogers, who would like to be a legal services attorney, but is attracted to the higher salaries of corporate practice, nods glumly.*]

Vernier: It may be that we'll have to wait another few years, until the current crop of black and minority law students graduates and gets some experience. We have some excellent prospects, including some members of your very class.

Rogers: [*Thinks: I've heard that one before, but says*] Well, thanks, Professor. I know the students will be disappointed. But maybe when the committee considers visiting professors later in the season it will be able to find a professor of color who meets its standards and fits our needs.

Vernier: We'll try our best. Although you should know that some of us believe that merely shuffling the few minorities in teaching from one school to another does nothing to expand the pool. And once they get here, it's hard to say no if they express a desire to stay on.

Rogers: [*Thinks: That's a lot like tenure. How ironic; there are certain of your colleagues we would love to get rid of, too. But says*] Well, thanks, Professor. I've got to get to class. I still wish the vote had come out otherwise. Our student committee is preparing a list of minority candidates that we would like to see considered. Maybe you'll find one or more of them worthy of teaching here.

Vernier: Judith, believe me, there is nothing that would please me more.

In the above dialogue, Professor Vernier's account represents the stock story—the one the institution collectively forms and tells about itself. This story picks and chooses from among the available facts to present a picture of what happened: an account that justifies the world as it is. It emphasizes the school's benevolent motivation ("look how hard we're trying") and good faith. It stresses stability and the avoidance of risks. It measures the black candidate through the prism of preexisting, well-agreed-upon criteria of conventional scholarship and teaching. Given those standards, it purports to be scrupulously meritocratic and fair; Henry would have been hired had he measured up. No one raises the possibility that the merit criteria employed in judging Henry are themselves debatable, *chosen*—not inevitable. No one, least of all Vernier, calls attention to the way in which merit functions to conceal the contingent connection between institutional power and the things rated.

There is also little consideration of the possibility that Henry's presence on the faculty might have altered the institution's character, helped introduce a different prism and different criteria for selecting future candidates. The account is highly procedural—it emphasizes that Henry got a full, careful hearing—rather than substantive: a black was rejected. It emphasizes certain "facts" without examining their truth—namely, that the pool is very small, that good minority candidates have many choices, and that the appropriate view is the long view; haste makes waste.

The dominant fact about this first story, however, is its seeming neutrality. It scrupulously avoids issues of blame or responsibility. Race played no part in the candidate's rejection; indeed the school leaned over backwards to accommodate him. A white candidate with similar credentials would not have made it as far as Henry did. The story comforts and soothes. And Vernier's sincerity makes him an effective apologist for his system.

Vernier's story is also deeply coercive, although the coercion is disguised. Judith was aware of it but chose not to confront it directly; Vernier holds all the cards. He pressures her to go along with the institution's story by threatening her prospects at the same time that he flatters her achievements. A victim herself, she is invited to take on and share the consciousness of her oppressor. She does not accept Vernier's story, but he does slip a few doubts through cracks in her armor. The professor's story shows how forceful and repeated storytelling can perpetuate a particular view of reality. Naturally, the stock story is not the only one that can be told. By emphasizing other events and giving them slightly different interpretations, a quite different picture can be made to emerge.

B. *The Same Event Told by John Henry*

Scene. John Henry has just received his rejection letter from the head of the appointments committee. The letter is quite cheerful. It tells Henry how much the faculty enjoyed meeting him and hearing his presentation on trends in civil rights litigation. It advises him that because of curricular concerns, the school's prime emphasis this year will be on filling slots in the Commercial Law and Corporations area. It concludes by encouraging Henry to remain in contact with the school and wishes him luck in his search for a teaching position. It nowhere tells him that he has been rejected.

A few days after receiving the letter, John Henry is having lunch with a junior colleague from the Fund. The colleague, who is also black, wants to teach some day and so quizzes Henry about his experiences in interviewing at school *X.*

Henry: It was, how shall I put it? Worse than I hoped but better than I feared. I'm not going to get an offer, although they of course never came right out and said so. And, from what I saw I'm not sure I would want to teach there, even if I had gotten one. If school *X* is any sample of what blacks can expect in this supposedly colorblind, erudite world of legal education, I think I prefer Howard, where, incidentally, I'm interviewing next week. I got more than a whiff of these attitudes when I went to law school almost 15 years ago, but I had dared to hope that things might have changed in the interim. They haven't.

Junior colleague: But how did they treat you? Did you give a colloquium?

Henry: You bet I gave a colloquium, and that's where it began. A good half of the faculty looked bored or puzzled and asked no questions. A quarter jumped down my throat after I had spoken maybe ten minutes, wanting to know whether I would advocate the same approach if the plaintiff were white and the defendant black. The old "neutral principles" idea, thirty years later. In the question-and-answer period, several younger professors tried to rescue me; one even changed the subject and asked about my philosophy of teaching. That brought everybody to the edge of their chairs. I got the impression many of them merely wanted assurance that I would write *some* articles, even if they were mediocre. But they were *all* extremely concerned that I be a good teacher. I think many of them were looking for a mascot, not a fellow scholar—someone who would counsel and keep the students in line, not someone who could challenge his or her colleagues at their own game.

During the small-group interviews, many of them didn't even show up. The ones that did asked me about curricular matters, what courses I would like to teach, how I enjoyed going to law school at Michigan and whether I took courses from their friend, so-and-so, who teaches there. The few who asked me anything about my colloquium ignored what I had said but asked me questions based on recent law review articles, written by their friends, most of which, of course, I had not read. They all seemed to deal with issues of equality, but none seemed to bear much connection to my work and litigation perspective.

Several asked what my grade point average was in law school—fifteen years ago, can you believe it!—and whether I was on the law review. They had my resume in front of them, so they knew the answer to that perfectly well. The first two who asked seemed dumbfounded when I said I had been invited to join the review and even more so when I said I had declined in order to work part-time in a prison law program. After a while I just answered the question by saying no.

Don't get me wrong. They're a good law school; I could see myself teaching there. But I think they're looking for someone they will never find—a black who won't challenge them in any way, who is just like them. I tried telling them about the cases I have argued and the litigation strategies I have pioneered. Most of them couldn't have cared less. Their eyes glazed over after three minutes, or they changed the subject.

Junior colleague: John, let me ask you something flat out. You don't have to answer this if you don't want to. You know that I practiced corporate law in a large firm in Atlanta for three years before coming to the Fund. I could see myself teaching business subjects some day, in addition of course to civil rights. The school you interviewed at is advertising that they need professors of business law. Do I want to teach there?

Henry: [*Slowly*] That's a tough one. If I went there, my greatest fear is that I would be marginalized and ignored—either that or co-opted into the mainstream. I doubt they would see my work in civil rights as on a level with theirs in, say, property. You might have a different experience, though, teaching corporate and business law courses. Are you serious about applying?

Junior colleague: I think so.

Henry: Okay, my man. Let me call the Asian professor I met there. His name is Chen, I think. He seemed sympathetic, and I guess he would level with us. I'll ask him what he thinks the climate would be like for someone like you. Maybe in the process I'll learn something about how I was seen and get some pointers on how to conduct myself the next time I interview at a white, elite law school—if I have to. I think Howard is quite interested in me, and frankly I'm tempted to just accept an offer there if they make one. It would simplify life a great deal.

Junior colleague: I would appreciate that. You're a good buddy. Let me know what you find out.

Henry and his younger colleague's story is, obviously, quite different from the institution's story. Their story shows, among other things, how different "neutrality" can feel from the perspective of an outsider. Henry's story emphasizes certain facts, sequences, tones of voice, and body language that the stock story leaves out. It infers different intentions, attitudes, and states of mind on the part of the faculty he met. Although not completely condemnatory, it is not nearly so generous to the school. It implies that the supposedly colorblind hiring process is really monochromatic: School *X* hires professors of any color, so long as they are white. In Henry's story, process questions submerge; the bottom line becomes more important. The story specifically challenges the school's meritocratic premises. It questions, somewhat satirically, the school's conception of a "good" teaching prospect and asks what came first, the current faculty (with its strengths and weaknesses) or the criteria. Did the "is" give birth to the "ought"? Henry's account, although less obviously slanted than Vernier's, contains exaggerations of its own. This is perhaps natural and understandable; Henry wanted his younger colleague to think well of him. His account is self-serving. For example, he implied that many of the faculty asked him about his law school grades, when in fact only two did. And, although Henry does struggle to free himself from the process trap to which Vernier succumbed, he does not succeed entirely. He charges that his "hearing" at the law school was substantively biased by racism and inappropriate criteria. But he also charges that the hearing was afflicted by ordinary defects: For example, many of his hearers did not bother to show up—it was a mock hearing. Henry still accepts the system's dominant values, wants to play, and win, by its rules. Perhaps this explains the calmness, the tone of resignation about Henry's story. Whether this is because he has internalized some of his victimizers' consciousness, has a good alternative coming up next week at Howard, or simply despairs of changing School *X* we do not know. But this situation soon changed drastically.

Following Henry's lunch with his younger colleague, Henry telephoned Chen and one other younger, bearded faculty member he met at the law school. The other professor, who is white, had visibly warmed up to Henry. He had asked him to call any time if Henry had questions. As a result of talking with these two at length, Henry learns facts that leave him seriously upset. No longer resigned, Henry consults with several colleagues at the Fund about a lawsuit. After receiving an offer from Howard, Henry retains private counsel. The following two stories are the result.

C. *The Legal Complaint and Judge's Order*

1. *The Complaint*

About a year after his unsuccessful interview, and ten months after speaking with Chen and the white professor, Henry files the following complaint in the superior court of College County of State *X:*

> *Henry v. Regents, et al.* Comes now the plaintiff and alleges as follows.

> [Following various jurisdictional and exhaustion-of-remedies allegations]: 8) That the defendant has intentionally engaged in an unlawful employment practice in that the defendant has discriminated against plaintiff by denying him an appointment as Professor of Law, because of his race and color; that defendant has denied plaintiff employment as Professor of Law because of his

engagement in civil rights activities; that defendant has denied plaintiff employment as Professor of Law because as a black Professor teaching Civil Rights he would not "fit in"; and that the above mentioned acts of discrimination violate 42 U.S.C. section 1981 in that they were based on race, color, and civil rights activities and orientations.

9)   That the plaintiff has lost wages by reason of the illegal employment practices of defendant and has earned less money in other employment than he would have earned had he received appointment as Professor of Law at defendant institution.

Whereupon plaintiff prays that this Court find that the defendant has intentionally and illegally denied plaintiff employment because of his race, color, and civil rights activities, and because as a black man he would not "fit in"; that the Court enjoin defendant from engaging in these and similar practices; that the defendant be ordered to pay plaintiff all lost wages because of said unlawful employment practices; that the defendant pay plaintiff's reasonable attorney's fees; and that defendant be ordered to pay all costs in this action.

> Phyllis M. Leventhal
> Attorney for Plaintiff
> Address: 49 State Building
> Capitol City, State *X*

2.   *The Judge's Order Dismissing the Action*

After a short period of discovery, the judge dismissed Henry's suit with a brief opinion:

The defendant's motion for summary judgment is granted.

Even viewing the evidence in the light most favorable to Plaintiff, it is clear to this Court that he cannot prevail. Plaintiff has adduced no evidence, save his own assertion that he was not hired, that he has suffered unlawful employment discrimination. Given the historic shortage of qualified minorities in the applicant pool, it is not surprising that white faces should preponderate on a law faculty. This imbalance is not irrelevant but by itself does not constitute invidious discrimination. It is of no greater or less significance than the proportion of blacks to whites on the school's athletic teams.

Even assuming that he is qualified to teach at School *X*, Plaintiff has not made out a claim that his failure to be hired there is a product of discrimination. If he could adduce even one example of obvious discrimination—for example, if he had been told that his lack of authorship disqualified him, but he could prove that some white faculty members had neither published nor perished—this would be a far different case. But there is no such smoking gun. Plaintiff believes he was blackballed as a potential "troublemaker," someone who might use his position atop the ivory tower to cry out against the university, to bite the very hand that had uplifted him. But a propensity toward disloyalty is simply one of the competing considerations in the hiring process, the weight of which our scales of justice shall not attempt to assay. There is, however, nothing intrinsically wrong with requiring a college professor to be true to his school.

Nor do we find that differential standards were applied to Plaintiff's application. It may be that the law faculty devalued his potential contributions as a teacher and scholar of civil rights law. But a faculty is entitled to make judgments that one class or area of study is more urgently needed to round out the school's curriculum than another.

Moreover, this Court would be most hesitant to substitute its own standards for those of the professors who make up the faculty of *X* School of Law. The Law School is an eminent institution, one of the nation's finest. The decisions of such a body are necessarily judgmental and highly subjective. It is not an appropriate function for this Court to tell the faculty whom they should hire. That is a matter for their professional judgment, and short of manifest unfairness or illegality, this Court cannot and will not interfere. The factors that make a good law professor are many, subtle, and eminently professional in character. They are best made by those who, had he been hired, would have been Plaintiff's peers. It would ill serve the Plaintiff to force him on an unwilling institution. We find no actionable wrong. This case is dismissed.

Both the complaint and the order dismissing it are stylized versions of Henry's story. Both use existing statutory and case law as a type of "screen" that makes certain facts relevant and others not. Henry's lawyer struggled to present her client's story in terms a court would accept. She failed. Unless reversed on appeal, the complaint's story will remain a renegade version of the world, officially devalued.

Putting the facts in the linguistic code required by the court sterilized them. The interview was abstracted from its context, squeezed into a prescribed mold that stripped it of the features that gave it meaning for Henry. It lost its power to outrage. In a sense, even if successful the complaint would have legitimated the current social order. As Cornel West and others have warned, litigation and other seemingly revolutionary activity can serve this end. Civil rights litigation also demeans, humbles, and victimizes the victim, draining away outrage and converting him or her into a supplicant.

Stories do not pose these risks. Stories do not try to seize a part of the body of received wisdom and use it against itself, jiujitsu fashion, as litigation does. Stories attack and subvert the very "institutional logic" of the system. On the rare occasions when law-reform litigation is effective for blacks, the hard-won new "rights" are quietly stolen away by narrow interpretation, foot dragging, delay, and outright obstruction. Stories' success is not so easily circumvented; a telling point is registered instantaneously and the stock story it wounds will never be the same.

John Henry's complaint was doubly unsuccessful. It was dismissed, its failure validating the dominant story, its principal opponent so far. It also gave the judge an opportunity to tell his own story—dismissive, curt, verging on insult, and give it circulation and currency.

D. *Al-Hammar X's Counter-story*

None of the above stories attempts to unseat the prevailing institutional story. Henry's account comes closest; it highlights different facts and interprets those it does share with the standard account differently. His formal complaint also challenges the school's account, but it must fit itself under existing law, which it failed to do.

A few days after word of Henry's rejection reached the student body, Noel Al-Hammar X, leader of the radical Third World Coalition, delivered a speech at noon on the steps of the law school patio. The audience consisted of most of the black and brown students at the law school, several dozen white students, and a few faculty members. Chen was absent, having a class to prepare for. The Assistant Dean was present, uneasily taking mental notes in case the Dean asked her later what she heard.

Al-Hammar's speech was scathing, denunciatory, and at times downright rude. He spoke several words that the campus newspaper reporter wondered if his paper would print. He impugned the good faith of the faculty, accused them of institutional if not garden-variety racism, and pointed out in great detail the long history of the faculty as an all-white club. He said that the law school was bent on hiring only white males, "ladies" only if they were well-behaved clones of white males, and would never hire a black unless forced to do so by student pressure or the courts. He exhorted his fellow students not to rest until the law faculty took steps to address its own ethnocentricity and racism. He urged boycotting or disrupting classes, writing letters to the state legislature, withholding alumni contributions, setting up a "shadow" appointments committee, and several other measures that made the Assistant Dean wince.

Al-Hammar's talk received a great deal of attention, particularly from the faculty who were not there to hear it. Several versions of his story circulated among the faculty offices and corridors ("Did you hear what he said?"). Many of the stories-about-the-story were wildly exaggerated. Nevertheless, Al-Hammar's story is an authentic counterstory. It directly challenges—both in its words and tone—the corporate story the law school carefully worked out to explain Henry's non-appointment. It rejects many of the institution's premises, including we-try-so-hard, the-pool-is-so-small, and even mocks the school's meritocratic self-concept. "They say Henry is mediocre, has a pedestrian mind. Well, they ain't sat in none of my classes and listened to themselves. Mediocrity they got. They're experts on mediocrity." Al-Hammar denounced the faculty's excuse making, saying there were dozens of qualified black candidates, if not hundreds. "There isn't that big a pool of Chancellors, or quarterbacks," he said. "But when they need one, they find one, don't they?"

Al-Hammar also deviates stylistically, as a storyteller, from John Henry. He rebels against the "reasonable discourse" of law. He is angry, and anger is out of bounds in legal discourse, even as a response to discrimination. John Henry was unsuccessful in getting others to listen. So was Al-Hammar, but for a different reason. His counterstory overwhelmed the audience. More than just a narrative, it was a call to action, a call to join him in destroying the current story. But his audience was not ready to act. Too many of his listeners felt challenged or coerced; their defenses went up. The campus newspaper the next day published a garbled version, saying that he had urged the law faculty to relax its standards in order to provide minority students with role models. This prompted three letters to the editor asking how an unqualified black professor could be a good role model for anyone, black or white.

Moreover, the audience Al-Hammar intended to affect, namely the faculty, was even more unmoved by his counterstory. It attacked them too frontally. They were quick to dismiss him as an extremist, a demagogue, a hothead—someone to be taken seriously only for the damage he might do should he attract a body of followers. Consequently, for the next week the faculty spent much time in one-on-one conversations with "responsible" student leaders, including Judith Rogers.

By the end of the week, a consensus story had formed about Al-Hammar's story. That story-about-a-story held that Al-Hammar had gone too far, that there was more to the situation than Al-Hammar knew or was prepared to admit. Moreover, Al-Hammar was portrayed *not* as someone who had reached out, in pain, for sympathy and friendship. Rather, he was depicted as a "bad actor," someone with a "chip on his shoulder," someone no responsible member of the law school community should trade stories with. Nonetheless, a few progressive students and faculty members believed Al-Hammar had done the institution a favor by raising the issues and demanding that they be addressed. They were a distinct minority.

E.   *The Anonymous Leaflet Counterstory*

About a month after Al-Hammar spoke, the law faculty formed a special committee for minority hiring. The committee contained practically every young liberal on the faculty, two of its three female professors, and the Assistant Dean. The Dean announced the committee's formation in a memorandum sent to the law school's ethnic student associations, the student government, and the alumni newsletter, which gave it front-page coverage. It was also posted on bulletin boards around the law school.

The memo spoke about the committee and its mission in serious, measured phrases—"social need," "national search," "renewed effort," "balancing the various considerations," "identifying members of a future pool from which we might draw." Shortly after the memo was distributed, an anonymous four-page leaflet appeared in the student lounge, on the same bulletin boards on which the Dean's memo had been posted, and in various mailboxes of faculty members and law school organizations. Its author, whether student or faculty member, was never identified.

The leaflet was entitled, "Another Committee, Aren't We Wonderful?" It began with a caricature of the Dean's memo, mocking its measured language and high-flown tone. Then, beginning in the middle of the page the memo told, in conversational terms, the following story:

'And so, friends and neighbors (the leaflet continued), how is it that the good law schools go about looking for new faculty members? Here is how it works. The appointments committee starts out the year with a model new faculty member in mind. This mythic creature went to a leading law school, graduated first or second in his or her class, clerked for the Supreme Court, and wrote the leading note in the law review on some topic dealing with the federal courts. This individual is brilliant, personable, humane, and has just the right amount of practice experience with the right firm.

Schools begin with this paragon in mind and energetically beat the bushes, beginning in September, in search of him or her. At this stage, they believe themselves genuinely and sincerely colorblind. If they find such a mythic figure who is black or Hispanic or gay or lesbian, they will hire this person in a flash. They will of course do the same if the person is white.

By February, however, the school has not hired many mythic figures. Some that they interviewed turned them down. Now, it's late in the year and they have to get someone to teach Trusts and Estates. Although there are none left on their list who are Supreme Court clerks, etc., they can easily find several who are a notch or two below that—who went to good schools, but not Harvard, or who went to Harvard, yet were not first or second in their classes. Still, they know, with a degree verging on certainty, that this person is smart and can do the job. They know this from personal acquaintance with this individual, or they hear it from someone they know and trust. Joe says Bill is really smart, a good lawyer, and will be terrific in the classroom.

So they hire this person because, although he or she is not a mythic figure, functionally equivalent guarantees—namely first- or second-hand experience—assure them that this person will be a good teacher and scholar. And so it generally turns out—the new professor does just fine.

'Persons hired in this fashion are almost always white, male, and straight. The reason: We rarely know blacks, Hispanics, women, and gays. Moreover, when we hire the white male, the known but less-than-mythic quantity, late in February, *it does not seem to us like we are making an exception.* Yet we are. We are employing a form of affirmative action—bending the stated rules so as to hire the person we want.

The upshot is that whites have two chances of being hired—by meeting the formal criteria we start out with in September—that is, by being mythic figures—and also by meeting the second, informal, modified criteria we apply later to friends and acquaintances when we are in a pinch. Minorities have just one chance of being hired—the first.

To be sure, once every decade or so a law school, imbued with crusading zeal, will bend the rules and hire a minority with credentials just short of Superman or Superwoman. And, when it does so, *it will feel like an exception.* The school will congratulate itself—it has lifted up one of the downtrodden. And, it will remind the new professor repeatedly how lucky he or she is to be here in this wonderful place. It will also make sure, through subtle or not-so-subtle means, that the students know so, too.

But (the leaflet continued), there is a coda.

If, later, the minority professor hired this way unexpectedly succeeds, this will produce consternation among his or her colleagues. For, things were not intended to go that way. When he or she came aboard, the minority professor lacked those standard indicia of merit—Supreme Court clerkship, high LSAT score, prep school background—that the majority-race professors had and believe essential to scholarly success.

Yet the minority professor is succeeding all the same—publishing in good law reviews, receiving invitations to serve on important commissions, winning popularity with students. This is infuriating. Many majority-race professors are persons of relatively slender achievements—you can look up their publishing record any time you have five minutes. Their principal achievements lie in the distant past, when aided by their parents' upper class background, they did well in high school and college, and got the requisite test scores on standardized tests which test exactly the accumulated cultural capital they acquired so easily and naturally at home. Shortly after that, their careers started to stagnate. They publish an article every five years or so, often in a minor law review, after gallingly having it turned down by the very review they served on as editor twenty years ago.

So, their claim to fame lies in their early exploits, the badges they acquired up to about the age of twenty-five, at which point the edge they acquired from Mummy and Daddy began to lose effect. Now, along comes the hungry minority professor, imbued with a fierce desire to get ahead, a good intellect, and a willingness to work 70 hours a week if necessary to make up for lost time. The minority person lacks the merit badges awarded early in life, the white professor's main source of security. So, the minority's colleagues don't like it and use perfectly predictable ways to transfer the costs of their discomfort to the misbehaving minority.

So that, my friends, is why minority professors

'(i)   have a hard time getting hired; and,

'(ii)   have a hard time if they are hired.

When you and I are running the world, we won't replicate this unfair system, will we? Of course not—unless, of course, it changes us in the process.

* * *

This second counterstory attacks the faculty less frontally in some respects—for example it does not focus on the fate of any particular black candidate, such as Henry, but attacks a general mindset. It employs several devices including narrative and careful observation—the latter to build credibility (the reader says, "That's right"), the former to beguile the reader and get him or her to suspend judgment. (Everyone loves a story.) The last part of the story is painful; it strikes close to home. Yet the way for its acceptance has been paved by the earlier parts, which paint a plausible picture of events, so that the final part demands consideration. It generalizes and exaggerates—many majority-race professors are *not* persons of slender achievement. But such broad strokes are part of the narrator's art. The realistically drawn first part of the story, despite shading off into caricature at the end, forces readers to focus on the flaws in the good face the dean attempted to put on events. And, despite its somewhat accusatory thrust, the story, as was mentioned, debunks only a mindset, not a person. Unlike Al-Hammar X's story, it does not call the chair of the appointments committee, a much-loved senior professor, a racist. (But did Al-Hammar's story, confrontational as it was, pave the way for the generally positive reception accorded the anonymous account?)

The story invites the reader to alienate herself or himself from the events described, to enter into the mental set of the teller, whose view is different from the reader's own. The oppositional nature of the story, the manner in which it challenges and rebuffs the stock story, thus causes him or her to oscillate between poles. It is insinuative: At times, the reader is seduced by the story and its logical coherence—it is a plausible counter-view of what happened; it has a degree of explanatory power.

Yet the story places the majority-race reader on the defensive. He or she alternately leaves the storyteller's perspective to return to his or her own, saying, "That's outrageous, I'm being accused of. . . ." The reader thus moves back and forth between two worlds, the storyteller's, which the reader occupies vicariously to the extent the story is well-told and rings true, and his or her own, which he or she returns to and reevaluates in light of the story's message. Can my world still stand? What parts of it remain valid? What parts of the story seem true? How can I reconcile the two worlds, and will the resulting world be a better one than the one with which I began?

These are in large part normative questions, which lead to the final two issues I want to explore. Why *should* members of outgroups tell stories? And, why *should* others listen?

II. WHY OUTGROUPS SHOULD TELL STORIES AND WHY OTHERS SHOULD LISTEN

Subordinated groups have always told stories. Black slaves told, in song, letters, and verse, about their own pain and oppression. They described the terrible wrongs they had experienced at the hands of whites, and mocked (behind whites' backs) the veneer of gentility whites purchased at the cost of the slaves' suffering. Mexican-Americans in the Southwest composed *corridos* (ballads) and stories, passed on from generation to generation, of abuse at the hands of gringo justice, the Texas Rangers, and ruthless lawyers and developers who cheated them out of their lands. Native American literature, both oral and written, deals with all these themes as well. Feminist consciousness-raising consists, in part, of the sharing of stories, of tales from personal experience, on the basis of which the group constructs a shared reality about women's status vis-a-vis men.

This proliferation of counterstories is not an accident or coincidence. Oppressed groups have known instinctively that stories are an essential tool to their own survival and liberation. Members of outgroups can use stories in two basic ways: first, as means of psychic self-preservation; and, second, as means of lessening their own subordination. These two means correspond to the two perspectives from which a story can be viewed—that of the teller, and that of the listener. The storyteller gains psychically, the listener morally and epistemologically.

* * *

CONCLUSION

Stories humanize us. They emphasize our differences in ways that can ultimately bring us closer together. They allow us to see how the world looks from behind someone else's spectacles. They challenge us to wipe off our own lenses and ask, "Could I have been overlooking something all along?"

Telling stories invests text with feeling, gives voice to those who were taught to hide their emotions. Hearing stories invites hearers to participate, challenging their assumptions, jarring their complacency, lifting their spirits, lowering their defenses.

Stories are useful tools for the underdog because they invite the listener to suspend judgment, listen for the story's point, and test it against his or her own version of reality. This process is essential in a pluralist society like ours, and it is a practical necessity for underdogs: All movements for change must gain the support, or at least understanding, of the dominant group, which is white.

* * *

NANCY LEVIT, *RESHAPING THE NARRATIVE DEBATE*
34 SEATTLE UNIVERSITY LAW REVIEW 751 (2011)

Levit is Associate Dean for Faculty and Curators' Professor and Edward D. Ellison Professor of Law at the University of Missouri-Kansas City School of Law. Her work was introduced earlier in this chapter.

In *Reshaping the Work-Family Debate: Why Men and Class Matter*, Joan Williams sets out to alter the terms of the public discussion about working, caregiving, and work-family conflicts.

* * *

Whether she intends it or not, Williams does something else that is extremely significant: she reframes part of the conversation about the use of narratives in legal analysis and policymaking.

This Essay describes the debate about narrative, or storytelling, in the legal academy. Two decades ago, a pitched jurisprudential battle surfaced in the pages of law reviews about the value of storytelling as legal scholarship. Since that time, narrative has sifted into academic texts in myriad ways; people are telling stories all over the place. Importantly also, research is emerging in cognitive neuroscience about the value of stories to human comprehension. And law schools are beginning to consciously recognize that part of what they do is to train storytellers.

Another narrative phenomenon has also become more pronounced during this same time frame. The overwhelming majority of the information people acquire comes from press accounts rather than reading original materials. The media have a singular ability to prioritize public issues and mold perceptions. Thus, press-constructed stories have become an increasingly powerful tool impelling or obstructing policy change. Stories such as the "boy crisis in education," "global cooling," and the "litigation explosion" capture the public's attention, prompt policy discussions, and at times spur legislation. It is this aspect of narrative for which Joan Williams's methods are particularly illuminating. In the first several chapters of her book, she unpacks the "opt-out narrative" created by the press—the story that says women are choosing to leave the fast track of professional advancement in favor of stay-at-home motherhood. Her methodology of empirically interrogating this storyline is incredibly valuable for academics wondering what to do about media mythology.

I.   THE STORYTELLING DEBATE IN THE LEGAL ACADEMY

More than twenty years ago, some groundbreaking theorists in the legal academy made a case for legal scholarship to incorporate the stories—the lived experiences—of outsiders. Neutral legal principles, they observed, were not really neutral; those legal rules encompassed racist and sexist norms. Traditional scholarship for centuries had excluded the perspectives of subordinated groups—voices from "the bottom."

The stories contributed by feminists and critical race theorists found a home in some of the most prestigious law reviews in the country. They revealed the types of discrimination faced by people outside the mainstream—biases associated with dress, language, accent, or "foreignness." The stories described the experiences of a black man who was prohibited from buying a suburban home even though he could afford it. They told about the brutality of police intimidation and the phenomenon of Driving While Black. The stories illuminated stereotypes of third- and fourth-generation Asian-Americans: "You speak such good English." They told of maternal-wall discrimination: the attorney who returned from maternity leave and was given the work of a paralegal, and who said, "I had a baby, not a lobotomy." Gay and lesbian legal theorists told stories too, so that their relationships would no longer be invisible in law—such as stories of losing a "domestic partner" in the 9/11 tragedy and the need for workers' compensation benefits for the family. Personal stories like these enriched understandings of the situations of disempowered people.

The storytelling movement met major resistance from traditional theorists. Stories, said opponents, are not an appropriate methodology of legal scholarship. One of the primary critiques was that stories posed problems of reliability and validity: stories are, in many respects, nonfalsifiable, and they might not be representative of universal experiences. To the extent that they describe personal experiential truths, the argument went, personal stories contain subjective impressions and cannot be verified. Opponents also argued that stories are not analytical—they present a one-sided, emotionally painted view of a situation. Other skeptics suggested something of the opposite—that narratives even failed on the psychological front because outsiders did not have a unique perspective. In the view of objectors, stories were irrational, emotional, unverifiable, and incendiary.

What was the outcome of the narrative battle over the past couple of decades? In important dimensions, stories changed the way legal academics thought about scholarship. People in the legal academy began to understand something scholars in other disciplines had known for a long time—that people comprehend events in narrative form. Storytelling became part of a reconstructive project of reimagining law.

* * *

II. IT'S STORIES, ALL THE WAY DOWN

Philosopher William James once explained what an "absolute moralist" believed by describing a series of rocks, one rock resting atop another foundational one: "it was rocks all the way down." A perhaps apocryphal story growing out of this, maybe influenced by Hindu cosmology, which posits that the Earth rests on the back of a giant turtle (and probably promoted by Dr. Seuss's *Yertle the Turtle*), is that "[i]t's turtles all the way down." This metaphor became important in jurisprudence circles when critical legal studies scholars began to explain how power worked. It is an explanation that applies to narrative as well. Everyone tells stories: People in power tell stories too. It's stories all the way down.

* * *

B. *Understandings about Narrative and Neuroscience*

* * *

Over the same couple of decades that stories began to abound in the legal academy, cognitive psychologists were beginning to empirically demonstrate that stories are the way people understand the world. Creating a storyline is fundamental to how humans comprehend and remember events. "The brain is structured, or 'wired,' to detect patterns" and encoding ideas in story form is a better way than simply conveying facts to "encourage . . . the recognition of new patterns and relationships among objects and ideas." People retain about one-fifth of what they read, but will remember about four-fifths of the images they form in their minds. Stories are recalled much better than sterile facts because stories are essentially remembered as symbols or images.

Cognitive neuroscientists have documented that narratives provide a holistic learning experience. Narratives trigger a release of neurotransmitters that affect both hemispheres of the brain. Stories activate both the rational (the frontal cortex) and the emotional (midbrain neural centers) parts of the brain. People processing narratives engage with them both factually, as argument, and emotionally, because they create an affective response. "Thus, stories are . . . more interesting, more memorable, and more persuasive than other narrative forms." Stories don't just entertain, they provide a structure for organizing and understanding a chain of events.

Narrative is more than a powerful method of learning; it is also an extremely influential method of persuasion. Stories provoke interest, they invite involvement, and they encourage empathetic imagination. Stories create a connection between the teller and the listener. At the end of the day, "a trial is not a debate; it's a contest of stories. The strongest . . . most persuasive, most inspiring story will win. Juries pick the story they want to win; they don't pick the stack of facts they want to win . . . ."

* * *

IV. CONSTRUCTING NEW NARRATIVES

The difficulty is that press-constructed narratives have enormous staying power. Women in the workforce may draw on narratives that are in the ether—and the opt-out narrative may remain until a powerful competing narrative materializes. The need, then, is to go beyond rebutting the myth of the opt-out narrative and to create a new story to explain our reality. Williams hints at a counternarrative that is emerging, but frames it in terms of acquiring a broader-based political coalition rather than as a story.

She does note that women need to work and that employers need women's labor, but the way it plays out by class is problematic. What seems to be impeding a compelling counternarrative is class differences. It is this story that needs flesh: the story of flexible workplaces, even for blue-collar jobs; the economic benefits for employers—in employee retention and reduced turnover—of affording workplace choices and making workplaces family friendly; and the remaking of gender attitudes to accommodate different notions of male-female partnerships. While this latter process is underway, and further along for the middle class than the working class, the missing piece of the transformation is reaching the public with the message.

Perhaps it is this storyline that both academics and journalists can create going forward. In a later writing, Williams has applauded the *New York Times* for focusing "not on mothers' choices but on the ways the labor market pushes mothers out of good jobs." Looking for the good is helpful in nudging the press toward greater accuracy in reporting.

Law is tremendously important in creating more family-friendly workplace norms. So is taking the message to the public about ways to remake workplaces to allow more flexibility for men and women in balancing work and family obligations. Other academics are also realizing that reaching outside of sterile academic tracts to communicate with a popular audience has tremendous potential to create cultural shifts. Perhaps the challenge in the academic realm is to retain and tell the authentic stories of experience that "humanize the continuing struggle for equality."

CHAPTER 2

HISTORICAL PERSPECTIVES ON WOMEN LEADERS

■ ■ ■

INTRODUCTION

The history lessons that pervade our cultural experience often exclude critical details involving women who have made a difference or served in leadership roles. Any discussion of the contemporary experience of women and leadership necessarily requires taking a moment to reflect on the rich history that serves as a backdrop for where we are today.

It is difficult to select an exact point in time in which to begin such an inquiry. Some of the earliest efforts by American women to systematically organize manifested with an 1848 gathering in Seneca Falls. The gathering consisted of women and men, including the influential Elizabeth Cady Stanton and Frederick Douglass. The two worked closely for a time and were both active abolitionists against slavery, but Stanton eventually focused exclusively on women's equality to the exclusion of other causes. Douglass spoke passionately on behalf of women's rights, especially the right to vote. Their relationship became divisive, however, and Stanton eventually spoke out against the 15th amendment extending voting rights to African-American men. The rift is emblematic of both historic and contemporary divides that exist in the fight for equality.

The meeting in Seneca Falls culminated in the drafting of the *Declaration of Sentiments*. The resulting document highlighted a list of grievances that women of that day experienced. It functioned much like a blueprint for change, not unlike more contemporary endeavors such as the *Austin Manifesto on Women in Law*, drafted in 2009 by a group of the nation's leading lawyers at the inaugural Women's Power Summit on Law and Leadership hosted by the Center for Women in Law at the University of Texas School of Law.

Feminism's first wave focused on securing the right to vote, which was one of the primary issues expressed by women at Seneca Falls. The suffrage movement, led by well-known activists like Susan B. Anthony, Alice Paul, and Elizabeth Cady Stanton, was marked by different perspectives on not only the best way to achieve the desired end of securing the franchise for women, but also racial divisiveness. As but one example, in 1913, during a parade to highlight the suffrage cause in Washington, DC, Alice Paul demanded that black women march at the back of the parade, if at all. These racial tensions among women have persisted throughout the feminist movement in history and continue today.

After the passage of the 19th amendment securing the right to vote for women in 1920, some of the same activists then focused their attention on securing broader rights. Alice Paul introduced the Equal Rights Amendment ("ERA") in 1923. Fifty years later the amendment was finally introduced in Congress and sent to the states. As of late 2019, it still has not been ratified by a sufficient number of states. Racial tensions also surrounded the ERA movement, and the amendment has been a target of criticism by political conservatives.

Alongside the more prominent historical events, in these same years there were a number of unseen battles waged by women lawyers and law students. Many schools were initially closed to women, although a determined cohort of women (like Florence Allen, featured below), did earn law degrees and broke through barriers that would have previously kept them from accessing positions of leadership in the profession.

One lesser known effort took place among female students at the University of Michigan Law School in these same years as Seneca Falls. Beginning in 1848, the organizing of a small group of women resulted in the formation of the nation's first women lawyer's organization, the Equity Club. These women were among the nation's early female law students and they relied on one another and those in law schools across the country (and world to some extent) for support and guidance throughout their education. These women wrote letters to one another about the myriad issues they faced as law students. Historian Virginia Drachman has published these letters in her book, WOMEN LAWYERS AND THE ORIGINS OF PROFESSIONAL IDENTITY IN AMERICA: LETTERS OF THE EQUITY CLUB, 1887–1890, an excerpt of which appears later in the chapter.

Credit: Courtesy of the Ohio History Connection

Florence Allen, a prominent suffrage activist, became the first female judge to serve on a federal appellate court. President Franklin Delano Roosevelt appointed her to the Sixth Circuit Court of Appeals in 1934. She also was the first woman to appear on a shortlist for the United States Supreme Court. Though she could not, of course, legally marry another woman at that time, she nevertheless engaged in several same-sex romantic relationships throughout her life. Some historians speculate this interfered with her potential appointment to the Supreme Court when she was later considered by other presidents. But it did not keep her from achieving an incredibly successful career in the law.

There are many other under-reported or untold stories of women who have blazed trails over the course of history, and this is especially true for women of color. We include an article chronicling the rich history of black women lawyers later in this chapter.

We also uncovered a series of these untold stories buried in the midst of an empirical research project we embarked on almost a decade ago when we were exploring media coverage of nominees to the United States Supreme Court. That project, which resulted in the article, *Rethinking Gender Equality in the Legal Profession's Pipeline to Power: A Study on Media Coverage of Supreme Court Nominees,*[1] began as a reaction to the media's portrayal of then-Supreme Court nominees Sonia Sotomayor and Elena Kagan. We were struck by headlines like *Then Comes the Marriage Question* in the New York Times[2] and *The Supreme Court Needs More Mothers* in the Washington Post,[3] and an online story on AbovetheLaw.com, *Elena Kagan v. Sonia Sotomayor: Who Wore it Better?*[4] Our research was driven in part by our curiosity about whether the bias and stereotyping evidenced in these news stories might be reflective of perceptions and practices in the workplace that keep women from ascending to positions of power.

The research revealed how the media frequently commented on the female nominees' attire, sexual preferences, dating life, and childlessness,

---

[1]   Hannah Brenner & Renee Knake, *Rethinking Gender Equality in the Legal Profession's Pipeline to Power: A Study on Media Coverage of Supreme Court Nominees*, 84 Temple L. Rev. 325 (2012).

[2]   Laura M. Holson, *Then Comes the Marriage Question*, N.Y. Times, May 14, 2010.

[3]   Ann Gerhart, *The Supreme Court Needs More Mothers*, Washington Post, May 16, 2010.

[4]   David Lat, *Elena Kagan v. Sonia Sotomayor: Who Wore it Better?*, AbovetheLaw.com (June 28, 2010), https://abovethelaw.com/2010/06/elena-kagan-v-sonia-sotomayor-who-wore-it-better/.

among other topics completely unrelated to their competency for judicial office, in stark contrast to coverage of their male counterparts. Our content analysis of media coverage also showed that women are portrayed and critiqued in explicitly gendered and often unfavorable ways. Furthermore, in contemplating the impact of our findings, we observed how the gender discourse surrounding the Supreme Court typically focuses on the four women who have served as justices, and that there is little, if any, ongoing attention paid to women who were shortlisted, but never nominated. This latter inquiry resulted in the discovery of nine women who were shortlisted for the Supreme Court, dating as far back in time as the 1930s when President Hoover and then President Roosevelt each considered Florence Allen (featured above). You can learn more about Allen and the other women in our book SHORTLISTED: WOMEN IN THE SHADOWS OF THE SUPREME COURT (forthcoming New York University Press 2020).

THOUGHT QUESTIONS

As you read the articles excerpted below, consider the following questions:

1.   Why is it important to learn about key women leaders in history?

2.   Reflect on your own experience learning about history throughout your educational years. What do you recall from these lessons, if anything, about key women leaders? Do you feel as though you have been adequately exposed to women's presence in history?

3.   After reading the Declaration of Sentiments, what are your reactions to the list of grievances expressed by women in 1848? Have all these grievances been resolved? If not, which ones remain? What would appear on a contemporary Declaration of Sentiments if you were charged with drafting the document today?

4.   What are your impressions of the Equity Club? Are the experiences of early women law students anything like your own? Describe similarities and differences.

ELIZABETH CADY STANTON, *DECLARATION OF SENTIMENTS* (AUTHOR)

JULY 1848

Drafted in Seneca Falls, New York, at one of the first organized gatherings of women to express dissatisfaction with their status in life, the document includes a list of grievances to guide future organizing efforts. Stanton was a primary author of the document.

FREDERICK DOUGLASS, *DECLARATION OF SENTIMENTS* (SUPPORTER)

JULY 1848

Douglass gave an impassioned speech at the gathering in Seneca Falls, urging the adoption of women's right to vote as an issue in the Declaration of Sentiments. Douglass worked closely with Stanton for many years, but the two parted ways due to racial divisiveness that characterized the women's rights movement.

When, in the course of human events, it becomes necessary for one portion of the family of man to assume among the people of the earth a position different from that which they have hitherto occupied, but one to which the laws of nature and of nature's God entitle them, a decent respect to the opinions of mankind requires that they should declare the causes that impel them to such a course.

We hold these truths to be self-evident; that all men and women are created equal; that they are endowed by their Creator with certain inalienable rights; that among these are life, liberty, and the pursuit of happiness; that to secure these rights governments are instituted, deriving their just powers from the consent of the governed. Whenever any form of Government becomes destructive of these ends, it is the right of those who suffer from it to refuse allegiance to it, and to insist upon the institution of a new government, laying its foundation on such principles, and organizing its powers in such form as to them shall seem most likely to effect their safety and happiness. Prudence, indeed, will dictate that governments long established should not be changed for light and transient causes; and accordingly, all experience hath shown that mankind are more disposed to suffer, while evils are sufferable, than to right themselves, by abolishing the forms to which they are accustomed. But when a long train of abuses and usurpations, pursuing invariably the same object, evinces a design to reduce them under absolute despotism, it is their duty to throw off such government, and to provide new guards for their future security. Such has been the patient sufferance of the women under this government, and such is now the necessity which constrains them to demand the equal station to which they are entitled.

The history of mankind is a history of repeated injuries and usurpations on the part of man toward woman, having in direct object the establishment of an absolute tyranny over her. To prove this, let facts be submitted to a candid world.

He has never permitted her to exercise her inalienable right to the elective franchise.

He has compelled her to submit to laws, in the formation of which she had no voice.

He has withheld from her rights which are given to the most ignorant and degraded men—both natives and foreigners.

Having deprived her of this first right of a citizen, the elective franchise, thereby leaving her without representation in the halls of legislation, he has oppressed her on all sides.

He has made her, if married, in the eye of the law, civilly dead.

He has taken from her all right in property, even to the wages she earns.

He has made her, morally, an irresponsible being, as she can commit many crimes, with impunity, provided they be done in the presence of her husband. In the covenant of marriage, she is compelled to promise obedience to her husband, he becoming, to all intents and purposes, her master—the law giving him power to deprive her of her liberty, and to administer chastisement.

He has so framed the laws of divorce, as to what shall be the proper causes of divorce; in case of separation, to whom the guardianship of the children shall be given, as to be wholly regardless of the happiness of women—the law, in all cases, going upon the false supposition of the supremacy of man, and giving all power into his hands.

After depriving her of all rights as a married woman, if single and the owner of property, he has taxed her to support a government which recognizes her only when her property can be made profitable to it.

He has monopolized nearly all the profitable employments, and from those she is permitted to follow, she receives but a scanty remuneration.

He closes against her all the avenues to wealth and distinction, which he considers most honorable to himself. As a teacher of theology, medicine, or law, she is not known.

He has denied her the facilities for obtaining a thorough education—all colleges being closed against her.

He allows her in Church as well as State, but a subordinate position, claiming Apostolic authority for her exclusion from the ministry, and with some exceptions, from any public participation in the affairs of the Church.

He has created a false public sentiment, by giving to the world a different code of morals for men and women, by which moral delinquencies which exclude women from society, are not only tolerated but deemed of little account in man.

He has usurped the prerogative of Jehovah himself, claiming it as his right to assign for her a sphere of action, when that belongs to her conscience and her God.

He has endeavored, in every way that he could to destroy her confidence in her own powers, to lessen her self-respect, and to make her willing to lead a dependent and abject life.

Now, in view of this entire disfranchisement of one-half the people of this country, their social and religious degradation,—in view of the unjust laws above mentioned, and because women do feel themselves aggrieved, oppressed, and fraudulently deprived of their most sacred rights, we insist that they have immediate admission to all the rights and privileges which belong to them as citizens of these United States.

In entering upon the great work before us, we anticipate no small amount of misconception, misrepresentation, and ridicule; but we shall use every instrumentality within our power to effect our object. We shall employ agents, circulate tracts, petition the State and national Legislatures, and endeavor to enlist the pulpit and the press in our behalf. We hope this Convention will be followed by a series of Conventions, embracing every part of the country.

Firmly relying upon the final triumph of the Right and the True, we do this day affix our signatures to this declaration.

Lucretia Mott	Phebe King
Harriet Cady Eaton	Julia Ann Drake
Margaret Pryor	Charlotte Woodward
Elizabeth Cady Stanton	Martha Underhill
Eunice Newton Foote	Dorothy Mathews
Mary Ann M'Clintock	Eunice Barker
Margaret Schooley	Sarah R. Woods

Martha C. Wright

Jane C. Hunt

Amy Post

Catharine F. Stebbins

Mary Ann Frink

Lydia Mount

Delia Mathews

Catharine C. Paine

Elizabeth W. M'Clintock

Malvina Seymour

Phebe Mosher

Catharine Shaw

Deborah Scott

Sarah Hallowell

Mary M'Clintock

Mary Gilbert

Sophrone Taylor

Cynthia Davis

Hannah Plant

Lucy Jones

Sarah Whitney

Mary H. Hallowell

Elizabeth Conklin

Sally Pitcher

Mary Conklin

Susan Quinn

Mary S. Mirror

Lydia Gild

Sarah Hoffman

Elizabeth Leslie

Martha Ridley

Rachel D. Bonnel

Betsey Tewksbury

Rhoda Palmer

Margaret Jenkins

Cynthia Fuller

Mary Martin

P. A. Culvert

Susan R. Doty

Rebecca Race

Sarah A. Mosher

Mary E. Vail

Lucy Spalding

Lavinia Latham

Sarah Smith

Eliza Martin

Maria E. Wilbur

Elizabeth D. Smith

Caroline Barker

Ann Porter

Experience Gibbs

Antoinette E. Segur

Hannah J. Latham

Sarah Sisson

The following are the names of the gentlemen present in favor of the movement:

Richard P. Hunt

Samuel D. Tillman

Justin Williams

Elisha Foote

Frederick Douglass

Henry Seymour

Henry W. Seymour

David Spalding

William G. Barker

Charles L. Hoskins

Thomas M'Clintock

Saron Phillips

Jacob P. Chamberlain

Jonathan Metcalf

Nathan J. Milliken

S.E. Woodworth

Edward F. Underhill

George W. Pryor

Elias J. Doty

John Jones

William S. Dell

James Mott

William Burroughs

Robert Smallbridge

Jacob Mathews

Joel D. Bunker

Isaac Van Tassel

Thomas Dell

E. W. Capron

Stephen Shear

Henry Hatley

Azaliah Schooley

BRADWELL V. ILLINOIS

Supreme Court of the United States
83 U.S. 130 (1872)

Despite meeting the requisite qualifications, Myra Bradwell (pictured) was denied access to the practice of law in Illinois because she was a woman; she appealed her case to the United States Supreme Court and lost. She founded the newspaper, the Chicago Legal News, which was the first legal publication that was edited by a woman. Late in her life, the Illinois Supreme Court reversed its earlier course and admitted her to the practice of law.

MR. JUSTICE MILLER delivered the opinion of the court.

The record in this case is not very perfect, but it may be fairly taken that the plaintiff asserted her right to a license on the grounds, among others, that she was a citizen of the United States, and that having been a citizen of Vermont at one time, she was, in the State of Illinois, entitled to any right granted to citizens of the latter State.

The court having overruled these claims of right founded on the clauses of the Federal Constitution before referred to, those propositions may be considered as properly before this court.

As regards the provision of the Constitution that citizens of each State shall be entitled to all the privileges and immunities of citizens in the several States, the plaintiff in her affidavit has stated very clearly a case to which it is inapplicable.

The protection designed by that clause, as has been repeatedly held, has no application to a citizen of the State whose laws are complained of. If the plaintiff was a citizen of the State of Illinois, that provision of the Constitution gave her no protection against its courts or its legislation.

The plaintiff seems to have seen this difficulty, and attempts to avoid it by stating that she was born in Vermont.

While she remained in Vermont that circumstance made her a citizen of that State. But she states, at the same time, that she is a citizen of the United States, and that she is now, and has been for many years past, a resident of Chicago, in the State of Illinois.

The fourteenth amendment declares that citizens of the United States are citizens of the State within which they reside; therefore the plaintiff was, at the time of making her application, a citizen of the United States and a citizen of the State of Illinois.

We do not here mean to say that there may not be a temporary residence in one State, with intent to return to another, which will not create citizenship in the former. But the plaintiff states nothing to take her case out of the definition of citizenship of a State as defined by the first section of the fourteenth amendment.

In regard to that amendment counsel for the plaintiff in this court truly says that there are certain privileges and immunities which belong to a citizen of the United States as such; otherwise it would be nonsense for the fourteenth amendment to prohibit a State from abridging them, and he proceeds to argue that admission to the bar of a State of a person who possesses the requisite learning and character is one of those which a State may not deny.

In this latter proposition we are not able to concur with counsel. We agree with him that there are privileges and immunities belonging to citizens of the United States, in that relation and character, and that it is these and these alone which a State is forbidden to abridge. But the right to admission to practice in the courts of a State is not one of them. This right in no sense depends on citizenship of the United States. It has not, as far as we know, ever been made in any State, or in any case, to depend on citizenship at all. Certainly many prominent and distinguished lawyers have been admitted to practice, both in the State and Federal courts, who were not citizens of the United States or of any State. But, on whatever basis this right may be placed, so far as it can have any relation to citizenship at all, it would seem that, as to the courts of a State, it would relate to citizenship of the State, and as to Federal courts, it would relate to citizenship of the United States.

The opinion just delivered in the *Slaughter-House Cases* renders elaborate argument in the present case unnecessary; for, unless we are wholly and radically mistaken in the principles on which those cases are decided, the right to control and regulate the granting of license to practice law in the courts of a State is one of those powers which are not transferred for its protection to the Federal government, and its exercise is in no manner governed or controlled by citizenship of the United States in the party seeking such license.

It is unnecessary to repeat the argument on which the judgment in those cases is founded. It is sufficient to say they are conclusive of the present case.

JUDGMENT AFFIRMED.

MR. JUSTICE BRADLEY:

I concur in the judgment of the court in this case, by which the judgment of the Supreme Court of Illinois is affirmed, but not for the reasons specified in the opinion just read.

The claim of the plaintiff, who is a married woman, to be admitted to practice as an attorney and counsellor-at-law, is based upon the supposed right of every person, man or woman, to engage in any lawful employment for a livelihood. The Supreme Court of Illinois denied the application on the ground that, by the common law, which is the basis of the laws of Illinois, only men were admitted to the bar, and the legislature had not made any change in this respect, but had simply provided that no person should be admitted to practice as attorney or counsellor without having previously obtained a license for that purpose from two justices of the Supreme Court, and that no person should receive a license without first obtaining a certificate from the court of some county of his good moral character. In other respects it was left to the discretion of the court to establish the rules by which admission to the profession should be determined. The court, however, regarded itself as bound by at least two limitations. One was that it should establish such terms of admission as would promote the proper administration of justice, and the other that it should not admit any persons, or class of persons, not intended by the legislature to be admitted, even though not expressly excluded by statute. In view of this latter limitation the court felt compelled to deny the application of females to be admitted as members of the bar. Being contrary to the rules of the common law and the usages of Westminster Hall from time immemorial, it could not be supposed that the legislature had intended to adopt any different rule.

The claim that, under the fourteenth amendment of the Constitution, which declares that no State shall make or enforce any law which shall abridge the privileges and immunities of citizens of the United States, the statute law of Illinois, or the common law prevailing in that State, can no longer be set up as a barrier against the right of females to pursue any lawful employment for a livelihood (the practice of law included), assumes that it is one of the privileges and immunities of women as citizens to engage in any and every profession, occupation, or employment in civil life.

It certainly cannot be affirmed, as an historical fact, that this has ever been established as one of the fundamental privileges and immunities of the sex. On the contrary, the civil law, as well as nature herself, has always recognized a wide difference in the respective spheres and destinies of man and woman. Man is, or should be, woman's protector and defender. The natural and proper timidity and delicacy which belongs to the female sex evidently unfits it for many of the occupations of civil life. The constitution of the family organization, which is founded in the divine ordinance, as well as in the nature of things, indicates the domestic sphere as that which properly belongs to the domain and functions of womanhood. The harmony, not to say identity, of interest and views which belong, or should belong, to the family institution is repugnant to the idea of a woman adopting a distinct and independent career from that of her husband. So firmly fixed was this sentiment in the founders of the common law that it became a maxim of that system of jurisprudence that a woman had no legal existence separate from her husband, who was regarded as her head and representative in the social state; and, notwithstanding some recent modifications of this civil status, many of the special rules of law flowing from and dependent upon this cardinal principle still exist in full force in most States. One of these is, that a married woman is incapable, without her husband's consent, of making contracts which shall be binding on her or him. This very incapacity was one circumstance which the Supreme Court of Illinois deemed important in rendering a married woman incompetent fully to perform the duties and trusts that belong to the office of an attorney and counsellor.

It is true that many women are unmarried and not affected by any of the duties, complications, and incapacities arising out of the married state, but these are exceptions to the general rule. The paramount destiny and mission of woman are to fulfil the noble and benign offices of wife and mother. This is the law of the Creator. And the rules of civil society must be adapted to the general constitution of things, and cannot be based upon exceptional cases.

The humane movements of modern society, which have for their object the multiplication of avenues for woman's advancement, and of occupations adapted to her condition and sex, have my heartiest concurrence. But I am not prepared to say that it is one of her fundamental rights and privileges to be admitted into every office and position, including those which require highly special qualifications and demanding special responsibilities. In the nature of things it is not every citizen of every age, sex, and condition that is qualified for every calling and position. It is the prerogative of the legislator to prescribe regulations founded on nature, reason, and experience for the due admission of qualified persons to professions and callings demanding special skill and confidence. This fairly belongs to the police power of the State; and, in my opinion, in view of the peculiar characteristics, destiny, and mission of woman, it is within the province of the legislature to ordain what offices, positions, and callings shall be filled and discharged by men, and shall receive the benefit of those energies and responsibilities, and that decision and firmness which are presumed to predominate in the sterner sex.

For these reasons I think that the laws of Illinois now complained of are not obnoxious to the charge of abridging any of the privileges and immunities of citizens of the United States.

MR. JUSTICE SWAYNE and MR. JUSTICE FIELD concurred in the foregoing opinion of MR. JUSTICE BRADLEY.

THE CHIEF JUSTICE dissented from the judgment of the court, and from all the opinions.

RENEE KNAKE, *THE PROGRESS OF WOMEN IN THE LEGAL PROFESSION*
29 PACE LAW REVIEW 293 (2009)

Knake is one of the authors of this casebook. You can read more about her background in the Introduction.

* * *

While the number of female and male law school graduates has been almost equal for nearly a decade, the number of women remaining and advancing in the field does not reflect gender equality within the profession.

* * *

Given that women have been practicing law for over one hundred years, statistics like these necessarily lead to the question: What has kept women from making more progress within the legal profession? Two recent books from Canadian scholars attempt to answer this question by addressing the progress (or lack thereof) made by women in the legal profession. One book is a history of the first women lawyers from countries around the world, and the second book is a contemporary assessment of modern women lawyers based upon a study conducted in Ontario, Canada.

In comparing the books, it is striking to note that certain elements of the struggles faced by the first women lawyers continue in various forms today, in particular, the effort to reconcile the "double consciousness" associated with being a lawyer and being a woman, a tension illustrated by the quotations listed above. This review evaluates how these books contribute to the growing body of scholarship on women in the legal profession. Each book fills a particular gap in the interdisciplinary scholarship on women lawyers. Read together, these books provide an essential background for understanding the progress achieved toward gender equality in the legal profession and identifying the work that remains to be done in this regard.

The first book examined in this review is The First Women Lawyers: A Comparative Study of Gender, Law and the Legal Professions ("First Women Lawyers") by Professor Mary Jane Mossman. The book presents the stories of a number of individuals who devoted their lives to opening the legal profession to women at the turn of the twentieth century. Mossman's study is grounded in historical and sociological research. Her work spans the globe, including the stories of the first women lawyers from North America, Western Europe, Asia, and Australia. Mossman focuses not only on the personal path that each woman took in her efforts to pursue a legal career, but also on their paths in the context of the women's movement at that time. Furthermore, to the extent possible, she addresses how their paths crossed, whether literally through the exchange of letters or symbolically as they encountered similar barriers to the profession. A familiarity with this history is necessary for addressing the continued challenges faced by contemporary women lawyers around the world. Mossman raises important questions based upon the lives of the first women lawyers that resonate with women lawyers today.

The second book examined in this review is Bar Codes: Women in the Legal Profession ("Bar Codes") by Professor Jean McKenzie Leiper. Her work focuses on the current situation of women lawyers and the future of gender equality in the profession. The book is based upon a study of approximately one hundred Canadian women lawyers conducted from 1993–2002. Bar Codes recognizes that while women's access to the legal profession certainly has progressed since the first women became lawyers a century ago, stark gender differences remain, most notably with respect to opportunities for advancement. Furthermore, Leiper observes that certain aspects of the masculine resistance faced by the first women lawyers continue in present practice. The stories documented in this book can play a vital role not only in understanding the present situation for women lawyers, but also in shaping the future for women who take up law as a career.

* * *

I.   A History of Progress: Examining the Efforts of the First Women Lawyers

First Women Lawyers is a seminal work on the history of women in the legal profession. Professor Mossman's historical account is careful and comprehensive, unique in its attempt to present a global, comparative study of the first women lawyers. At the outset, Mossman asserts that "the history of the first women lawyers is relevant to an understanding of contemporary issues of gender and professionalism," and she commits herself to meticulously making this point throughout the book. The book is divided into six chapters, each representing the first women lawyers from different countries around the world. Though the book is not comprehensive in documenting the experience of all early women lawyers in their respective communities (as Mossman herself readily concedes), the stories typify the common effort by women in North America, Asia, and Europe to find a place within the law. Each chapter could stand on its own as a separate project, but presenting them as a cohesive work allows Mossman to convey a much more dramatic (and accurate) picture of the pioneering accomplishments of the first women lawyers.

While in some ways scholarship on the history of women in the legal profession may be considered an emerging field, as noted, Mossman certainly is not the first to examine the early efforts of women to become lawyers. Her study stands apart from others, however, in several respects. For one, as she moves from country to country, she draws associations between the stories of the featured lawyers and the entry of women into the profession in the other countries. These associations include the common cultural or political movements at the time, for example suffrage, as well as the infrequent but important instances where the women's lives overlapped directly.

Furthermore, First Women Lawyers is not merely a compilation of existing scholarship on the entry of women into the profession. Mossman has conducted independent research of historical records, court documents, news accounts, archived letters, and diaries, all of which she draws upon with an intent to give context to the work of others and to reach conclusions of her own. Where her research diverges from the work of others, she carefully makes the case for her own findings. For example, much of the existing scholarship on the first women lawyers seems to characterize them as leading feminists, but Mossman's research, in some cases, suggests otherwise.

At least two additional distinctions separate Mossman's work from others documenting the history of women lawyers. First, Mossman takes an expansive view of the term lawyer, including in her definition women who practiced law despite never being formally admitted. Second, Mossman recognizes the "contradictions and ambiguities" inherent in her endeavor to scrutinize both the personal paths chosen by early women lawyers, as well as the larger historical context in which they made their way.

By the late 1860s and 1870s, some, but certainly not all, American state bars began to admit women. Mossman includes the stories of Arabella Mansfield, the nation's first woman admitted to a state bar, and Myra Bradwell, who was famously denied admission to the Illinois bar just a few months later by both the Illinois Supreme Court and the Supreme Court of the United States. Mossman explains that this inconsistency laid the groundwork for subsequent bar admission attempts by women in other states, with some courts granting admission and others deferring to state legislatures. In the late 1880s, American women lawyers had established the Equity Club, a group formed as a resource and encouragement to women lawyers in the United States, largely through the exchange of written correspondence—correspondence which provides Mossman a true inside perspective in her research.

Mossman takes care to place women's efforts to enter the legal profession within the larger picture of the pursuit of women's rights generally, such as suffrage. She observes that recognition of the emerging goals of the women's movement in the late nineteenth century is critical to appreciating the history of women's desire to enter the legal profession, though at times these women lawyers were at odds with the overall movement. She makes clear that while women lawyers and suffrage activists were "closely connected immediately after the Civil War, they increasingly diverged in the latter decades of the nineteenth century; indeed, it seems that a number of successful women lawyers gradually adopted a professional identity as lawyers, one that increasingly distanced them from other women activists," thus establishing a troubling dichotomy for women lawyers that persists today.

Mossman also addresses legal education for women in the United States. She remarks that while the women's movement encouraged education, law schools "responded unenthusiastically, and sometimes with resolute opposition to women's interest in studying law." Moreover, those women who managed to enter a legal education program encountered a variety of obstacles in obtaining their degrees, not to mention the additional hurdles faced when attempting to seek admission to the bar or to secure jobs after graduation.

By devoting the first chapter to the efforts of American women, Mossman lays the framework for a comparative analysis of efforts by women in other countries. In Chapter 2, Mossman continues to focus on North America, reviewing the progress of the first women lawyers in Canada. Canadian women began to seek legal education and entry into the profession at the end of the nineteenth century, notably later than the women of the United States. Mossman states that Britain, "where women were formally excluded from becoming solicitors or barristers until after World War I," had greater influence over the Canadian legal profession and courts than it had in America. Accordingly, she questions, "it is important to assess whether the history of women's admission to the legal profession in Canada reveals a fissure in current theories about a common professional project in law in North America, or whether there is some other explanation for this divergence between the United States and Canada . . . ."

In making this assessment, Mossman studies the arguments presented by women in specific court cases, as well as the court opinions rejecting women's arguments for entry into the Canadian legal profession. While American cases are cited in the arguments, the "decisions reveal how courts continued to defer to jurisprudence in Britain, a jurisprudence of male exclusivity for both barristers and solicitors." In contrast, however, a number of the Canadian provincial legislatures passed legislation permitting women to become lawyers, so long as they did so " 'on the same terms as men,' an approach which simultaneously granted women admission to the bar and also confirmed the profession's fundamental maleness." Mossman concludes that hinging women's admission on "the same terms as men" had the effect of pushing women to the margins of the profession. As in the United States, for many Canadian women, legislative action was required before they could enter the legal profession.

The next three chapters stand in contrast to Mossman's studies of the American and Canadian female lawyers in definitive ways. First, most of the North American women's experiences involved litigation regarding their admission to the legal profession, whereas the women in the other common law jurisdictions began to practice law without initiating a legal challenge in court regarding their admission to practice. Second, and perhaps because of the first reason, Mossman spends a significant amount of time on detailed biographies of the individual women who represent the regions beyond North America. For example, in moving overseas to Britain in Chapter 3, Mossman focuses predominantly on Eliza Orme, who established a law office in 1875 and maintained her practice without seeking admission to the bar. Orme's activities in the law and in the suffrage movement receive over thirty pages of attention, compared to the handful of pages or paragraphs dedicated to the lives of the women lawyers, such as Myra Blackwell and Clara Brett Martin, chronicled in Chapters 1 and 2.

Chapter 4 turns to the efforts of women in Australia and New Zealand. The chapter opens with a general historical account, including highlights such as the admission of the first Australian woman, Grata Flos Greig, in 1905 and the delay experienced by Ada Evans in New South Wales, who was not admitted to the bar until nearly twenty years after her graduation from the University of Sydney's law school in 1902. Mossman connects the experiences of these women to others in the world, writing that "the pattern for the first women lawyers in Australia was one of sporadic litigation and ongoing lobbying efforts to achieve legislation in each state, a pattern that was similar for women who aspired to become lawyers in other former British colonies, including Canada."

The heart of Chapter 4, however, directs the reader to the path that one woman took in her quest to practice law in New Zealand. Ethel Benjamin was the first woman lawyer admitted to practice in New Zealand, having gained admission in 1897 without the challenges or delays experienced by most of the women featured in this book. While she was entitled as a matter of law to be admitted to the bar, the culture of the profession was not very welcoming. Mossman notes that Benjamin was excluded from certain activities of the professional bar, and she had difficulties at times sustaining her legal practice, though this also may have been due to her youth and Jewish background. Mossman cites Benjamin's difficulties and the fact that other women did not seek to enter the legal profession in New Zealand for many years as confirmation of the impact that the strong male exclusivity had on the profession.

Additionally, as with the early American and Canadian women lawyers, Mossman declares that "Benjamin did not fit comfortably into the women's movement in New Zealand." Nevertheless, Benjamin's practice included a substantial amount of family law work on behalf of women and children, though she also represented clients whose interests were not aligned with women's issues. As with the biography of Orme, Mossman devotes a sizeable portion of the book to Benjamin's life (over thirty pages), permitting a fuller understanding of such seeming inconsistencies and the role that gender played in her legal career.

Chapter 5 follows the pattern of Chapters 3 and 4 with particular attention centered on the life and career of one woman, this time an Indian woman, Cornelia Sorabji. Sorabji was the first woman to study law at Oxford University, sitting for examinations in 1892, despite the fact that women were neither entitled to Oxford degrees nor eligible to sit for the bar. Nevertheless, she had a substantial legal career, including court appearances to the extent judges would permit her to appear on behalf of her clients. In 1904, after many years of practicing law (while simultaneously facing repeated roadblocks in her effort to become admitted to the bar), she received a special government appointment as a legal advisor with the Court of Wards, the administrative agency charged with providing assistance to widows and children in Northern India. Only after World War I was she admitted as a barrister. Interestingly, a major source for Mossman's research on Sorabji is her own autobiographic memoir, India Calling.

The final chapter of First Women Lawyers includes an overview of the efforts by Louis Frank, a Belgian barrister, to facilitate women's admission to the legal profession in European countries, including the struggle for admission of Lydia Poet in Italy, Jeanne Chauvin in France, and Marie Popelin in Frank's home country of Belgium. Frank exchanged written correspondence with all three women (as well as others encountered earlier in the book) and met two in person as he worked to assist them in presenting their claims for admission, largely through the 1898 publication of his treatise, La Femme-Avocat, a comprehensive sociological analysis and historical documentation of women's roles, legal status, and efforts to practice law. As Mossman discerns, these women's stories are significant because they show both the pioneering efforts on behalf of women in the law and the confrontation of civil-law based arguments against women in the law. They thus provide "interesting comparisons with women's claims for admission to the bar in common law jurisdictions."

The content of this final chapter is fascinating on two fronts. First, as in the prior chapters, Mossman's detailed biographies of the featured women once again are effective at illustrating the tensions and concerns in these specific women's lives and in the women's movement generally. Her account of Frank's work is equally deliberate and compelling, aided by her successful effort to place it in the context of the work of early women lawyers around the world, many of whom the reader already has become acquainted with in the preceding chapters.

In her final reflections, Mossman considers how the experiences of these early women lawyers might illuminate "contemporary issues about gender and professionalism in the twenty-first century." In many ways the greatest strength of this book is Mossman's ability to weave the stories of the first women lawyers across borders and oceans to create a cohesive history. Mossman conveys, with historical accuracy and intimate, personal detail, the unique and at times inconsistent paths taken by women striving for the common goal of becoming lawyers. Notably missing, however, are stories from women in other parts of the world. Yet, Mossman sets a high bar for those who may come after her to document the stories of women from other countries in Europe, Latin America, South America, Africa, and the Middle East that remain to be told. Her work lays the foundation for future scholarship and demonstrates the real need for further work in this regard.

* * *

J. CLAY SMITH, *BLACK WOMEN LAWYERS: 125 YEARS AT THE BAR: 100 YEARS IN THE LEGAL ACADEMY*

40 HOWARD LAW JOURNAL 365 (1997)

Smith was a law professor and dean of Howard University. Early in his career, Jimmy Carter appointed him to the EEOC. He served as interim chairman of the agency in the early 1980s, during which time he defended protections on workplace sexual harassment. He authored the book, Emancipation: The Making of the Black Lawyer, 1844–1944" which included a foreword by Supreme Court justice Thurgood Marshall.

I.   The Beginning

A.   Charlotte E. Ray

The accomplishments of the modern black woman cannot be fully explored without paying tribute to the illustrious Charlotte E. Ray, the world's first black woman lawyer.

* * *

Born on January 13, 1850 into a country gripped and drunken with slavery and its atrocities, Charlotte E. Ray became the first black woman admitted to practice law in the United States. She was the first black woman to graduate from an American law school and the first woman lawyer admitted to the bar of the District of Columbia. This is a tremendous accomplishment given that the District of Columbia had just ten years earlier abolished slavery.

Ray's admission to law school and admission to the bar was remarkable given that the laws and mores of the times were hostile toward women. The status of women was crippled by the archaic common law concept of inherent incapacities. It was not until 1869 that Belle A. Mansfield became the first woman admitted to the bar in the United States (Iowa), "mark[ing] the beginning of a new era."

It is incredible that black women, who during slavery were routine victims of rape, separated from their families and made to do incredibly inhumane work, can now rise and accomplish any vocation in life they choose. Without the benefit of the Civil Rights Movement and the proposed Equal Rights Amendment, Ray was one of the few women of her time, white or black, to achieve access to a profession that had been reserved solely for white men.

One begins to appreciate just what an accomplishment Charlotte Ray's admission to the bar represented by looking at the environment in which she lived. In 1871, when she was seven years of age, the Supreme Court pronounced the Dred Scott decision which held, among other conclusions, that the Negro had no rights as a citizen under the Constitution. During Ray's childhood, John Brown, an abolitionist, who took action to free slaves by force, led the insurrection at Harper's Ferry.

Slavery, the Civil War, the impending Emancipation, the assassination of President Lincoln, and the Reconstruction era may have been some of the events that stuck incessantly in the forefront of Ray's mind. The Reconstruction era "was especially important to Blacks, including Black women, for the Thirteenth, Fourteenth, and Fifteenth Amendments to the United States Constitution were ratified. However, both blacks and [white] women were soon to learn that ratified amendments did not mean rights, freedoms, and full citizenship in America."

During Ray's entire life she witnessed and experienced the antagonism of racism and the refusal of equal rights for black women. Despite such opposition, Ray witnessed the strength and defiance of the abolitionist movement in her family and in the black community. In fact, black women like Ray, who became the nation's first lawyers, may have roots in the abolitionist movement. It must have been truly inspiring for Ray to see, hear or learn about Sojourner Truth in action.

* * *

Upon acceptance to the law school she continued to teach at Howard University's Normal and Preparatory Department and attended law school in the evenings. While at Howard, Ray was known to be illustrious and accomplished during her studies and graduated with a concentration in commercial law. At the commencement ceremony, Ray presented a paper on "chancery." In February 1872, she graduated from Howard's law school and was admitted to the bar in Washington, D.C. In the same year, the Illinois Supreme Court refused a white woman, named Myra Bradwell, the right to practice law in that State.

* * *

In spite of this clear signal of male disdain for women in the legal profession, Ray opened her own law practice in Washington, D.C., where she established a reputation for being one of the best lawyers in the area of corporations law. However, "in spite of outstanding achievement and recognition as a legal authority on corporation law, Ray was unable to maintain a law practice because of the lack of business." This stifled the opportunity for America's first black woman lawyer to carve a niche in corporate law, which, had it occurred, may have established future streams of commercial benefits for black people. We can only speculate on the extent to which black lawyers, particularly black women lawyers, would have advanced as corporate lawyers, but in Ray's case, it is likely that "corporate law practice represent[ed] a plausible mechanism for advancing [black community] interests" which could not be furthered because of racial discrimination.

Ray's courageous attempts to become a successful corporate lawyer in the District of Columbia likely made her more determined to support black and women's issues. She was an active member in the National Association of Colored Women and attended various women's conventions on women's suffrage. Thus, while racism and sexism were seemingly responsible for the demise of Charlotte Ray's law practice, she chose and continued to fight on another front.

* * *

B.   Black Women Lawyers—Getting To Know Them

Women in the legal profession were generally unknown during the Colonial period of American history. Although there was a period during ancient times when women were advocates, and also during a period in German history, the recognition of their accomplishments has been minimal. Historians and social and political scientists, both male and female, appear to be unaware about the role that black women lawyers have played in American law. There is a dearth of studies solely on black women lawyers and their status in the black community and within the legal structure, perhaps "because [they face] dual subjugation: being Black and female."

In the 1980s, Juanita Kidd Stout complained before the National Bar Association about the "scant mention of the black woman lawyer" in American history. The contributions of black women lawyers has neither been captured by scholars nor understood by the general public, thus, leaving them obscure in American law. Although progress has been made, "the [legal] profession has ... been extremely hierarchical in nature, granting women and minorities only very limited access to its more prestigious and remunerative positions." The limited access to the legal profession coupled with the lack of opportunity because of racism and sexism, may be the reason for the low interest in the documentation of black women lawyers.

The progression of black women in the field of law was not thwarted only by white men, but black men as well. Although there is evidence that some black male lawyers supported the role of a career woman, some did not. Yet, it may be an over-generalization to conclude that the subordination of all women who aspired to the professions were limited by sexism. For example, in 1912, a year after the death of Charlotte E. Ray, a black man asserted that "when [we] have advanced to that stage where the intrinsic worth of the purity of womanhood is known and appreciated we will then realize the degrading influences of American slavery."

One of the first known accounts by a black lawyer in recognition of the equality of black and white women was William J. Whipper, one of the first black lawyers admitted to practice in South Carolina during Reconstruction. During the South Carolina Constitutional Convention, he argued that the right to suffrage should not be denied because of sex. David Augustus Straker and Robert Brown Elliott, both black lawyers in South Carolina were "Feminist supporters" during the 1870s. Black lawyers in the North, such as George Washington Williams and Calvin Chase also voiced strong support of black women. In 1883, Williams, also a noted historian, proposed a resolution to credit the role that black women had played during the Civil War.

Black women recognize the assistance of black men in aiding them in the area of law. For example, Constance Baker Motley credits Thurgood Marshall as a mentor. Marshall hired Ms. Motley to the staff of the NAACP Legal Defense Fund after she graduated from Columbia University's law school. Marshall "admired Black women who had the courage to enter the legal profession."

* * *

Yvonne Burke, another black female lawyer, credits her interest in law to the work of Loren Miller, a brilliant civil rights lawyer in California, who fought to have racially restrictive covenants declared unconstitutional. Black male and female lawyers began to associate with one another professionally. Helen Elsie Austin and Henry J. Richardson, Jr. practiced law together in the state of Indiana in 1940, becoming the first black law firm in the state headed by a black man and black woman. Other evidence points to the fact that black male lawyers assisted black women during and after law school to develop their skills and to employ women in their law firms. For example, in 1940, Lucia Theodosia Thomas, a recent graduate of the Robert H. Terrell Law School, "joined the law firm of George A. Parker," founded by a prominent black lawyer in the District of Columbia. In 1948, Ruth Cavers Flowers, also a graduate of the Robert H. Terrell Law School, was tutored through her first criminal trial in the local court of the District of Columbia by a black lawyer prior to graduating. In Chicago, Richard E. Westbrooks, one of the leading black lawyers in the nation, hired at least three black women during the 1940s. One of these women was Lucia Theodosia Thomas, who, in 1942, had recently moved to Chicago from the District of Columbia. Ms. Thomas reports that "I knew Mr. Westbrooks did not discriminate against women lawyers before I joined the firm because both Georgia Jones Ellis and Barbara [Watts] Goodall were associated with his firm."

* * *

As opportunities in the field of law have increased for both black women and black men, it is more probable today that black children are associating with law firms headed by their parents. The research on daughters joining law firms headed by their mothers is scant. For example, the husband and wife team, Annie Louise Brown Kennedy and Harold Lillard Kennedy, Jr. both graduated from Howard University's law school in 1951. In 1953, Ms. Kennedy opened a sole practice and one year later, in Winston-Salem, N.C., her husband joined her firm, forming the law firm of Kennedy and Kennedy. Ms. Kennedy is one of the first black women to open a law firm in the South and to establish a law firm to which her spouse and sons became associated. In 1977, Harvey Kennedy, a 1977 graduate of Harvard Law School, joined the firm. The following year, Harvey's twin brother, Harold Lilliard [sic] Kennedy III, a 1977 graduate of the

University of Michigan School of Law joined the firm forming Kennedy, Kennedy, Kennedy & Kennedy.

Black women have struggled to overcome both racial and gender discrimination. This discrimination slowed, redirected and eliminated their power as black women lawyers to influence law and politics.

* * *

Because there have never been more black women lawyers than white women lawyers in the legal profession, it is likely that they also trail their white sisters in several areas in the profession.

II. Education

A. Education Made Black Women Rival Claimants in Law

Macon Bolling Allen was the first black lawyer in America. He was admitted to the bar of the state of Maine in 1844. It was not until after the Civil War that black lawyers were admitted to American law schools. In 1869, George Lewis Ruffin became Harvard University's first black law graduate and the first black person to graduate from a chartered law school in the nation. The following year Albany Law School graduated James Campbell Matthews. In 1871, Howard University School of Law graduated the first class of black lawyers in the world. These black men received most of their education in the North, as did several black lawyers who were admitted to the bar in the late nineteenth century.

Black women received formal education training as early as 1851, the year that the Miner School (named for Myrilla Miner, a white founder of the school) was established in the District of Columbia. However, the first black woman did not graduate from a college until 1862, which "mark[ed] the beginning of higher education for Negro women in the United States."

After the Civil War, several "coeducational colleges for Negroes sprang up in various places . . . and the real education of Negro women began." Among the first Historically Black Colleges and Universities were Fisk University and Shaw University, founded in 1865, Atlanta University and Howard University, founded in 1867, and Tougaloo College and Straight University, founded in 1869. These black institutions and others "are among the important institutions which admitted women and men on the same basis." Thus, black women in the South competed against black men in liberal educational environments. At Howard University, Professor Kelly Miller, a prominent black educator, advocate for the need for more black lawyers, and sympathizer to the plight of black women's rights, believed in a "strong domestic science department for women, advocating that this was a woman's greatest educational need." With few exceptions, views held by Professor Miller's generation predominated in segregated schools in the South based on a belief that women were most needed in the home.

By 1908, the year that Professor Kelly voiced his opinion on the need for domestic education of black women, they had already determined not to be limited solely to the domestic front of education or life. Charlotte E. Ray's historic graduation from Howard University School of Law in 1872 and her admission to the bar of the District of Columbia had irreversibly unlocked the lid of "genie's jar" on the role that women would play in law and politics. It had made her "a rival claimant for at least some of the wealth monopolized by her stronger brother." Because of the dearth of research on the role of black women in the law, we are left to wonder the extent to which these women have gained wealth and stature in a profession significantly occupied by males.

White women pointed to Ray's admission to the bar and to her law practice to justify their admission to the bar. Ray's name was cited before the Supreme Court of Wisconsin in 1872 in order to justify the right of women to be admitted to the bar in the states of the nation. In an article entitled, The Negro Ahead of the White Woman, white women appear to object to the progress that black lawyers were making in law in advance of their own interests.

While the initial admission of black women to law schools and to the bar was sporadic, their initial entry into the legal profession was rooted in black and some white law schools. For example, in 1883, Mary Ann Shadd Carey (sometimes spelled Cary) was graduated from Howard University School of Law. Carey became a formidable leader in both the women's movement and for the liberation of black people. Ida G. Platt, who had first been interested in a musical career, switched to law and in 1894 graduated from the Chicago Law School. Platt became the first black woman admitted to the bar in the state of Illinois.

Despite efforts to limit black women to domestic duties, some of them escaped or were encouraged to seek higher education to compete for jobs that would help to secure themselves and their families. Beyond that, they entered the legal profession and broke new ground wherever opportunities were open to them.

B.   First Woman Law Professor in an American Law School

Lutie A. Lytle, a native of Kansas, attended Central Tennessee Law School, a black school, where she was one of the top students. In 1897, the year that Lytle graduated from the law school, she was hired as a professor of law and the law librarian at Central Tennessee Law School having the dual distinction of being the nation's first woman to teach in an American law school and lawyer-librarian at a law school. Professor Lytle also became the first black woman admitted to the bar in the South (Tennessee) and in the West (Kansas).

The factual record of Professor Lytle's experience at Central Tennessee Law School is sparse. This is understandable, as no American woman had entered the front of a law school class to teach men. One hundred years have passed since Lutie A. Lytle betrayed all stereotypes that a woman, particularly a black woman, could not master legal abstractions and teach law. To date, the significant achievements of Professor Lytle appear to be unknown, and if known, she remains unacknowledged as a pioneer in the legal academy. Nevertheless, she represents the beginning of women in legal education in America.

C. World War and Affirmative Action Provided the Opportunity for Legal Education

* * *

Two phenomena influenced the increase in the number of women in law school during the twentieth century: for black women, it was the opportunity to attend college, World War II (which depleted the ranks of males in law schools) and the civil rights litigation which desegregated public colleges. For white women, it was World War II. Around 1940, black women began to outnumber black men receiving baccalaureate degrees (3,244 and 2,463, respectively). This may account for the increased enrollment of black women in law schools during the early 1950s. The limited opportunities for black men returning from the war may also have resulted in the opportunity for black women to be admitted to law schools. Hence, between 1952–1953, "the surge of Black women" receiving degrees from historically Black Colleges and Universities was significant: "They received 62.4 percent of all degrees" from these institutions. In 1957, "1.6 per cent of all negro men in the population 14 years of age and over [had] completed four-years-or-more of college as compared to 2.1 per cent of negro women." In contrast, the figure was 6.0 and 4.4 percent, respectively in the white group.

Throughout the 1950s black women in higher education decided that "[t]raining for a particular occupation or profession was ... first in importance." However, some black women did not practice law until the early 1970s, an era influenced by important affirmative action programs which increased the number of minorities in the legal profession. For example, as a result of the Earl Warren Legal Training Program, black women and men were admitted to and graduated from southern state law schools in the early 1970s. These women remained in the South after graduation, settling in Mississippi, Arkansas and Georgia.

It is ironic that a war and affirmative action spurred the growth of women in the law. One is left to wonder where white and black women lawyers would be today if men had not been called to war and if affirmative action policies had not been initiated. It is likely that there would be fewer white and substantially fewer black women at the bar and certainly even fewer of both in the legal academy.

III. Civil Rights

A. Black Women Lawyers Exert Power for Their Rights

Lois Ada Sipuel, a brave young black woman was denied admission to the University of Oklahoma School of Law because of her race. At that time, states could legally provide segregated law schools under the Equal Protection Clause of the 14th Amendment. Because Oklahoma did not have a black law school Sipuel sued. It took two efforts by Thurgood Marshall, Counsel-Director of the NAACP, before the U.S. Supreme Court ordered the state of Oklahoma to admit Sipuel to the law school or to provide one for her. In 1949, when Sipuel was finally admitted to the University of Oklahoma's law school, she was forced "to sit in a raised chair apart from the other students, behind a sign reading 'Colored.' " She was also required to enter the law school through a side door to the cafeteria and eat alone under the watchful eye of a uniformed guard. Sipuel graduated from the University of Oklahoma in 1951, a year after her brother received his law degree from Howard University School of Law.

Whether the victory of Sipuel inspired black women to enter the struggle to desegregate public white law schools in the nation is unknown, but the sheer weight of determination to break down the racial barriers at the University of Oklahoma could not have gone unnoticed by black women across the nation who desired to enter the legal profession. In 1992, the historic feat of Sipuel did not go unnoticed by the national press when she was appointed to the Board of Regents of the University of Oklahoma, forty-six years after being denied admission to the law school.

In 1967, in the midst of the Civil Rights Movement, Eli Ginzberg observed that "most Negroes have little opportunity to enjoy the good things of life that are available to the large majority of white Americans." Ironically, it was because of the lack of opportunities and the denial of fundamental freedoms that several black women decided to become lawyers. These women dedicated their lives to civil rights and their efforts were key to reversing the disparity of inadequate incomes, educational attainment, and to breaking down other barriers which thwarted the entry of blacks into the mainstream of American life.

During the past thirty years black women lawyers have been in the forefront to free themselves and their people from all forms of "discrimination that have characterized American society." In 1995, the Lawyers' Committee for Civil Rights Under Law held a conference on "African American Women and the Law: Exerting Power, Reclaiming Our Communities." The conference presenters (almost exclusively black women lawyers) presented a legal perspective on a broad range of civil and human rights issues affecting the daily lives of women on both the domestic and international scenes. Prior to the conference, Barbara R. Arnwine, the Executive Director of the Lawyers' Committee for Civil Rights Under Law, declared that the conference would "address an array of issues pertaining to the status of African American women and the extent to which the U.S. legal system serves as a tool and a barrier to their improved condition." Just as Anna J. Cooper hoped that the twentieth century would be turned upside down by black women, the African-American Women and Law Conference, coming at the end of the twentieth century is a renewal of Cooper's expectations for black women lawyers in the twenty-first century.

The call for black women to become involved in civil rights came early in the twentieth century. In 1928, Mary Church Terrell, who headed the legislation committee of The National Association of Colored Women, emphasized the need for black women to pay close attention to civil rights, particularly as related to the on goings of Congress. She proclaimed that it was the duty of the black woman "to her country, her State and the city or town in which she lives [to learn] all she can about the laws enacted" so that she could address the barriers of her status as a black woman and as a citizen. Terrell believed that "women have a very powerful weapon which they can easily use to help secure just and wise legislation, if they will only do so."

The fight for civil rights on the streets and in courtrooms has not been waged solely by black and white men. In 1950, the beginning of the civil rights movement, Juanita Kidd Stout, a black woman lawyer, declared that her life's work would be to help gain "the rights of women and the colored man's equality." Black women have long been leaders in the civil rights movement, but the systematic role that black women lawyers played in the advancement of equality for themselves and for others has been largely ignored. Also ignored has been the cooperation between black women activists, many of whom are lawyers, and black men, in the struggle for gender and racial equality, but "black female activist [have] not receive[d] the public acclaim awarded black [and white] male leaders."

Black women lawyers have been pioneers in the civil rights struggle for some time. During the 1960s, the presence of Constance Baker Motley in Mississippi to litigate civil rights cases was unprecedented. No black woman lawyer had stirred so much attention in Mississippi since 1885, the year in which Mary Ann Shadd Carey gave speeches on civil rights on the court-house steps in Mayersville, Mississippi. Derrick A. Bell, Jr., describes an occasion during the early 1960s when the assistant attorney general of Mississippi declined to extend his hand to Motley, who was the principle lawyer attempting to enjoin the University of Mississippi from refusing to admit a black applicant, James Howard Meredith. Bell observes that " '[n]othing in the Southern lawyers' background could have prepared them for [Motley]. To them, Negro women were either mammies, maids, or mistresses. None of them had ever dealt with a Negro woman on a peer basis, much less on a level of intellectual equality, which in this case quickly became superiority.' "

In 1966, Motley was appointed to the U.S. District Court of New York by President Lyndon B. Johnson, becoming the first black woman appointed to any federal court. The struggle that she faced as a black woman lawyer did not cease when she became a federal judge. Soon after her confirmation to the court Judge Motley's race, sex and experiences as a civil rights litigator were questioned by defense lawyers in a sex discrimination employment case.

* * *

It was not generally expected that the civil rights movement would find black women lawyers on the front lines of the struggle. However, an important element of the civil rights movement was the role black women and black women lawyers played to advance social and political rights for themselves. The advocacy and protest of black women raised essential issues for justice, their minds provided strategic planning for the movement and their hands were directly involved in the execution of the plans to achieve racial and gender equality. Yet, the record of the achievements and the views of the black woman lawyer in the area of civil rights remain underdeveloped. For example, the only discovered expression on the right to vote by a black woman lawyer is that of Gertrude Elzora Durden Rush. In 1919, the year before the Nineteenth Amendment was ratified, Rush, who had just been admitted to the Iowa bar made a speech at a woman's convention auxiliary of the National Baptist Church on "What The Ballot Can Do." The text of this speech is not available. However, the minutes of the meeting reporting on Rush's remarks provides important insights about the content of Rush's speech.

* * *

As more research is done on the role that black women lawyers have played in the civil rights movement and in the courts, on the streets, in the classrooms, in politics or as mobilizers in women's organizations, more "sheros" will emerge and claim responsibility for the enlargement of liberty and progress of blacks in America before and after Brown v. Board of Education.

* * *

VIRGINIA DRACHMAN, *THE EQUITY CLUB IN HISTORICAL PERSPECTIVE,* IN *WOMEN LAWYERS AND THE ORIGINS OF PROFESSIONAL IDENTITY IN AMERICA: LETTERS OF THE EQUITY CLUB, 1887–1890*

(1993)

Drachman is the Arthur Stern Jr. Professor of American History at Tufts University. Her research focuses on the history of women in male-dominated professions, particularly medicine, law, and business.

On the evening of October 6, 1886, seven women lawyers and law students at the University of Michigan in Ann Arbor met at the home of law student Letitia Burlingame for an all-women's dinner. The purpose of the evening was to honor the new female law students as they began their legal studies. By the end of the evening, this small group of women had formed the Equity Club. Though local at its founding, the Equity Club quickly developed into a correspondence club for women lawyers and law students throughout America and in other countries as well.

Measured against large and powerful professional institutions and well-established women's organizations, the Equity Club was a modest venture. It lasted only four years and had only thirty-two members. But despite its short life and small size, the Equity Club was the first national organization of women lawyers in American history. Moreover, with several European members, the Equity Club was the first international association of women lawyers as well. Many larger and longer lasting women's legal institutions followed, including state and county women's bar associations, legal sororities, and the *Women Lawyers' Journal.* But the Equity Club was the first of these all-women's professional organizations in law. As such, it's founding in 1886 marked the budding of professional identity among women lawyers in the late nineteenth century.

The women of the University of Michigan founded the Equity Club in an age of organizational growth in the legal profession. The decade of the 1870s marked the beginning of this era. Lawyers organized city and state bar associations throughout the country to bring lawyers together at the local and state level while the American Bar Association [ABA] was founded in 1878, elevating this period of professional organization to the national level. The mission of these associations was to raise the standards of the legal profession through reforms, tightened educational requirements, and an elite membership of wealthy, white, American-born male lawyers.

The Equity Club was at once part of and apart from the legal associations of the era. Like the ABA, it was a national association that strove to unite lawyers throughout the country. At the same time, it functioned on an intimate, personal level like the local bar associations of the day. But unlike the mainstream legal associations, the Equity Club was inclusive, rather than exclusive, open to all women lawyers and law students. Its members, all women, were excluded from practically all of the professional organizations of the day. In an era when membership in legal associations became a new professional standard, the Equity Club was the only legal organization open to most women lawyers.

The women lawyers at Michigan founded the Equity Club in the midst of a decade when the number of women lawyers in America more than doubled from a sparse 75 in 1880 to 208 in 1890. Scattered across the country, it was difficult, if not impossible, for these women to become acquainted with each other, much less to develop a sense of professional community and collective professional identity. The Equity Club provided women lawyers and law students with a way to transcend the geographic distance that separated them and to build a community of women with similar professional interests and concerns. In the span of only four years, its small membership identified and grappled with a range of pressing issues. These issues fell into three general categories: professional matters, the dilemma of marriage and family, and the intimate details of health and sexuality. In grappling with the issues in these three areas, the women of the Equity Club defined the professional agenda for all women lawyers of their generation. Moreover, in doing so, they confronted their dual roles in the public arena of the workplace and the private arena of the home and identified the universal challenge that faced all professional women of their day-how to strike a balance between their femininity and their professional roles. This was the essential challenge that lay at the heart of all the issues the Equity Club members discussed and that defined the parameters of professional identity for women lawyers as it emerged in the late nineteenth century. The founders of the Equity Club were part of the first generation of women to enjoy the benefits of higher education. All of the original members-Letitia Burlingame, Corinne Douglas, Almeda Hitchcock, Rebecca May, Martha Pearce, and Margaret Wilcox-were graduates of the Law School of the University of Michigan. Their educational training set them apart from many young lawyers of their day-male or female-for formal legal education was typically not a requirement for admission to practice law in the late nineteenth century. Instead, most would-be nineteenth-century lawyers followed the route of apprenticeship into law practice. Under the apprenticeship system, an aspiring lawyer read law for several years with a practicing attorney before going out into practice on his or her own.

In the last quarter of the nineteenth century, legal education in law schools gradually became an alternative to the apprenticeship system. While elite law schools such as Harvard, Yale, and Columbia remained closed to women into the twentieth century, women made inroads into other university law schools in the late nineteenth century. Washington University in St. Louis and the University of Iowa led the way in 1869. Union College of Law (Northwestern) graduated the first woman lawyer, future Equity Club member Ada Kepley, in 1870. The University of Michigan and Boston University admitted women to their law schools in 1870 and 1872, respectively. Other law schools admitted women in the last third of the nineteenth century, including Hastings College of Law in San Francisco, Buffalo Law School, University of Pennsylvania, and New York University.

It is no accident that the law department of the University of Michigan was the locus of the founding of the Equity Club. The University of Michigan was not only a pioneer institution in its early admission of women into the law school; it had a long record of admitting women throughout the university well before other institutions of higher learning. When it opened its doors to women in 1870, it was one of the first eight state universities in the country to become coeducational, and its medical department was the first university medical school to admit women.

But the University of Michigan did not always embrace the idea of coeducation. Rather, the admission of women in 1870 was preceded by twenty years of debate and agitation. While the university's original statute of incorporation in 1837 provided that the university should be open to "all persons" regardless of sex, for decades women who applied to the university were rejected. Beginning in the 1850s, the question of accepting women at the University of Michigan became a widely debated topic. At its annual meeting in 1855, the state Teachers' Association, with its large female membership, officially endorsed coeducation at the university. Over time they were joined by reformers-men and women-who supported the principle of coeducation, as well as taxpaying parents who wanted their daughters to enjoy the same educational opportunities as their sons. But the champions of coeducation faced formidable opposition from the Michigan State Board of Regents, a majority of the university's faculty and university presidents Henry Tappan and Erastus Haven. After much debate, the University of Michigan opened its doors to women in 1870 under the temporary leadership of acting president Henry S. Frieze. Women finally had access to one of the most prestigious universities in the country.

In the fall of 1870, a total of thirty-four women studied at the University of Michigan, fourteen in the literary department, eighteen in the medical school, and two in the law department. Opposition to women on campus persisted, however. Initially, the faculty ridiculed or patronized the new female students, while residents of Ann Arbor often snubbed them in town and in church. The medical faculty vehemently opposed the presence of female medical students, arguing that the sensitive nature of medical topics required separate classes for the female students. Male students opposed female medical students as well, derisively referring to them as "hen-medics."

Despite this resistance to coeducation at Michigan, the university, under the progressive leadership of President James Burrill Angell, emerged as one of the most popular institutions of higher learning for women in the late nineteenth century. Women flocked to the University of Michigan for liberal arts education as well as professional training. In 1871, Sarah Killgore Wertman, who later joined the Equity Club, became the first woman to graduate from the law school. Jane Slocum and Ellen Martin, also future Equity Club members, followed Wertman in 1874 and 1875, respectively. The founders of the Equity Club-Burlingame, Douglas, Hitchcock, May, Pearce, and Wilcox-were among the group of women who attended the law school in the 1880s.

While the acceptance of women into the University of Michigan provoked controversy, the actual experiences of the early female graduates of the law school revealed little of the acrimony that preceded their arrival. "The Law Department encountered no difficulty in the admission of the new female students," Henry Frieze claimed in his President's Report in 1871.7 Unlike the male students in the medical school who resisted the presence of women, most of the male law students welcomed women into their classes. The students of the Webster Society led the way.

* * *

While the women law students were welcomed by their male classmates, they were graciously received by the faculty as well. Professor James V. Campbell and the dean of the law school, Judge Thomas Cooley, made them feel welcome and safe. "Judge Campbell's scholarly and benign face smiled upon us from the desk at regular intervals," Slocum recalled. Referring to Campbell and Cooley, she continued: "The generous interest of these distinguished jurists will never be forgotten by the grateful women who were treated not only as students who were welcome there, but as friends whom they were glad to aid in their life work."

In reality, Cooley was condescending even as he was accepting of the women students. In a letter to the president of Cornell University in 1871, the year before Slocum arrived on campus, he revealed his ambivalence toward the new female students: "The number who come is small, and for the most part of the unlovely class, some of them afford the boys some amusement. . . ." Still, Cooley acknowledged that women not only could compete academically with the male students but were often held to higher standards than the men. "You are misinformed if you are told the standard for admission is lowered. The tendency has been in the other direction."

But Cooley's ambivalent views did not seem to interfere with his respectful treatment of the women law students. For her part, Slocum was aware of only courteous and kind treatment from Cooley. In a letter to him she freely expressed her deep gratitude for his respect and kindness toward her.

"It would in any case be impossible for me to express the gratitude which I feel for all your kindness and courtesy and for the advantages I have been permitted to enjoy here. One cannot know what a little cordial help is to any woman who tried to do something out of the beaten tracks, which makes people look with cold criticism if not with suspicion upon every motive and act, so you will never know how your abundant kindness will be treasured."

Years after Cooley confessed his inner thoughts, female graduates of the law department continued to speak appreciatively of their treatment at the law school. In 1889, Cora Benneson, a graduate of the law school in 1880 and a member of the Equity Club, summarized the good will the women students enjoyed from both the faculty and male students. In an essay she wrote for the *Woman's Journal* entitled "Life of Women at Michigan University," she explained that the women students took their place beside their male classmates "as if no lengthy discussion had ever been held in regard to the fitness of co-education."

While the spirits of the women law students at the University of Michigan were high, their numbers remained low. As President Angell reported in 1900, "the number of women in the law school is always small." Throughout the nineteenth century, women law students were a remarkably small and isolated group within the large community of male students. In 1870, when the University of Michigan first accepted women, there were more than 300 male students in the law school. In 1872, Jane Slocum was one of only three female students among 327 men in the law school. In 1886, the year after Burlingame graduated, and the year that the Equity Club was founded, there were seven women in the law school, the largest number of female students since women were first admitted in 1870. But for almost four decades thereafter, the number of women at the law school did not reach as high as seven again. It was not until 1924, when there were eleven women in the law school, that the number of women surpassed seven. By 1900, over 6,000 men had graduated from the law school. Ten years later, after forty years of coeducation, fewer than forty women had received law degrees from the University of Michigan.

The University of Michigan was not alone in its low enrollment of women law students among law schools that accepted women. Boston University, from which came the next largest group of Equity Club members, was another example. From its founding in 1870, Boston University Law School was open to women. But no woman graduated from the law school until Equity Club member Lelia Robinson in 1881. Robinson was followed by Equity Club members Jessie Wright Whitcomb and Mary Anne Greene, who became the second and third female graduates of the law school in 1887 and 1888, respectively. Together, Robinson, Whitcomb, and Greene were part of a group of seventeen women and 985 men who graduated from Boston University Law School in the late nineteenth century. Like the women at the University of Michigan, they studied law among a sea of men.

Despite the fact that most of the male law students at the University of Michigan accepted women into their school, it was not easy for most young women in the late nineteenth century to attend law school in an environment dominated by men. In 1884, shortly before she left her home in Joliet, Michigan, for Ann Arbor, Letitia Burlingame worried about going to the University of Michigan precisely because she knew there would be so few other women law students. "With my dreadful bashfulness, which age seems very little to banish, I realize what a trial a course in the University, in a large class with few, if any, ladies will be, but I guess grit will conquer shyness, for I feel that I can really make a successful lawyer let me once get admitted to the bar."

But lack of female friendship was not the only problem women law students faced; at the same time that they had few other women to turn to, they also had to be careful to maintain a respectable distance from their male classmates. Burlingame resolved the matter of overcoming her loneliness and preserving her reputation in a way that was not unusual for other female University of Michigan students of her day; her mother went with her to live in Ann Arbor. While Letitia attended law school, her mother ran a boarding house for students of the university. In this way, Letitia's mother recreated a home away from home for her daughter, thereby protecting her from the loneliness and dangers young single women faced in a city alone. But in doing this for Letitia, the Burlingames temporarily broke up their nuclear family, for Letitia's mother left her husband for almost two years in order to stay with her daughter. This was no small sacrifice. Letitia recalled how difficult the breakup of her family was, particularly for her mother. "Such a general breaking up at home and leaving Papa behind awakened sad thoughts. . . .Thus sadness was mingled with joy, for I knew it was all done for me, and Mama cried for hours as if her heart would break." The enormity of this sacrifice reveals the lengths to which the Burlingame family was willing to go to enable Letitia to attend law school at the University of Michigan.

The women law students at the University of Michigan were a very small group within the large community of male law students. But their isolation brought them closer to each other. While they enjoyed cordial relationships with most of their male classmates, they found their deepest friendships and their strongest support among themselves. Burlingame, for example, established strong friendships with several other women lawyers and law students, including Martha Pearce, Rebecca May, and Margaret Wilcox. During the summer after her first year at law school, Burlingame had the opportunity to spend some leisurely time with other women. "Those were golden hours," she recalled. "How I feel refreshed and strengthened by the sympathy of kindred minds. . . ." The friendships Burlingame and the others built were deep and enduring. Burlingame was particularly close to Martha Pearce. "It will be a long while before I shall find another friend in whom I can confide so unreservedly," she wrote in the midst of her second year of law school. Moreover, these friendships lasted well beyond the days the women spent together in Ann Arbor. Three years after she graduated from law school Burlingame wrote to Rebecca May, who was practicing law in Topeka, Kansas, to invite May into joint practice. "I have some cases that it would be very difficult to manage alone," Burlingame wrote to May. "Would you at all consider a proposition to come here and go into partnership with me?" Unfortunately, Burlingame and May never had the opportunity to work together because Burlingame became ill just two weeks after she had written to May and died seven months later.

But during their years together in Ann Arbor, Letitia Burlingame, Martha Pearce, Rebecca May, Margaret Wilcox, Almeda Hitchcock, and Corinne Douglas built a small community of women lawyers and law students. The heart of this community was the Equity Club. Its founders had often discussed the formation of a correspondence club. Catharine Waugh had written to the women at the University of Michigan and suggested the idea as well. With this goal in mind, Burlingame and Pearce invited the new female law students to dinner in 1886. They borrowed the idea for the dinner from the women of the literary department and the medical school, who traditionally invited the new female students of their respective departments to a special annual dinner. But the idea for a correspondence club was unique to the women in law, and they formed a local group to organize a correspondence club for women lawyers. They chose Burlingame as chair and Pearce as corresponding secretary.

The founders of the Equity Club made their organization as inclusive as possible, hoping to build a broad professional community for women lawyers. Their motto, "All the allies of each," reflected their commitment to bringing together as many women in law as they could. All women lawyers and law students, as well as nonpracticing women lawyers, were welcome to join. This set the Equity Club apart from the bar associations run by men, which were exclusionary in their admissions policies and hierarchical in their organizational structure. In contrast, the Equity Club, run by women for women, was a unique example of the women's institution building of its day.

* * *

The Equity Club deviated somewhat from the model of sexual discrimination and female culture that lay at the heart of most nineteenth-century women's institutions. Its founders endured isolation within the male-dominated institution of the University of Michigan Law Department rather than outright exclusion from it. The creation of the Equity Club revealed women's attempt to nurture their female identity in a situation where, despite their acceptance into the law department at the University of Michigan, their numbers were so small that their presence was a matter "of entire indifference," according to Judge Cooley.

Women's so-called benign isolation from the male lawyers and law students at the University of Michigan foreshadowed a situation that did not characterize that of women doctors until the early twentieth century when they began to attend male-run medical schools and hospitals instead of their own all-women's medical institutions. In 1905, the noted surgeon Dr. Bertha Van Hoosen, a graduate of the medical school at the University of Michigan, lamented the consequences of this new situation. "A generation earlier, women doctors were on the outside standing together, now they were on the inside sitting alone." Women doctors responded to this isolation in much the same way as the women lawyers at the University of Michigan had years before, founding their own professional organizations to retain their female community. It is no accident that the all-women's American Medical Women's Association was founded in 1915, precisely the same year that the American Medical Association finally opened its doors to women. In the early twentieth century, women doctors finally discovered what the women lawyers in the Equity Club understood years before-that entry into the male-dominated mainstream was only the first step on the long road for women who sought to make careers in a male-dominated profession.

While professional isolation rather than exclusion fueled the founding of the Equity Club, the club shared with other women's organizations of its day a strong commitment to the unique needs and values of women. In fact, its members made it clear that the very appeal of the Equity Club was that as an all-women's organization, it provided women lawyers with friendship and understanding from other women lawyers. Martha Pearce, the corresponding secretary of the club, expressed this sentiment in her letter to the club in 1887. "Our need of sympathy and encouragement has led each one of us at some time-at many times, perhaps,-to wish to clasp the hand and look into the eyes of someone who could understand without a word

. . . . For what can be so refreshing to an aspiring soul, that has been stifled in a narrow conventionalism, as to be simply *understood?*"

* * *

While the purpose of the Equity Club was to create a female professional community to address the unique needs of women in law, its founders at the University of Michigan took careful steps to ensure that they would not offend their male colleagues in the process. Appreciating the fair treatment they had received from men at the law school, and recognizing how dependent they were upon the good will of these men, the founders of the Equity Club wanted to continue to cultivate these friendly professional relationships. With this in mind, the selection of a name for their club demanded careful consideration. On the one hand, the founders wanted a name that would convey the club's special commitment to the needs of women lawyers. At the same time, they sought a name that would encourage support rather than ignite antagonism from their male colleagues. "We tried to avoid using any name that could raise a suspicion of opposition or rivalry," explained Pearce. In particular, the founders wanted to avoid selecting a name that would convey the erroneous message that they had established a separate all-women's bar association. They feared that a women's bar would not only antagonize male lawyers, but would seem to exclude many potential members, particularly students and nonpracticing lawyers. With the number of women lawyers in the country so small, they needed a name that would welcome as many women in law as possible without alienating male lawyers in the process.

The founders of the Equity Club recognized the need to convey a message of moderation to male lawyers, and they also sought a name that would strike a balance for its members between their roles as women and their roles as lawyers. From this point of view, the very naming of the Equity Club was itself an example of women lawyers' perpetual struggle to balance their femininity with their professional identity. Ironically, it was a man, Harry Burns Hutchins, Professor of Equity at the University of Michigan, who provided the founders with the name they sought. His statement, "Equity has been the saviour of woman," conveyed precisely the message the founders wanted, and they seized upon it to name their group the Equity Club.

* * *

In the long run, the founders of the Equity Club did not seek pure equality with male lawyers, nor did they wish to sacrifice their ties to female culture as they established their professional identity. Rather they sought to bring their femininity to their professional lives. Whereas men claimed that the practice of law demanded an objective mind, most nineteenth-century women lawyers insisted that law required an understanding heart as well. By calling their organization the Equity Club, its founders invoked an age-old legal tradition and reassured men and women alike that women lawyers would complement their male colleagues, not compete with them.

Having settled on the name or their organization, the founders of the Equity Club sent invitations to sixty-two women to join. Requirements for membership were simple: an annual letter and annual dues of twenty-five cents. The dues covered the costs of postage, stationery, copyright, and printing. The letters formed the backbone of the club and were the primary requirement for membership. A woman who sent dues without a letter was not admitted as a member. On the other hand, if a woman sent a letter without dues, she was occasionally accepted depending on the circumstances.

Of the sixty-two women invited to join, only fourteen women responded with letters for circulation in the first year. Significantly, ten were either alumnae or students of the University of Michigan Law School. Over the course of the four years of the Equity Club's life, a total of thirty-two women participated. Membership varied by year; while only fourteen women joined in 1887, twenty-two participated in 1888. Sixteen were new members, and six had been members the year before. Eight of the original group from 1887 dropped out. The year 1888 marked the peak of membership in the Equity Club. In 1889, there were no new members and ten women dropped out, leaving only twelve women in the Equity Club. In 1890, the last year of the Equity Club, two new members joined, but they were part of an even smaller group of eleven members.

Despite the turnover in membership, there was some continuity as well. Nine women were members for at least three years, five of whom were members all four years. Of this group of five, three-Martha Pearce, Almeda Hitchcock, and Margaret Wilcox-were among the original founders back in 1886. The other two were Lelia Robinson and Mary Greene, the first two graduates of Boston University Law School.

Altogether the thirty-two members of the Equity Club wrote sixty letters. They sent their letters to Martha Pearce who, as corresponding secretary, was responsible for collecting the letters and preparing them for circulation among the members. The original plan was to print the letters each year and to distribute a copy of the printed collection to each member. But the initial membership fee of twenty-five cents was too small to cover the cost of printing and mailing the letters. Hampered by a lack of funds in the club's first year, Pearce had to send out the original letters. One by one, individual club members received the collection of letters for 1887 and often held onto them until they made personal copies before they sent them on to others. In 1888, Pearce received twenty-two letters, many of which were significantly longer than any she had received the year before. With the dues increased to two dollars, Pearce was able to publish the letters as the

Equity Club Annual, and she included an extensive secretary's report in which she detailed the history of the club's founding as well as its purpose, organization, and structure. In addition, Pearce raised issues and asked questions regarding social and professional matters, and she made suggestions for the future direction of the club. Her hope was that members would discuss these matters with each other in their future letters.

The time involved in producing the *Equity Club Annual* in 1888, plus the dramatic decline in the number of letters to twelve in 1889, combined to discourage Pearce from continuing in her position as corresponding secretary. At the same time, she was disheartened by the decline in members. "The letters she longed for never came," she lamented. Moreover, she felt burdened by the time and responsibility her job as corresponding secretary demanded. In 1889, Pearce called for someone to replace her, but no one volunteered to take her place. As a result, the *Annual* was not published in 1889 and 1890. Instead, the letters were copied into a letter book and the original letters were circulated as in 1887.

The thirty-two women who comprised the membership of the Equity Club shared certain characteristics in common. All were white, American-born, and middle class. Women of color, different ethnic groups, or working-class backgrounds did not enter the legal profession in any measurable numbers until the turn of the century. The opening of part-time evening law schools such as Portia Law School in Boston and Washington College of Law in Washington, D.C., permitted working-class and immigrant women to study law at night while they continued to work during the day. In addition, the admission of women to the law school of Howard University in Washington, D.C., made it possible for a small number of African-American women to study law as well. But the Equity Club members were part of an earlier era when women lawyers, and male lawyers as well, comprised a homogeneous profession in terms of race, class, and ethnicity.

In other ways, the members of the Equity Club were a diverse group. They came from urban centers such as Boston and Chicago, smaller cities like Omaha, Nebraska, and Iowa City, Iowa, and small towns such as Hutchinson, Kansas, and Tiffin, Ohio. In addition, there were three European members, one from England, France, and Switzerland, respectively. While they spanned the country from Massachusetts to California, a majority of twenty were from the Midwest and West, where law schools and state bars had a tradition of accepting women, while only seven lived in cities and towns in the East. Nine lived in large cities, three each from Boston, Chicago, and Washington, D.C., which were accustomed to women in professional work, social reform, and other activities in the public arena.

The members of the Equity Club ranged in age from their mid-twenties to their late fifties. At one end of the spectrum were young women such as

Almeda Hitchcock, Jessie Wright Whitcomb, and Catharine Waugh McCulloch who, in their mid-twenties, were just embarking on their legal careers. Most of the Equity Club members were in their thirties and forties. They had completed their legal training and had settled into the pattern of their adult lives, whether it was legal practice, reform work, or care of home and family. Only two members, Belva Lockwood and Catharine Waite, were in their fifties. At the ages of fifty-seven and fifty-nine, respectively, they were the Equity Club's link with the first generation of the Woman Movement in antebellum America. Waite, a leader in the post-Civil War woman suffrage movement, did not enter law school until she was fifty-six. At the Union College of Law (Northwestern), she befriended a fellow student, young Catharine Waugh, and introduced her to another classmate, Frank McCulloch. Waugh married Frank McCulloch and became known as Catharine Waugh McCulloch. After Waite graduated, she went on to publish a legal journal, the *Chicago Law Times,* and became president of the International Woman's Bar Association.

Belva Lockwood was the first woman admitted to practice before the United State Supreme Court. She was the quintessential pioneer among nineteenth-century women lawyers, having overcome sexual discrimination to open the doors for herself and other women to the legal profession. She gave inspiration to younger women and served as the model of success for generations of women lawyers who followed after her.

While certainly the most well known of all nineteenth-century women lawyers, Lockwood was by no means the only pioneer among the Equity Club members. In fact, there was an impressive number of members who were the first among women to break barriers in the legal profession. Ada Kepley, a graduate of Union College of Law (Northwestern) in 1870, was the first woman to earn a law degree in America. Sarah Killgore Wertman was the first woman to graduate from the law school of the University of Michigan and the first woman admitted to the Michigan State Bar. Similarly, Lelia J. Robinson was the first woman to graduate from Boston University Law School and the first woman to gain admission to the bar of Massachusetts. Mary Wilkinson was the first woman to graduate from the University of Iowa Law School. Ada Bittenbender, Mary Greene, and Almeda Hitchcock were the first women to break the sexual barriers to the state bars of Nebraska, Rhode Island, and Hawaii, respectively. Several Equity Club members were ground breakers in other ways. Laura de Force Gordon, along with another California woman, Clara Foltz, brought a law suit against the University of California that opened the Hastings College of Law in San Francisco to women. Emma Gillett, along with a friend of hers, Ellen Spencer Mussey, opened the Washington College of Law, a law school for women in Washington, D.C. Though Gillett and Mussey were willing to admit men to their law school, their primary goal was to provide legal education to women. Catharine Waite managed and edited the *Chicago Law Times,* the law journal she owned with her husband.

With so many club members accomplishing so much, the women of the Equity Club were certainly an impressive group. In pursuing their own careers with conviction and persistence, they broke long-established barriers against women in the legal profession and opened the way for women to follow after them.

* * *

While many Equity Club members shared the experience of teaching with other women of their day, they also participated with them in a number of reform activities. As thousands of women in the last decades of the nineteenth century left their homes to work on behalf of a wide range of reforms, many of the Equity Club members joined them in this Woman Movement, particularly to fight on behalf of suffrage and temperance. Some even took leadership roles. Bittenbender, for one, served as legal counsel for the Women's Christian Temperance Union, while McCulloch, Gillett, and Gordon were leaders in the suffrage movements in Illinois, Washington, D.C., and California, respectively. McCulloch, Robinson, and other women lawyers in the Equity Club also expanded the parameters of the Woman Movement by bringing their knowledge of the law to the question of women's legal rights, particularly property rights and custody rights. These were issues that only women lawyers, with their legal training, were qualified to address among all other nineteenth-century feminists. By contributing their legal expertise to the suffrage and temperance movements, the women lawyers of the Equity Club did more than participate in the Woman Movement; they took their place at its very center.

This diverse group of thirty-two women came together once a year through their letters. The Equity Club provided a way for them to ask questions, give advice, express their hopes and fears, and share the successes and setbacks in their professional and personal lives. While a few wrote tentatively, intimidated somewhat by the accomplishments of some of the members, they all participated enthusiastically and expectantly. The long silences between their annual letters tested their patience as they waited months to hear from one another. But their persistence revealed their need for each other and their commitment to the Equity Club at a time when they had few if any other opportunities to share their thoughts with other women lawyers. Moreover, their letters from year to year revealed a remarkable continuity in their subject matter as they responded to each other's queries, though twelve months later. At the same time, a great deal transpired in their lives over the course of a year, and members shared with each other some of the most significant professional and personal moments in their lives. Some graduated from law school, others passed the bar, while still others had important legal victories. A few married and one had a baby, while others had to stop work to care for sick relatives. As they communicated these events with each other from year to year, Equity Club members created a strong though short-lived network of support for each other. They were candid and trusting with each other as they addressed controversial professional matters and asked each other for advice. They were not afraid to disagree, but they always did so with respect and good humor. And they willingly shared some of the most intimate details of their personal lives.

The specific matters the Equity Club members discussed in their letters grew out of the realities of their public and private lives. They sought each other's advice on a range of issues including how to dress as lawyers while retaining their femininity, whether women lawyers belonged in the courtroom, whether they could succeed in the business of law while preserving their ties to charity and reform, how to balance marriage and career, and whether a woman had the physical constitution to withstand the demands of law practice. The diversity of these issues reveals the spectrum of concerns for women lawyers in the late nineteenth century. At the same time, at the heart of all of these issues was a common theme: how to be both a lady and a lawyer in the late nineteenth century. As women lawyers in the Equity Club corresponded about a range of issues, they simultaneously grappled with this dilemma of how to strike a balance between femininity and professional identity.

Lelia Robinson was one of the first members to raise the sticky problem of the place of femininity in women lawyers' professional lives. *"Do not take sex* into the practice," she wrote in her letter to the Equity Club in 1887. "Don't be 'lady lawyers.' Simply be *lawyers,* and recognize no distinction-no existence of any distinction between yourselves and the other members of the bar." Robinson's straight-forward advice launched a debate among the members of the Equity Club over how to balance their femininity and their professional identity. The letters from Ellen Martin and Emma Gillett the following year supported Robinson's advice to emphasize their responsibilities as lawyers over their roles as women. But others such as Ada Kepley and Sarah Killgore Wertman disagreed and urged their sister club members to emphasize their womanhood in their practice of the law. The result, Kepley claimed, would be "sweeter manners-purer laws." But Kepley and Wertman did not have the final word. The dialogue continued in 1889 when Florence Cronise, in response to Kepley, declared herself "too matter of fact" to sympathize with her "sisters of the Equity Club who think woman's mission in the profession is to purify."

In fact, the question of the role of femininity in their professional lives underscored every matter the Equity Club members discussed. From their debate over the professional question of the propriety of the bonnet in the courtroom to their discussion of the very private matter of the sexual rights of the married woman lawyer, the Equity Club members could not escape the gnawing problem of how to be at once a lady and a lawyer. For example, the matter lay at the very center of their debate over the place of philanthropy and reform in their professional lives. Victorian-American society created a clear distinction between business and charity. Business was defined as men's domain because it demanded the objectivity and hard-heartedness believed to be inherent to manhood. Charity and reform were accepted as part of women's domain because they relied on the supposedly womanly virtues of nurturance and sentimentality. This sharp division between men's business and women's charity and reform created another source of tension for women lawyers in the late nineteenth century. As women, it was appropriate for them to engage in charity and reform. But as lawyers, it was more acceptable for them to restrict themselves strictly to business and professional concerns.

* * *

While the women lawyers in the Equity Club grappled with the question of the place of charity and reform in their professional lives, they also tried to reconcile the problem of how to balance marriage and career. Lelia Robinson, perhaps contemplating marriage to her future husband, first brought up the issue in her letter to the Equity Club in 1889. "Is it practicable for a woman to successfully fulfill the duties of wife, mother, and lawyer at the same time? Especially a young married woman?" she asked. Robinson's query was part of an ongoing discussion among Equity Club members about the relationship of marriage and family to their professional lives.

Single members of the Equity Club typically chose not to marry precisely because they believed that marriage imposed too many domestic obligations on women and was, therefore, incompatible with a serious career. "A glance through the [Equity Club] Annual," wrote Gillett, "would seem to indicate that the majority of the practitioners who are sticking to their work and plodding on in the sure and safe way to win success are unmarried." Believing that they had to make a choice between marriage and career, single women sacrificed the former in hopes of establishing productive professional lives. Even Marion Todd, who had been married once but was a widow by the time she joined the Equity Club, insisted that she had no intention of remarrying, declaring that, from her experience, marriage was "too great a responsibility."

While many Equity Club members followed the path of the single life that was typical of most nineteenth-century professional women, more than one-half (seventeen) of the members of the Equity Club were married. These married Equity Club members mirrored the marital patterns of women lawyers of their day. When Equity Club member Lelia Robinson sought to gather information on as many women lawyers in the country as possible, she found that one-half of the 120 women lawyers and law students she identified in 1890 were married. As Robinson concluded, the late nineteenth-century woman lawyer "exists to quite a numerical degree in the married state as in that of single blessedness." Moreover, in contrast to the Victorian notion that marriage and career were incompatible for women, most of the seventeen married women in the Equity Club continued to practice after they married. Among this group of married, working women, eight were married to other lawyers and were in practice with their husbands. For these women, marriage enhanced rather than impeded their careers. In contrast to single women who typically had to confront sexual discrimination and the difficult search for work on their own, women lawyers who were married to lawyers usually found that their husbands not only shielded them from public disapproval but provided them with a secure and welcoming place in which to work.

* * *

The debate over the appropriateness of courtroom work for the woman lawyer was a matter of great concern to the members of the Equity Club, whether they were married or single. The courtroom was considered the epitome of the male domain in the legal profession. To most contemporary observers, this arena of legal combat where lawyers encountered "all the unclean issues of society" and where only the strongest of lawyers survived, was no place for a lady. In contrast, the office was deemed the appropriate arena for women in the legal profession. While the courtroom duplicated the rough and tumble of the public arena, the office mirrored the privacy of the home. Office work demanded the same focus on organization, efficiency, and detail that was expected of the Victorian lady in her home. It was the site of negotiation, compromise, and settlement, the skills of the ideal wife and mother.

Despite the prevailing view that the office was women lawyers' proper arena of work, the Equity Club members did not reach a consensus on the matter. Simply put, they were not all willing to turn over the courtroom to men. Some explained that they could not sufficiently service their clients from within their offices. Others admitted that they preferred the activity and publicity of the courtroom to the privacy of the office. Still others explained that courtroom work was more lucrative than office work.

But not all women lawyers in the Equity Club claimed equal rights to the courtroom. Many members preferred to restrict their practice to office work. Though they sometimes had to go to court, single women such as Gillett and Robinson tried to handle all their work in the office. In contrast, married women whose husbands were lawyers, such as Haddock, LeValley, and McCulloch, could rely on their husbands to handle courtroom matters while they stayed exclusively within the privacy of the office.

Emma Haddock, for one, explained that because she worked with her husband, she did not need "to take public part in the practice," and that, in fact, she "preferred the preparation of a case to its argument." Laura LeValley described her situation similarly. "I have never made an effort to take an active part in court. In fact I never intended to do so, but have been assisting my husband in the office, and have given much time to stenography and office work. . . ."

* * *

The question of women's place in the courtroom led naturally to another matter of debate taken quite seriously by members of the club-the appropriate attire for the woman lawyer who had to go to court. Again, Lelia Robinson posed the question for the Equity Club. "Shall the woman attorney wear her hat when arguing a case or making a motion in court," she asked in 1888, "or shall she remove it?" With this query, Robinson once again confronted her sisters in the Equity Club with the challenge of reconciling their traditional roles as women with their new roles as lawyers. From the point of view of social convention, which required a lady to wear a hat in public, it was appropriate for a woman lawyer to wear a hat when she ventured into the courtroom. But professional etiquette dictated that as a lawyer she remove her hat when she entered the courtroom, just as her male colleagues did. Thus, the matter of the hat, seemingly a frivolity of fashion, posed in actuality a perplexing problem for the woman lawyer seeking to balance her femininity and her professional identity.

The Equity Club members lined up on both sides of the question. Robinson spoke on behalf of the hat. She acknowledged that she followed her feelings on the matter and wore her hat in court because it made her feel more comfortable before the judge and jury. Catharine Waugh McCulloch objected to Robinson's willingness to succumb to sentiment and urged the Equity Club members "on principle" to remove their hats in the courtroom just as men did. Other Equity Club members, including Burlingame and Wilcox, rejected both Robinson's ties to tradition and McCulloch's quest for equality and claimed, instead, every woman lawyer's right to make the decision for herself. "I maintain it is the inalienable right of each lady to follow her 'own sweet will,' " wrote Wilcox in her letter in 1889.

The hat debate focused on the most public of arenas, the courtroom. In contrast, the issue of women lawyers' health and sexuality forced the Equity Club members to face the innermost sanctums of their private lives. More than any other issue, the matter of women's health and sexuality reveals how deeply the problem of balancing their dual roles as women and as lawyers penetrated women lawyers' personal lives. Female health was a highly controversial issue in the late nineteenth-century United States and one which the Equity Club took very seriously. Their debate about women's physiological ability to endure the strains of law practice occurred within the context of the larger social debate about the fragility of women's health.

* * *

RENEE KNAKE, *HIDDEN WOMEN OF HISTORY: FLOS GREIG, AUSTRALIA'S FIRST FEMALE LAWYER AND EARLY INNOVATOR*
THECONVERSATION.COM, JULY 24, 2019

Knake is one of the authors of this casebook. You can read more about her background in the Introduction.

When Grata Flos Matilda Greig walked into her first law school class at the University of Melbourne in 1897, it was illegal for women to become lawyers. But though the legal system did not even recognise her as a person, she won the right to practice and helped thousands of other women access justice. In defying the law, Greig literally changed its face.

That she did so is a story worthy of history books. And how she achieved this offers key insights for women a century later as they navigate leadership roles in the legal profession and beyond.

Flos, as she was known, grew up in a household full of possibilities unlimited by gender boundaries. Born in Scotland, as a nine-year-old she spent three months sailing to Australia with her family to settle in Melbourne in 1889. Her father founded a textile manufacturing company. Both parents believed that Flos and her siblings—four sisters and three brothers—should be university educated at a time when women rarely were.

She grew up firm in the knowledge that women could thrive in professional life, and witnessed that reality unfold as older sisters Janet and Jean trained to become doctors. Another sister, Clara, would go on to found a tutoring school for university students. The fourth sister, Stella, followed Flos to study law.

Women could not vote or hold legislative office, let alone be lawyers, when 16-year-old Flos began to study law. Yet she did not let this deter her. As she approached graduation she focused on, "the many obstacles in the path of my full success. I resolved to remove them".

Other feminine aspirants, she noted, had previously wished to enter the profession, "but the impediments in the way were so great, that they concluded, after consideration, it was not worthwhile".

Flos felt otherwise. She declared, even in 1903 when women were largely excluded from public life: "Women are men's equals in every way and they are quite competent to hold their own in all spheres of life."

'The Flos Greig Enabling Bill'

Six years after entering the University of Melbourne, Flos witnessed the Victorian Legislative Assembly's passing of the Women's Disabilities Removal Bill, also known as the Flos Greig Enabling Bill. Suddenly, women could enter the practice of law. How had she made this happen?

While childhood had provided Flos with role models from both sexes, she did have to rely upon a series of men to navigate her entry into the exclusively male club of the legal profession. Her male classmates had initially questioned the capabilities of a woman lawyer and resisted her presence, but she soon persuaded them otherwise.

Not only did Flos graduate second in her class, but the men took a vote to declare—affirmatively—that women should be allowed to practice law. Their support undoubtedly fuelled her ambitions.

Next, Flos turned to one of her lecturers, John Mackey, who happened to also be a member of the Victorian Legislative Assembly. Together they worked with other supporters to craft the legislative change. Mackey argued that by passing the law, Parliament could ease the concerns of women who believed they could not get justice from a legislative body made up only of men.

Still, Flos needed to complete a period of supervised training known as "articling" before she could be sworn into the bar. No Australian woman had ever engaged in the "articles of clerkship" before. A Melbourne commercial law solicitor Frank Cornwall employed her, and she was officially admitted to the practice of law on August 1, 1905.

At her swearing-in ceremony, Chief Justice John Madden described Flos as "the graceful incoming of a revolution". He also expressed some skepticism about her future success: "Women are more sympathetic than judicial, more emotional than logical. In the legal profession knowledge of the world is almost if not quite as essential as knowledge of the law, and knowledge of the world, women, even if they possess it, would lie loth to assert."

Flos would prove him wrong about her knowledge of the world, both in law and in her other passion, travel.

'What did I wear? Don't ask me!'

At the ceremony, her name was the third called—in alphabetical order—before what was reportedly an "unusually large gathering of lawyers, laymen, and ladies . . . seldom seen in halls of justice". Attendees noticed smiles that "flickered over the faces of the judges as they entered the crowded chamber" at the sight of Flos among her "somberly-clad male" counterparts.

News accounts focused more on the physical attributes of the first lady lawyer than her qualifications. When questioned by a reporter about her clothing choice for the occasion, Flos blushed, "What did I wear? Don't ask me!" But then confessed, "Well, if you insist! I wore grey, with a greenish tinted hat, trimmed with violets!"

Another news reporter critiqued the flower-adorned hat as "a most unlegal costume". As if there was any basis for making such an assessment—until that moment the nation had never seen the "costume" of a female lawyer. The media's fixation with female lawyers' appearance endures more than a century later.

Flos soon established a solo practice in Melbourne focusing on women and children. Among other endeavours, she represented the Women's Christian Temperance Union in lobbying to establish the Children's Court of Victoria.

Media fascination with Flos's attire did not diminish once admitted to practice. She delivered a speech in 1905 to the third annual National Congress of Women of Victoria on a paper she wrote titled, "Some Points of the Law Relating to Women and Children".

The reporter noted that Flos "treated her subject in a masterly manner, and gave an immense amount of useful and, at times, startling information". But Flos's "stylish, yet simple, gown of grey voile, with cream lace vest" was equally newsworthy as were "her pretty black hat and white gloves". The fashion choices of other (male) speakers went unmentioned.

Flos also helped open the legal profession to other women. She founded The Catalysts' Society in 1910. Two years later it became the prestigious Lyceum Club in Melbourne, devoted to advancing the careers of women and offering networking opportunities.

After the launch of the Women's Law Society of Victoria in 1914, Flos was elected its first president. She cared deeply about the right of all women to vote, arguing in a 1905 debate that if "politics were not fit" for women, "the sooner they were made so the better." (In 1908 Victorian women won the right the vote.)

Law was not Flos's only pursuit. She travelled extensively. Two decades after graduating from law school, she took a lengthy trip through Asia, spending time in Singapore, China, Bali, Java, Malaysia and two weeks in the Burma jungle. She stayed in local homes and on her return, spoke to audiences about the experience, delighting them with tales of "leopards, tigers, wild pigs, peacocks, . . . and wild jungle fowl". She lectured publicly and on radio stations about the geography, religion and race.

The end of her career took Flos to Wangaratta in Northern Victoria. She practiced at a law firm headed by Paul McSwiney, and was known to explore the countryside in a "Baby Austin" tourer. She remained an activist, supporting higher education for women and the Douglas Credit Party, a political party that aimed to remedy the economic hardships of the 1930s depression.

Flos died in 1958. While she did not live to see other female firsts, such as the appointment of the first female Chief Justice of the Supreme Court of Victoria in 2003, Flos' capacity to envision women as equals under the law places her among the profession's greatest innovators.

CHAPTER 3

INTERSECTIONALITY IN LEADERSHIP

■ ■ ■

INTRODUCTION

The pervasive inequality that exists in positions of leadership and power is not restricted solely to gender. Our identities are made up of multiple layers including ability, class, ethnicity, gender, geography, race, religion, sexual orientation, socio-economic status, and more. Chapter 3 explores intersectionality in identity and considers its interplay with systemic bias and discrimination. Invariably, these factors further complicate the gender dynamics and impede the progress for women explored in Chapters 1 and 2.

As illustrated in the previous chapters, numerous studies document the lack of women lawyers in positions of power. But those statistics, by lumping together women as a group, without distinguishing between facets of identity like race, ethnicity, or sexual orientation, tell only part of the story and render some women invisible. Even reporting numbers for "minority" attorneys is problematic as it does not distinguish among different groups, sometimes leading to inaccurate conclusions about diversity. Here we begin to fill in the narrative to offer a more accurate picture with the important caveat that it is merely a starting place. NALP's *2018 Report on Diversity in Law Firms*[1] reveals that the percentage of LGBT lawyers hovers around 2.86 percent, which is a slight increase from the last reporting period. The numbers are higher for associates than for partners. Asian women make up 1.38 percent of partners and 6.64 percent of associates. Black/African American women comprise 0.68 percent of partners, and 2.55 percent of associates. And Hispanic women make up 0.77 percent of partners and 2.45 percent of associates. The data varies widely depending on geography and size of firms. Taken together, this information informs the reality that while equality is slowly improving in law firms and the legal profession generally, this is not universally the case for all women.

The judiciary is really no different than law firms. Women began assuming positions on state and federal courts in the early 20th century. But it was not until 1982 that the first minority woman, Justice Dorothy

---

[1]   *2018 Report on Diversity in U.S. Law Firms*, NALP (Jan. 2019), https://www.nalp.org/uploads/2018NALPReportonDiversityinUSLawFirms_FINAL.pdf.

Comstock Riley, a Latina, served on a state supreme court (Michigan). The first black female state supreme court justice, Juanita Kidd Stout of the Pennsylvania Supreme Court, did not sit on the bench until 1988. Joyce Luther Kennard was the first Asian American/Pacific Islander justice, who joined the California Supreme Court in 1989. Virginia Linder of the Oregon Supreme Court was the first openly lesbian on a state supreme court when she took office in 2007. No openly transgender judge sits on a state supreme court, but Phyllis Frye became the first in the nation to sit on a court, appointed as an associate judge for the City of Houston Municipal Courts by mayor Annise Parker in 2010. Leah Ward Sears became the first black woman to serve as the chief justice of a state supreme court in 2005 on the Supreme Court of Georgia, and the first openly lesbian to do so is Maite Oronoz Rodriguez, appointed as Chief Justice of the Supreme Court of Puerto Rico in 2016. A minority woman serving on any court remains very much a rarity today. Much of the statistical research that explores inequality distorts the systemic lack of representation by lumping together all minorities or women of color into one category. Not only does this contribute to visibility bias, or the idea that when we see a minority in a given workplace we actually assume that there are many, but it also leads to the dangerous practice of treating one woman's experience as representative of the experiences of all women.

The readings in this chapter explore intersectionality in the legal profession through the lens of the judiciary to determine whether and how gender, race, and other attributes make a difference in leadership.

Credit: Creative Commons Attribution 3.0 License

When **Sonia Sotomayor** graduated from Princeton University in 1976, she did not see herself attaining the ultimate position of power in the legal profession. Yet, three decades later she went on to become the first Hispanic and Latina on the U.S. Supreme Court. In her autobiography MY BELOVED WORLD, she offers the following advice for those aspiring top roles: "The idea of my becoming a Supreme Court Justice— which, indeed, as a goal would inevitably elude the vast majority of aspirants—never occurred to me except as the remotest of fantasies. But experience has taught me that you cannot value dreams according to the odds of their coming true. Their real value is in stirring within us the will to aspire." Consider how the intersectionality of her identity as a Latina—a minority woman—impacted her rise to the Supreme Court as you read the excerpts in this chapter. To better understand this, read her autobiography.

THOUGHT QUESTIONS

As you read the articles excerpted below, consider the following questions:

1.   How does the intersection of multiple parts of identity like ability, class, ethnicity, gender, geography, race, religion, sexual orientation, and socio-economic status impact leadership capacity? Are there related aspects of identity that we should consider in answering this question that have not been identified?

2.   Consider the multiple facets of your own identity. Can you come up with examples where these different dimensions caused internal or external conflicts for you?

3.   Can you recall an experience where you specifically identified with someone because you shared commonalities in identity or you contemplated pursuing a specific path because you were inspired by someone who "looked" like you?

4.   Two authors from the reading excerpts have become law school deans since authoring these articles. Angela Onwuachi-Willig is the first African American female dean of Boston University, and Theresa Beiner is the first permanent female dean of the William H. Bowen School of Law at the University of Arkansas Little Rock. Before becoming deans, both were highly regarded academics whose research focused on issues of race and gender in the legal profession. (A third author whose work is included in Chapter 5, Carla Pratt, became the first African American and Native American female dean of Washburn Law School after writing the piece we include there.) How do you think their scholarly work might have impacted their career trajectories?

JONATHAN K. STUBBS, *A DEMOGRAPHIC HISTORY OF FEDERAL JUDICIAL APPOINTMENTS BY SEX AND RACE: 1789–2016*

26 BERKELEY LA RAZA J. 92 (2016)

Stubbs is a Professor of Law at the University of Richmond Law School where he writes about race and civil rights, and teaches courses on constitutional law and international human rights.

In 2009, President Barack Obama jettisoned a 220-year-old precedent by nominating then-Second Circuit Judge Sonia Sotomayor to become a

Justice of the Supreme Court of the United States. No president of the United States had ever nominated a woman of color for the highest Court.

Not long after Judge Sotomayor's nomination, a controversy erupted involving a speech that she had delivered nearly a decade earlier. Speaking to a distinguished group of legal professionals, law students, and others, Judge Sotomayor asked a simple question: "what [would it] mean to have more women and people of color on the bench?" Being a conscientious jurist, Judge Sotomayor voiced concern about how her own background might impact her impartiality:

> I am reminded each day that I render decisions that affect people concretely and that I owe them constant and complete vigilance in checking my assumptions, presumptions and perspectives and ensuring that to the extent that my limited abilities and capabilities permit me, that I reevaluate them and change as circumstances and cases before me requires

In fact, Judge Sotomayor forthrightly acknowledged her human frailty: "I can and do aspire to be greater than the sum total of my experiences but I accept my limitations." In essence, she showed sensitivity to seeing things not just from her own viewpoint, but also from a variety of perspectives.

During her speech, however, Judge Sotomayor also stated, "I would hope that a wise Latina woman with the richness of her experiences would more often than not reach a better conclusion than a white male who hasn't lived that life." This "wise Latina" remark ignited a vigorous discussion—some might say a firestorm—that obscured the central question of Judge Sotomayor's speech—namely, what the effects would be of having a federal bench that included more women and people of color She later apologized for making the "wise Latina" statement, a comment many people found offensive.

The controversy surrounding the confirmation of Justice Sotomayor to the Court also shed light upon a misperception that the American federal judiciary boasts more diversity than it actually does. In their insightful article "The Realism of Race in Judicial Decision Making," Professors Pat Chew and Robert Kelley commented upon this phenomenon: "Given all the media attention dedicated to race, affirmative action, post-racial politics, and political correctness, it would not be surprising that people believe that the judiciary is diverse and that minorities fare well in the judicial system. The reality is more complicated and less heartening."

With this background, a synopsis of this Article's three main foci and a few practical illustrations follow. First, this Article assesses America's progress in its 226-year odyssey to desegregate the originally all-White and all-male federal bench. Thus, the primary diversity focal points involve sex and "race." Race is placed in quotes because, as Dr. Craig Venter, a chief researcher for the Human Genome Project has reportedly said, "No serious scholar in this field now considers race to be a scientific concept. . . . It doesn't matter what the genetic trait is, there are few if any of them that are related to what society calls race or ethnicity." Nevertheless, for discussion purposes, this Article accepts the current nomenclature that suggests that humans comprise more than one race and that groups like African Americans, Whites, Latin(o/as), Asian Americans, and American Indians constitute discrete racial categories.

For reasons discussed in more detail later, this Article concludes that it may take decades before the federal judiciary more fully reflects the diversity of the American population. Consider a brief example: over the past seven years, President Obama has appointed more women to the federal bench than did any of his predecessors. Nevertheless, even if all of Obama's successors follow his example and appoint women to the federal bench at the same rate as he did, the United States will never have a judiciary that mirrors the general population because, while most Americans are female, a majority—58 percent—of Obama's appointees have been male This unrepresentative 58–42 split is all the more remarkable as the best ratio that any president has achieved.

This Article's second concern revolves around Justice Sotomayor's query regarding the practical effect of a more diverse federal bench. Relevant scholarship suggests that a more demographically inclusive federal judiciary will better administer justice. This Article preliminarily agrees that a more diverse judiciary is likely to have a positive, substantive impact. Nevertheless, a caveat is in order: we must avoid stereotyping on the basis of secondary demographic characteristics, like a judge's sex or racial identity.

* * *

Finally, this Article preempts some common concerns and objections to the diversification of previously segregated institutions like the federal courts. Such concerns include, for example, the assertion that we cannot find enough qualified women and men of color to serve as judges.

Another short illustration: since Ronald Reagan's presidency, American presidents have appointed, and the Senate has confirmed, 1,567 judges to federal courts of general jurisdiction. In other words, American presidents have averaged forty-six appointments per year. One might ask: in 2016, what are the advantages and disadvantages of seeking to appoint women to at least half of judicial vacancies? Stated differently, at any given time, are there twenty-three women in the United States who are competent, available, and willing to serve as federal judges? For those with open minds, concrete facts can help answer these questions.

* * *

For the first 145 years of the American federal judiciary (1789–1934), all 869 confirmed judicial appointees to courts of general jurisdiction were White men. However, in 1934, President Franklin Roosevelt appointed, and the Senate confirmed, the first woman to a lifetime appointment on a federal court of general jurisdiction. Fifteen years later, President Harry Truman appointed the first person of color. From President George Washington through President Dwight Eisenhower (1789–1960), the demographic profile of the American federal judiciary, comprised of 1,337 confirmed judicial appointments, may be depicted as follows: 1,333 White males, two White females, one African American male, and one Asian American male.

* * *

The table which follows sets forth more detailed demographic information regarding the judicial appointments from President Kennedy's administration through much of President Obama's second term. (January 20, 1961–March 10, 2016)

Judicial Appointments to Federal Courts of General Jurisdiction (John F. Kennedy–Barack H. Obama)

Presidential Appointments

Ethnicity	Kennedy	Johnson	Nixon	Ford	Carter	Reagan	GHW Bush	Clinton	GW Bush	Obama
Af. Am. Males	3	8	6	3	30	6	9	46	15	34
Am. Ind. Males	0	0	0	0	1	0	0	1	0	0
As. Am. Males	1	0	1	2	3	2	0	4	3	11
Latinos	1	3	2	1	15	13	5	18	18	23
Pac. Is. Males	0	0	0	0	0	0	0	0	0	1
White Males	119	153	210	55	169	308	137	194	214	118
Af. Am. Females	0	1	0	0	7	1	2	15	8	26
Am. Ind. Females	0	0	0	0	0	0	0	0	0	1
As. Am. Females	0	0	0	0	0	0	0	1	1	9
Latinas	0	0	0	0	1	1	3	5	12	13
Pac. Is. Females	0	0	0	0	0	0	0	0	0	0
White Females	1	2	1	1	32	27	31	83	50	88

* * *

II. THE MYTH AND SUBSTANCE OF FEDERAL JUDICIAL DIVERSITY

The data in the preceding pages show that men—and White men especially—have historically dominated and continue to dominate the federal judiciary. This section more closely scrutinizes Justice Sotomayor's query as to what it will mean to have more women and people of color in the federal judiciary. The conclusions are preliminary because, as stated previously, much more in-depth empirical and qualitative research needs to be done to support broader claims. Nevertheless, for the reasons that follow, a well-founded basis exists for (cautious) optimism regarding the continuation of the diversification (that is, desegregation) of the federal courts, as well as the improvement of judicial decision making.

Because many members of the general public seem to have misperceptions regarding the extent to which the federal judiciary is diverse, we begin with those flawed perceptions.

A. Diversity Mythology

The federal judiciary has been segregated by sex and ethnicity for so long that when the Senate confirms a person of color or a woman to the bench, members of the general public find the event newsworthy. For instance, the recent elevation of Diane Humetewa to the federal bench broke the 225-year precedent of excluding Native American women from federal judicial service. Judge Humetewa's elevation to the bench exemplifies that while the pace of change is modest, the media often broadly reports breaches of deep-rooted barriers. As Professors Chew and Kelley observed, perhaps such attention at least partially explains the widespread misimpression that the federal judiciary has more diversity than it does. Chew and Kelley stated, "[A]lthough more minority judges sit on the federal bench today than fifty years ago, providing evidence of progress within the last half century, it still is a long way from representing the faces of America."

Furthermore, in an incisive article on gender equality, Professors Hannah Brenner and Renee Newman Knake stated that "[o]ne explanation for these misperceptions comes from a 'tendency to overestimate the proportion of a minority group present in a given population;' this phenomenon has been characterized as 'visibility bias.'" Citing Professor Rosemary Hunter's work on discrimination against women barristers in Australia, Professors Brenner and Knake offered the following specific example of such bias: "[O]ne solicitor estimated that between twenty to thirty percent of the barristers he selected in his work were female, when the actual figure was closer to ten percent, which resulted in solicitors believing they were giving women ample opportunities."

In the United States, such misperceptions are not new. For example, a poll conducted during debates about immigration reform in the mid-

1990s revealed a striking example of visibility bias among White members of the general public:

Percentage of the United States population that White Americans think is Hispanic: 14.7.

Percentage that is Hispanic: 9.5.

Percentage that Whites think is Asian: 10.8.

Percentage that is Asian: 3.1.

Percentage that White Americans think is Black: 23.8.

Percentage that is Black: 11.8.

Percentage that Whites think is White: 49.9.

Percentage that is White: 74.

Similar observations have been made regarding the status of racial minority groups like Asian Americans, who are perceived as "model minorities" and are perceived as being immune to racial discrimination.

* * *

The short answer to Justice Sotomayor's query is that it is probably too early to definitively tell what the impact of increased diversity will have on the bench. As the preceding discussion points out, empirical data and persuasive arguments suggest that a more diverse bench is likely to have a number of positive impacts.

* * *

Nevertheless, in responding to Sotomayor's question, significant analytical issues remain. For instance, here is a nonexhaustive list of possible concerns:

1.   Process Concerns

What criteria would be most appropriate to use in evaluating whether adjudication by a more diverse bench is qualitatively better than a less diverse one? Suppose for example, that a case involves a low-income, single, pregnant woman who seeks a second-trimester abortion. In those circumstances, here are just a few examples of questions that could arise:

a.   To what extent would having a woman interpret existing law be preferable to having a man do so?

b.   To what degree would one need to scrutinize the arguments that were advanced before the court? For instance, must we consider each argument or only the ones that we perceive to be significant?

c.   How does one decide the weight to give each argument?

d.   How should one evaluate situations in which neither the court nor the parties raise a particular pertinent contention? For instance, suppose an interested party seeks joinder to the litigation but is excluded?

e.   How far would one need to consider the impact of a decision maker's personal biography (perceptual prism) upon how a decision maker views the facts and law before her?

2.   Qualitative Queries

Aside from concerns about the process by which we evaluate the decisions of a more diverse bench, we must also consider how we would know substantive justice (fairness?) when or if we see it. To take another contemporary example, how should a court interpret "equal protection of the laws" in a case involving a gay or lesbian person who claims sex discrimination in employment? Again, a few pertinent issues:

a.   How much weight should be given to the history and text of the Fourteenth Amendment?

b.   How persuasive should a court perceive decisions in analogous cases involving race or religion?

c.   To what extent should the judge be sensitive to how her own life experiences (perceptual prisms) affect her perspectives regarding the case? As Justice Sotomayor pointed out:

> I am reminded each day that I render decisions that affect people concretely and that I owe them constant and complete vigilance in checking my assumptions, presumptions and perspectives and ensuring that to the extent that my limited abilities and capabilities permit me, that I reevaluate them and change as circumstances and cases before me requires.

d.   Stated differently, should a heterosexual judge ask herself a question like, "Suppose I were a gay or lesbian person and knew that heterosexual individuals had recognized rights which protected them from employment discrimination and I did not. How might viewing the law from the perspective of such a gay or lesbian person affect my view of equal protection of the laws?"

e.   How might the court's decision practically impact the societal understanding of what constitutes equal justice?

f.   Might a judge need a practical decision-making default? For example, should the judge ask how she might perceive the justice of her decision if she were the plaintiff (or defendant)? If she were one of the lawyers? A member of the general public?

g.   How far should empathy matter in interpreting the law—in other words, seeing "more angles." Another way of posing the question might be to ask whether equal protection of the laws is a shorthand description of "The Golden Rule."

Questions like this could multiply. They are worthy of some consideration, and could occupy significant time and energy resources. Such questions are beyond the parameters of this Article. Suffice it to say for now that further research is required to explore in depth the impact of judicial diversity upon judging.

KIMBERLE WILLIAMS CRENSHAW, *TWENTY YEARS OF CRITICAL RACE THEORY: LOOKING BACK TO MOVE FORWARD*
43 CONNECTICUT LAW REVIEW 1253 (2011)

Crenshaw teaches at UCLA Law School and Columbia Law School and is a leading authority in the area of civil rights, black feminist legal theory, and race, racism and the law. She is one of the founders of the Critical Race Theory movement (along with Richard Delgado, whose work appears in Chapter 1). She also introduced the concept of intersectionality, which is a framework for understanding the ways that the multiple aspects of our identities combine to create unique experiences and for exposing societal privilege and oppression.

In the summer of 1989, twenty-four scholars of color answered a call to attend a "New Developments in CRT [Critical Race Theory]" workshop at the University of Wisconsin. Meeting oddly enough in a convent, they all had agreed to submit something written as a ticket for admission. It was not at all clear, however, that this would be an event worth lining up to attend. After all, the title was a bit misleading. The "New Developments in CRT" was premised on the assumption that there was already something old. But prior to the moment that the invitation was drafted, there really was no CRT as such. The name was made up. It represented more of a possibility than a definitive project. Although the terms did make sense in light of the group's aspirations, the billing suggested that there was a "there there" that wasn't really there yet.

The committee that sent that letter and the invitees that they solicited represented a motley crew of minority scholars who populated the backdoor speakeasies at the American Association of Law Schools (AALS) and Critical Legal Studies (CLS) annual gatherings. These speakeasies were usually hotel rooms and other small enclaves where a certain cohort congregated, drawn by word of mouth, to discuss the events and dynamics transpiring on the main stage. The group might be described as intellectual nomads, folks who were attracted to both liberal antidiscrimination and Critical Legal Theory discourses at a time when the two traditions were connected only at the margins. The organizers had all gravitated in some way or another toward the environs of CLS: among them was an Asian American law professor who had attended the very first CLS conference about a decade earlier, and three others who had first approached CLS as students at Harvard Law School during the late 1970s and 1980s. That group was, respectively, Neil Gotanda, Stephanie Phillips, Terri Miller, and this Author. Joining this group were Richard Delgado and later Linda Greene, both linked to the project through earlier integration struggles at Harvard, and who were by then professors at the host site, Wisconsin Law School.

We were all veterans, in one way or another, of particular institutional conflicts over the nature of colorblind space in American law schools. * * *

This gathering was thus underwritten by specific institutional and organizational struggles over how racial power would be articulated in a post-civil rights America. There were by this time many fights, both within the academy and in society at large, over how far and to what ends the aftershocks of white supremacy's formal collapse would travel. These tensions were evident in struggles ranging from the raw contestations over schools and public resources in the public sphere to the more refined debates about "diversity" in the walled-off worlds of the nation's editorial rooms and faculty lounges. Among the many tremors at the fault lines of race reform and retrenchment were contestations that stand out as defining moments because of their unique role in both synthesizing the multiple strains of racial politics of that moment, and serving as a point of departure for series of related events. The eruption that served as a point of departure in CRT's trajectory was the institutional struggle over race, pedagogy, and affirmative action at America's elite law schools.

* * *

. . .[T]he links between the visions of colorblindness in the 1980s and more recent embrace of post-racialism are robust. Yet while both cast a foreboding shadow over racial injustice frames, there are nuanced differences between them with respect to their stances toward racial power. These differences are best captured by lining up their descriptive and performative analogues-colorblind merit and post-racial pragmatism. The differences between them can be traced in part to their contextual origins. The former arose in the context of elite institutions where a certain degree of bureaucratic rationalism lay at the center of the contestations around "colorblind merit." Post-racialism by contrast is most readily identified with an electoral event, an exercise of political power where the outcomes are dictated by mass preferences. These differences help explain the new conditions that any broadened notion of CRT will confront.

In the context of institutional struggles in higher education and other elite spaces, the notion of colorblind merit came to define the baseline for measuring whether the relative absence of racial minorities is the product of discrimination or the unhappy reality of the uneven distribution of "qualifications." At least with respect to merit, the assertion-although contested-was that merit stood apart from racial power. Merit was value set apart from the economy of racial power, qualities that may well be maldistributed but not racially inscribed.

Importantly, it was not necessary to believe that merit constituted a here-and-now justification for who got what in American institutions in order for adherents to embrace the idea of colorblind merit. Indeed, defenders of meritocracy might be called idealists in that their belief in colorblind meritocracy did not necessarily turn on its current reality but instead on a normative defense of a metric of just deserts that was utterly disconnected from the subjective preferences of the evaluator or the evaluated. One could believe that contemporary practices were stacked or even that a different set of institutional rules might be in place had the relevant history been different, yet hold nonetheless that these realities did not justify the abandonment of the colorblind ideal. The normative commitment to a certain vision of race neutrality in turn foregrounded prescriptive commands that located the seeds of transformation in the willingness of the Other to acquire the skills, attitudes, and hard work needed to succeed in these institutions. Race consciousness of any sort would be a departure from colorblind merit. Such departures might be justified temporarily for a variety of institutional purposes, but race itself was ideally irrelevant in assessing a candidate's intellectual performance and deservingness. Ideally, both the candidate as well as the institution should be colorblind.

Post-racial pragmatism as it is unfolding is less beholden to the ideal of colorblind merit and more grounded in reckoning with white preferences and values to develop the tactical means of engaging them. In contrast to the debates in the 1980s where the racial contours of institutional standards were obscured in an idealist discourse of merit, in electoral politics one is hard pressed to say that racial power is effectively hidden within American "democracy." In contrast to the idealism of colorblind merit where the promise of hard work and the right values elevates the possibility of success, post-racialism's North Star is majority preferences. Freedom and progress turn on the recognition that race need not stand as a barrier to those who satisfy majority sensibilities. Pragmatism locates deservingness not as an objective quality intrinsic to the candidate but in the resourceful adaptation to the projected preferences of those who have power to determine what matters. This is not the idealism of meritocracy but the realism of racial power, now tamed to the limited extent that whiteness can be erased as a prerequisite for accepting a lifeline from someone with a funny name and brown skin.

Politically and institutionally, what post-racial pragmatism suggests is that maneuvering around racial power is not only possible and productive, but in virtually all cases normative. Taken up and popularized in public discourse, post-racial pragmatism sets a standard not only for campaigns and for governance, but for racial justice constituencies, advocates and stakeholders as well. This form of pragmatism is an adjustment to and negotiation with existing power while ensuring that such power remains unmarked. It is a position that urges scaling racial obstacles while declining to name them, walking on water without calling attention to this fact. The ability of some to perform such feats soon becomes the responsibility of all. The rose that grows through the cracks confirms that concrete is fertile after all; the slave who manages to escape proves that those who remain in captivity do so out of choice. It is not the instinct to find a way forward that is problematic here, but it is the inattention to the asymmetrical conditions out of which this post-racial performance is launched. Post-racialism thus raises the baseline to another higher level. While formal equality grounds the legitimacy of the racial status quo in race neutrality, the calling card for post-racial pragmatism is maneuverability.

Of course, the terms of the maneuver are neither available nor acceptable to all. What might be standard practice in politics, especially in mass elections, may not be transferable to ordinary social life. What may be possible for particular individuals might not guarantee trickle down opportunity for others confronting racial obstacles, preferences, and outright exclusions. History makes the fairly obvious point that while some exceptional performers were able to break through racial barriers, this implied little about the lifting of barriers for others. Jackie Robinson still played in front of segregated audiences. White audiences' taste for Black performers at the Cotton Club did not whet the desire to share the dress circle or even the same row with other African Americans, much less neighborhoods, schools, and any other social space. Yet the magnitude and very public nature of Obama's political win has created a narrative of transcendence that operates as though all lesser obstacles disintegrate when the greater one gives way. It is as if the moment Jackie Robinson signed with the Dodgers, all other manifestations of segregation fell apart right then and there.

The difference post-racialism makes-if there is one-is that it facilitates a re-alignment between critics of the racial injustice narrative and those who push back against its repudiation. Post-racialism's cool pose with respect to the thicket of racial obstacles that continue to shape the social terrain permits a deeper alignment with forces that deny that significant racial barriers remain. In the face of the conservative celebration of arrival, the bargain that post-racial pragmatists strike is silence about the racial barriers that continue to shape the life chances of many people of color. This failure to engage racial power jeopardizes racial justice agendas by giving license to those who seek to stigmatize all discourse pertaining to ongoing inequalities. The difference between the post-racial stance and its colorblind predecessor-and this may be slight indeed-is that with respect to colorblind merit, there is at least an opening to argue about its racially-inflected construction. Race Crits came to be through early attempts to critique colorblind merit while liberals disagreed even as they sometimes "suspended" their commitment to it, but at least there was space for a debate. The relevant frames overlapped just enough to provide some possibility that the liberal investment in rooting out "bias" could open up a conversation about rethinking meritocratic standards more broadly. Post-racial pragmatism allows for relatively few interventions of this sort because the issue at base is not whether the standards are fair and race neutral. The question instead is that given what they are, whether they constitute a total bar to all racial Others or whether, as is likely to be the case, some, few, or even One, can make it through. If it is indeed possible, perhaps miraculously so, that one racial Other can overcome, the assumption becomes that any other inequality or barrier is simply an excuse, a failing to make good on opportunity that is now provably there.

While critiques of racism are losing ground, not all discourse about race has been swept under post-racial sanction. Race remains available both to mark non-white delinquency and to deploy disciplinary power to contain it. The differential sanction between talk about racism versus talk about race is apparent in the contrasting reactions to Obama's entreaties to voters not to let his non-traditional image stand in the way of his becoming president (condemned as playing the race card) versus the warm reaction to his Father's Day speech lecturing Black fathers on paternal responsibility (portrayed as courageous truth-telling). One might infer a similar disciplinary impulse in the widespread criticism Obama received for commenting on the controversial arrest of notable Harvard scholar Henry Louis Gates in his Cambridge home. Although the President declined to definitively denounce the arrest in the common parlance of racial profiling, his comment that the police acted stupidly in arresting a man in his own home was widely denounced as out of line. In the controversy that followed, it was apparently beyond the pale to so much as intimate that Henry Louis Gates might have been the victim of racism yet it was almost axiomatic to many commentators that the insult to Sergeant James Crowley was racially-tinged.

In crossing a line that was until that moment undefined, the President also revealed the strings attached to his dizzying post-racial triumph. Indeed, while it was Professor Gates who was visibly carted away in handcuffs, the more lasting image was the discursive constraints that tied the tongue of the President of the United States. The beer summit that tidied up the controversy reproduced President Obama's Philadelphia script in positioning the conflict in the symmetrical terms of a misunderstanding between racial equals. Of course even the Philadelphia script contained a subtext of asymmetrical responsibilities for African Americans that was implicitly written into this one as well. Obama's earlier line-crossing comments had given some credence to an asymmetrical perspective-veering off script in both the sense that it suggested that the scene might have been racially inflected and that something more might be going on than Black sensitivity to past racism. The great upshot of this "teachable moment" was the famous beer summit where the President, the Professor, and the Officer-joined by the completely uninvolved Vice-President-presented a photo-op that recalibrated the President's more candid response to fit the Philadelphia frame. At no moment was the Professor's indignation about being arrested for what many saw as talking back to power in his own home framed as a legitimate or even understandable reaction to his perception of having been racially profiled.

Conveyed in the casual image of four dudes kicking back a cold one in the Rose garden was the message that racial conflict could be managed, even finessed, largely on terms carefully chosen to extinguish the lingering sting of racial accusation. Racial protest was thus doubly arrested in the episode, and President Obama has not been seen in these parts since.

Admittedly speculative, it is hard to fathom that the President's utterance in that unguarded moment was an aberrant thought unrelated to a broader view that race still matters in ways that are contemporary and real rather than post-traumatic projections from an ugly but distant past. Yet the President is constrained by the terms upon which his acceptance by and future ability to win white voters is predicated. That the most powerful man on earth may be silenced and surveilled is a particularly sensitive barometer of the wages of post-racialism. These constraints-this post-racial entrapment-is particularly acute for the President and others who skirt the margins of the majority's racial comfort zone in a way that suppresses any hint of racial complaint. The strategy carries consequences not only for a politician seeking votes, but for any person or group seeking to operate under a less accommodationist sensibility. To borrow a page from post-racialism's "greater accomplishments includes all lesser ones" one might ask, "If the President can't speak Truth to Power, is it possible that lesser mortals can?"

Post-racial pragmatism entraps not only the President, but racial justice advocates and constituencies as well. The bargain comes with strings attached-or perhaps more accurately, discursive handcuffs. The measured agnosticism toward racial power that is characteristic of the post-racialist stance makes it that much harder to affirm, on occasion, that racial injuries actually exist. Like a reverse Chicken Little, repeated assurances that racial harmony can be purchased without breaking the embargo on racial grievance becomes a trap. Where racial complaint is a predicate for understanding and moving against racial harms, the messenger who has promised no racial drama compromises his credibility if he hints that he not only understands the complaint but might share it.

The post-racial pragmatist must be guarded so as to preclude a replay of the unsightly vision of the President being carted away to the virtual slammer.

Although the triumph of a competent Black man in the White House offered reason to hope for an Administration uniquely responsive to racial inequality, fidelity to the terms of post-racial pragmatism virtually guaranteed continuing silence about the crisis in communities of color. Like the colorblind gloss on formal equality, post-racialism's stance toward the remainder of racial power leaves little room for critique and contestation. For racial justice constituencies, the election brought with it an old lesson: winning and losing can be part of the same deal.

This entrapment born of the post-racial bargain is perhaps the ultimate example of contemporary frame misalignment. While broad constituencies found pleasure and hope in what was widely regarded as a shared breakthrough, the terms of success buttressed a deadly silence about the disproportionate and growing losses suffered by wide swaths of people of color. The challenge faced by civil rights constituents and other stakeholders is to find new ways to talk about the reproduction of racial inequality in a political era in which race is left off the table by the very representatives they have supported.

Patterns and practices such as standardized tests and universalistic naturalized conceptions of meritocracy, complex systems that produce the school-to-prison pipeline and the disproportionate impact of the mortgage-foreclosure crisis, material disparities that limit both the quality and length of life such as the wealth gap, the health gap, and so on are dynamics that are becoming unremarkable features of the post-racial world. As these conditions are being swept under post-racialism's "rising tide" mythology, there is in effect, a critical drama playing out in America with no narrative frame under which it might be told. The loss is not simply material and discursive, it is political as well. Without some version of a racial justice frame, the possibilities for collective action are similarly jettisoned. Moreover, this abandoned space does not remain narrative free. As post-racialism takes racial injustice out of the equation, it also widens the bandwidth of other race discourses that naturalize the status quo-recast and rebranded but effectively serving the same purposes as the biological and cultural explanations of the past.

The virtual abandonment of the racial injustice frame is perhaps the most significant misalignment between critical race theorists and the various cohorts with which we have occasionally allied and struggled. Its antecedents pre-exist the rise of post-racialism, and extend well beyond the front-line of presidential politics and media punditry. The disintegration of the injustice frame began the instant the contradictions upon which it was premised yielded to reformist demands. Contradiction-closing reforms such as the repeal of white-only rules and the collapse of formalized white supremacy offered legitimating cover to the ongoing material inequalities that gave rise to the demands in the first place. Transformation and legitimation have been flip sides of the same coin, however ambivalence and tension within the liberal civil rights coalition about colorblindness, meritocracy and the terms of integration continued to erode the powerful vision that inspired millions to move against the status quo. By the time colorblindness became attached to a powerful cultural force that changed the complexion of presidential politics, there was little in the discursive arsenal from which to resist the overnight reframing of racial injustice as racial grievance. Entrapment was the natural if not inevitable outcome.

Some part of the vulnerability to this post-racial malaise points to the limited field of vision that has long characterized the discourses of the liberal/civil rights establishment. The community's contradictory orientation towards affirmative action, as demonstrated in the Harvard debacle, was just one of many episodes that revealed the deep divisions between the mainstream understanding of racial under-representation and more critical frames that foregrounded the notion of meritocracy as one of many repositories of racial power. The subsequent embrace of diversity in the context of affirmative action symbolized a broader concession about how to understand racial disparity at a wider societal level. In embracing the language of diversity, the civil rights coalition endorsed a shift from a discrimination paradigm, already somewhat limited in its capacity to capture the fuller dimensions of racial power, to its distant cousin-diversity. In the same way that diversity erased the particular dimensions of racial subordination in education, especially its institutional and structural synergies, the widespread articulation of diversity as the stand-in for race reform helped to marginalize racial injustice as a contemporary phenomenon.

Today, civil rights pragmatism is reflected in beltway politics that rely on polls and focus groups with an eye toward branding and messaging. Moving in concert with a professionalized notion of racial justice advocacy, this generation takes cues from communications specialists who provide expert advice on whether and how persuadables-largely white voters-might be convinced to support various social justice objectives. Of course, there may be no way to get to some destinations, given the existing geographies of race and public opinion. Where there is no way to get to Peoria, post-racial pragmatism provides little direction.

The distance between the world of civil rights advocacy now and civil rights advocacy of the 1950s and 1960s is not just the difference in the target, but also a difference in the stance itself. Where King's civil disobedience and Marshall's appeal to equal citizenship both sought to broaden and transform the boundaries of racial equality, today's more pragmatic orientation seems limited to those issues that can be advanced within the limited sensibilities of persuadable (white) voters. Needless to say, had Martin Luther King, Jr. or Thurgood Marshall looked to dominant opinion to sort out a strategy in mid-20th century America, it is doubtful whether and how the March on Washington and the campaign to end school segregation would have unfolded. Missing from much of contemporary racial politics is the recognition that short term campaign-based advocacy is not a social movement. Pollsters might be able to fashion a strategy for the former, but the larger goal of broadening and sustaining racial equality discourses cannot be sustained within the limited parameters of current opinion.

The media also helped normalize a particular erasure of racial power in its coverage of racial disparities and conflict. By rarely situating affirmative action or any other race-conscious policies within a frame that pointed to contemporary practices of racial discrimination, the media helped frame racism as a thing of the past. Those who resisted this interment of race were increasingly positioned as outside the mainstream.

As the colorblind offensive continues to move against doctrines and ideas that were partial but hard-won victories, civil rights advocates and constituencies find themselves reigned in and the field of contestation substantially narrowed. In the space that remains, debates about key racial issues have either suppressed the racial dynamics that underscore key social issues or have reversed the frame altogether. As a consequence, those who were formerly recognized as the racially-entitled are turning into racism's new victims and established legal remedies are re-emerging as intolerable civil wrongs.

Consider the way in which post-racial discourses distort understandings of contemporary social problems, often by banishing the racial histories pertaining to these problems to the land of unspeakables. The widely acclaimed Waiting for "Superman" is a particularly compelling example. The portrayal of our deteriorating public school system conjures up images of racial isolation, yet the film manages to narrate a story about the tragic abandonment of public education without any reference to the racial history that shaped public education today. Neither the landmark case of Brown v. Board of Education and the massive white flight that it eventually prompted, nor the interventions such as tracking and magnet schooling that arose in its aftermath, are told as events pertaining to race. Racial power is neither spoken nor acknowledged, although it is shown in almost every frame. Waiting for "Superman" is like a silent film, one in which the viewer can see dynamics that are unfolding, but can hear nothing that vocalizes the actions that are being shown.

Waiting for "Superman" is more than a silent movie about race in America. It is a triumph of the post-racial paradigm. Its ability to engage, move, and inspire millions of Americans, many of whom are destined to live within the racialized contours of opportunity that it fails to name, makes it one the most significant accomplishments of post-racialism to date. It manages to generate support for interventions that are in many ways the product of resistance to Brown's basic commands, even among those who have been left behind by a jurisprudence that has largely insulated public education from meaningful reform.

Whereas "Superman" repudiates racial injustice frames in its failure to name racial injustice, the case lodged against the then-Supreme Court nominee Sonia Sotomayor in the summer of 2009 represents an even more sobering case of outright reversal. The case against Sotomayor was that Obama's search for "empathy" in his nominees and her outsider origins would manifest as open bias against white men. Sotomayor's race and her judicial opinions were lined up to indict the nominee within the emerging discourse of post-racialism while her supporters largely declined to defend the vision of racial justice for which she was being excoriated. Judge Sotomayor's participation in Ricci v. DeStefano's appellate decision to uphold prevailing interpretations of Title VII disparate impact law against the claims of white males seemed to only confirm for her opponents the need to oppose Sotomayor in the language of reverse racism. This framing, ultimately upheld by the Supreme Court, was itself a reversal of the basic assumptions underlying disparate impact doctrine. Accordingly, employers who are attentive to the possibility that their employment practices may unnecessarily exclude minority candidates may also be vulnerable to allegations that this very attentiveness discriminates against whites. The zero-sum frame that is evident in beliefs that more opportunity for racial minorities constitutes less opportunity for whites has been further amplified in Ricci. By tightening the reigns on how and when an employer can act to preclude a disparate outcome, the Court added yet another layer of insulation around the status quo. At the same time, the kind of racial discrimination that disparate impact had traditionally been deployed to remedy was itself erased, defined away by the Court's failure to seriously consider the job-relatedness of the criteria. The stigma of discrimination was visited upon City officials who accepted their responsibility to disrupt the unnecessary exclusion of minority firefighters rather than on those who rallied to prevent the reconsideration of practices that had created a racially skewed status quo.

This attack on the principle of disparate impact became a direct attack on Sotomayor herself. Critics seized on Sotomayor's embrace of her own background as a source of a judicial wisdom and married that to her vote in Ricci to build an image of the judge as a reverse racist, one who will simply hurt white male interests if permitted to serve on the Supreme Court. Yet consistent with the contradictions of post-racialism, white male justices whose backgrounds were invoked as markers of their ethnic identities remained free of such racial sanction even when their rulings functionally benefit white men. The attack on Sotomayor and the broader mischaracterization of disparate impact law warranted little response from the Administration and a rather tepid response from the civil rights community more broadly. No doubt part of this deflection was grounded in the pragmatic understanding that there was little point in engaging in a fist-fight when the votes for confirmation were already secure. But a longer-term loss was evident in the fact that there was virtually no conversation about the devastating consequences of Ricci itself nor a strategy to regain the ground-both conceptually and legally-that was lost by the Court's gesture toward equating disparate impact doctrine with reverse discrimination. Although the handwriting about the eventual confrontation between Congress and the Supreme Court on the scope of Congressional power to address disparate impact is on the wall, there seem to be no readily discernible plans to defend this vital terrain. Experts will no doubt warn that framing issues around race and discrimination are losing propositions, and thus, defending the scope of Title VII's protections must be rebranded or jettisoned.

At the end of the day, there are limits to the degree that racial justice can be finessed; while bridges to white opinion can be built through analogies and commonalities, at some point the rubber meets the road and the specific burdens of race must be addressed. Concessions made to occupy only the space that is pragmatically useful limits the ability to explore possibilities not yet discovered, to tell stories and counter-narratives that hold the possibilities of broadening rather than constraining the terrain of social discourse.

* * *

Critical race projects have occupied both deconstructionist and interventionist spaces; there is no necessary inference that allegiance to the former precludes investment in the latter. Critical Race Theory, both in its traditional iterations and in an expanded articulation, can and should disrupt racial settlement and push for conceptual tools that may, for a short time, push things in a different direction. Certainly there are no final answers, no blueprints for transformation, but something more than the post-racial agnosticism seems warranted by today's milieu.

More importantly, it is not necessary for every writer or researcher with an interest in race to think critically about the apparatuses that they use, nor about the possible ways that their work can help illuminate new patterns of thought and action that might spur incremental change. What is necessary is that a critical mass engages these questions collectively with a certain intention. Whether to understand more fully the context of the university as a historical site of racial power, or to harness these resources to facilitate a more effective resistance to the social settlement that post racialism carries, it is decidedly a project that resists post-racialism's agnosticism on race and that replaces it with an engaged, alternative set of possibilities. Whether these alternatives are framed as racial injustice narratives or something else is up for grabs. Something else might come into its place. Indeed, in the same way that post racialism builds on colorblindness but re-popularizes it, a new critical approach might build on the remnants of racial injustice to fashion a new intellectual frame.

* * *

Our challenge is to develop a broader project, one that interrogates the limitations of contemporary race discourse both in terms of its popular embodiment and its epistemic foundations. It is not a project of fitting inside prevailing sensibilities and disciplinary paradigms, but of broadening them. As Martin Luther King, Jr. once said, "[a] genuine leader is not a searcher for consensus but a molder of consensus." If this is indeed the task of a broadened, interdisciplinary CRT-to remap the racial contours of the way that people see the world that we live in-then in so doing we create a new set of possibilities for racial-justice advocates. Of course, any call to re-imagine the world we live in is one that puts participants at odds not only with prevailing institutional practices, but with allies as well. It requires a certain resistance to "friendly fire," recognizing that some of the most trenchant, invested and rewarded critics may reside closer to home. Yet having such critics, whether near or far, puts us in good stead. It has been reported that Malcolm X once said that if you have no critics, you'll likely have no success. If indeed having critics is the key to success, then critical race theorists have every reason to be wildly optimistic.

THERESA BEINER, *IS THERE REALLY A DIVERSITY CONUNDRUM?*
2017 WISCONSIN LAW REVIEW 285 (2017)

Beiner is a civil rights law scholar. In 2018, she became the first permanent female dean of the William H. Bowen School of Law at the University of Little Rock.

There is consistent agreement among scholars that diversity on the federal bench is a good thing. However, there is some disagreement on the rationale for encouraging this diversity. While some political scientists have focused their research on differences in judges' voting patterns based on each judge's personal characteristics—such as race or sex—others have criticized this approach as a justification for diversifying the bench. While most studies of voting patterns of state and federal judges find no difference or inconsistencies in differences in voting patterns based on these characteristics, there are areas of the law in which they appear to make a difference in judges' approaches, at least in certain types of cases.

This Article begins by canvassing some of the common arguments for diversifying the bench. It also addresses the current demographics of the federal bench, which has become increasingly diverse, thanks in large part to the judicial appointments of President Barack Obama and earlier Democratic presidents. It then discusses the few areas of the law in which studies have shown some differences in outcomes correlating with the race or gender of the judge. Finally, this Article attempts to address the tension that results from focusing on differences in case outcomes based on the race or sex of the judge in a judicial system that aspires to impartiality.

I.   THE VALUE OF A DIVERSE BENCH

Political scientists, law professors, and others have identified a variety of reasons that a diverse bench—in particular, the federal bench—is a good thing. Some arguments emphasize the difference "nontraditional" judges bring to the courts. For example, nontraditional judges contribute an "outsider" perspective—particularly in areas involving sexual preference, race, employment, and constitutional law—that might have an impact on the outcome of a case. This is akin to arguing that women, or members of minority groups, will judge cases differently—what Hanna Fenichel Pitkin refers to as "substantive representation"—"what the representative actually does on behalf of the interests of the group he or she is associated with." Relatedly, nontraditional judges may help narrow and subvert prejudices based on their outsider statuses.

Nontraditional judges also increase public confidence in the courts. Courts that reflect the country—the people who are seeking justice before them—inspire more public trust in the entire judicial system. Indeed, one can easily see how appearing before a judge who cannot relate to one's life experience would lead a person to question the fairness of such a judicial system. Law professor Niemke Grossman argues that sex representation, in particular, influences the sociological legitimacy of courts. She explains that if men and women see situations differently and that different perspective results in different outcomes in cases, normatively, this requires both sexes represented or the results run the risk of bias—or at least the perception of bias—in decision making. As the American Bar Association's Commission on the 21st Century Judiciary opined in a report well over ten years ago, "[w]ithin communities of color [in the United States] . . . concern that they receive unequal, inferior treatment in the courts is compounded by a lack of confidence due to the lack of diversity throughout the judiciary."

Closely related to public confidence arguments is the fairness/representation rationale. This is what Pitkin referred to as descriptive representation—"resembling or reflecting the constituent elements of the community that it governs." Such representation strengthens "at least the appearance of judicial impartiality, as well as the judiciary's legitimacy as a democratic institution." As Sally Kenney argued in her book *Gender and Justice: Why Women in the Judiciary Really Matter*, "Justice must not only be done; it must be seen to be done." Judges who represent the community, Kate Malleson posits, increase the judiciary's legitimacy as a political institution. But is the judiciary a representative branch like other branches of the United States government? Analogizing to jury duty cases, Kenney argued that members of minority groups and women are stigmatized and told that they are essentially less than full citizens when this civic duty—being a member of the judiciary—is denied to them. Thus, there is an argument for judicial diversity from an equity perspective as well. As Malleson put it the context of international courts, "it is inherently unfair that men enjoy a near monopoly on judicial power."

II. PRESIDENT OBAMA'S DIVERSE BENCH

In spite of these arguments, diversification of the federal bench has been slow to develop, beginning with President Jimmy Carter, who was the first president to emphasize diversity in his appointments. While President Bill Clinton also stressed diversity in his judicial nominees, diversity got its biggest boost during President Obama's two terms in office. President Obama was, at first, criticized for his administration's initial slow focus on federal judicial appointments during his first term in office. Since his first term, however, President Obama appointed judges who are the most diverse group in terms of gender, race, ethnicity, and sexual orientation that have ever been appointed. In his first six years in office, he appointed as judges the highest number and proportion of women (40% of district court appointees, 60% of court of appeals appointees), the highest proportion of African Americans (over 20% of district court appointees, 5% of court of appeals appointees), the highest number and proportion of Hispanic Americans (over 11% of district court appointees), and the highest number and proportion of Asian Americans (over 6% of district court appointees, 5% of court of appeals appointees). He also appointed ten openly gay judges in this period. He made diversity on the bench, rather than just judicial ideology, one of the important components of his selection process. But there may be a cost to focusing on diversity.

The appointment process during President Obama's time in office was very slow. Republican senators engaged in delay tactics, even though President Obama's appointees seemingly were not ideologues. Indeed, "judicial selection accounts . . . highlighted the first-term efforts of the [Obama] administration to nominate confirmable moderates to the circuit bench." But still, the process was slow. In the 112th Congress, President Obama had the highest "index of obstruction and delay" (this index includes nominees who were not confirmed and any who took over 180 days to be confirmed) for his district court and court of appeals appointees of any other president. It is thought that this was delay for delay's sake—only 18 of the 250 nominated involved a "sincere real dispute." This, along with delays in appointing judges to the D.C. Circuit, led to Senator Harry Reid's invocation of the "nuclear option"—whereby Senate Democrats changed Senate rules so that the Senate could attain cloture with a simple majority instead of sixty votes. While President Obama had lower rates of success in appointments during his first term, he did very well in the first two years of his second term. In the 113th Congress, he had an 88.6% confirmation success rate.

Edward DuMont provides an example of some of the obstruction President Obama ran into during the judicial nomination process. Professor Carl Tobias, one of the organizers of this symposium, wrote an article about the nomination failure of Mr. DuMont, the first openly gay nominee to a federal court of appeal. President Obama's withdrawal of Mr. DuMont's nomination after a year and a half of delay made it clear that the Senate would not confirm his appointment, in spite of his stellar credentials.

Looking at the appointees from his first six years in office, President Obama's nontraditional judges also came from different experiential backgrounds than his white male appointees. Most had judicial or prosecutorial experience. Only 24.7% of his nontraditional appointees lacked such experience. This compares notably to his traditional appointees—40.2% of whom had neither judicial nor prosecutorial experience. A higher percentage of his nontraditional appointees had law degrees from prestigious law schools. In general, President Obama appointed an elite bunch of judges; he had the highest proportion of all five prior administrations of judges receiving an Ivy League undergraduate and law school education.

The emphasis President Obama placed on judicial experience can be problematic for nontraditional nominees. "The Gavel Gap," a recent study by Tracey George and Albert Yoon, shows that women and members of minority groups are under-represented in state court systems—an excellent pipeline for those who would like to obtain the type of judicial experience that would provide a pathway to a federal judicial appointment. Their study showed that white men make up 30% of the population and hold 57% of state trial court judgeships and 58% of state appellate court judgeships. Indeed, the researchers gave twenty-seven states Fs on their courts' gender diversity report card and thirty-two states Fs on racial and ethnic diversity. Thus, if judicial experience is one of the main prerequisites to a federal judicial appointment, this criterion may limit opportunities for women and members of minority groups interested in such appointments. Still, President Obama did a remarkable job appointing a diverse bench.

III. DO WOMEN AND MINORITY JUDGES MAKE A DIFFERENCE?

So, in what ways, if at all, does the race or sex of a judge make a difference in the judiciary? Overall, race and/or gender of the judge have little impact on case outcomes. But in some rare cases, it does make a difference. Studies have shown influences in two different ways: how the judges vote in discrimination cases and their influence on their colleagues in these cases. In addition, at least some judges believe their backgrounds play a part in how they view cases. And, occasionally, the case law appears to bear this out.

In terms of case outcomes, in most cases the race, ethnicity, or gender of the judge does not make a difference or studies at best are mixed that it does. Kenney notes, in particular, that there is little evidence that male and female judges decide cases differently. For example, with respect to differences based on sex of judge, Christina L. Boyd, Lee Epstein, and Andrew D. Martin's review of the existing research summed it up well: Of the thirty studies of judicial voting behavior based on sex, "roughly one-third purport to demonstrate clear panel or individual effects, a third report mixed results, and the final third find no sex-based differences whatsoever." Results, therefore, are mixed and inconclusive, except for one area of the law that is a particularly important one: sex and race discrimination cases.

Boyd, Epstein, and Martin found no effect in eleven of the twelve areas of the law they studied, but they did find an effect based on sex of judge in Title VII sex discrimination cases. The probability of a woman voting in favor of a plaintiff in the cases they studied was 10% higher than that of a male judge. They also found panel effects. "[W]e observe causal effects ranging from 0.12 to 0.14—meaning that the likelihood of a male judge ruling in favor of the plaintiff increases by 12% to 14% when a female sits on the panel." They opined that this effect may be underestimated because of the many cases that settle.

Political scientist Nancy Crowe found different results than Boyd, Epstein, and Martin in a study of the impact of race and sex of judge on employment discrimination cases decided by the federal courts of appeal between 1981 and 1996. Crowe found that having a woman on the panel had no impact on outcomes, and having an African-American judge actually had a negative impact on white male judges' propensity to rule for a race discrimination plaintiff. These differing results might be a result of the cases Crowe studied—all were non-consensual cases. In other words, the panels were all non-unanimous.

Before exploring other findings with respect of panel composition, it's important to note that there is a norm of unanimity in the federal appellate courts. Federal appellate panel decisions are overwhelmingly unanimous; dissent rates range from six to eight percent. So, federal appellate judges' tendency to agree with each other may result in more conservative judges leaning in the direction of his or her more pro-employment discrimination plaintiff female and minority colleagues.

Sean Farhang and Gregory Wawro also found an impact based on panel composition in a study of federal appellate employment discrimination cases decided between 1998 and 1999. Their study found that the presence of a female judge on a federal panel increased the probability that a male judge would vote for a plaintiff in an employment discrimination case by nineteen percent. The addition of a second woman did not have an additional impact. Overall, the addition of one woman to a court of appeals panel increased the probability of a pro-plaintiff outcome by about twenty percent, and ideological composition of the panel had an effect as well. Interestingly, addition of a racial minority judge had no impact.

Similarly, a study by Jennifer Peresie of sexual harassment and sex discrimination cases decided in the federal courts of appeals between 1999 and 2001 found that plaintiffs were twice as likely to prevail when a female judge was on the bench. Unlike Farhang and Wawro's study, however, Peresie found that having a second woman on the panel also increased the likelihood of a pro-plaintiff outcome. There was no statistically significant difference between male and female judges who were appointed by a Democratic president. She noted that judicial ideology, as reflected by the political party of the president appointing the judge, was the "most powerful alternative explanation" for her results. Even after controlling for political ideology, she found "both liberal and conservative female judges were more likely than their male counterparts to support plaintiffs."

Other studies have found an impact based on race of judge in employment discrimination cases. . . . Studies have found that the political party of the president appointing the judge generally correlates with judges' voting patterns. However, studies have shown a shift in voting based on the composition of the panel. Studies of the federal circuit courts suggest that judges appointed by the opposite party "tend to acquiesce to their colleagues' preferences." So, a Republican appointee with two Democrat appointees will lean liberal and a Democrat appointee will lean conservative. In their study of federal courts of appeals through 2012, Susan Haire, Barry Edwards, and David Hughes found President Obama's white male judges were more likely to support the liberal position than his minority and/or female judges. The opposite held true for President George W. Bush's appointees—his minority and/or female judges were more likely to support a liberal position.

Aside from the studies, there are anecdotal examples from judges that suggest their life experiences influenced how they approached cases. Justice Ruth Bader Ginsburg provides a useful illustration, but the same may be said of Justice Sandra Day O'Connor—in *Planned Parenthood of Southern Pennsylvania v. Casey*, for example. This Article uses Justice Ginsburg as an example because the cases involving her approach are more recent and are consistent with her expressed feminist ideology.

Justice Ginsburg's decision and discussion in *Safford Unified School District v. Redding* provides an excellent example. In this case, the Supreme Court of the United States considered whether the strip search of a thirteen-year-old girl to locate ibuprofen and naproxen—"drugs" her school considered contraband—violated Section 1983. The oral argument in the case made it look like the plaintiff would lose. Even Justice Breyer, who is typically sympathetic to civil rights plaintiffs, commented that the strip search was akin to changing for gym class.

After oral argument, Justice Ginsburg commented that her male colleagues "have never been a 13-year-old girl . . . . It's a very sensitive age for a girl. I didn't think that my colleagues, some of them, quite understood." Although the Court ultimately held that the search was unreasonable, a majority of the Court agreed that the administrator who ordered it was protected by qualified immunity because the law was not clearly established that this type of search was unreasonable at the time the school administrator ordered it. Justice Ginsburg, dissenting in part, disagreed, arguing that the search violated "clearly established" law, and therefore school officials were not entitled to immunity. In particular, Justice Ginsburg focused on the continued humiliation of plaintiff Savanna Redding even after school officials found no contraband during their strip search. As she explained,

> To make matters worse, Wilson did not release Redding, to return to class or to go home, after the search. Instead, he made her sit on a chair outside his office for over two hours. At no point did he attempt to call her parent. Abuse of authority of that order should not be shielded by official immunity.

In *Safford*, the majority agreed with Justice Ginsburg that a strip search of a thirteen-year-old girl for ibuprofen and naproxen was unconstitutional, but the Court still afforded the plaintiff no relief. Given the statements of some Justices during oral argument, it would be interesting to know if Justice Ginsburg's understanding of a thirteen-year-old girl's perception swayed some of her fellow justices to agree that, going forward, courts would consider such a search unconstitutional.

* * *

It is not that men cannot understand the perspective of women who are faced with sex discrimination. Indeed, all-male courts decided early United States Supreme Court cases with outcomes favoring women in sex discrimination cases. However, as studies suggest, having a woman on the Court may help bring that perspective into focus for men not so inclined to see it for themselves from the start.

IV. PROBLEMS WITH FOCUSING ON DIFFERENCE

This brings me back to the fundamental conundrum in arguing that women and members of minority groups make a difference on the bench. It presents as a typical double-edged sword. By making these arguments, political scientists such as Sally Kenney argue that advocates for a diverse bench fall into an essentialist trap regarding the differences between male and female judging. Discussing these differences assumes that women or particular minority group members, such as Americans of African descent, all view situations similarly. Yet, like initial advocates of legal feminism, it is privileged members of the group whose views are publicly supported. This is especially true of federal judges, who, because of the elite background of most women and members of minority groups who would be good candidates for the federal bench, are less likely, for example, to have working class roots. Indeed, even President Obama's very diverse nominees are a rather wealthy and elite group, given their backgrounds.

Arguments suggesting that women and members of minority groups will judge cases differently also appear to conflict with the goal of judicial impartiality. After all, the outcome of a case is not supposed to depend on the background of the judge, but instead on an impartial view of the law and the facts involved in the individual case. One way to avoid this criticism is to question the foundation of what is currently deemed "impartial." Indeed, if a male and a female judge or a white and minority judge view the same fact pattern differently, one would have to make the normative judgment about which judge was being impartial. History and compelling scholarly argument show that many legal rules were and are not impartial with respect to race and gender, at least in their application and impact. The United States Supreme Court itself acknowledged this by raising the level of scrutiny in cases involving race and gender discrimination. Thus, if an impartiality "correction" of sorts is needed, it would be in a direction that incorporates the experiences of women and members of minority groups. Otherwise, the worldview that is privileged in judicial decision making is white and male.

Of course, gender and race of judge are clearly not the end all, be all of how judges make decisions, and Kenney and others are wise to caution that these characteristics should not be overemphasized as a justification for appointing a diverse bench. Justice Ginsburg herself expressed skepticism regarding studies suggesting a difference in judging based on gender. As she noted, "I certainly know that there are women in federal courts with whom I disagree just as strongly as I disagree with any man." Indeed, in the examples of cases where Justice Ginsburg's perspective arguably provided a differing view of the case than her fellow male justices, there were always male justices who agreed with her position. A majority of the Court agreed in *Safford* that the strip search of a teenage girl for pain relievers was unconstitutional.

The main case studies that show a consistent difference in voting patterns based on race and/or sex are employment discrimination cases. In addition, a study of voting rights cases found that the addition of an African American judge to a panel resulted in more favorable rulings for plaintiffs than panels that had all white judges. So, maybe that there are few cases with consistent differences in voting patterns is a good enough reason to abandon any talk of different approaches between judges of diverse backgrounds. This would avoid the essentialist trap created by such arguments.

However, employment discrimination cases and voting rights cases are important. Jobs are fundamental to the ability of individuals to feed, clothe, and house themselves and their families. Jobs are also access points to greater economic opportunities. Voting rights provide opportunities for women and members of minority groups to see their interests supported by elected officials. Thus, the differences in these cases is important to acknowledge and think about when considering the advantages of a diverse bench. Otherwise, the judiciary runs the risk of privileging a world view (at least in the critical areas of jobs and voting) that does not reflect the perspectives and understandings of the larger community.

Kenney and Malleson have both argued that arguments based on difference are strategically dangerous. Malleson suggests that arguing that women judge a particular way is of a piece with women lawyers being pigeonholed into "women's" law, such as domestic relations work. She further argues that this "difference" often is elided with "better," which results in women suddenly having to be better judges than their male counterparts. Finally, it is likely that any differences will be perceived as "lesser," given that female characteristics consistently have been devalued. Because of the strategic problems with difference arguments, Kenney suggests a representative argument makes more sense and is a more justifiable basis upon which to hang the "diversity on the bench" hat. Ultimately, both Kenney and Malleson rely on judicial legitimacy, including public confidence in the courts, as a better argument that does not depend on what women judges may or may not do in actual cases.

A representative approach is not without its problems when it comes to the federal judiciary, which is not considered a "representative" branch in the traditional sense. The design of the United States Constitution is to keep judges above the political fray by appointing them with guaranteed job security and salaries. Thus, they are not intended to be "representative" in the same sense that legislators and the President of the United States are representative of those who elected them. As Alexander Hamilton pointed out in the *Federalist Papers*, the judiciary was designed as a "distinct and independent bod[y]." Judges were people of "independent spirit . . . essential to the performance of so arduous a duty." Chief Justice Roberts recently underscored this in his opinion in *Williams-Yulee v. Florida Bar*. Justice Roberts, in the context of upholding campaign limitations placed on elected state judges, explained that the state has a "vital" interest in "safeguarding 'public confidence in the fairness and integrity of the nation's elected judges.'" In distinguishing judges from other elected officials, Justice Roberts explained:

> In deciding cases, a judge is not to follow the preferences of his supporters, or provide any special consideration to his campaign donors. A judge instead must "observe the utmost fairness," striving to be "perfectly and completely independent, with nothing to influence or control [sic] him but God and his conscience."

Kenney argues that the case for women judges is akin to the case for including women on juries. It's not that they will decide a case differently, but instead that this is a civic function that should be open to all in the community. The same argument works for judges who are members of racial and ethnic minority groups. As Kenney explains, "[t]he best case for a gender-diverse bench does not rest on difference. The most persuasive arguments appeal to democracy and legitimacy, recognize the symbolic role of judges, call for simple nondiscrimination, and draw analogies between gender and geographic representation." As Justice Felix Frankfurter explained over sixty years ago, "justice must satisfy the appearance of justice."

Kenney and Malleson surely are correct that appeals to difference, though common, are likely not the best approach for making the case for a diverse bench. Indeed, there is no evidence of any widespread differences in decision making based on race and/or gender of the judge. However, one should not forget, as Boyd, Epstein, and Martin point out, though a female panel member on a court of appeals panel "rarely" makes a difference, "[r]arely, though, is not never."

* * *

AMBER FRICKE & ANGELA ONWUACHI-WILLIG, *WHY FEMALE "FIRSTS" STILL MATTER FOR WOMEN OF COLOR*

2012 MICHIGAN STATE LAW REVIEW 1529 (2012)

Fricke (right) is Legal Counsel for the State of Iowa Legislative Services Agency. Onwuachi-Willig (left) is a scholar of civil rights and racial/ gender inequality. In 2018, she became dean of Boston University Law School. They wrote this article together while Fricke was Onwuachi-Willig's student at the University of Iowa College of Law.

This Article argues that diversifying the federal judiciary with more women and men of color, but particularly with more women of color, is essential to moving forward and strengthening this country's democracy. Specifically, this Article responds to arguments by prominent feminists that having female "firsts" on the bench is not as critical as having the "right" women on the bench—"right" meaning those women who are invested in and supportive of what are traditionally viewed as women's issues. In so responding, this Article acknowledges the appeal of such arguments regarding judicial service from the "right" women, but contends that, while achieving "firsts" (and "seconds" and more) on the bench for white women may not be as important as it was in the past, it is still crucial for women of color, who are nearly absent from the federal bench. Much like the "firsts" of white female judges all over the nation held important symbolic meaning for the advancement of white women and helped to change societal perceptions about who is and should be a judge, so, too, will the same "firsts" for women of color. However, for women of color to have a similar impact on society as their white sisters, appointments of women of color to the federal bench must occur in meaningful numbers; they must represent more than mere tokenism, and they should include women of color with a variety of backgrounds and viewpoints.

* * *

While progress for women on the bench, overall, has been slow, for some groups of women, it has been even slower. Women of color are just beginning to make real inroads into the federal judiciary. Indeed, women of color's access to Article III judgeships has been slow-coming and in small numbers. As noted previously, the first woman of color to serve in an Article III judgeship, Constance Baker Motley, was not appointed until 1966. Furthermore, it was not until President Carter's administration and his deliberate diversity push—which included appointing forty female judges and thirty-seven African-American judges (seven of whom were African-

American women)—that an African-American woman was appointed to an appellate judgeship. That woman, Amalya Kearse, was appointed to the U.S. Second Circuit Court of Appeals in 1979. Even so, it took more than forty years from Judge Motley's appointment to the U.S. District Court for the Southern District of New York and over thirty years from Judge Kearse's appointment to the U.S. Second Circuit Court of Appeals for a woman of color to be appointed to the U.S. Supreme Court. In 2009, Justice Sonia Sotomayor, a Latina, was appointed to the U.S. Supreme Court by President Barack Obama.

* * *

In addition to having low numerical representation within the federal judiciary, women of color, much like their white female peers, have faced and continue to face the barriers and challenges . . . . This gender barrier, however, is racialized, which, as Kimberle Crenshaw's theory of intersectionality explains, means that women of color judges encounter gender-related challenges that are distinct from those faced by white female judges. Lynn Hecht Schafran has explained this issue by using the sociological concept of a "status set." Schafran explicates that a "status set" is used:

> to describe the expectation that an individual who holds one status in the world will also hold certain others. The status set for judges is still white and male. Thus, white women judges are one step removed from the "norm." Women of color judges are two steps removed. This lack of fit with peoples' expectations has many implications for how women judges, particularly women of color, are perceived and treated by a wide array of people.

In general, as Schafran provides, it is more difficult for women than men to gain respect from court employees and litigants, and that problem is exacerbated for women of color. For example, women of color likely face more hostile reception from attorneys and litigants in judicial evaluation surveys. Women of color also encounter race- and gender-based requests for recusal in the courtroom. For example, in one case, the defendant in an employment discrimination lawsuit sought to disqualify Judge Motley from sitting on his case based on the rationale that she, as a black woman, had been discriminated against and would identify with those who have suffered race or sex discrimination. Judge Motley declined to recuse herself, explaining:

> "[I]f background or sex or race of each judge were, by definition, sufficient grounds for removal, no judge on this court could hear this case, or many others, by virtue of the fact that all of them were attorneys, of a sex, often with distinguished law firm or public service backgrounds."

In other words, although all judges, including white male judges, have a race or a sex that can affect their outlook, judges of color, and especially female judges of color, are primarily the ones who have their ability to be neutral arbiters challenged. These actions reveal how both whiteness and maleness have been defined as the norm in society.

Similarly, while all women are often ranked lower than equally performing men for not conforming to feminine gender stereotypes, such as failing to act lady-like, women of color may be particularly vulnerable to such mistreatment as a result of stereotypes, such as the fiery Latina, the angry black woman, or submissive Asian flower. For example, black women and Latinas may often be assumed to be harsh, rude, and overbearing all traits that are in line with the stereotype of the Sapphire. Even if a black woman or Latina deliberately "works her identity" to counter and disprove this stereotype, she still may not benefit from her behavior. Rather, attorneys who are responding to the evaluation may be more predisposed to remember the Latina or black woman judge as the Sapphire and may unfairly rate her negatively, regardless of her objective demeanor.

* * *

Such realities in the experiences of women of color on the bench are in part the result of stereotypes about women of color, but they are also in part the result of the near complete absence of women of color from the bench. When women of color are absent from the bench, the implicit messages sent are that women of color lack the competence, temperament, and ability to serve as judges and that, when they act as their white male counterparts do, what they are doing is wrong or unnatural.

III. The Need for More Women of Color in the Federal Judiciary (Without Regard to Political Affiliation)

Now that there is a critical mass of women on the federal bench, a number of advocates for gender diversity have argued that the mere representation of women on the bench alone is not material. "Firsts" are no longer critical, they say; rather, the focus should be on getting women who are concerned about women on the bench. In effect, these advocates downplay the importance of "firsts" for women on the bench, choosing instead to place an emphasis on getting the "right" women on the courts. However, this argument, while very appealing politically, neglects the fact that there is no essential female experience. The argument is, in some sense, essentialist, meaning it implies that there is "a unitary, 'essential' experience [for women that] can be isolated and described independently of [gender,] race, class, sexual orientation, and other realities of experience," and it ignores Professor Crenshaw's point about intersectionality, which is that different groups may experience events and treatments differently based on the differing intersections of identity-categories—here, race and sex. In other words, the feminist argument against a focus on female judicial "firsts" (and "seconds") is problematic for the same reason that the first two waves of the feminist movement were: failure to account for women of color's experiences. The fact is that women of color have not broken many barriers within the federal judiciary nor have they achieved many "firsts" on the federal bench; consequently, their placement on the bench, particularly as "firsts," would still hold strong symbolic meaning, and it also will likely enrich the process of judging, particularly where panels are involved; instill greater confidence in the courts for all the litigants who come before them; and increase general confidence in the system of democracy in the country.

Great importance should be placed on ensuring intersectional, race and gender (with gender including sexuality) representation when selecting judicial nominees—and for reasons apart from and, more controversially, separate from the political ideology that the nominee may be perceived as advancing. While society has not reached a point where gender representation on the bench is no longer material, it particularly has not reached this point with regard to women of color.

A. The Symbolic Value in Seeing Female Judges of Color

Many reasons have been proffered for promoting gender and racial diversity on the bench. The strongest argument for increasing the number of women of color in the judiciary is symbolism. For women of color, "first" appointments to the bench are essential, regardless of political affiliation. The symbolic value of having more women of color serve on the federal bench is significant because it can illustrate to society and the legal community that people who are not white males, or even white females, are capable of becoming federal judges and administering justice equitably. It removes from the public's mind what is implied when women of color are absent from the bench. It removes the unspoken statement that women of color are not good enough or competent enough to serve on the bench. Justice Ruth Bader Ginsburg made similar comments about the potential impact of having three female justices now sitting on the U.S. Supreme Court when she said, "When the schoolchildren file in and out of the court and they look up and they see three women, then that will seem natural and proper—just how it is." It is important for our society, too, to readily see that service on the bench by women of color is natural and proper.

But, before the sight of female judges, including women of color, comes to be viewed as natural and proper, there is often an adjustment period for society in experiencing such changes. The very image of more female judges, both white and of color, may be a befuddling experience for spectators. Consider, for instance, former U.S. Tenth Circuit Court of Appeals Judge Deanell Reece Tacha's description of the first time that an all-female judge panel presided over a case in her circuit. Retired Judge Tacha, now the Dean of Pepperdine University School of Law, noted that when the first all-female panel in her circuit was convened, it was thought to be a newsworthy event. Implicit in the press's coverage of the panel was the assumption that an all-female judicial panel was unnatural and foreign. Judge Tacha stated, "The reports in the press were comical for their non-newsworthiness. The press reported comments, such as 'they were very well prepared,' and 'they asked good questions.'" As such commentary illustrates, despite claims and perceptions of gender equality in society, the public may strangely be surprised when women perform a job traditionally reserved for men and do so with the same competence expected from men. However, with time, and increased emphasis and follow-through on confirming more women, particularly women of color, to the bench, their presence will not be noted as extraordinary due to their gender or to their race and gender.

In the end, having women of color serve on the federal bench will carry great symbolic value, not just for women and girls of color, but also for white women and girls and men and boys of all races. After all, women of color judges serve as role models through their mere presence, and role models are important because they provide hope and demonstrate to individuals, especially those who see themselves in the models, that such aspirations are within reach for "someone like me."

* * *

B.   Meaningful Numbers

But, simply having a few more female judges of color is not enough. Women of color must join the federal judiciary at rates greater than mere token representation. Having a critical mass of women of color on the bench makes it possible for women of color judges to perform their jobs without being saddled with the additional duty of speaking for all women of color. Judge Anna Blackburne-Rigsby of the District of Columbia Court of Appeals expressed this point when she wrote that "[o]ur varied experiences illustrate the necessity of having a 'critical mass' of black women on our nation's state and federal appellate courts so that no single black woman feels 'isolated or like [a] spokesperson[ ] for [her] race [and gender].'"

In addition to lessening the burden of being a spokesperson for other women of color, having a critical mass of women of color on the bench helps to ensure diversity of experience and exposure to diversity of experience from the bench. In summarizing her article on black women judges, Judge Blackburne-Rigsby wrote: "I have seen that being both black and female brings an important additional voice to the deliberative process, but that voice is varied because there is no singular 'black woman' perspective." In other words, having a critical mass of women of color on the bench helps to highlight the diversity of thought, perspective, and judicial philosophy among women of color. Shining a light on this diversity of thought serves as an effective tool for dulling the effects of unconscious prejudice and quelling stereotypes about whom a judge should be. For this reason, diversity of political ideology and background amongst female judges of color becomes very important in selection, as such diversity among women of color can further facilitate the breaking down of stereotypes about women of color and their viewpoints by challenging the preconceived notion that all women of color think the same way.

One good example for illustrating this point is the contrast between the only two black U.S. Supreme Court Justices: Justice Thurgood Marshall and Justice Clarence Thomas. Both Justices grew up black in the United States and experienced racism; however, one was liberal, and the other is conservative. Both of the Justices' viewpoints were shaped and have been shaped by their racialized experience. They simply had and have two different "voices of color." If one were to rely on an essentialist notion of race, one would have predicted that the two Justices would decide all cases the same or, in the alternative, would attempt to rationalize Justice Thomas's approach by de-blackening him, calling him a race-traitor, or in some way denying him the ability to describe his reality.

* * *

Finally, meaningful numbers of women of color on the bench will help to counter the opposition that women of color nominees often face because of race and gender bias. Just increasing the number of women of color judges will make it more difficult for racist and sexist arguments, such as women of color's success being the result of special treatment through affirmative action or exceptionalism, to be put forth. For example, it would become harder to explain Justice Sotomayor as an "exception" to her race, a proclamation that implies that most other Latinas are incompetent or unworthy of being federal judges. In conclusion, women of color with diverse backgrounds and political ideology should be appointed to the federal bench in order to combat racial and gender stereotypes, respect difference, and create a more welcoming, conducive work environment for women of color judges.

C. Ensuring Democracy

Additionally, having women of color on the bench is beneficial because it conforms with our democratic principles of inclusion and participation. A democracy is not at its best if all of its citizens are not included. Courts should reflect the composition of the populations that they serve. Like white women and men of color, women of color, too, must be included within our democracy.

Furthermore, the presence of women of color will benefit all members of the citizenry by strengthening the legitimacy of the judiciary in the eyes of communities of color, communities that are currently more likely to feel (and be) disenfranchised than Whites, for example. Race and gender diversity on the bench helps to instill trust in the courts, and in the system of government as a whole. Defendants, plaintiffs, and attorneys of all races and sexes will all have greater trust in a court system that is reflective—at least on its face—of their realities. This is particularly true of the criminal justice system, which many communities of color do not view as a fair and legitimate institution. By increasing the access to and visibility of women of color in the judiciary, the legitimacy of the judiciary, too, will be increased.

D. Improving Decision Making

Finally, creating greater diversity within the federal judiciary by nominating and confirming more women of color will strengthen decision making on affected courts—leading those members of the judiciary to think more broadly about legal issues and to consider more frequently life experiences that are foreign to them. This will enhance the deliberative decision-making process on panels. The ability of a judge to understand an experience provides valuable context for adjudicating issues in an informed manner. One person will not have the experiential knowledge to adjudicate every case in an informed manner, but appellate courts provide crucial opportunities for judges to discuss cases, provide insight from their own experience, bring underlying assumptions in parties' arguments to the surface, and ensure that biases do not take the discussion off-track and deny justice to a party. Diversity on the bench encourages all members on an appellate court to think more broadly. Chief Justice Peggy Quince of the Florida Supreme Court, the first black women to serve in this position, said that "[s]he feels that having black women judges at the appellate level makes a difference." She explained:

> "Just your mere presence makes people stop and listen. Your colleagues may not agree and your perspective may not make a difference in the particular case at issue, but it opens the minds of your [colleagues] to different perspectives to the table that would not otherwise have had a voice."

Studies of appellate courts also bear out the tangible effects that a woman or a person of color may have on the outcome of a case. Studies have shown that the presence of one woman on an appellate panel increases the likelihood that a female sex discrimination plaintiff will prevail. Similarly, the presence of an African American on an appellate panel has been found to increase the likelihood that a panel will find in favor of the racial minority who is alleging race discrimination. In many cases, there will not be a tangible, quantifiable outcome-determinative effect of diversity on appellate courts. Nevertheless, anecdotal evidence suggests that racial and gender diversity on appellate courts is still important.

* * *

Conclusion

In conclusion, female "firsts" on the bench in any area and on any court still matter, but especially for women of color. Women of color still have hurdles and obstacles to overcome that their white sisters do not, both in terms of symbolism and numbers. While there may be a need for "feminist" or "womanist" judges, and for good reason, that call is a different one than the call for women of color judges.

PAT CHEW, *JUDGES' GENDER AND EMPLOYMENT DISCRIMINATION CASES: EMERGING EVIDENCE-BASED EMPIRICAL CONCLUSIONS*
14 JOURNAL OF GENDER RACE & JUSTICE 359 (2011)

Chew is the Judge J. Quint Salmon and Anne Salmon Chaired Professor at the University of Pittsburg School of Law, and a past-chair of Association of American Law Schools Section on Women in Legal Education. The youngest of six children, she grew up in El Paso, Texas in a Chinese-American family.

* * *

I.   Introduction

Both the legal community and society have become particularly intrigued with the topic of women judges. In part, increasing visibility and number of women judges, jump-started by numerous judicial appointments of women in the Carter, G.H. Bush, and Clinton Administrations, explain this interest. Recent high-profile events brought attention to women in political life generally. The presidential campaigns of both Hillary Clinton and Sarah Palin highlighted their remarkable, but still novel, roles as female candidates for national office. And certainly Justice Sonia Sotomayor's confirmation hearings and the uproar surrounding her "wise Latina" comment confirmed that both the gender and ethnicity of judges remain hot-button issues.

The increase of women on the bench has intrigued legal and social science researchers. It has prompted theoretical and empirical explorations of the importance and consequences of the increasing presence of women on the bench. Some have considered the symbolic value of more gender diversity in the judiciary, while others have noted the substantive value of women judges. While the symbolic value of a more diverse judiciary can be very meaningful, it is distinguishable from the substantive effect women judges may have through different interpretations of legal principles, resulting in different case outcomes.

Researchers utilizing different models of judicial decision making put forth different predictions about whether the gender of judges will make a substantive difference in case outcomes. In particular, the legalistic and professional-socialization models contrast with the realistic and personal-attribution models. Those who subscribe to the legalistic model think that judicial decision making is largely a mechanical and essentially formulaic process, and would likely predict that judges' gender or other personal attributes are unlikely to make a difference. The professional socialization model further complements this legalistic model. It argues that judges, through their legal and judicial training, are repeatedly socialized to the profession's norms and that this socialization prevails over any personal attributes or experiences. Thus, a judge's gender would not likely affect the decision-making process.

In contrast, those who believe that the judicial decision-making process involves some personal discretion (realistic model) are more likely to predict some relationship between judges' gender and case outcomes. The personal attribution model similarly complements this realistic model. It argues that judges do not leave their humanness at the courtroom door. Judges' lives, including personal attributes and experiences, consciously or unconsciously influence how they interpret case facts and legal principles.

* * *

III. Macro-Level Review of Empirical Evidence

Using a range of sources the Author, to the best of her knowledge, identified all empirical studies on federal court cases since 1990 that focus on the relationship between judges' gender and outcome in employment discrimination cases in general, and sexual discrimination in particular. Fourteen studies were identified, all of which are listed in the Appendix. State court cases and federal cases that are on other subject areas are not included. While a handful of studies looked at data prior to 1990, their application to our current understanding of the relation between judges' gender and judicial decision making is limited and possibly misleading given the age of their data. This review of studies on the effects of a judges' gender reveals that more empirical research exists in employment discrimination, particularly sex discrimination, than any other particular non-criminal law topic. The comparative richness of this existing body of work allows us to better understand the role that gender plays in judicial decision making. This macro review reveals a number of notable patterns.

A. Judges' Gender in Sex Discrimination Cases

To the extent that female and male judges differ in how they resolve legal cases, the frequent hypothesis is that those differences would most likely appear in employment discrimination cases, particularly sex discrimination. The weight of the empirical evidence supports this hypothesis. For example, studies have found that female judges in the federal appellate courts have different decision-making patterns than male judges when it comes to sexual discrimination cases: namely, female judges are more likely to hold for the plaintiffs. The recent study by Boyd, Epstein, and Martin illustrates this. Likewise, the Crowe study, Massie study, and Peresie study on sex discrimination and sexual harassment cases reach the same conclusion. In contrast, the Kulik study on district court cases and the Westergren study on appellate court cases did not find gender differences in the judges' decision-making patterns.

The Boyd study is based on a data set from appellate court cases on a range of different legal subjects between 1995 and 2002, compiled by Cass Sunstein and his colleagues for their project on the effect of political ideology on judicial decision making. Boyd and her colleagues study two questions: Do male and female judges decide differently (individual effects)? Does the presence of a female judge on a panel cause male judges to behave differently (panel effects)? Their paper is distinctive in part because of its elaborate discussion of research methodology in judge studies, including a description of the most dominant methodology and an alternative method that the researchers advocate.

The Boyd study found strong significant differences in sex discrimination cases at the appellate level (although it did not find gender differences in other subject areas). When dealing with sex discrimination suits, the study found significant differences in the way female and male judges ruled, with female judges finding in favor of plaintiffs more frequently than male judges. Furthermore, it was more likely for a male judge to rule in favor of the plaintiff if at least one female judge sat on the appellate panel. The difference between all-male versus mixed-gender panels had measurable consequences for litigants.

* * *

B. Judges' Gender in Employment Discrimination Cases

A review of the broader category of employment discrimination cases, including sexual discrimination and discrimination based on other protected statuses, revealed the pattern is significantly similar to the studies on just sex discrimination cases. Davis and her colleagues, as well as Farhang and Wawro, for example, found that the gender of the judges makes a significant difference in appellate-level discrimination cases. Similarly, the Massie study of appellate cases dealing with civil liberties (including sex discrimination cases) also found gender differences. In each of these studies, women judges were more likely to hold for the plaintiffs. In contrast, two studies of the district courts, one by Manning and one by Segal, did not find gender differences. The Manning study sampled Hispanic and non-Hispanic judges, and the Segal study sampled Clinton judicial appointees. Given the mixed results in appellate and district court cases, perhaps there is a difference in the collective decision making that occurs on appellate panels versus the individual decision making in district courts.

Farhang and Wawro studied whether women and racial-minority judges impacted case outcomes in 400 federal appellate court employment discrimination cases from 1998–1999. Their research inquiries included whether women and minority judges influenced the decisions of other panel members. They found male judges voted more liberally (in favor of the plaintiff) when one woman served on the panel compared to all-male panels. Furthermore, the gender composition of the panels influenced the way all the judges voted. When there was at least one woman judge on the panel, the probability of an outcome favoring the plaintiff increased by about twenty percent. Interestingly, adding another woman to the panel did not increase the likelihood that the plaintiff would win. The general ideological make-up of the panel also mattered, but the racial composition did not.

Farhang and Wawro offered a contextual analysis of their empirical results by relating them to the institutional norms of appellate judicial decision making. They determined that decisions on federal appellate panels are overwhelmingly unanimous, with dissent rates averaging only six percent to eight percent across circuits. They suggest this norm of consensus on appellate panels is "motivated by a view among judges that unanimous court opinions promote the appearance of legal objectivity, certainty, and neutrality, which fosters courts' institutional legitimacy, while dissenting opinions create legal uncertainty, erode courts' credibility, and may even provoke opposition to a decision."

* * *

Furthermore, according to this model, judges confer "in a spirit of 'give-and-take' (or accommodation) in an effort to reach a decisional consensus and thus avoid public dissension." Farhang and Wawro argue that their finding that mixed-gender appellate panels are more likely to hold for the plaintiff is evidence of women judges' effect over their male colleagues. Farhang and Wawro "conclude that under a strong norm of unanimity on federal appellate panels, elements of both deliberation and bargaining— alternative perspectives, persuasive argument, and horse-trading— explain how women on a panel are able to influence the way male judges on the panel vote."

C. Judges' Gender and Non-Gender-Related Cases

In addition to the separate analyses of studies on sex discrimination and on employment discrimination cases (including sex discrimination), the author reviewed employment discrimination studies that expressly do not include any gender-related cases (such as sex discrimination cases). This research of non-gender-related cases offers a contrasting conclusion on the effect of the judges' gender. Namely, the judges' gender did not make a difference in case outcomes dealing with race-related disputes.

Two studies on racial harassment cases by Chew and Kelley found that judges' gender does not make a difference in how the cases turned out. In contrast, the judges' race did make a difference. Crowe's study of appellate court race discrimination cases reached similar conclusions, as did Cameron's study of race-based affirmative action cases.

Chew and Kelley studied racial harassment cases in both the federal district courts and the appellate courts over an extensive time period (1981 to 2002). Judges' gender did not make a significant difference in case outcomes, with plaintiffs being successful before female judges about twenty-six percent of the time versus twenty-one percent of the time before male judges. However, other judge characteristics, such as the judges' race and political ideology, did make a significant difference in case outcomes.

In a second study of racial harassment cases, Chew and Kelly studied only district court cases from 2002 to 2008 to obtain a clearer picture of individual decision making (rather than the collective decision making that occurs on appellate panels) and to offer a more contemporary analysis of judicial decision making. While the research focused on the race of judges and plaintiffs, the research also analyzed a number of other variables, including the judges' gender. Consistent with their first study, the researchers found that the judges' gender did not make a significant difference in the case outcomes: plaintiffs before female judges had a win rate of twenty-seven percent compared to a win rate of twenty-three percent before male judges.

Crowe's study of federal appellate judges also reveals a telling comparison of judges' gender in sex discrimination and race discrimination cases. Her analysis indicated that female judges are more likely than male judges to vote in favor of plaintiffs in sex discrimination cases. In race discrimination cases, however, there were no differences among judges based on the judges' gender.

IV. Conclusion

* * *

A macro review of the research indicates three general patterns. First, considerable evidence supports the hypothesis that the gender of the judge does make a difference in sex discrimination cases. Female judges are more likely than male judges to hold for the plaintiffs; and a mixed-gender appellate panel is more likely to hold for the plaintiff, suggesting that female judges do influence male judges in their decision making. Second, in studies of employment discrimination cases in general (studies that include a range of discrimination claims including sex discrimination), the pattern of gender differences is also the consensus. It may be, however, that the sex discrimination cases in those studies drive this result. A third pattern supports this possibility: in the few studies with employment discrimination cases that were not gender related, including race discrimination and racial harassment cases, the gender of the judge did not appear to make a difference. In other words, male judges were as likely as female judges to hold for the plaintiffs. No evidence of a significant difference in their decision-making patterns surfaced.

Why does evidence of gender differences among judges diminish as the cases move from cases dealing with sex discrimination to those that do not? Numerous explanations are possible. To begin with, perhaps the gender of judges makes a difference in cases in which women and men perceive the factual situation differently. Those differing perceptions are likely to occur where gender is the focus of the underlying claim, such as in sexual discrimination or sexual harassment claims. In contrast, differing gender perceptions are not as likely to occur in cases in which gender is not the focus, such as in race-based disputes. It may also be that the gender of the judge makes a difference when one gender of judges can more readily identify with the plaintiff's assessment of the situation. For example, women judges might identify with the female plaintiff as the target of sexual harassment but not identify particularly with African-American plaintiffs as the target of racial harassment.

CHAPTER 4

THE GLASS CLIFF, EMOTIONAL TAX, SHORTLISTING, LIFE ADMIN, #METOO AND OTHER POST-FEMINISM DISCRIMINATION

■ ■ ■

INTRODUCTION

Chapter 4 identifies and explores forms of gender bias and discrimination that may not readily appear as impediments to advancement in leadership. Many believe that as women entered professional education and the workforce, they naturally would ascend into leadership roles. The legal profession long explained the lack of women judges, law firm partners, general counsels, and professors as simply the reality of women having been formally excluded from legal education and law practice for so many decades. But, as discussed in the previous chapters, women have entered legal education in numbers equal to or greater than men for decades and yet the leadership ranks do not reflect this equality. To understand why, researchers and scholars have started identifying other structural and institutional barriers that hold women, or those individuals who assume traditional child-rearing and/or homemaking roles, back from advancement. You will find it even more disheartening, but perhaps not surprising, to learn that minority women are even more negatively impacted by these phenomena.

It has long been understood that women are impacted by unique dynamics (typically not experienced by men) in the workplace, all of which contribute to gender disparity in leadership. Law professor Catharine MacKinnon first defined the concept of "sexual harassment" as illegal discrimination in her 1979 book, SEXUAL HARASSMENT OF WORKING WOMEN, though it did not become a household term until Anita Hill raised sexual harassment allegations against Clarence Thomas during his confirmation hearings for the United States Supreme Court. Legal ethicist Deborah Rhode, the second tenure-track female faculty member hired at Stanford Law School in 1979, coined the phrase "the no-problem problem" in the late 1990s to describe a then-common assumption that gender issues were believed to no longer be a concern as women began to advance in the workplace.[1] Many women work full-time jobs both in and outside the home, as documented by sociologist Arlie Hochschild in what she called "the second shift" in 1989.[2] Communication scholar Kathleen Hall Jamieson described this issue as "double-binds" in 1995, identifying a series of false dichotomies that compromise women in the workplace: (1) "womb/brain," (2) "femininity/competency," (3) "silence/shame," (4) "sameness/difference," and (5) "aging/invisibility."[3]

Scholars in the early part of this century have built upon this previous work by continuing to raise awareness of enduring gender-based biases and barriers, giving them new labels and framing. One example is the selection of women for advancement only when organizations are already in trouble, termed the "glass cliff." Scholars also have documented harms associated with phenomena like "life admin" (or "admin" for short), "emotional tax," "sidelining" and "shortlisting." You will read more about each of these in the articles excerpted below.

In 2018, the #MeToo movement brought the reality of workplace sexual harassment that many women have lived with for years to the forefront of public consciousness. It is important to note, however, that the origins of the #MeToo movement pre-date 2018 by at least a decade, when Tarana Burke first began the movement. As a black woman, Burke has largely been rendered invisible. The more recent movement empowered women to vocalize harms they have suffered, which is a beneficial goal. It seems, however, to have had the unintended consequence of potentially creating yet another hurdle—if not outright barrier—for aspiring female leaders. As reported by the World Economic Forum, men expressed reluctance over mentoring or working with women after the rise of #MeToo. We turn to solutions in the final chapter of the book, Chapter 9, and you should keep in mind this example as one of the unexpected results or backlash that potential strategies or reforms might hold. Look for others as you consider how these concepts play out in all leadership arenas, whether the general counsel's office, the judiciary, the law firm, politics, or other professions.

Take a moment to consider what other dynamics in both personal and professional lives might also impact women more harshly than men in the pursuit of leadership and power. The concepts highlighted in this chapter are not meant to be an exhaustive list, but rather are intended to help you re-examine existing institutional structures, laws, and policies that could be reformed to enhance rather than encumber those who aspire to lead. They are also meant to equip you with a new vocabulary for describing the

---

[1] DEBORAH L. RHODE, SPEAKING OF SEX: THE DENIAL OF GENDER INEQUALITY 1–2 (1997).

[2] ARLIE HOCHSCHILD AND ANNE MACHUNG, THE SECOND SHIFT: WORKING FAMILIES AND THE REVOLUTION AT HOME (1989).

[3] KATHLEEN HALL JAMIESON, BEYOND THE DOUBLE BIND: WOMEN AND LEADERSHIP (1995).

bias that endures against women and inspire you to continue this effort in the spirit of those included here.

Credit: Tim Pierce [CC BY-SA 4.0 (https:// creativecommons.org/ licenses/by-sa/4.0)]

When **Anita Hill** began working for Clarence Thomas at the Department of Education and later at the Equal Employment Opportunity Commission ("EEOC"), the concepts of sex discrimination and harassment were not recognized as they are today. Hill endured harassment from Thomas at both workplaces, but did not speak out about it publicly until his U.S. Supreme Court hearings in 1991. Hill was treated disrespectfully by the media and the senators themselves. Decades later, Senator Joe Biden, then Chair of the Senate Judiciary Committee, called Hill in 2019 to express his regret for this mistreatment (though he did not formally apologize). Thomas, of course, was confirmed. Hill went on to become the University Professor of Social Policy, Law, and Women's, Gender and Sexuality Studies at Brandeis University. In the wake of her testimony, Congress passed legislation giving victims of sexual harassment the right to receive federal damages, including back pay and reinstatement. Complaints to the EEOC increased by fifty percent in the year following her speaking out.

THOUGHT QUESTIONS

As you read the articles excerpted below, consider the following questions:

1.   Why might it be important to identify and label the forms of bias, discrimination, or institutional structures that keep women from attaining leadership roles?

2.   Have you experienced any of the phenomena identified in the excerpts? If so, did you recognize this at the time as a potential barrier or hardship? How do these phenomena impact minority women differently than white women?

3.   Can you identify other forms of bias or discrimination that hold women back from leadership that still do not have labels or names? If so, how would you name them?

4.   Naming is an important first step. But how can we move from identifying or labeling barriers to helping more women attain leadership roles?

JULIE ASHBY, MICHELLE RYAN & ALEX HASLAM, *LEGAL WORK AND THE GLASS CLIFF: EVIDENCE THAT WOMEN ARE PREFERENTIALLY SELECTED TO LEAD PROBLEMATIC CASES*

13 WILLIAM & MARY JOURNAL OF WOMEN & LAW 775 (2007)

Ryan (pictured) is a Professor of Social and Organisational Psychology at the University of Exeter, UK and a (part-time) Professor of Diversity at the University of Groningen, The Netherlands. Haslam is the Professor of Social and Organizational Psychology and Australian Laureate Fellow at the University of Queensland. Ashby previously was a scholar at the University of Exeter.

Despite evidence that women are beginning to break through the glass ceiling (the invisible barrier preventing them from achieving leadership positions), gender equality in organizational life has yet to be achieved. On a positive note, just under half of all women in full-time work in Britain are in managerial, professional, and associate professional jobs. Indeed, the last fifteen years have seen the number of female executives double. Yet in spite of this increase, women still only represent thirty-five percent of all professionals and "are less than half as likely as men to work in higher managerial or professional occupations." Moreover, in terms of remuneration, women's hourly earnings remain significantly lower than men's. The picture is much the same in the United States. Although women comprise just over fifty percent of all employees in management, professional, and related positions, they are more likely to occupy lower and middle ranks.

Nonetheless, the fact that cracks are beginning to appear in the glass ceiling has led many researchers to shift their focus from the barriers standing in the way of female leaders to the experience of those women who do manage to achieve leadership positions. This type of research tends to look at the relative dissimilarities (or similarities) between male and female leaders. Here it seems that women leaders are still treated with some skepticism and may face less favorable evaluations than their male counterparts. This bias appears to be especially pronounced for women who violate gender expectations by holding positions that are overtly "masculine" in nature or are held predominately by males, such as a CEO position. For Schein this phenomenon reflects and contributes to a "think manager-think male" bias, whereby males, by virtue of their gender, are perceived as more likely than women to have the characteristics associated with managerial success.

In terms of leadership effectiveness this individualistic approach has, for the most part, portrayed female managers in a positive light. Nevertheless, by focusing on the individual abilities of female and male leaders, important situational factors may have been underestimated. Attempting to redress this oversight, recent research by Ryan and Haslam has shifted the focus from women leaders per se to the context surrounding their appointment. Importantly, such research has uncovered evidence that women are placed in very different leadership positions than are men.

* * *

The Glass Cliff

Research into the "glass cliff" was partially stimulated by a [2003] front-page newspaper article entitled Women on Board: Help or Hindrance?. Based on evidence that the most successful companies on the UK FTSE 100 tended to have all-male boards while those with the most women on the board tended to perform least successfully, this article suggested that women had "wreaked havoc" on British companies' performance and shares. Ryan and Haslam questioned this claim in an archival study that examined the share price performance of FTSE 100 companies before and after the appointment of a male or female board member. Focusing on key situational factors, in particular the time of appointment and fluctuations in company performance, the researchers found that "[i]n a time of a general financial downturn in the stock market, companies that appointed a woman had experienced consistently poor performance in the months preceding the appointment." On this basis, Ryan and Haslam suggested that the causal sequencing of [the] 2003 analysis was wrong: it was not that women board members caused poor company performance, but that poor company performance caused women to be appointed to company boards. Coining what turned into something of a corporate buzzword, the researchers suggested that women leaders are exceptionally likely to be placed on top of a "glass cliff," such that they are more likely than males to be appointed to leadership positions in problematic organizational circumstances.

* * *

In an attempt to validate their alternative causal analysis, Ryan and Haslam replicated the tendency to appoint women to glass cliff positions in a series of experimental studies. In these, participants were given the task of appointing one of two possible candidates to a leadership role: a male and a female both equally qualified for the position. The results of the first study revealed that international management students were more likely to appoint a female candidate to the position of financial director when company performance, defined by share price performance, was decreasing than when it was increasing. Along similar lines, in the second study, community college students were more likely to appoint a female candidate to the position of youth representative of a festival when its popularity was declining than when it was increasing.

Factors relating to the decision makers, such as their attitudes towards feminism and their evaluations of the candidates, as well as factors relating to the position, such as how desirable it was, were also examined in both experiments. Intriguingly, contrary to Ryan and Haslam's initial predictions, none of these factors were found to play a significant role in the appointment of women to risky leadership positions. Although more research was therefore called for to clarify issues of underlying process, what this research made clear was that glass cliff appointments represent subtle but substantial hurdles for females attempting to climb the leadership ladder.

Extending this research beyond the business realm, this conclusion is also reinforced by a series of archival and experimental studies in the sphere of politics. These studies again found clear evidence of the glass cliff phenomenon with female candidates being more likely to be selected to contest elections considered unwinnable.

* * *

Given existing gender inequities in the legal profession and anecdotal evidence of the glass cliff, the present study sought to establish empirically whether women are differentially selected to take on problematic legal tasks. In the first instance, the obvious research strategy that suggests itself is archival or survey research examining the distribution of particular types of legal work among male and female members of the legal profession. However, although such research could certainly have value, it presents four serious practical and methodological problems. First, unlike the business and political domains in which "objective" indicators of precariousness exist (e.g., fall in share price, the margin that an electoral candidate needs to make up), there are no comparable (and readily accessible) indicators relating to legal work. Second, even if one could find such indicators, the resulting data would provide little insight into the causal structure of any relationships between gender and work responsibilities that emerged from analysis. This is important, as prior research has highlighted a need to differentiate between potential explanations of the glass cliff, specifically in terms of (a) relatively malign processes (e.g., sexism, ingroup favoritism on the part of men, degrading stereotypes of women) and (b) more benign processes (e.g., a desire to signal change, beliefs about the distinctive competencies of women, women's desire to take on challenges). Third, to the extent that any such measures relied on self-reports, they would potentially be subject to a range of self-presentational and strategic biases. Finally, even if they were not in any way distorted, such reports would be able to provide limited insight into underlying psychological and socio-structural process.

To circumvent these problems, the present study used an experimental procedure modelled on previous work by Haslam and Ryan. In this study, undergraduate law students were provided with descriptions of one of two legal cases: one precarious and associated with high risk, the other low risk. Participants were then presented with biographical details of three lawyers who could potentially step up and take over the case. One candidate (a male) was obviously much weaker than the other two. These two focal candidates had matching qualifications and experience but one was a man and the other a woman. The participants' task was to select the candidate they felt was best suited to lead each case.

In line with previous research, the study's main hypothesis was that the female lawyer would more likely be chosen to lead when the case was associated with a high rather than a low level of risk. However, to explore the mechanisms that might underpin this outcome, participants were asked not only to select their preferred candidate but also a number of questions that would provide insight into the issue of whether the processes implicated in glass cliffs are benign or malign. Among other things, these questions aimed to establish (a) whether appointment decisions were associated with the participants' level of feminism and sexism, and (b) whether precarious positions were seen as something to be avoided or as a good opportunity for women to further their careers.

* * *

Participants and Design

Participants were one hundred fourteen undergraduate law students from a British university who participated in the study during a class exercise. Their median age was twenty years; seventy-two were female and thirty-six were male (six did not specify their gender). Participants received information about a legal case that was either described as being high risk or low risk and then evaluated three candidates (including two focal candidates, a male and a female) for the position of leading lawyer. The study thus had a 2 (riskiness of case: high risk, low risk) × 2 (gender of candidate: male, female) × 2 (gender of participant: male, female) design, with repeated measures on the second factor.

* * *

Discussion

The results of the present experiment provide an important replication of Ryan and Haslam's previous demonstrations of the glass cliff phenomenon in the realms of business and politics. In line with the study's main hypothesis, the female candidate was seen as being significantly more appointable to a position as lead counsel on a high-risk legal case (one associated with negative publicity and criticism) than an equally qualified male candidate. On the other hand, gender was not a determining factor when deciding who to appoint to a position as leading counsel on a low-risk legal case (one described as easy and trouble free). This pattern of results was also apparent in the evaluations of the candidates, such that when the case involved high risk, the female candidate was evaluated more positively (being seen as more suitable, having better leadership skills, and being more likely to have a positive impact) than the male candidate, although this was not true when it involved low risk. In this, the findings demonstrate that the processes that contribute to glass cliffs can be reproduced in a legal context, an additional field in which gender discrimination has previously been identified as a significant and obdurate problem.

* * *

Yet this study did more than merely reproduce experimental evidence of the tendency for people to preferentially appoint women to precarious leadership positions in a new domain and with a new participant population. Significantly, it extended previous research by examining participants' perceptions of risky leadership positions, and was thus able to shed some light on the motivations that are likely to contribute to the appointment of women to glass cliff positions. In particular, in earlier commentary it had been assumed that high-risk positions, with their increased risk of failure, were inherently less desirable and attractive than low-risk positions, but this assumption had not been tested directly. Such a test proves to be important in light of suggestions that the glass cliff phenomenon can be explained simply by women's desire to take on risky leadership roles. For example, Patricia Peter, Head of Corporate Governance at the British Institute of Directors has argued, "I know of women who don't want to sit on a board that isn't a challenge, and who feel that if they go to a company that's doing quite well, they might not be noticed." As Vinnicombe puts it, "[i]t may be that women are choosing to go for the most challenging positions where they can make the most difference. Insofar as the present findings provide evidence that, prior to taking them on, the high-risk positions for which women are preferred are not seen to be more desirable than the low-risk ones (and indeed, as we had assumed, tend to be seen as less desirable, at least insofar as they are less likely to be recommended to a friend), they suggest that such alternative accounts may be post hoc rationalizations to reduce cognitive dissonance rather than reflections of genuine a priori motivations.

The findings also revealed that although participants acknowledged that a position associated with poor publicity and a higher risk of failure was indeed more risky, perceptions of risk also depended on their choice of candidates. Thus only those participants who chose the male candidate (a minority, particularly when the case was described as risky) recognized this increased risk. Those participants who chose the female candidate did not. Along related lines, when the case involved low risk, participants saw it as providing an equally good opportunity for the male and female candidates, but when it carried a high risk it was seen to provide a much better opportunity for the woman.

At the most basic level these patterns point to the context-dependence of perceptions of risk and opportunity, since the dangers and merits of any given position were not recognized uniformly but varied depending on whether that position was going to be occupied by a man or a woman. However, in line with Ryan and Haslam's previous arguments, these findings also demonstrate the subtlety of the gender discrimination that contributes to glass cliffs. Participants clearly were only attuned to the problems inherent in any given position to the extent that it was to be filled by a man. Second, for a woman, the high-risk case was construed more as a "golden opportunity" than as a "poisoned chalice," presumably a reflection of participants' sensitivity to the fact that women lawyers have fewer opportunities than their male counterparts. Compatible with this world view, participants felt that losing the case, whether it was risky or not, would be more likely to have a detrimental impact on the leader when they had chosen a male candidate than when they had chosen a female candidate. This would seem to suggest that men are seen to have more to lose than women if there is a possibility of things going wrong.

Taken together, these findings present a coherent picture of a constellation of perceptions and understandings that have the potential to contribute to the creation of glass cliffs. Rather than being the product of overtly sexist intent (in this study at least), the preferential selection of a woman for a risky leadership position appears to be associated with beliefs that high-risk positions are less risky for women than men, presumably because they are seen to have less to lose and more to gain. Given the underlying facts (i.e., that women are coming from a position of disadvantage), there may be some sense in which this is true. Indeed, given that men have more options to choose from than women, they may be better advised to wait for a sure-fire opportunity to arise than to take a chance when they do not have to do so. Nevertheless, the insidious consequences of this system of beliefs are not hard to discern, not least because it has the capacity to corral women into high-visibility, high-risk positions where failure, blame, and scapegoating are more likely.

* * *

The present study not only provides clear experimental evidence for the glass cliff but also demonstrates that the phenomenon can be generalized beyond the business and political arenas into the domain of law. The fact that the participants here were legal students who themselves were aspiring to take up legal positions also makes the relevance of this phenomenon more pronounced. Certainly, to the extent that the female students end up being chosen for, and choosing for themselves, positions that are more risky than those taken up by men, we should not be surprised to find that glass ceilings in the legal profession are also accompanied by glass cliffs.

Moreover, the study has built on Ryan and Haslam's previous research into the glass cliff by building a case that discriminatory beliefs relating to perceptions of risk and opportunity play an important role in the phenomenon. What we see here is not only that the opportunities that are open(ed) to men and women are not equal but, much more subtly, that the very definition of opportunity is gender-specific. Paradoxically, this has the consequence that those who appoint men and women to leadership positions can maintain beliefs in equality of opportunity—and practices that are totally consonant with those beliefs—while at the same time perpetuating forms of systematic discrimination. To the extent that this is true, it suggests that the link between equal opportunity ideology and genuine equality of opportunity may be much more thorny than is commonly supposed.

ELIZABETH F. EMENS, *ADMIN*

103 GEORGETOWN LAW JOURNAL 1409 (2015)

Emens is an Isidor and Seville Sulzbacher Professor of Law at Columbia Law School. Her principal areas of publishing and teaching include disability law, family law, anti-discrimination law, contracts law, and law and sexuality. Her book LIFE ADMIN: HOW I LEARNED TO DO LESS, DO BETTER, AND LIVE MORE was published in 2019.

The complexity of modern life generates a characteristic form of labor that this Article calls *admin*. The growth of the administrative state, on the public side, and the expanding technology of communication and consumerism, on the private side, spur individuals to spend substantial time and energy managing the administrative details of their lives. Admin includes the work we do to administer our own individual lives and also, for many people, the lives of others. This form of work raises important questions of efficiency—that is, how much time is spent on this labor and can that time be reduced for everyone? Admin also raises questions of distribution—namely, who is spending time on these tasks within the family and is that allocation transparent and fair?

By *admin*, I mean all of the office-type work that people do to manage their lives, work that is generally thought to be a means to an end, rather than an end in and of itself. Examples of admin include setting up utilities, scheduling doctors' appointments, opening bank accounts and paying taxes, ordering new supplies and returning broken ones, arranging transportation, and applying for benefits or government-issued identification. Distinct from traditional chores, like cooking and cleaning, the category of admin comprises both the managerial and the secretarial side of household labor.

Though consisting mainly of small tasks, admin has big consequences. Consider home mortgage refinancing. One study estimates that approximately twenty percent of U.S. households that could benefit from refinancing fail to do so—in part for reasons as simple as neglecting to open a letter or make a phone call—resulting in a foregone savings of 5.4 billion dollars. Admin not only takes time but also influences life outcomes, as studies of financial aid suggest. By one estimate, the Free Application for Federal Student Aid (FAFSA) will cost families one hundred million hours this year, and a recent study shows that pro bono assistance with completing the FAFSA makes students more likely to apply to—and attend—college.

Admin affects people differentially by age and especially at some junctures in life. Disability and illness typically come with substantial admin burdens (what we might call *disability admin*), and the admin work created by the death of a significant other, such as a spouse or parent, can practically overwhelm a person already weighed down with grief (*death admin*). Happier events can also involve substantial labor of this type (think *wedding admin* or *bat mitzvah admin*).

Admin burdens are heavily shaped by class and culture. A person's financial means will influence whether her admin burdens consist of calling references for a prospective housekeeper or negotiating excess charges on a cable bill, on the one hand, or filing paperwork for bankruptcy or applying for government benefits, on the other. Demographics and discriminatory laws also influence a person's admin profile. Prior to *Obergefell v. Hodges*, same-sex couples who lived in states that would not marry them needed to spend substantial time and resources with lawyers if they wanted to access the subset of marital rights and responsibilities available by contract; transgender individuals must navigate a complex matrix of demands for documentation of their identities.

Admin presents special challenges in relationships. Because admin is often not seen as labor, partners rarely divvy up this work in a transparent manner—even partners who explicitly allocate housework and, where applicable, childcare. Feminists have illuminated several kinds of labor that have been largely invisible and that disproportionately burden women. Some of these categories of labor overlap with admin but none of the existing categories captures admin in its entirety.

Admin's particular location in women's lives, and in all our lives, inspires new terminology. Working women's responsibility for the household has come to be known as the "second shift" because this work is completed after a long day's paid work in the marketplace. Admin is best understood, more precisely then, as the "parallel shift." Admin so often takes place in the interstices of life—through multitasking or in stolen moments between other endeavors—that it is like another job that runs alongside our work, leisure, and sleep. The parallel shift operates in tandem with the rest of life and thus imposes costs across the range of our experiences.

The disproportionate effects of admin on women serve here as a kind of "miner's canary" for the broader social costs of admin for everyone. That women do more admin raises distributional concerns because admin is, by definition, a means to an end. It is something that few people consider valuable in its own right. Women's heavier admin burden, particularly if it is unwanted or unacknowledged, warrants a response. Moreover, admin produces distributional inequities not only for women, but also for people of many stripes; because admin is "sticky," it tends to stay where it lands. Ultimately, the unequal allocation of admin highlights a broader concern: how much time everyone spends doing—or facing the consequences of avoiding—unappealing administrative labor just to manage our own lives. The feminist literature thus far has not linked the problem of the gendered distribution of admin work with the onerous life admin burdens that cut across gender lines, and therefore has not yet recognized the possibilities for regulatory and structural responses to these pervasive challenges of modern life.

Thus, different lives require different kinds of admin, arising from a varied mix of public and private sources. But admin demands of one kind or another affect virtually everyone above a certain age. This labor can consume substantial amounts of our time and energy, often at otherwise challenging or joyful moments in life. Admin therefore warrants elaboration, analysis, and, in some contexts, regulatory attention.

Government creates a sizable portion of this admin: The federal government alone required 9.45 billion hours of paperwork in fiscal year 2013. We know this because the federal government is also ahead of most sectors of society in attempting to track and contain the admin costs it imposes. The Paperwork Reduction Act (PRA) requires agencies to justify any information collection in terms of the need for the information and the means adopted. Paperwork is only one type of admin labor, but the PRA is nonetheless remarkable for its attention to costs so rarely acknowledged: the costs of admin.

Private law has no equivalent to the PRA. On the contrary, civil suits typically exclude damages for lost personal time. Despite the truism that time is money, individuals generally have no recourse if companies or other individuals burden them with time-consuming admin. Far from evincing sympathy, the few courts to consider questions in this vein seem *not even to see* the harm involved. This is, I suggest, an artifact of admin's relative invisibility as a form of labor.

The few laws that do permit individuals to recover against the state or against one another are a start. Yet allowing recovery for lost personal time is just one example of the legal and structural responses needed here. Government should work systematically to police and incentivize private, as well as public, entities to reduce the admin burdens that they impose. What will help in the family? Direct legal intervention in the distribution of familial labor is neither appealing nor feasible. But the state can help to make admin more salient by recognizing its value, for instance, in marital property determinations and custody proceedings, as a few courts have done. More concretely, state and local governments have made limited inroads into doing admin *for* people, though such initiatives are not understood in these terms. More could be done in this direction. Structurally, though, the most promising path to addressing admin distribution will be to confront the admin problem for everyone. Reducing overall admin should have disproportionate benefits for those who do it most. Thus, the miner's canary operates as a chiasmus: A problem of gender distribution sets into relief a problem that affects everyone, and addressing the problem for everyone should particularly reduce the distributional inequities.

Recognizing that admin has costs does not tell us whether changing particular laws to reduce admin is a good idea. Whether a particular form of admin should be reduced, by law or other means, depends on multiple inputs and considerations. The costs of admin are only one such input. Two aspects of the way forward are clear, however. First, we need to start asking the "Admin Question"—that is, we need to ask how admin may be influencing the effectiveness of any social policy or personal project. Second, in order to ask that question across contexts, we need to recognize and understand admin and its pathways.

This Article therefore aims to make admin more salient, both analytically, by developing an account of its features and costs, and practically, by identifying a range of possible public and private interventions.

* * *

A caveat before beginning: Admin may initially seem a trivial topic. This is part of its dangerous logic. By appearing to be small and unimportant, admin rarely commands our full attention or inspires sustained protest. But anyone who is considering enrolling in an insurance plan, buying a consumer item, planning a wedding or party, moving to another state or country, having a child, or applying for college or financial aid is heading down a road lined with the admin demands that accompany that decision. Each path will involve choices, conscious or not, whether to do admin, avoid admin, or redistribute admin to someone else. These are decisions about how we spend our time and about what demands we place on others' time. Few things could be more important.

* * *

Explaining a relatively unseen and diffuse category is not easy. In legal circles, admin has concrete and well-known meanings. In U.S. law schools, "admin" is a familiar term for the course in Administrative Law, which covers the "establishment, duties, and powers of and available remedies against authorized agencies in the executive branch of the government." Relatedly, the current President's appointments and staff are often referred to simply as "the Administration." In everyday usage, the word "administration" means "[t]he action of carrying out or overseeing the tasks necessary to run an organization [or] bring about a state of affairs." An "admin" is also a popular shorthand term for an administrative assistant—that is, the person who does the typically lower-status portion of the admin work required to run an office.

This Article aims to elaborate a meaning of admin that is less well-known and less often discussed: the office-type work involved in running a life.

* * *

Admin encompasses a wide range of activities, which could be categorized in a variety of ways. What follows is a nonexhaustive list that should illustrate what household admin entails:

- *Completing institutional paperwork*—for example, completing applications for identity documents or public benefits, filling in school enrollment or financial aid forms, and signing liability releases for one's home, kids, or activities.

- *Managing medical matters*—for example, finding doctors, making appointments, completing new patient forms, locating past records, managing insurance claims and appeals, and submitting documentation for income-capped health benefits.

- *Completing and following up on small commercial transactions remotely*—for example, shopping for necessities and communicating with retailers, online or by phone, to replace or obtain compensation for broken or inadequate products.

- *Managing inflow and outflow of paper, goods, and communications*—for example, collecting and sorting mail, opening mail and packages, mailing letters and packages, scanning and sending household documents, answering the phone, and listening to messages and communicating them to others.

- *Keeping track of the quantity and location of supplies in the home*—for example, food, clothing, and staples.

- *Creating shopping lists and, where applicable, ordering supplies remotely*—for example, food, clothing, and staples.

- *Handling finances*—for example, opening bank accounts and credit cards, creating budgets or otherwise managing income and expenses, paying bills, managing a financial aid application process, preparing tax returns directly or through an accountant, choosing and managing a retirement plan, managing any investments, responding to queries about any of these, interacting with bill collectors, and filing for bankruptcy.

- *Managing utilities*—for example, setting up utilities in a new home, paying and disputing bills, coordinating and supervising any service calls, and managing reconnection of disconnected utilities.

- *Keeping track of important documents*—for example, saving, organizing, and finding legal documents—such as contracts, leases, and wills—and official forms of identification—such as birth certificates, social security cards, passports, and immigration status documentation—as well as other household records.

- *Managing the selection, purchase, upkeep, and sale of any property*—for example, leasing or buying a car or bike, renting or buying a home, obtaining insurance to cover property where necessary, investigating these endeavors, obtaining financing, and doing the associated paperwork.

- *Managing personnel*—for example, identifying, hiring, scheduling, and paying people for housework, childcare, household maintenance and repairs; managing terminations and subsequent obligations like references; and, where applicable, filing any employee paperwork, keeping track of hours, and paying taxes.

- *Maintaining correspondence and gift exchanges*—for example, buying and preparing gifts, keeping track of birthdays and special events, deciding what relationships to maintain and how, helping to connect other people with resources like doctors or babysitters, and writing thank-you notes.

- *Planning special events*—for example, planning birthday parties, holiday celebrations, and special outings.

- *Managing and coordinating schedules*—for example, planning dates and playdates; coordinating work schedules to cover care for children, pets, or other dependents; and generating, researching, and arranging plans for solo or shared leisure time.

- *Arranging transportation*—for example, figuring out best routes, schedules, and fares for public or private transportation, booking travel and lodging, and preparing gear for journeys.

- *Planning for and picking up after emergencies*—for example, deciding whether to create disaster plans, creating such plans, and handling the aftermath of home intrusions (whether by people or pests), such as making police reports or contacting exterminators.

* * *

Admin often happens in the interstices of life—through multitasking at work or at home, or in competition with our sleep at night—as this epigraph dramatizes. Admin has no right time or place; as a cultural matter, there is no part of the day or week designated for filling out forms or researching doctors or planning schedules. Admin therefore threatens to occupy people's minds and draw their energy away from whatever they are meant to be doing in a given moment.

The "second shift" has become a popular term for all the household labor that burdens women after a hard day's work in the paid labor force. In her book by that name, Arlie Hochschild shows how women married to men continue to do the lion's share of the household labor, even when they work outside the home. If the work done *after* a woman gets home from her job is the "second shift," admin is best understood as what I call the "parallel shift." Admin work is largely completed in the margins of an already busy life, on a parallel track with the paid work, play, sleep, and relationships we value.

The second shift raises both distributional and efficiency concerns. By distributional concerns, I mean that many people—especially, but not only, women—may do more than their share of admin work. Partners, I suggest here, often distribute admin activities in a relatively thoughtless way, which ends up burdening one partner more than the other. By efficiency concerns, I mean that many individuals—female or male, partnered or not—may be spending substantial time and energy on admin, which, by definition, they do not value in its own right.

* * *

The empirical research on who does admin is still at an early stage. The subset that has received the most research attention is "household management," described in one study as the "[e]ssential planning, coordinating, and budgeting . . . above and beyond the physical demands of household work." But even the extant category of household management, which typically leaves out several aspects of admin, has been characterized as "the least researched aspect in the allocation of household labor" and "the last barrier to gender-egalitarian marriages." The research thus far is nonetheless revealing.

a.   *Male-Female Couples.* Research supports the anecdotal observation that women are doing more household admin than their male partners. Several studies find that women spend significantly more time on "household management" and "childcare management" than their male partners. These studies typically distinguish management activities (such as making grocery lists, planning meals, or scheduling medical appointments) from the accomplishment of specific "tasks" (such as shopping for groceries, cooking meals, or taking children to the doctor). Some of the "tasks" in these studies would also typically fall under my category of admin, though—for instance, interacting with childcare providers, corresponding with extended family, or preserving family memories—and in general women do more of the task labor as well as the management labor than their male partners. Interestingly, the Bureau of Labor Statistics American Time Use Survey (ATUS or "the Survey") reports less gender inequality in time spent on "household management," compared with other kinds of household labor. The 2013 ATUS notes that, of the respondents who engaged in household management, men spent an average of 43.8 minutes per day; women, 46.2 minutes. When averaged over the general population, including those who did not engage in any household management work, those numbers fell to 6 minutes and 9.6 minutes, respectively. The Survey suffers from several limitations, however—most notably, that it does not count activities done simultaneously, which is a particular problem for work that is so often done through multitasking. This makes it likely that the Survey systematically underestimates the time individuals spend on household management, which in turn makes the Survey of limited use in evaluating the amount and distribution of admin. Even if we take its results at face value, however, the Survey supports the argument that women are doing more of this work than men.

Some forms of admin are obviously gendered as a cultural matter, such as kin work or planning birthday parties. Other areas seem less so. For instance, handling finances might sound like a traditionally masculine domain. Generally speaking, however, as part of feeding and clothing the family, these days women more often pay the bills; as to who makes financial decisions, there is no clear trend toward men or women. More specifically, though, there is reason to think that men more often handle money when there is money to burn (or invest), but women take over when there is a need to make ends meet, for instance, at the point of bankruptcy.

The only significant outliers from this trend toward women doing more admin involve responsibility for outsourcing stereotypically masculine activities such as home repairs or car repairs. If men are not doing these activities themselves, then they are more likely than women to be the ones arranging for others to do them. Notably, though, once masculine labor turns into the admin of outsourcing, that labor also becomes somewhat less gendered than the underlying tasks; that is, more couples share equally the task of arranging for home or car repairs than share equally the task of actually repairing home or car.

To some extent, partners disagree about how much household admin they do. The general trend is towards men reporting that they do more admin than their female partners say the men do. This is consistent with the broader finding that men report doing more household labor and childcare than their partners say. One study found that men and women reported doing similar amounts of household management, but on closer examination of several metrics, found that women reported spending approximately twice as many hours on management tasks as their male partners did.

b.   Same-Sex Couples and Others. Same-sex couples appear to split the work of managing their households somewhat more equally, though the empirical work in this area is even more limited. Greater equity around admin would be unsurprising, given the general observation that same-sex couples split all forms of household labor more equally. One distributional trend is that the same-sex partner with the higher income tends to have more responsibility for the finances. In addition, where one partner is the "bio mom," she tends to do more childcare and perhaps also more childcare management as well. Despite the greater equity in same-sex couples, trends undoubtedly develop for particular couples. In terms of interactions with the outside world, it appears that gender if not sex plays a role in how admin is distributed: Multiple anecdotal sources report that, at schools that do not ask parents to name a primary contact parent, other parents try to figure out who in a same-sex parenting couple is the "mom" for these purposes, in order to decide whom to contact about playdates, parties, and parent participation in school activities.

A woman need not be coupled with a man—or coupled at all—to be doing more admin than the men around her. Single women are more likely to be taking care of children or ailing parents than are single men, and thus to be handling the admin that such caretaking entails. In families involving more than two co-parents, it would be interesting to know how the admin is divided up, and what role sex or gender plays in that division. Research suggests that, even after divorce, women tend to do more of the mental work of managing their children's lives.

Though beyond the scope of this Article, it is also worth noting that the gendering of admin work at the level of the family has a corollary at the institutional level: Whole labor sectors devoted to admin, most obviously secretarial work, are populated disproportionately by women. But even among people who have the same jobs, women may end up doing more (and often unrewarded) admin. Various scholars have studied and written about the ways that female faculty at some institutions end up shouldering a disproportionate share of the administrative burden. Some scholars argue that formerly prestigious tasks and roles suffer a drop in prestige when women begin doing them. The family dynamics surrounding admin seem to repeat themselves at the institutional level in some contexts.

* * *

There are at least two common frames for the unequal, gendered distribution of these activities, each with an informal and a formal version. These frames seem to operate rhetorically to justify the conventional distribution of admin along gender lines.

The first is what we might call the "female superiority" frame. Informally, this comprises claims that "women are better at this stuff," on the one hand, or of a partner's claims of incompetence in these domains (whether feigned or real), on the other. Formally, this ties in with the "women as multitaskers" thesis. The latest incarnation of the opt-out revolution news story—Lisa Miller's "The Retro Wife" in *New York* magazine in the spring of 2013—presents the formal version this way: "A number of those I spoke to for this Article reminded me of a 2010 British study showing that men lack the same mental bandwidth for multitasking as women." Miller perhaps chose her words carefully here, assigning responsibility for this reference to others; that study apparently has not been published and the upshot of the research on multitasking seems to be that women are not any better at multitasking than men. Women do appear to *do* much more multitasking and also typically to suffer through it.

The second is what we might call the "female dominance" (or "maternal identity") frame. Informally, this takes the form: "She just won't let me do any of this stuff." Formally, this is termed "maternal gatekeeping," the psychological term for "a reluctance to relinquish family responsibility by setting rigid standards, . . . a desire to validate a maternal identity, and . . .

differentiated conceptions of family roles." As one writer puts it, "Many women will also admit to the frisson of superiority, of a particular form of gratification, when they are the more competent parent."

* * *

The contemporary moment presents nearly constant opportunities for distraction from what matters. While our beliefs about what matters will vary widely across individuals, there is something that generally does *not* matter—that we by and large do *not* value—that is constant across individuals: admin. The subject of this Article is, by definition, something an individual does not value. More precisely, the time we spend doing admin is a means to an end, not an end in itself.

This Article therefore draws our attention to something that most people do not think much about, something most people do not want to think much about. But we should think about admin because its effects are significant, both individually and relationally. Though seemingly trivial, admin is critically important because it takes up time and energy we could spend on other things. Moreover, because so much of it happens remotely, it draws our attention away from things that matter to us even when we are doing something else. Admin can interfere with our ability to think creatively, to get into a flow with work or play. Admin can prevent us from relating effectively to the person right in front of us, pulling us into an "away."

Distraction can happen because we have our devices constantly with us, drawing us out of the present moment. Concerned commentators—scholarly and popular, secular or spiritual—will recommend putting away the devices. Strategic efforts to go off the grid, whether for a dinner or a weekend, may have various benefits individually or relationally. But going off the grid does not solve the problem of admin.

If admin is pressing enough, it may still be on our minds: We may still be solving a problem of planning or scheduling, or, less productively, we may be preoccupied by a more generalized anxiety at the prospect of forgetting what needs to be done. Admin sucks up our time, even if we do not do it through multitasking that pulls us away from our focus on the task at hand, on another person, or on our leisure. If admin needs to be done, then putting it aside now will mean missing out on another activity later.

* * *

The task of devising the best time and place to do all these things may be helped by making the admin demands of modern life more visible—by starting a conversation about them. And developing techniques for more fairly distributing these tasks across households, or for compensating those who do them in other ways, may also come from drawing our attention to this hugely time consuming aspect of family life.

All of us—partnered or single, with dependents or without—have an interest in a simpler set of changes in this regard: reducing the amount of admin that we have to contend with. The state already contributes to admin burdens; it adds to them or reduces them, directly and indirectly, through a variety of laws and administrative functions laid out in this Article. It sets legal frameworks, like the lack of damages for lost personal time in breach of contract suits, that shape the incentives of private actors in the market. It has the capacity to reduce admin and encourage private actors to do the same. In these and many other ways, the state could become not merely a partner, but a leader, in reducing the admin burdens that distract us all.

DNIKA J. TRAVIS AND JENNIFER THORPE-MOSCON, *EMOTIONAL TAX—A CHALLENGE COMPANIES CAN'T AFFORD TO IGNORE*

DAY-TO-DAY EXPERIENCES OF EMOTIONAL TAX AMONG WOMEN
AND MEN OF COLOR IN THE WORKPLACE (CATALYST, 2018)

Travis (left) is the Vice President, Research at Catalyst. She holds a PhD in in social work from the University of Southern California, and was named a "2017 Woman Worth Watching" by Profiles in Diversity Journal. Thorpe-Moscon (right) is the Senior Director, Research Data & Innovation Lab at Catalyst. She holds a PhD in social psychology from New York University, and is the author of How Geek Girls Will Rule the World (2013).

This report examines the Emotional Tax levied on Asian, Black, Latinx, and multiracial professionals in the United States as they aspire to advance and contribute to their organizations. In particular, we focus on an important aspect of Emotional Tax: the state of being on guard—consciously preparing to deal with potential bias or discrimination. Our findings show that:

- Asian, Black, Latinx, and multiracial professionals pay an Emotional Tax at work when they feel they must be on guard to protect against racial and gender bias.

- This experience was shared by nearly 60% of the women and men of color we surveyed.

- Employees who feel on guard are most likely to want to leave their employers and face challenges to their well-being.

- A majority of those who are on guard have a strong drive to contribute and succeed—suggesting that the loss of their talent would be detrimental to the organization.

- To retain these valuable employees and address potential reasons for being on guard, leaders must cultivate inclusive workplaces.

We show that it's not only employees of color, but the organizations they work for that pay the Emotional Tax in the form of lost talent and potential loss of revenue. Throughout this report, we present actions that you can take today to address and reduce the consequences of Emotional Tax and ensure that the people of color working at your company can thrive, contributing their best talents.

[Casebook authors' note: the full report can be found at this website link http://www.catalyst.org/knowledge/day-day-experiences-emotional-tax-among-women-and-men-color-workplace.]

LAURA A. ROSENBURY, *WORK WIVES*
36 HARVARD JOURNAL OF LAW & GENDER 345 (2013)

Rosenbury is the dean and the Levin, Mabie & Levin Professor of Law at University of Florida Levin College of Law. Previously, she was a professor of law and vice dean at Washington University School of Law in St. Louis. She also has served as a visiting professor at Harvard Law School, Stanford Law School and University of Chicago Law School.

Traditional gender roles continue to infuse many workplaces and families even as women have achieved massive gains in politics, in labor markets, and within the home. Law reform efforts over the past forty years have attempted to counter those roles. States and courts have embraced gender-neutral family laws, so that husbands are no longer required to be breadwinners or wives caregivers, as well as expansive interpretations of employment discrimination statutes designed to root out sexualization and other stereotyping at work. These moves toward legal gender neutrality have created opportunities for many individuals to reimagine the roles of both men and women within families and workplaces, but traditional notions of those roles persist even in the face of legal change. Traditional constructs of gender remain remarkably tenacious, maintaining gendered conceptions of work and home life.

This Article analyzes the challenge of gender tenacity, examining one way that traditional gender roles are reinscribed even as they are altered: through the metaphor of the work wife. By analyzing ways that gender flows between home and work through the phenomenon of the work wife, the project fills a void in scholarship concerning family law, employment discrimination, and feminist legal theory. Some such scholarship has previously acknowledged how gender roles are shaped both at home and at work, with expectations and patterns from each realm influencing the other. But by focusing solely on relationships subject to explicit legal regulation, specifically the marriage relationship and the employer-employee relationship, past scholarship has generally overlooked the ways that gender roles persist in unregulated relationships of connection and care. This Article, in contrast, analyzes how gender is constructed both in and out of law, through multiple daily interactions that resist easy classification or regulation.

The concept of the work wife is particularly instructive because it has moved from the structural to the discursive over time. Understandings of the work wife first evolved at a time when women had access to executive suites only through the secretarial pool. Women in professional workplaces were thus relegated to providing support that frequently looked like the care wives provided to their husbands at home, albeit in a more efficient form. For example, Faith Baldwin, in the foreword to her 1929 novel, The Office Wife, asked: "How many business men wish futilely that their homes could be run as well as their offices and their wives comprehend their needs as swiftly and silently as their secretaries?" Rosabeth Moss Kanter's sociological study of a large corporation in the early 1970s likewise found that the marriage metaphor was frequently used to describe the relationship between bosses and secretaries.

* * *

This marriage metaphor remains even though women in professional workplaces are no longer limited to secretarial roles. The passage of Title VII of the Civil Rights Act of 1964, which prohibits sex discrimination in the workplace, and the revival of women's movements in the 1970s eliminated many of the impediments to women's workforce participation. Work wives thus are no longer structural features of most workplaces. Yet portrayals of work wives remain to this day, in relationships defined less by hierarchy but still involving emotional bonds.

* * *

The persistence of the marriage metaphor does more than signal a close relationship. The marriage metaphor also keeps gender front and center at work despite legal changes designed to cleanse the workplace of oppressive gender roles. After all, the law of marriage has long been "a codification of a society's attitudes about women." Although legal marriage no longer makes distinctions between the roles of wives and husbands, the care provided within many marriages remains gendered, with wives more often than their husbands performing or overseeing child care and housework, as well as engaging in more of the emotional work of family life. Pleas to maintain "traditional marriage" in the face of same-sex marriage also reveal the ways that marriage plays a role in maintaining the gender order to this day. Using the language of marriage to describe close workplace relationships thus necessarily means that gender seeps into the workplace, even if in multiple and shifting ways.

This Article's examination of the work wife phenomenon therefore illustrates one means by which gender remains tenacious even as law attempts to lessen the effects of traditional gender roles. The dynamics of marriage flow between the public and private divides of work and home, creating a feedback loop that inserts gender into both domains in multiple ways. The concept of marriage at work may therefore influence assessments of job performance and workplace roles in ways that reinforce gendered expectations rather than challenge them. At the same time, however, the concept of marriage at work may also permit both women and men to experience intimacy and support in new forms that escape traditionally gendered dynamics of care without eschewing gender altogether. New performances of gender might result—performances that lie between gender hierarchy and the aspirations of gender neutrality that pervade both family law and employment discrimination law today.

At bottom, then, laws aspiring to gender neutrality and gender blindness at home and work have not, and likely cannot, eliminate the relevance of gender in either domain. Such laws have eliminated egregious instances of gender hierarchy, thereby enabling more diverse gender performances, but gender remains relevant in ways that both reinforce and challenge traditional gender roles. Those seeking to promote gender equality at home, work, and beyond must therefore develop a deeper understanding of the dynamics that contribute to gender performance and, ultimately, to the construct of gender itself. Analyzing work wives provides a new way to engage in that project.

* * *

"I Need a Wife"

The term wife thus remains culturally salient in a way that the term husband does not. In many ways, though, women's participation in the market has served to separate, at least partially, the role of wife from the wife (or spouse) herself. Female spouses often no longer are defined solely by their wife role, and many do not have the time or desire to perform all of the tasks traditionally performed by wives. But the package of tasks traditionally performed by wives remains defined by the term wife. Gendered and hierarchal notions of care thereby persist in the role of wife even if individual wives cannot or choose not to engage in the carework previously mandated by the state.

Consider the common plea, "I need a wife." That plea rarely means the speaker wants to get married to just any woman or even wants to get married at all; indeed, the speaker is often a heterosexual woman. Instead, the speaker desires someone in her (or his) life who will pick up the dry cleaning, keep track of appointments, do the laundry, take the kids to soccer practice, get dinner on the table, manage the social calendar, and vacuum, dust, and scour the tub. In other words, the speaker wants someone to perform the caregiving tasks that legal wives previously were required to perform when marriage was a gendered hierarchy, with men at the top and women at the bottom.

Yet, while the speaker seeks someone to fill the wife role, that role is often detached from legal marriage. In fact, the speaker may already be married, may be seeking a spouse who will be an equal partner rather than a servant, or otherwise may not view marriage as the path toward finding someone to fill the wife role. "I need a wife" therefore signals a desire for subservient care in a world where many marriages no longer provide that care in a comprehensive way. Marital roles remain gendered even as the parties to marriage have come to embody those roles in different ways.

Consider also the role of the wife in same-sex relationships. Such relationships are often assumed to transcend traditional gender role divisions, as discussed above. Many commentators thus have argued that same-sex marriage will make the institution of marriage less gendered and oppressive. However, some same-sex couples replicate gendered divisions of care in order to emphasize that their relationships are no different from the mixed-sex unions recognized and supported by the state. The role of wife may therefore be inhabited by a man caring for another man or by a woman caring for another woman. Even if same-sex couples do not replicate gendered divisions of care, individuals outside of the couple may still ask who is the wife and who is the husband. The roles thus trump gender, while remaining deeply gendered in form.

Against this backdrop, the terms "wife," "work wife," "spouse," and "work spouse," carry multiple meanings, embodying different gender performances. At one end of the spectrum are those wives, real or desired, who perform the package of caregiving tasks traditionally mandated by the state, whether at home or at work. The interests of these wives are generally viewed as subordinate to the interests of their husbands or bosses, as the wives take care of the details of life in order to support their husbands' or bosses' success. At the other end of the spectrum are those spouses who support each other at home or at work in ways unmoored from traditional gender roles. Such spouses just happen to be male or female; the sex of the participants is irrelevant to the support provided. As such, the terms wife and work wife can refer to the person who picks up the dry cleaning and keeps the calendar or to a close confidant and supporter whose sex is mere happenstance.

* * *

Deploying Existing Sex Discrimination Doctrine

With the passage of Title VII in 1964, most employers could no longer explicitly exclude women from their workplaces. Advocates for women's equality soon realized, however, that women could be excluded, pushed out, or denied advancement in more subtle ways. Formal equality theory, purporting to provide women with the same opportunities traditionally provided to men, was inadequate to deal with these forms of discrimination. Feminist legal theorists and activists thus developed more nuanced conceptions of sex discrimination, designed to achieve substantive equality, in addition to formal equality, in the workplace. Two of these conceptions—sexual harassment and sex stereotyping—provide insight about the potential of employment discrimination law to address dynamics found in some portrayals of marriage at work.

1.   Sexual Harassment

In 1986, the Supreme Court held that unwanted sexual advances in the workplace may constitute discrimination on the basis of sex if they are "sufficiently severe or pervasive to alter the conditions of [the victim's] employment and create an abusive working environment." The Court emphasized that sex discrimination could be found even if the employee was not threatened with termination or other adverse action for failure to submit to the advances, or if such threats were unfulfilled. The Supreme Court has repeatedly affirmed this "hostile work environment" conception of sexual harassment, even extending it to same-sex sexual harassment so long as employees provide that it actually constituted "discrimination 'because of . . . sex.'"

This conception of sexual harassment directly grew out of feminist theories, largely developed by Catharine MacKinnon, arguing that men's sexual domination of women defines gender relationships throughout society, including at work. This so-called "dominance theory" thus challenges the notion that paid work might easily be separated from the dynamics that pervade the private, domestic sphere even in a legal regime committed to formal equality, or gender neutrality, at work. In contrast to formal approaches to workplace equality, then, hostile work environment conceptions of sexual harassment reject a clear divide between work and home, instead acknowledging the ways that male norms in the domestic sphere may influence workplace practices, thereby limiting women's ability to compete at work. Law therefore must do more than open the doors of workplaces to women; law must also change workplace practices built around male needs and norms.

Portrayals of work wives may highlight another way in which the gendered practices of the home have shaped workplace norms. In a workplace structured around male needs, women may be confined to a limited range of roles: either they are sexualized as potential girlfriends or playthings, or they are viewed as nurturing caregivers who are expected to assume at least some of the functions of the traditional wife. As Katherine Franke has emphasized when discussing the potential range of sexual harassment, "I now ask my students which practice they would find most humiliating, objectifying, or objectionable: having a male boss ask you, out of nowhere, to (i) kiss him, (ii) babysit for his kids, or (iii) be responsible for serving coffee at staff meetings." Although dominance theory has long focused on kisses and other forms of sexual conduct as the essence of sexual harassment, Franke reports that "[f]ew of my female students select the kiss as the most objectionable encounter."

The use of the marriage metaphor at work may therefore provide new insight about the diversity of oppressive gendered practices that remain prevalent at work despite Title VII's antidiscrimination mandate. Such practices are not necessarily perpetuated in order to maintain male dominance; instead, they may be the result of attempts "to secure familiar working conditions or re-establish a comfort level, rather than resist change or preserve explicitly masculine norms." In fact, some women and men may affirmatively embrace the metaphor of marriage at work even as they remain committed to workplace equality. Yet dominance theory has long interrogated women's choices to take on gendered roles, including caring, nurturing roles, under conditions of gender hierarchy, and has sought to deploy law to free women from such expectations. For example, some women may (consciously or unconsciously) embrace work wife portrayals in order to protect themselves from sexualization at work; if they are perceived to be work wives, they may be insulated from the sexual advances of other male employees. Other women may embrace the work wife label, in relationships with male or female employees, in order to fit into a work culture that provides a limited range of acceptable social roles for women.

Even men may be constrained by networks of gendered practices at work. As Angela Harris writes, "all men experience the pressure not to be women and not to be 'faggots.'" At first glance, portrayals of straight men serving as work wives to other men could be viewed as resisting that pressure. But, upon closer examination, such portrayals may in fact be responding to such pressure, not resisting it. A close relationship between two men, at work or otherwise, often raises questions about the men's sexuality and masculinity. The work wife label may insulate men from that suspicion, emphasizing that they are not gay and still masculine. Here, the desexualization of marriage, and particularly of work wives, is vital; the metaphor of marriage at work signals that no sex is occurring within the relationship even if it is otherwise close and supportive. At the same time, the male gender of the participants clearly distinguishes these work wives from traditional ones. In this way, then, the work wife label is used as a joke to signal that men involved in close relationships with each other are neither gay nor women.

Portrayals of work wives therefore elucidate a broader range of gendered practices at work than has been previously acknowledged by hostile work environment doctrine. To the extent these practices reinforce masculine norms in the workplace, advocates of gender equality may want to extend the doctrine to contexts in which women or men feel subordinated by work wife portrayals or the expectations that flow from them. Scholars such as Kathryn Abrams and Katherine Franke have already urged courts and advocates to focus less on sexual advances at work and more on the ways sexualized practices "preserve[ ] male control or entrench[ ] masculine norms in the . . . workplace," or reinforce "a system of gender norms that envisions women as feminine, (hetero)sexual objects, and men as masculine, (hetero)sexual subjects." If the metaphor of marriage at work participates in that gendered system, it too could be brought into the fold of sexual harassment theory and doctrine.

* * *

2. Sex Stereotyping

The Supreme Court has also developed a doctrine of sex stereotyping to address situations in which employers open their doors to women but then penalize them for failing to conform to traditional understandings of femininity. In 1989, the Court held in Price Waterhouse v. Hopkins that

> [W]e are beyond the day when an employer could evaluate employees by assuming or insisting that they matched the stereotype associated with their group, for '[i]n forbidding employers to discriminate against individuals because of their sex, Congress intended to strike at the entire spectrum of disparate treatment of men and women resulting from sex stereotypes.'

The Court therefore upheld the lower court's finding that the employer was motivated by gender when, in denying partnership to a female employee, its decisionmakers described her as "macho" and suggested that she "walk more femininely, talk more femininely, dress more femininely, wear make-up, have her hair styled, and wear jewelry."

This doctrine, like the hostile work environment doctrine, acknowledges that expectations from the domestic sphere often infiltrate the workplace. Unlike the dominance theory that motivated the development of hostile work environment theory, however, advocates of anti-stereotyping doctrine generally do not seek to alter gender relations throughout society. Instead, they seek to increase the freedom of all people to succeed in the public sphere and market by eliminating sex-based roles and stereotypes in those zones. As such, the doctrine embraces the assumption that employees will be free to succeed at work according to their own merit once impermissible stereotypes are eliminated, often ignoring the ways that traditional inequalities in the domestic sphere may influence women's ability to perform at work. The elimination of sex stereotypes may free some men to take on caregiving duties in the private sphere, but that possibility is merely a byproduct of the doctrine's focus on eliminating sex stereotypes at work.

This sex stereotyping doctrine could be extended to cover gender-based expectations flowing from work wife portrayals. If the metaphor of marriage at work represents the transfer of gendered care from the realm of traditional marriage to the realm of work, then such expectations may be so infused with gender stereotypes as to violate Title VII. In particular, employers could be found to be engaging in sex stereotyping if they expect employees to be, or not be, work wives on the basis of sex. Indeed, although no reported case has alleged such facts, sex stereotyping doctrine seems poised to address such situations in its current form.

* * *

Gender Beyond Subordination

Portrayals of work wives insert gender into popular notions of the workplace. Given Title VII's mandate that gender be irrelevant to employment decisions, that insertion immediately seems suspect. Yet the metaphor of marriage at work may in fact further, not thwart, some forms of gender equality. This Section considers the potential value of such relationships and the ways in which they might produce new conceptions of gender, for both men and women.

1.   The Value of Workplace Relationships

Another theory of gender equality has long embraced the value of relationships and caregiving, critiquing those who seek success for women within traditional male frameworks (reformed or not) instead of embracing traditionally female activities and values. This so-called "difference feminism" or "relational feminism" may be particularly salient for analyzing the metaphor of marriage at work, as it has long emphasized that "[i] f caregiving is moral work, there is no reason to restrict its domain to family life." Yet difference theory to date has tended to focus on child care, to the exclusion of the care provided to husbands, other adult partners, or adult dependents, calling for policies that would better permit women to balance work and parenting and otherwise integrate childrearing into public life.

Work wives provide an opportunity to extend existing arguments in order to situate care within the larger market system. Joan Williams, drawing upon difference feminism, has already attempted to situate care in this manner by using the term "domesticity" to refer "not only to women's role in the home but also to a particular organization of market work and family work, and to the conceptions of masculinity and femininity that support breadwinner/primary caregiver gender roles." Williams thus recognizes that the carework women have traditionally performed within the home has effects outside of the home, in particular by serving as the (feminine) work against which (masculine) wage-work is defined. Williams's definition overlooks, however, the ways that carework is also performed outside of the home.

Portrayals of work wives fill this gap by providing an example of the ways domesticity and care not only organize market work, but may also pervade market work. In crossing the divides between public and private realms, these dynamics of care may reinforce male authority or thwart women's autonomy, as both hostile work environment doctrine and sex stereotyping suggest. But such dynamics of care may also operate in multiple ways beyond male dominance and female submission. Care may even, in some instances, be vital to workplace satisfaction and success.

Studies of "old-boys networks" and other forms of social networking have long provided support for the notion that workplace relationships, in addition to other considerations of work performance, often determine employee success. Judge Richard Posner recently recognized this potential in McReynolds v. Merrill Lynch, a Title VII case alleging race discrimination. In determining whether class certification was warranted, Judge Posner considered a company-wide "teaming" policy, in which brokers, rather than their managers, were authorized to form teams to share clients. He emphasized that "there is no doubt that for many brokers team membership is a plus; certainly the plaintiffs think so." And that is what made the policy suspect as potential "disparate impact" employment discrimination. Judge Posner emphasized that the African-American plaintiffs described the teams as "little fraternities (our term but their meaning), and as in fraternities the brokers choose as team members people who are like themselves. If they are white, they, or some of them anyway, are more comfortable teaming with other white brokers."

In McReynolds, then, the plaintiffs invoked Title VII to gain access to workplace relationships, not to be freed from them. Women and men may similarly seek to benefit from relationships portrayed as work marriages.

Indeed, unlike old-boys networks or the Merrill Lynch teams, marriage at work is portrayed as providing an additional layer of support at work that is not simply about making connections or ingratiating oneself with the right people. Instead, the relationship may offer a trusted sounding board and daily care that helps one or both work spouses endure uncertain work situations. Such support is similar to the support long provided by wives in the home, but many workers may desire support in both domains in light of increasing workplace demands and women's increased workforce participation.

Moreover, women may have more access to relationships portrayed as work marriages than they have to other relationships at work. Men often make work connections, and find other sources of workplace support, through sports and fraternities, as Judge Posner suggests. While most women have difficulty breaking into such structures, they may more easily be able to step into relationships analogized to marriage. Female workers may in fact benefit from the gendered nature of traditional marriage, in that women, more so than men, may assume nurturing roles at work without disrupting gendered expectations. And, unlike the uncompensated work of the traditional wife, such care may be compensated at work through promotions and pay raises (or the avoidance of layoffs and pay cuts), as well as other forms of workplace stability, power, and prestige.

2.   Opportunities for New Gender Performances

The metaphor of marriage at work may also do more than hurt or benefit individual women, or men, in the workplace. In contrast to the approaches to gender equality already discussed, other approaches have focused on the ways gender is constructed and performed in multiple contexts, including work. Postmodern, anti-essentialist theories resist any one characterization of women or women's needs. These theories instead emphasize that "gender itself is a product of power and language and social institutions, including law, not a reality that preexists those structures." This emphasis is postmodern in that it embraces an understanding of the subject as "decentered, polymorphous, contingent"; it is anti-essentialist because it challenges the notion that women are "ontologically distinct from men" or that there otherwise exists a universal conception of woman that transcends differences of race, class, sexual orientation, and other identity categories. Such theories seek to understand how gender construction operates in order to destabilize that system, in part by recognizing the multiple, fluid, and shifting gender performances amidst the constraints of law and other social practices that construct gender.

Portrayals of work wives provide insight into the complexity of gender constructions and the multiple ways of performing gender within those constructions. In some portrayals, work wives are subordinated; in others they are privileged and rewarded; in still others they may operate outside of familiar, or even intelligible, power relations. There is no one work wife. The law's placement of such relationships outside of marriage law or employment discrimination law permits each of these multiple possibilities, and infinite others, to exist. Yet each possibility arises within a legal regime that still makes distinctions between work and home, recognizing marriage at home, but not at work, and prohibiting discrimination at work, but not at home. The law thus shapes portrayals of work wives even as no law explicitly recognizes or regulates the relationship.

Most importantly, this divide between work and home was traditionally gendered de jure, and it remains deeply gendered de facto. Given this history and ongoing reality, it is tempting to engage in analysis designed to eradicate such gendering for good. Yet such reform would participate in the construction of gender even as it attempts to challenge existing gender dynamics. Gender, and the gendered division of labor, might be constructed somewhat differently, creating different possibilities for gender performances, but gender dynamics would not be eradicated. At least for now, and maybe for eternity, gender would remain at work and elsewhere.

Portrayals of work wives thus highlight the ways that gender is reproduced and maintained by multiple forces, including portrayals of work marriage and legal responses, or nonresponses, to it. Although persistent, these gender dynamics are neither static nor do they operate in ways that are always detrimental to women. As previously discussed, if the market for work marriage mirrors that for legal marriage, then African-American women may have less access than white women to relationships portrayed as work marriages. This could be good or bad. On the one hand, African-American women could benefit from being viewed as workers, not wives, with their work performance evaluated more on work product than on care. On the other hand, they could be denied support and connections that contribute to workplace success and satisfaction.

Even more so, however, it is unlikely that the market for work marriage would always mirror the market for legal marriage. Returning to the relationship between Condoleezza Rice and President Bush, for example, it is possible that African-American women in white-collar work settings may benefit from conceptions of sexuality that have de-sexualized them. That de-sexualization, among other factors, may contribute to lower rates of marriage among middle- and upper-middle class African-American women. Given the de-sexualized nature of work marriage portrayals, however, African-American women may in fact be more attractive work wives to powerful white men than are white women. Gender always intersects with other aspects of identity, but such intersections may play out differently in the work wife context than in other contexts.

Portrayals of marriage at work therefore resist any categorization as good or bad for women or men as categories. Other approaches to gender equality tend to assume that care and work occur either within a traditional gender framework or completely outside of it (once feminist reforms are adopted). Postmodern, anti-essentialist approaches embrace a much broader spectrum between traditional gender roles and complete freedom from those roles. Even though gender remains tenacious, multiple gendered performances of care and connection may exist along this spectrum.

* * *

Thinking Beyond the Limits of Employment Discrimination Law

* * *

The shifting meanings of the marriage metaphor at work call into question the very nature of Title VII's workplace equality project. Title VII addresses identifiable harm flowing from gender at work. Although harm may be a feature of some work wife portrayals, harm likely mixes with many other factors and may often be largely, or even entirely, absent. That does not mean, however, that the care at the core of such portrayals is necessarily less gendered. Rather, the care may be gendered in ways that do not map on to current understandings of either discrimination or equality.

Indeed, examining workplace care in all its complexity permits a new analysis of three important aspects of the theories undergirding employment discrimination law as a whole: merit, intent, and identity performance. This analysis highlights some of the limits and gaps in existing approaches to workplace equality and suggests paths for beginning to address such limits. Most importantly, the analysis reveals that identity—and gender itself—is not exogenous to the workplace but instead is produced, at least in part, by the interactions occurring within it.

First, with respect to merit, the metaphor of marriage at work provides yet another challenge to the concept itself. The very idea of the work wife indicates that something more than individual effort and talent may be necessary to succeed at work. Feminist legal theorists have long made a similar point, emphasizing the support that many male employees receive from sources outside of the workplace, namely the free domestic carework that husbands often receive from their wives. Such support is rendered largely invisible in workplace law, however, maintaining the myth of individual merit. Employees without access to such support, primarily women, are in turn disadvantaged.

Feminist legal theorists have not, until recently, examined the support that workers do or do not receive from personal relationships within the workplace itself. The ongoing traction of the marriage metaphor at work indicates, at the very least, a desire for the exchange of care and support at work, if not the actual exchange of such care and support. That the metaphor is even intelligible at work highlights that care is not confined to the private sphere but instead crosses the public-private divide, albeit often in complex and contradictory ways, disrupting attempts to separate individual merit from dependency and support.

Such flow of care complicates efforts to achieve gender equality in the workplace. Some advocates of women's equality have posited engagement with paid work as necessary for achieving women's equality with men, constructing work as the place where women are freed from the gendered caregiving expectations that pervade the domestic sphere. Yet women, like men, may need to engage in at least some forms of supportive relationships at work in order to succeed. To the extent that some of those relationships are loaded with caregiving obligations, they may at times impede women's abilities to assert their individual talents. Other relationships may give women access to care at work that was previously unavailable to them, however, supporting their ability to succeed at work rather than thwarting it. Finally, still other relationships may permit women to exchange care for access to power, achieving more than they could based on individual talent alone.

Second, with respect to employer intent, the metaphor of marriage at work illustrates the difficulties of separating discriminatory intent from all other workplace dynamics. The general deference to employer prerogatives in all hiring, firing, and promotion decisions, absent discrimination, assumes that discriminatory intent is a phenomenon distinct from all other workplace dynamics. This assumption merges with the emphasis on individual merit to support the theory that the workplace will promote equality so long as assessments of individual merit are not tainted by employer animus. Yet gender, race, and other aspects of identity flow through work in complex ways often unmoored from employer intent.

For example, if relationships contribute to workplace success and if some employees are more likely to be portrayed as work wives than others—whether for reasons of gender performance, race performance, or other factors—then employees who are not in the preferred categories may have to engage in additional work to succeed. Conversely, those employees easily considered work wives may have to engage in additional work to prove they have something beyond care or support to offer to employers. These forms of work may be unequally distributed on the basis of gender or race, but such inequality is not necessarily the result of discriminatory intent. Rather, it is a response to workplace structures and employees' desires to achieve a sense of belonging and respect in the workplace. These factors may affect work trajectories as much or more than does irrational discrimination, but antidiscrimination law does not currently include them in its analysis.

Finally, the metaphor of marriage at work provides a new lens to examine the complexity of gender performance. Such examination reveals new forms of inequality and empowerment, highlighting the limits of existing doctrine's aspirations of gender-neutrality. For example, although women generally may not be liberated from care expectations in the workplace, and supervisors and coworkers may thus subtly treat them differently than male employees, such expectations at work may be preferable to those in the home. Both women and men may, in fact, enjoy opportunities to experience, and experiment with, emotional ties in the workplace that are less subsumed by the domesticity and dependent care at the core of many marriages outside of work. Accordingly, some women may embrace the metaphor of marriage at work even as it continues to insert gender into the workplace.

That embrace leads neither to the conclusion that such women are freely choosing to engage in gendered care nor to the conclusion that they are falsely conscious. Instead, performances of marriage and gender at work may be the product of a complex combination of individual choice, the structural constraints of home and work, and the relationships that both mediate and contribute to those constraints. Only by acknowledging such complexity will scholars be able to develop more meaningful conceptions of equality and discrimination for the workplace and beyond.

Conclusion

Marriage works in multiple ways, flowing between the public and private divides of work and home. This feedback effect is key to understanding the tenacity of traditional gender roles both at home and at work. Law, of course, guides these relationships, but as this Article emphasizes, law is at times a catalyst for change and at others a mere backdrop for individual negotiations and performances of gender. Seemingly gender-neutral laws therefore are not necessarily so, and they are unlikely to eliminate the relevance of gender or its performance at home or at work.

The ongoing salience of the marriage metaphor at work specifically means that gender remains a fact in many workplaces despite antidiscrimination law. The metaphor inserts gender into the workplace in ways that may further or thwart gender equality or be indifferent to it. Some portrayals of work wives may continue to reinforce gender hierarchy by portraying women providing traditionally gendered care from positions of subordination, much like the relationships between many male executives and their secretaries prior to the passage of Title VII. But other portrayals of work wives may engage in strikingly different performances of gender than are generally available in legal marriages rooted in the home. Such performances may ultimately permit more individuals to reimagine the roles of both men and women within families and workplaces. Studying work wives therefore leads to new understandings of the limits and potential of Title VII, the complexity of gender tenacity, and the meanings of gender equality.

HANNAH BRENNER AND RENEE KNAKE, *SHORTLISTED: WOMEN IN THE SHADOWS OF THE SUPREME COURT*
NEW YORK UNIVERSITY PRESS (FORTHCOMING 2020)

Brenner and Knake are authors of this casebook, and you can learn more about them in the Introduction.

* * *

Contemporary discourse on gender and the Supreme Court in law, gender studies, political science, and media . . . has mostly focused on the stories of the women who are selected, not shortlisted. Reporters, commentators, and scholars frequently retell Justice O'Connor's story as the first woman to serve on the Court, followed by a discussion of the three successful female nominees who followed in the wake of her legacy. The year 1981 is remembered as a pivotal and celebrated year as President Ronald Reagan made history by nominating the first woman, Sandra Day O'Connor, to the United States Supreme Court. Over the course of the next thirty years, four more women would be nominated, three successfully appointed to the Court. Ruth Bader Ginsburg was nominated and appointed to the Court in 1993, followed by Sonia Sotomayor in 2009 and Elena Kagan in 2010. Harriet Miers was nominated but withdrew from consideration in 2005.

Coverage of the women nominated and confirmed to the Court is important, but here we expand the narrative to include the myriad untold stories stumbled upon in our media study, the stories of those shortlisted. It is valuable, as a preliminary matter, to tell their stories as part of the larger historical record of women's entry into the legal profession. But beyond that, however, their stories also expose barriers that endure whenever a candidate is shortlisted but not selected. Their collective history offers guidance for transcending modern shortlists.

Our work further builds upon earlier scholarly work that developed the theory of the "leaking pipeline," in other words, the idea that women enter the profession in numbers equal to men but do not advance into leadership positions at the same rate, if at all. One way the pipeline 'leaks' is via shortlisting, with qualified women considered in the mix of candidates but not selected.

Shortlists help to identify and explain latent discrimination and bias both within and outside of the judiciary. Many attempts to achieve diversity are effectively nothing more than window-dressing intended to create the appearance that diversity is valued. Take the so-called 'Rooney

Rule,' named for former president and owner of the Pittsburg Steelers Dan Rooney, which is a policy adopted by the National Football League requiring that at least one ethnic-minority be interviewed when hiring for head coaching and senior leadership positions. Some herald the rule as a success because it has increased the number of minorities who interview for these positions. They argue that even if a minority candidate is not selected, there is benefit in them having been considered. Aspirational policies like these, however, have done little to change the demographics of who is actually hired.

Some companies have experimented with similar policies. In 2017, the Diversity Lab launched the Mansfield Rule for law firms and corporate legal departments, named after Arabella Mansfield, the first woman admitted to practice law in the United States when she received a law license from the Iowa bar in 1869. The Mansfield Rule requires that employers consider diverse candidates for 30% of open positions in leadership or governance, thus for ten potential hires three must be women or minorities. With a significant cohort of prestigious firms and corporations committing to the effort, this seems promising, but it is too soon to assess the impact. In 2010, the Securities and Exchange Commission began requiring companies to disclose efforts to address diversity when choosing board directors in proxy statements, however, this effort has not increased the number of women on Fortune 500 boards. The data reveals a dismal picture where, even after implementation of the SEC rule, the number of women named to boards actually decreased by two percent, down from approximately 12 percent to 10 percent. We do not mean to diminish the importance of policies like these, but we are more concerned with who is actually selected, not just who appears on the shortlist.

* * *

Shortlisting happens to many women in competitive professional contexts, even if they are unlikely to find themselves on a president's list for a Supreme Court vacancy. Our mission, however, is to move more women and minorities from shortlisted to selected.

Shortlisting inevitably occurs with any pursuit of leadership or advancement, whether the judge in the courtroom, the CEO in the corner office, or the coach on the playing field. Women, and especially female minorities, regularly find themselves equally or more qualified than the white men on the shortlist, but they are far less likely to be selected. Shortlists thus project a façade of diversity with their inclusion of women and minorities but function to preserve the status quo.

Diverse shortlists are a prerequisite for producing diverse leaders, but they are not sufficient in and of themselves to achieve this goal. Moreover, sometimes individuals self-shortlist, for example, declining to be considered among a pool of candidates or forgoing a position even if offered because of other priorities, a lack of confidence, fear of an unwinnable situation, or the perception of being less than qualified despite objective evidence to the contrary. More often, however, shortlisting is at the hands of the decision-maker and is attributable to enduring discrimination, prejudice, bias, and the dominant group's desire to remain in control.

Diversity includes much more than gender or race or religion or ethnicity or sexuality or socio-economic status. Individuals sharing the same facets of their identity commonly vary in their perspectives on politics, policy, and in many other respects. Our point is simply that the symbolism of diverse shortlists is unlikely to increase diversity in leadership unless additional strategies are implemented to shift diverse candidates from shortlisted to selected. Systemic shortlisting women and minorities risks the hollow achievement of symbolic diversity at best, and at worst becomes a mechanism to actively hold back the underrepresented.

ANTHONY MICHAEL KREIS, *DEFENSIVE GLASS CEILINGS*
GEORGE WASHINGTON LAW REVIEW (FORTHCOMING 2020)

Kreis is a visiting assistant professor of law at Chicago-Kent College of Law, Institute for Law and the Workplace.

The #MeToo Movement is a grassroots effort mobilized by victims of sexual assault and sexual harassment to end sexual violence and sex-based discrimination against women. Though in its infancy, the movement has been a catalyst for significant legal and cultural reform. The movement has also brought to light credible accusations of various sex-based misconduct, causing the careers of prominent men to nosedive. Men have reacted by doubling down on decades old workplace sex-based inequities and practices to avoid women in the workplace and hedge against allegations of wrongdoing or the appearance of impropriety. The American workplace will be more sex-segregated if recent anecdotal evidence of men increasingly dodging women is indicative of a wider, long-term trend.

At the same time, women are punished on the job for being too friendly at work or because they are perceived as too attractive, mistreatment stemming from men's fears that they are unable to exercise self-control, that women are "overly sensitive," or that women might make baseless accusations against them. Too often courts have declined to recognize these invidious employment practices as unlawful sex discrimination because judges fail to see these behaviors manifestations of systemic gender policing. Judges, instead, chalk it up to a few bad apples misbehaving. The hue and cry of this paradigm-shifting moment is ripe to reconsider the law's prior understanding of sexual harassment and sex discrimination in the workplace.

This Article advances two primary arguments. First, employment practices that create different rules of workplace engagement, which are motivated by ambivalent sexism and are for the primary benefit of men, form defensive glass ceilings—a term first introduced by this Article. Second, because defensive glass ceilings are a structural barrier to women's employment opportunities, the employer practices that create them are prohibited under existing employment antidiscrimination laws.

* * *

Glass ceilings are a structural obstacle for women and sexual minorities in the workplace—they are "the unseen, yet unbreachable barrier that keeps minorities and women from rising to the upper rungs of the corporate ladder, regardless of their qualifications or achievements." Defensive glass ceilings are a kind of glass ceiling that destabilize the upward career trajectories of women who defy or want to defy sexist traditions of workplace interpersonal conduct that keep men and women separate.

The manifestation of workplace practices that defensively reinforce glass ceilings are deeply rooted in sexist ideology—they grow out of fears stemming from sex stereotypes about the types of relationships that are acceptable in the workplace, the combustible nature of interactions between ambitious women and men of weak constitutions, and the perception of women as temptresses using femininity to control men. In short, these sexist tactics are calibrated to cement the control of those who wield power in the workplace under the pretext of liability-avoidance or to protect a purported familial or general reputational dignitary interest.

* * *

Sometime between 1949 and 1950, the influential evangelist Billy Graham returned to his hotel room after finishing one of his famous Crusade meetings. To Reverend Graham's surprise, or so the story goes, a naked woman was lying in wait for him in his bed. Ever the dutiful husband, Graham reported that he immediately left the room and thereafter swore to never interact with a woman—including traveling, dining, or meeting—alone. Clergymen and businessmen followed Graham's model, adopting his rule for their own personal interactions. In 2002, then-Congressman Mike Pence told The Hill that he embraced a similar philosophy as Reverend Graham. Pence explained that, except for his wife, he never eats alone with a woman and does not attend events where alcohol is served without her. The rule also extended to his staffing policies. Pence only permitted male congressional aides to work late nights. Pence's office was not the only one on Capitol Hill to take sex based considerations into account for operations management. Women reported that female aides in multiple offices were restricted from attending evening events, traveling alone, and holding one-on-one meetings with their bosses. In the wake of his elevation to the vice presidency and national conversations about sexual harassment, Pence's sex-based socialization rules received renewed attention.

Some nationally prominent commentators championed the Graham-Pence Rule after proliferating allegations of workplace wrongdoing in 2017 and 2018. Writing for the National Review, David French offered a three part justification for the Pence Rule: sexual attraction is more likely to blossom in casual social environments outside the workplace, the potential for reputational is harm minimized by avoiding the appearance of impropriety, and women are protected from truly predatory colleagues. Another commentator argued the Pence Rule is ideal since "men do not like being held accountable by women" because it comes across as "nagging, an attack, or some feelings-based weirdness" and the Graham-Pence Rule is a better vehicle for male self-regulation. Charles C.W. Cooke not only praised Pence as a model of "decency" and "humility," but also advocated the policy's widespread adoption to protect marital relationships. Caution is no vice when the end is so undesirable," Cooke opined.

* * *

Survey data conducted by McKinsey and Company and Lean In revealed there are considerable numbers of anxious men worried about placing themselves in jeopardy at work.

* * *

Over 50 years ago, Congress took significant steps to eradicate artificial barriers to employment opportunities. The sweep of sex discrimination doctrine has dramatically evolved in that time since. Indeed, the law has appreciably developed through judicial interpretation and statutory amendments to combat forms of bias well beyond basic ontological sex discrimination. Today, employment anti-discrimination law works to protect workers from sexual harassment, gender nonconformity discrimination, sexual orientation bias, and the mistreatment of transgender persons. But for all its progress, employment discrimination doctrine's full potential is hampered by considerable blind spots. The law must continue to mature and afford robust protections to workers who are discriminated against because of anxious decision-makers and defensive workplace environments. The #MeToo Era is an appropriate moment to rethink the law's prior understanding of sexism and renew scrutiny of defensive employment practices that penalize individuals because of ambivalent sexism.

LESLIE P. CULVER, *THE RISE OF SELF SIDELINING*
39 WOMEN'S RIGHTS LAW REPORTER 173 (2018)

Culver is an identity scholar and professor of legal writing professor at California Western School of Law and Director of A.I.M. for Law, a diversity pipeline program to encourage college students from underrepresented communities to consider law school. She was a Visiting Professor of Lawyering Skills at UC Irvine School of law from 2018–2020 and previously practiced as an associate at Husch & Eppenberger (now Husch Blackwell Sanders).

I always thought that there was nothing an antifeminist would want more than to have women only in women's organizations, in their own little corner empathizing with each other and not touching a man's world. If you're going to change things, you have to be with the people who hold the levers.

—Justice Ruth Bader Ginsburg

* * *

This Article beckons awareness to expose yet another obstacle without a legal remedy that particularly affects women, the rise of which has a corrosive effect on the legal profession as a whole. That is, self sidelining. Self sidelining, as defined here, stems from impostor phenomenon effects being intensified through gender sidelining. Briefly, the impostor phenomenon, a psychological construct, emerged in 1978 by psychologists Dr. Pauline Clance and Suzanne Imes. The phenomenon describes the inability of high-achieving women and men to internalize their success, due to the distorted assumption that they are phonies in their respective field despite objective evidence to the contrary. While both men and women are susceptible to impostor feelings, research overwhelmingly indicates that the phenomenon is more limiting to women based on familial expectations and gender role socialization, both of which suggest women's natural and skilled place is inside the home, not in the workplace. A separate theory, gender sidelining, popularized in legal scholarship by Professor Jessica Fink, describes "the various ways in which women across a wide range of employment settings may find themselves sidelined, upstaged or otherwise marginalized [by men] in ways not reached by traditional antidiscrimination laws."

The Article's central thesis suggest that when the impostor phenomenon welds itself to gender sidelining, the latent effects run deep, placing women at risk of *self sidelining* to their personal and professional detriment. In other words, despite objective evidence of success, the high achieving woman internally feels like an intellectual fraud (i.e., impostor phenomenon), but when her ideas and contributions are discounted by men (i.e., gender sidelining), these negative experiences externally validate, albeit erroneously so, the belief that she is an intellectual phony, and she begins to believe that perhaps she does not belong. In turn, she intentionally shies away or walks away from opportunities for professional advancement based on falsely endorsed feelings of inadequacy. She falls prey to self sidelining. At the start, I am mindful of areas of divergence this work takes with existing scholarship. First, that some female faculty at colleges and universities depart their posts pre-tenure due to intense impostor feelings, but by and large the hallmark features of impostor phenomenon are anxiety, fear of failure, and self-doubt, not departure. Second, that Fink's use of the term gender sidelining as a reference to *women's* achievements and opportunities to advance are downplayed in comparison to *men*. By replacing the term "gender" with "self" to sidelining, I intentionally extend the theory of gender sidelining to suggest that *women* may in fact downplay or prevent their *own* achievements and opportunities to advance.

While this work draws upon interdisciplinary principles, it is anchored in critical legal scholarship focused on gender disparities. Similar to gender sidelining, self sidelining not only lacks legally actionable remedies (and rightfully so), but it also threatens to further silence, suppress, and shrink voices that make up a significant and integral mass within the legal profession—female law students, attorneys, and judges—unconsciously of their own accord. These voices are vital to the vibrancy and diversity of the legal profession. Legal scholarship continues to underscore gender disparities in opportunities for advancement in legal education, practice and the judiciary. For instance, the very formation of the American Bar Association's Commission on Women in the Profession in 1987, decades after formal legal reforms were initiated, signaled the need for continued conversations to remove persistent informal barriers. In many respects, the legal profession will remain shortsighted if it defines something as a problem only if there exists or should exist an identifiable legal remedy.

* * *

This Article attempts to bring awareness to a self-defeating phenomenon affecting women's professional growth, with emphasis on women in the legal profession. The first part provides a background of the impostor phenomenon, discussing where it appears in the legal profession, its social science origins, disparate gender outcomes, and other characteristics. The second part briefly provides an overview of gender sidelining, and the final part theorizes how gender sidelining can trigger and falsely affirm previously held impostor feelings, thus leading to the rise of self sidelining.

The work focuses on white women for two reasons. First, white women coined impostor phenomenon and popularized gender sidelining. And although their respective work does not consider the effect on women with multiple diverse identities, e.g., race, sexuality, disability, it may be foolish to assume that the absence of such explicit consideration deems the experiences of such diverse women automatically included in their findings. Second, while beyond the scope of this work, I would argue that the rise of self sidelining has a one-dimensional effect on white women, compared to a two-dimensional effect on women with multiple diverse identities. Even though white women are affected by *gender* bias, they still highly benefit from white privilege and white supremacy; that is, they are legitimized by their race. Therefore, even in the wake of experiencing impostor feelings, any gender sidelining by men is an affront to a white woman's ability to professionally advance based on patriarchy alone. Thus, when the white woman self sidelines, she only has to push past a one-dimensional concern based on gender. Compare this one-dimensional concern to, for example, women of color who live in a space of multiple diverse dimensions. Unlike white women who are only affected by gender bias, as compared to white men, women of color are affected by both *race* and *gender* bias and cannot be legitimized on either plane with white men. For women of color who experience impostor feelings, it is uncertain whether any gender sidelining that may follow is an affront by white men based only on patriarchy, on race, or both—a problem widely recognized as intersectionality. In this way, when a woman of color self sidelines, she has to consciously push past bias or presumed incompetency based on her race, as well as gender bias. This represents a two-dimensional concern (and in some cases three or more due to LGBTQ+ identity, living with a disability, or other diverse attributes as part of the women's identity).

While the focus is on white women, and at the risk of essentializing a monolithic woman experience, I believe there is value in the conversation of self sidelining for all women as an impetus against patriarchy. But the awareness of the unique way in which self sidelining may manifest in women with multiple diverse identities bears additional consideration in the face of white privilege, white supremacy, and white male domination.

* * *

A.   *Impostor Phenomenon Characteristics*

The genesis of impostor feelings is influenced largely by family dynamics and social contexts, i.e., gender role socialization. Dr. Clance's six potential characteristics identify someone affected by the impostor phenomenon.

1.   The Impostor Cycle

Certainly the first characteristic, *The Impostor Cycle*, is the most referenced in relevant literature, if not by name, than in content. Beginning with "a new opportunity . . . new project, or [the] start[ ] [of] any challenging occupational task," the Impostor Cycle starts running. With the onset of a new challenge, anxiety may set in, which results in a person over-preparing, or procrastinating until the last minute, and then "engag[ing] in a frenzy of activity." If they are successful by over-preparing, they will believe they must *always* over-prepare to compete with their colleagues, and that any success was due to immense effort and hard work. Likewise, if they are successful despite procrastination, they will presume it was sheer luck in pulling off a last minute task. In either case, the person "forfeits the affirmation of a job well-done" and accepts that they are an impostor. The person's belief about how success was achieved (e.g., effort or luck) makes the person feel like a fraud and that such success cannot be duplicated, thus triggering self-doubt and anxiety when another new task presents itself. The Impostor Cycle is repeated.

2.   The need to be special or to be the very best

This self-evident characteristic arguably creates an interesting conflict, placing the person on the losing end of his or her own measuring stick. Desiring to be the very best in a given situation, the person also realizes there are many talented and successful people around them, particularly at a university level, thus his or her own brilliance is no longer atypical and it is dismissed.

As an aside, this characteristic is animated in the Disney movie, *The Incredibles*, the endearing story of a family of superhero crime-fighters who are relegated to live as "normal" citizens after a stint of attempts to help their fellow man back-fired. In one scene, Dash, so named for his superhero speed, is frustrated by his mom's repeated denial of his request to join a sports team at school. Pleading with his mom to let him go out for sports, he promises to "only be the best by a tiny bit" and adds, "Dad always said our powers were nothing to be ashamed of; our powers made us special." With a heavy sigh his mom replies, "Everyone's special Dash," to which he sulkily remarks, "which is another way of saying no one is." Despite the son's need to be special or to be the very best, his mom is constructing this normalized belief that everyone is the same, that everyone has talent and is special. Thus, the subtext is that Dash's own talents as a superhero are really not special and, most relevant, that he should dismiss or suppress them. Sadly, Dash's face expresses the crushed spirit of someone who desires to be the very best, and simply cannot.

3.   Superman/Superwoman aspects

Related to the need to be the best, this *Superman/Superwoman* characteristic describes the proverbial perfectionist. The perfectionist's goals are high and "almost impossible" to reach; the failure to do so renders them overwhelmed and disappointed. To this point, relevant studies attribute impostor feelings to an unhealthy belief that perfectionism can and should be attained. For example, in one study of college students where the relationship between impostorship and perfectionism was tested, the study, unsurprisingly, "supported that perfectionism correlates to the extent that participants externalized success, set high standards for themselves, and self-analyzed." Interestingly, a later study confirmed the positive correlation between impostorship fears and perfection, but found that the fears were more associated with "displays of public perfection, not simply general self-presentation [sic] concerns."

4.   Fear of failure

The *fear of failure*, particularly when a new achievement-related task is assigned, results in a person overworking due to high levels of anxiety. The idea of "not performing at the highest standard precipitates feelings of shame and humiliation." To this point, those with imposter feelings, more so than those without, "experience greater concern over mistakes, overestimate the frequency of mistakes, have less satisfaction with their performance, and feel less confident about their performance." Even knowing that failure is unavoidable, the impostor "can[not] tolerate the thought of it and they avoid it at all costs." For some, the fear of failure may be so profound that they simply belittle their own ability and talent to be successful, assuming they cannot fail if "they don't reach too high." Or, perhaps from a childhood incident or the hallowed halls of family memories, the fear of failure is closely tied to "appearing foolish or stupid"—an identity the person with impostor feelings cannot bear. Thus, with the impossible goal of never being humiliated, they do not place themselves in situations where failure of this magnitude could even occur.

5.   Denial of competence and discounting praise

Observed in this characteristic, a person *discounts praise* or downplays positive feedback and "objective evidence of success," but actually takes the time to invest in arguments as to why they do not deserve any praise or attention for successes achieved. In other words, imposter feelings generate an individual's almost insistent need to negate any apparent evidence that would contradict their *self-belief* that they are really not intelligent.

6.   Fear and guilt about success

Interestingly, this final characteristic of *fear and guilt about success* is driven by external concerns. That is, unlike the other more internal characteristics, such as feeling special (or desiring to feel such), lofty goals, or the opposite extreme of overwhelming anxiety and self-doubt, this final fear rests in how others will perceive such success. To this fear, social science scholars Sakulku and Alexander write: "when their successes are unusual in their family or their peers, Impostors often feel less connected and more distant. They are overwhelmed by the guilt about being different and worry about being rejected by others."

In short, the literature on the impostor's feelings of inadequacy seem unending, with perhaps an attempt not to dim the reality that these individuals are generally exceptional academics and professionals. While both women and men are prone to the impostor phenomenon, the next section discusses its particular, and often limiting, effect upon women.

B.   *The Unique Effect of Impostor Phenomenon on Women*

Since success for <u>women</u> is contraindicated by societal expectations and their own internalized self-evaluations, it is not surprising that women. . .need to find explanations for their accomplishments other than their own intelligence—such as fooling other people.

—Drs. Pauline Rose Clance & Suzanne Imes

In their seminal clinical research, Clance and Imes found the impostor phenomenon occurred more in women than in men in both frequency and intensity, despite mixed opinions from males who testified to experiencing the phenomenon. They supported their early findings with the work of attribution theorist Kay Deaux, whose 1976 study of sex differences in attribution demonstrated that "women consistently have lower expectancies than men of their ability to perform successfully on a wide variety of tasks," thus women "attribute their successes to temporary causes, such as luck or effort, in contrast to men who are much more likely to attribute their successes to the internal, stable factor of ability."

Subsequent research, however, has confirmed that impostor phenomenon occurs fairly equally in women and men, foregoing its once feminist shadings. Yet because women exist in a male-normed society, women, more than men, suffer from imposter phenomenon in a more *particular* and intense way due to family dynamics and gender role socialization.

* * *

If the particularized impact of the impostor phenomenon on women was not discouraging enough, gender sidelining delivers yet another blow to the female gender.

II.   UNDERSTANDING GENDER SIDELINING

What to say when a male's three-way tie for second place is headlined over a female's world-record gold-medal dominance . . . at the Olympic games? Or when the photo of a former male president, circa 2001, makes the front page after a country nominates its first female in a presidential election . . . fifteen years later? This is Gender Sidelining. While one need not probe extensively to find ample research on men's achievements deemed superior to women's achievements of the same ilk, Professor Fink popularized this occurrence as "gender sidelining" in legal scholarship. The following section provides a brief overview of Fink's use of gender sidelining as well as illustrations of this phenomenon on the professional stage.

A.   *Defining Gender Sidelining*

Fink's discussion of gender sidelining arose from viewing a male's achievement literally and figuratively headlined over a female's far superior achievements on a national stage. On a momentous Olympic night in the summer of 2016, swimmer Katie Ledecky shattered world records (including her own), demonstrating her athletic prowess and becoming one of the greatest swimmers in sports history. That same night, Michael Phelps, most certainly with a celebrated record of his own, was part of a three-way tie for second place. To be sure, for any athlete to be competing and medaling at the Olympic games is no small feat; yet one small college newspaper's reporting of these events the next morning may forever mark them with a Scarlet A (or more appropriately an "S" for sexist) in media history. The August 13, 2016, headline of the *Bryan-College Station Eagle*, displayed a headline in large bold font reading "Phelps ties for silver in 100 fly" and beneath in "smaller and less prominent print . . . 'Ledecky sets world record in women's 800 freestyle.'" *The Eagle's* account is one example of biased media coverage nationwide that vividly demonstrates "gender sidelining."

Gender sidelining, according to Fink, describes "the various ways in which women across a wide range of employment settings may find themselves sidelined, upstaged or otherwise marginalized in ways not reached by traditional anti-discrimination laws." While Title VII provides some relief from gender discrimination, it does not provide protection from the subtle biases such as "a lack of access to certain opportunities, the diversion of credit for an idea, [and] a nagging sense of being held to a higher standard than their male peers."

* * *

III.   The Rise of Self Sidelining

According to the American Bar Association's (ABA) 2017 report on women in the legal profession, women are entering law school at nearly the same rate as men, but represent only 36% of the legal profession. Baffled by this statistic, ABA President Hilarie Bass, launched a national study in November 2017 called *Achieving Long-Term Careers for Women in the Law* to find out why more seasoned women are leaving law firms. While some women are making lateral moves for increased flexibility and mentorship, others are departing law firms for government employment, in-house counsel positions, or to start their own law firms, among other things. Decades of ABA statistics on women in the profession, including the 2017 study, and copious scholarship focused on the advancement, attrition, and retention of women, not only emphasize the gender gap in the legal profession, but also that parity for this marginalized group mandates conversation even absent a legal remedy—a sentiment central to this article's thesis. The theory of self sidelining is unlikely to resolve the inequity facing female attorneys, but it merits a seat at the table of conversation to raise conscious awareness concerning stagnant professional advancement of women in a culture of white male domination within the legal profession.

At the heart of the cycle that culminates in self sidelining there exists highly intelligent, capable, and successful women—certainly a norm within the legal profession. Their worthy accomplishments should not be overlooked. Sadly, the impostor phenomenon displaces this space of success with internal fears of unworthiness or incompetence; after which gender sidelining's devaluation of women, as compared to men, serves to falsely endorse a woman's preexisting internal impostor feelings. Finally, the resurgence of impostor feelings, now externally validated by gender sidelining, may prevent women from even staying in the game—this is self sidelining. More simply stated, gender sidelining can trigger previously held imposter feelings, placing women at risk of sidelining themselves out of career opportunities to their professional detriment.

To be clear, as previously stated, this Article recognizes that the term gender sidelining refers to *women's* achievements and opportunities to advance that are downplayed, or ignored entirely, in comparison to *men*. By replacing the term "gender" with "self," I am intentionally tailoring Fink's theory to suggest that external gendered forces may consciously or unconsciously make women discipline themselves to downplay or prevent their *own* achievements and opportunities to advance. The following sections anecdotally demonstrate the evolution from impostor to self sidelining, then, as an example, discusses two gender sidelining consequences that reawaken impostor feelings, and finally how those resurrected impostor feelings lead to self sidelining.

* * *

Finally, modern literature and feminist movements also recognize the work of self sidelining as evidenced by their rally cry to empower women generally and particularly in the workplace. In mainstream literature, some authors suggest that women are concerned about affecting professional relationships and thus, withdraw from professional ascent. The work of Babcock and Laschever in *Women Don't Ask*, supports the idea that a relationship heartstring can often act as a professional snare. They stated, "[w]omen often worry more than men about the impact their actions will have on relationships." Thus, spending more time ensuring all parties at the table are happy, rather than negotiating their own professional growth. Their research, spurred on by an initial observation of male graduate students teaching their own courses while many female graduate students served as teaching assistants, led them to question whether "women [are] really less likely than men to ask for what they want[.]" In a word, yes.

Arguably one of the most well-known modern books and taglines concerning women and their dim visibility in the professional realm is Sheryl Sandberg's, "Lean In," where she challenges an entire gender not to retreat from male dominated spaces, but instead to claim a seat at the table. In this work, she suggests the multiple roles that women play may contribute to their lack of self-promotion. Specifically, Sandberg draws attention to the negative images portrayed when women play the double or triple duty roles of wife, mother, and professional, commenting that "[w]e need more portrayals of women as competent professionals and happy mothers—or even happy professionals and competent mothers." As an impostor sufferer herself, she comments that the lack of such positive portrayals unnecessarily feeds a woman's disabling fears that she cannot do both, so why even try; and if she does try she's subject to the oft overused and bothersome phrase, "*I don't know how she does it.*"

For all the accolades and star power that arose from *Lean In*, this tagline has also been met with criticism, one in particular that this Article is sensitive to in the discussion of self sidelining. That is, the locus of gender inequality is on women; that women need to fix themselves. My guess is that was neither Sandberg's intended outcome nor prevailing thought, nor is it this Article's assertion. But the criticism surrounding this call to action as a well-meaning prescription raises larger issues of a social harm.

Do we have the right remedy, or worse still, have we undersold female empowerment as a remedy, and missed discussing the underlying layers of how gender socialization affects identity formation; and how, right or wrong, women must live in a state of readiness to push back against male norms to confidently perform their identity? As a society, do we oversimplify the message to women to lean in harder, have the will to lead, just be more empowered? In many respects, though, aren't many women doing this? Recent reports indicate that women are earning more college and graduate degrees than men. As previously discussed, in the legal profession women are entering law schools in equal, if not greater numbers, than men. Yet, after law school, despite female attorneys being represented on prestigious platforms such as organizational presidents, commissioners, and judgeships, they still comprise significantly less than half of the legal profession.

Undoubtedly, the preference toward maleness as the industry standard is rearing its ugly head, which arguably intensifies the inquiry. I suggest that it is the gravity of fraudulent feelings based on gender role socialization, which are continually reaffirmed by society's preference for the male standard, that may be conditioning women to discipline their professional choices. To the extent this socially constructed cycle of inferiority toward an entire gender is not legally actionable, it is offensive to suggest that there is no social harm deserving of a meaningful discussion and response.

The social harm resulting from self-sidelining may actually be worse than we believe if it causes women, even in small numbers, to exit their careers. This harm, for example, results in less female partners in our nation's law firms, fewer women in tenured law professor positions, fewer female judges in state and federal courts—simply fewer women at the top and with adequate job security and pay. If the remedy is to tell female attorneys to strengthen their will and resolve, to simply lean further in on the table, do we risk minimizing the emotional and perhaps psychological impact that has occurred behind the scenes? That is, the triple impact of the impostor phenomenon, gender sidelining, and self sidelining. This impact may generate considerable insecurity and anxiety, making some women unable to move forward in their profession, or have little courage to try.

It is clear from the body of literature that a woman's struggle with self-promotion and doubting her value is due, in part, to the aftermath of a history of rigid gender roles being shaped within a male normative social structure. That is to say, women, unlike men, have long been socialized *not* to promote themselves, *not* to speak their mind, *not* to take risks, and *not* to believe they are deserving of professional growth, thus causing veritable anxiety if they do ask for something at all. This struggle for value, for voice, for parity, is not a matter of apathy, and it unlikely is willed away—it is a forerunner to self sidelining.

CHAPTER 5

LEADERSHIP IN THE LEGAL PROFESSION

■ ■ ■

INTRODUCTION

The readings included in this chapter focus on issues related to leadership in the legal profession. The doors to law schools have been open to women for many years, and women and men have been graduating from law schools in relatively equal numbers for decades. Looking around your law school classrooms, we imagine you see relatively equal numbers of men and women. Despite the presence of women and minority students in law school and as new lawyers entering the profession, the upper echelons of power are still heavily dominated by white men. The data on the dearth of women at the top of the legal profession is extensive and the problem has been well documented. The American Bar Association released a new report in mid-2019 on the demographics of the legal profession that revealed 85 percent of lawyers are white and mostly male.[1] The report also confirmed that progress has indeed stalled, and the statistics have not changed significantly over the past decades.

According to the National Association of Women Lawyers *2018 Survey on Retention and Promotion of Women in Law Firms,* twenty-two percent of managing partners and twenty percent of equity partners in the nation's largest law firms are women.[2] This number shrinks to two percent when looking at the presence of women of color in these coveted leadership roles.[3] Across other sectors of the profession, women represent less than twenty-six percent of general counsels to the Fortune 500,[4] make up almost thirty-

---

[1] *ABA Profile of the Legal Profession*, 2019, https://www.americanbar.org/content/dam/aba/images/news/2019/08/ProfileOfProfession-total-hi.pdf (highlighting how white male lawyers in the legal profession are overrepresented as compared to the general population).

[2] Destiny Peery, *2018 NAWL Survey on Retention and Promotion of Women in Law Firms* (Chicago: National Association of Women Lawyers, 2018). Other studies reach a similar conclusion. For example, Julie Triedman reports that "the absolute number of women non-equity partners reported by The Am Law 200 surged by 9.5 percent between 2011 and 2014, while the number of female equity partners remained flat," and that "in 2014, 26 percent of nonequity partners were female, compared with 16.8 percent in the equity tier." Julie Triedman, *A Few Good Women*, THE AM. LAWYER (May 28, 2015), https://www.law.com/americanlawyer/almID/1202726917646/.

[3] *Id.*

[4] Am. Bar Ass'n Comm'n on Women in the Profession, *A Current Glance at Women in the Law*, CHICAGO: AM. BAR ASS'N 3 (2018), https://www.americanbar.org/content/dam/aba/administrative/women/a-current-glance-at-women-in-the-law-jan-2018.authcheckdam.pdf.

two percent of law school deans,[5] and account for thirty-two percent of tenured law school professors.[6] According to the most recently available data, only thirty-eight percent of law review editors-in-chief at top fifty U.S. law schools are women.[7] Only thirty-six percent of judges serving on state supreme courts or their equivalent are women.[8] Just a handful of states have a *majority* of women on their highest court, and many have only one.[9] Only twenty-three percent of lawyers who argue cases before the Supreme Court are women.[10] And although four women have served on the United States Supreme Court, we have never had a woman Chief Justice. The situation deteriorates even more when factoring in race, ethnicity, and sexual orientation.

Despite the ongoing exposure of this inequality in leadership, not much has changed over multiple decades. The causes are not entirely explained by numbers alone, nor are the causes always readily apparent. It is not just about the presence (or lack thereof) of women in various sectors of the profession, but also about the kind of work they do in these respective spaces. It is more than specifically where women lawyers are situated in the professional hierarchy, but what they are doing, how they are lawyering, and what they are paid for their work. A recent study exploring the position of female attorneys in civil and criminal trials, for example, revealed that male lawyers are significantly more likely to occupy lead roles (i.e., first chair) in these cases.[11] This chapter looks at some of the wide-ranging and problematic ways in which inequality manifests in the legal profession.

---

[5]   *Id.* at 4; Laura Padilla, *Women Law Deans, Gender Sidelining and Presumptions of Incompetence,* 34 BERKELEY J. GENDER, LAW & JUSTICE ___ (forthcoming, 2020).

[6]   American Bar Ass'n, *Data from the 2013 Annual Questionnaire, ABA Approved Law School Staff and Faculty Members, Gender and Ethnicity: Fall 2013*, CHICAGO: AM. BAR ASS'N, 2013, www. americanbar.org (of 5,398 tenured faculty members in 2013, only 1,766 were women).

[7]   *2012–2013 Law Review Diversity Report,* NEW YORK LAW SCHOOL, at 3 (Dec 2013), http:// www.nylslawreview.com/wp-content/uploads/sites/16/2013/12/Law-Review-Diversity-Report-2013.pdf; "In 2012–2013, women continued to lag behind their male counterparts in the Top 50 Sample, as women held 46% of leadership positions, and only 38% of EIC positions." *Id.*

[8]   Jennifer Horne, *Capitol Research: Women in State Government,* COUNCIL OF STATE GOVERNMENTS, 1 (2016), https://www.scribd.com/document/319010384/CSG-Capitol-Research-Women-in-State-Government-2016.

[9]   *Gender Diversity Survey,* THE AM. BENCH: JUDGES OF THE NATION, Forster Long 25 (2015) (the states with a majority of women serving on the highest court are Massachusetts, New York, Ohio, Washington, and Wisconsin. Idaho, Iowa, and Maryland had no women on each of the states' highest appellate courts in 2015).

[10]   Tony Mauro, *Supreme Court Specialists, Mostly Male, Dominated Arguments This Term,* NATIONAL LAW J. (May 11, 2016).

[11]   Am. Bar Ass'n, *First Chairs at Trial More Women Need Seats at the Table: A Research Report on the Participation of Women Lawyers as Lead Counsel and Trial Counsel in Litigation,* COMM'N OF WOMEN IN THE PROFESSION, 2015, https://www.americanbar.org/content/dam/aba/ marketing/women/first_chairs2015.pdf.

Credit: Library of Congress

Sandra Day O'Connor was the first woman to serve on the United States Supreme Court after decades of presidents shortlisting but never selecting women. She was appointed by President Reagan in 1981. She served on the Court as the lone woman until she was joined by Ruth Bader Ginsburg in 1993. At the time of O'Connor's nomination, the country appeared ready for a woman on the Court. A *New York Times*/CBS News Poll found that "72 percent of the public believed that it made no difference whether a man or a woman was appointed." Nonetheless, O'Connor sometimes ran into unexpected roadblocks, like the lack of a convenient woman's bathroom in the Court. Even though the justices stopped using the honorific "Mr." to refer to themselves (replacing it with "Justice") several months before her appointment, two years later, the *New York Times* still referenced the "nine men" sitting on "SCOTUS" in an editorial. She penned a letter to the editor to correct them: "According to the information available to me, and which I had assumed was generally available, for over two years now, SCOTUS has not consisted of nine men."[12] O'Connor retired in 2006 to care for her husband who was suffering from Alzheimer's disease. She devoted many years to civics education and judicial election reform. In 2018, she withdrew from public life herself, due to cognitive decline and health issues.

THOUGHT QUESTIONS

As you read the articles excerpted below, consider the following questions:

1.   What are some of the reasons that might explain the disconnect between the number of women graduating from law school and the number of women in leadership roles in the legal profession? Why has progress toward equality stalled? Does the legal profession have an ethical responsibility to address inequality among its own ranks?

2.   Have you experienced and/or witnessed bias or discrimination in law school or in professional legal settings? What have these situations looked like? Did you take steps, formal or informal, to report these issues? If so, how were your reports handled? If not, what were some of your reasons?

---

[12]   Sandra D. O'Connor, *High Court's '9 Men' Were a Surprise to One*, N.Y. TIMES, October 5, 1983.

3.   The National Association of Women Lawyers collects data from the nation's largest law firms on issues of inequality and publishes the *Survey on Retention and Promotion of Women in Law Firms* each year, available at https://www.nawl.org/p/cm/ld/fid=82# surveys. Select a handful of these surveys from different points in time and compare the data. What trends do you notice? What, if anything, has changed?

4.   When you think about female leaders in the legal profession, who are some of the women who come to mind? Create a list of these individuals. If the list is short, spend some time researching the names of women who serve in leadership roles in your state's bar association, in the local legal community, on your state supreme court, or other judicial bodies. Look at your own law school. Are there women who occupy leadership roles today or in the past?

5.   Does being a leader in the legal profession require being a dean of a law school, a judge, a general counsel, or managing partner of a law firm? Do you agree that sometimes leaving the practice of law is itself a form of leadership? What are some other forms of leadership that might be less obvious?

JUSTIN LEVINSON & DANIELLE YOUNG, *IMPLICIT GENDER BIAS IN THE LEGAL PROFESSION: AN EMPIRICAL STUDY*

18 DUKE JOURNAL OF GENDER, LAW, AND POLICY 1 (2010)

Levinson (pictured) is a leader in the field of implicit bias and the law and an expert in psychological decision-making in the legal system; his scholarship regularly employs experimental social science methodology. He is a professor of Law at the University of Hawaii at Manoa, William S. Richardson School of Law. Young earned her PhD from the University of Hawaii and is an Assistant Professor of Psychology at Manhattan College.

Introduction

Commentators have marveled at the continuing lack of gender diversity in the legal profession's most influential and honored positions. The passage of time, for years cited as a reason for hope, has failed to put a major dent in the huge disparities in both career advancement and pay. After achieving near equal numbers of male and female law school graduates for approximately two decades, the gap between men and women in law firms, legal academia, and the judiciary remains stark.

* * *

Scholarship focusing on the continuing gender gap has been detailed and interdisciplinary, offering a variety of potential explanations for the continued problem. Of these explanations, the most convincing have been science-based, relying on the powerful role of implicit gender stereotypes. Scholars have argued that due to negative stereotypes portraying women either as workplace cutthroats or, conversely, as secretaries or housewives, decision-makers continue to subordinate women to men in the highest levels of the legal profession. Despite these compelling arguments, many of which are grounded in social science theory, no empirical studies have tested whether implicit gender bias might explain the disproportionately low number of women attorneys in leadership roles.

In order to test the hypothesis that implicit gender bias drives the continued subordination of women in the legal profession, we designed and conducted an empirical study. The study tested whether people hold implicit gender stereotypes of women in the legal profession, and further tested whether these implicit stereotypes predict discriminatory decision-making. Specifically, the experiment consisted of several measures. First, based on the stereotype of male leaders and women clerical workers, we created and conducted a new Implicit Association Test (IAT), the "Judge/Gender IAT," a reaction-time based measure that tests whether people hold implicit associations between men and judges and women and paralegals. Next, due to the stereotype of men as professionals and women as homemakers, we employed a well-known IAT that tests whether people associate men with the workplace and women with the home and family. In addition to testing for implicit gender bias in the legal setting, we also tested whether gender stereotypes predict biased decision-making. We thus included three additional gender-based measures in our study: a law firm hiring measure (participants were asked to select a candidate to hire), a judicial appointments measure (participants were asked to rank the desirability of masculine and feminine traits in appellate judges), and a law student organization budget cut measure (participants were asked to reallocate funds in response to budget cuts).

The results of the study were both concerning and hopeful. As predicted, we found that a diverse group of both male and female law students implicitly associated judges with men, not women, and also associated women with the home and family. For these implicit measures, results of the study indicated that law students were much like other studied populations in related IAT studies: implicit gender biases were pervasive. In addition, the results showed that for both male and female participants, their implicit gender biases predicted some, but not all, of their decisions on the remaining studies. For example, the more strongly male participants associated judges with men in the Judge/Gender IAT, the more they preferred that appellate judges possess masculine (compared to feminine) characteristics. This result demonstrates that implicit gender biases can affect decision-making.

The results of the remaining studies offered hope, however. Participants were frequently able to resist their implicit biases and make decisions in gender-neutral ways. In fact, for the resume study, male law student participants even preferred female candidates to male candidates and held other pro-female job attitudes. Additionally, for the budget cut study, law student participants were no more likely to cut funds from a women's organization than from other organizations. Taken together, the results of our study highlight two conflicting sides of the ongoing gender debate: first, that the power of implicit gender biases persists, even in the next generation of lawyers; and second, that the emergence of a new generation of egalitarian law students may offer some hope for the future.

* * *

II.   Gender Stereotypes and the Legal Profession

* * *

B.   A Brief Primer on Gender Stereotypes

Before turning to legal scholarship linking gender stereotypes to the continuing subordination of women in the legal profession and beyond, we first provide a social science-based overview of gender stereotypes. One of the most telling facts about stereotypes is that they emerge early in life, often influencing children as young as three years old. These impressionable children, who are constantly engaged in interpreting the world around them, quickly learn to ascribe certain characteristics to members of distinct ethnic and social groups. Such associations derive from cultural and social beliefs, and are learned directly from multiple sources, including the children's parents, peers, and the media. As the children grow older, their stereotypes harden. Although they may develop non-biased (explicit) views of the world, their stereotypes remain largely unchanged and become implicit (or automatic). In the context of gender stereotypes, children are likely to learn at an early age that men are "competent, rational, assertive, independent, objective, and self confident," and women are "emotional, submissive, dependent, tactful, and gentle."

Once adults have ingrained implicit biases, the stereotypes they learned as children continue to affect the way they perceive the world. That is, people perceive information in ways that conform to their stereotypes. Gary Blasi provides two brief exercises that help illustrate how the simple associations people learn as children affect the way they think about gender and career: First, "try to imagine, in sequence, a baseball player, a trial lawyer, a figure skater, and a U.S. Supreme Court justice—without a specific gender or race. . . ." Did you succeed? Next, "try to imagine a carpenter. When you have that image settled in your mind, describe the color of her hair." Did you pause or do a double-take? Blasi's exercises help illustrate the simple gender-based hurdles the mind must make in even basic career related situations. If we immediately picture a man when we think about a trial lawyer, for example, what might that mean for women seeking to reach the pinnacle of the profession?

Although Blasi's examples are concerning enough, gender stereotypes can play even more complicated mental tricks than the previous perception tasks illustrate. They have, for example, been shown to affect the way people make judgments about others and even change the way people remember information. In a study testing how implicit gender stereotypes can change the way people evaluate others' traits and behaviors, Mahzarin Banaji and her colleagues primed gender stereotypes by exposing participants to phrases related to the female stereotype of dependence (e.g. some participants saw the phrase "never leaves home"). Banaji and her colleagues predicted that this simple act, exposing participants to dependence related phrases, would trigger a broader set of female stereotypes that would affect the way participants would later evaluate women's behaviors. Thus, after telling participants that they were beginning an unrelated study, the researchers asked participants to read short stories about a person (either male or female) and rate the person's level of dependence, inhibition, insecurity, and passivity (all confirmed female stereotypes). The results showed that study participants who previously had their gender stereotypes activated were more likely (than a control group whose stereotypes were not activated) to evaluate a woman's behavior as dependent, inhibited, insecure, passive, and weak. The study demonstrates the dangerousness and sensitivity of activated gender stereotypes, particularly their ability to change the way people interpret and attribute women's behavior.

A second study confirms the dangerousness of gender stereotypes, this time by focusing on how gender stereotypes can actually facilitate the creation of false memories. In this study, Alison Lenton and her colleagues presented participants with a list of words. Some of the word lists were stereotypic of women (such as secretary and nurse), and others were stereotypic of men (such as lawyer and soldier). After briefly distracting participants, the researchers asked the participants to identify the words they had seen. Results showed that participants used gender stereotypes in creating false memories. That is, they more often (incorrectly) reported that they had seen gender stereotyped words than non-gender-stereotyped words. Results also indicated that these false memories were elicited implicitly (i.e., automatically). Despite the nature of their errors, most participants were completely unaware of the gender stereotype theme of the word lists. The researchers expressed concern that the implicit creation of stereotype-consistent false memories may help to explain the "self-perpetuating nature of stereotypes and their resistance to change."

Research on stereotype biased perception, information processing, and memory each demonstrate the dangerous potential that implicit gender biases may have in the employer-employee relationship. We next turn to legal scholarship and review the ways legal scholars have argued that these gender stereotypes might explain continuing gender disparities.

C.   Do Gender Stereotypes Explain Gender Disparities?

Commentators have offered a variety of explanations for the continuing gender disparities, and the debate continues. Some of the most interesting scholarly arguments range from those downplaying the numbers in light of the potential promise of future amelioration (claiming the low number of women in law school thirty years ago explains the small number of women judges today) to relying on gender differences in intentional career choices (e.g. women disproportionately "opt out" of the leadership race). Perhaps the most compelling subset of scholarship, however, focuses on the ways in which gender stereotypes about women may affect women's hiring and career advancement and ultimately exclude large numbers of women from leadership positions.

Legal scholarship discussing the impact of gender stereotypes on the leadership progression of women has been both diverse and comprehensive, and taken together it tends to support three main themes: first, stereotypes linking women to the home and family affect their prospects for career advancement; second, stereotypes about women's work styles, character traits, and job competencies hinder their ability to land and advance in high level leadership positions; and third, because certain jobs are consciously or unconsciously perceived as male jobs, females will be evaluated less favorably for those positions. This subsection provides a brief overview of legal scholarship that connects gender stereotypes to women's limited career advancement, focusing on the three main themes stated above.

The first theme that has emerged in legal scholarship is that stereotypes linking women to the home and family affect women's prospects for hiring and career advancement. Deborah Rhode, a leading scholar in examining gender disparities in the workplace, argues that this "subtle side of sexism" manifests in a variety of automatic ways that may be neither obvious nor intentional. For example, gender stereotypes connecting women to the home and family may cause colleagues to provide different attributions for men and women during a variety of common workplace circumstances. Rhode explains, "[I]f a working mother leaves the office early, her colleagues may infer that the reason involves family obligations. A working father's absence may not trigger the same assumption." Relying on this example and others, Rhode argues that gender stereotypes account for a significant portion of the leadership gender disparity.

Joan Williams also argues that the deeply held cognitive association connecting women to the home and family continually affects the workplace assumptions made by employers. Williams uses the example of a traditional husband and wife couple who work for the same "high-hours employer": "[a]fter she had a baby, she was sent home at 5:30 p.m. every night—she had a baby to take care of. He, on the other hand, was kept later than before the baby's birth—he had a family to support." Williams also provides another example from case law: a woman who had children was not considered for a promotion because her superiors assumed she would not want a position that required travel. The impact of Rhode and Williams' examples is intuitive: if people automatically and unintentionally use stereotypes to help them evaluate women in the workplace, these stereotypes will undoubtedly have negative impacts on career opportunities.

The second theme that has emerged in legal scholarship is that stereotypes about women's work styles, character traits, and job competencies hinder women's ability to land and advance in high level leadership positions. Although this theme is related to the first in that they are both based on gender stereotypes that hinder career advancement, it differs in that the first theme deals with women's perceived choices (commitment to the home and family), while the second theme relies on generalizations about women's personalities (work styles and character traits). Williams provides two clear examples of how character or trait based gender stereotypes may arise in the workplace: first, assertiveness in a female makes her perceived as "a bitch," while for a male it is perceived as a sign of strength; and second, social bonding behavior among men is considered to be work related (he's mentoring or rainmaking), but is considered to be frivolous among women (she's chatting or gossiping).

These pervasive and pernicious character-related stereotypes begin a complex interaction in which women may attempt to dispel stereotypes by changing workplace behavior. As Holning Lau proposes, a female lawyer concerned with stereotypes of female passivity, for example, may choose not to talk about her children "because her colleagues may be prone to infer that women who adhere to nurturing stereotypes also adhere to passivity stereotypes."

* * *

The third theme that has emerged in legal scholarship is that because some jobs are consciously or unconsciously perceived as male jobs, females will be evaluated less favorably for those positions. As Diane Bridge contends, because males have traditionally dominated certain positions, potential employers' choices will be affected by gender stereotypes about the ideal candidate for those positions. This type of stereotype effect becomes magnified in leadership jobs. Williams summarizes, "when a task or setting is stereotypically masculine, as are most 'high-powered' jobs, the setting will activate assumptions that associate competence with masculinity, thereby increasing the perceived competence of men." Thus, in addition to the litany of stereotypes that may hinder women professionals generally, the highest-level women professionals may face an additional layer of stereotypes related to the association between certain high-level jobs and masculinity. One might expect these masculine stereotypes to be most potent in powerful legal jobs, such as appellate judge positions.

Legal scholarship thus argues that women are hindered from career advancement by stereotypes that peg them as home and family-focused, as well as those that construe their personalities as weak and gossip-driven (or conversely, as workplace cutthroats). Additionally, women in contention for high-level positions are hindered by job-specific associations people have between certain jobs and the men that have historically held those positions. This powerful framework of stereotypes led us to develop our empirical study, which tested not only whether people hold many of the implicit gender biases described in this section, but whether those biases lead to discriminatory decision-making in the legal profession. Before detailing the study, however, we first describe existing empirical work that has investigated gender bias in the legal profession.

III. Examining Gender Disparities in the Law

A. Empirical Studies

As gender disparities among practicing lawyers and judges have continued despite twenty years of near numerical equality among law school graduates, a limited number of scholars have begun devising empirical studies designed to investigate the sources of these gender disparities. This subsection reviews the few existing empirical studies on gender disparities in the legal profession and also reviews related studies of gender disparities in academia. This review concludes that women are disproportionately affected in the legal profession and academia due to workplace expectations of masculinity and in-group preferences among male hiring attorneys. No empirical studies, however, have examined implicit gender biases among members of the legal profession.

A fascinating study of gender bias in law firm hiring investigated the relationship between hiring criteria and ultimate hiring decisions. Elizabeth Gorman hypothesized that the masculinity and femininity of law firms' published hiring criteria would be related to gender disparities in hiring decisions. To pursue this hypothesis in a sample of over 700 firms during one hiring year, Gorman first reviewed each firm's published hiring standards. Using previously established research on masculinity and femininity in language, Gorman counted the number of stereotypically masculine (e.g. assertive, decisive, or energetic) and feminine traits (e.g.

cooperative, friendly, or verbally oriented) in each firm's published standards. She then compared the number of masculine and feminine traits for each firm's standards to the number of male and female associates they hired. The results of the study showed that for every additional masculine characteristic listed by a firm, a woman's chance of getting hired decreased by approximately five percent. This finding was significant both for entry-level attorney hires as well as for lateral hires. Gorman explains this result by focusing on the power of gender stereotypes.

* * *

Further analysis revealed that firms that relied on more feminine hiring criteria were only more likely to hire women attorneys at the entry level. They did not hire more female "lateral" (i.e. higher level) attorneys. Gorman analyzed this result by focusing on the strength of gender stereotypes at the more senior levels of law firms. Although gender stereotypes at entry hiring levels may still pose a formidable obstacle for women, as her study showed, the additional connection between the highest level jobs and historically male roles may create an additional hurdle.

* * *

Finally, Gorman analyzed whether law firms with female hiring partners were more likely than firms with male hiring partners to hire women associates. The study's results confirmed this hypothesis. Firms with women hiring partners were in fact more likely to hire more female entry-level candidates. However, this effect diminished in firms where women had already achieved a greater gender balance among firm partners. This result confirms that the gender of the primary decision-maker matters, an effect consistent with what social psychologists call "in-group bias."

In a separate project, Gorman collaborated with Julie Kmec to investigate women's promotion to partner in corporate law firms. Examining data on a national basis, Gorman and Kmec compared law firms' hiring of incoming associates and tracked the firms' partnership decisions when that associate group became eligible for partner. The results of the study found consistent gender bias at the upper levels of the corporate firms. Women who were hired as entry level associates by firms were much less likely than their male counterparts to be promoted to partner. Gorman and Kmec predicted that these findings would likely hold true in other high level jobs both inside and outside of the legal field. As long as decision-makers consciously or automatically rely on gender stereotypes in making hiring and promotion decisions, Gorman and Kmec concluded, continuing disparities should be expected.

* * *

Notwithstanding this scholarly progress in empirically understanding gender inequality, studies have yet to investigate whether implicit biases might help explain the perpetuation of gender disparities within the legal profession. We thus devised an implicit social cognition-based empirical study designed to test the role of implicit gender stereotypes in the legal profession. The next subsection describes how we devised a study that attempted to bridge scholarly discourse on gender stereotypes with existing knowledge of gender disparities in the legal profession and academia.

B. Crafting an Empirical Study that Responds to Gender Disparity Research

In planning our empirical study, we established two goals: first, test whether members of the legal community harbor implicit gender biases, and second, test whether gender stereotypes affect decision-making at various levels of the legal profession. These goals, of course, were influenced by both the strengths and limitations of existing discourse. For the first goal, to test whether members of the legal community harbor implicit gender biases, we strived to respond as directly as possible to the themes set forth by legal scholars. That is, we set out to craft a test that would examine whether members of the legal community implicitly associate women with home and family, as well as whether they associate certain high level legal positions (such as judges) with males. As we describe in the next subsections, we turned to the science of implicit social cognition (and in particular, the Implicit Association Test) to find an empirical test that would allow us to achieve our goal.

For the second goal, to test whether gender stereotypes affect decision-making at various level of the legal profession, we responded to the literature by choosing to test three separate potentially discriminatory areas of the legal profession. First, in light of Gorman's findings demonstrating that masculine and feminine job-related expectations might be at least partially to blame for some of the legal profession's gender disparities, we decided to test directly whether, for leadership positions in law, people believe that the best legal thinkers should have masculine rather than feminine characteristics. For this area, we decided to focus on the relationship between masculinity and femininity and one of the most renowned positions in the legal profession, the appellate judgeship. Second, considering that Rheinpreis and others have found that some decision-makers evaluate male-named CVs more favorably than identical female-named CVs, we resolved to create our own resume test to see if members of the legal community display the same biases when evaluating law student resumes. And third, because implicit stereotypes have been shown to predict decisions such as economic decision-making (moving funds away from already disadvantaged groups), we decided to test whether members of the legal community, during a hypothetical fund shortage, would disproportionately shift funds away from women's lawyers organizations. Each of these studies would also allow us to examine whether in-group biases affect male and female participants' decisions.

In creating our study, we also needed to decide whom to test. In the case of gender bias in the legal profession, there are several possibilities. One might choose to focus on existing decision-makers (those professionals already making hiring and promotion decisions, such as law firm partners or members of a state judicial selection committee), or on future decision-makers (those who are likely to be making the key decisions in the future, such as young lawyers or law students). We were interested in both groups. However, due to practical considerations, such as the ease of participant recruitment, we chose to focus our study on future decision-makers. Because we are university-based researchers, obtaining a law student sample—and based on recent history, likely a strong sample of future decision-makers—would not be difficult.

* * *

IV. The Empirical Study

We designed an empirical study to test whether implicit gender biases may be driving gender discrimination in the legal profession. This Section reports on the details of study, including the research methods, study materials, and results.

* * *

B. Methods

Participants were recruited from the law school library at the University of Hawai'i William S. Richardson School of Law. Fifty-five participants completed the study. Data for five of the participants was dropped because those participants had lived outside of the United States for more than ten years. The remaining fifty participants included eight 1L's, thirty 2L's, and twelve 3L's. There was gender balance in the participant pool. Twenty-four of the participants were male and twenty-six were female. The population was ethnically diverse. Forty-six percent identified themselves as Asian American, twenty-four percent as White/Euro-American, twelve percent as multi-racial, eight percent as Native Hawaiian, six percent as Pacific Islander, two percent as Latino/Hispanic, and two percent identified as Other. The mean age of the participants was 26.48. Two female research assistants recruited participants and conducted the study. Participants completed the study in a laboratory with two separate computer stations. Participants first completed the non-implicit measures, which were given to them in counterbalanced order. Next, participants completed the IATs, which were also given to them in counterbalanced order. At the end of the study the participants provided demographic information.

* * *

C.   Results

1.   Implicit Associations between Judge/Male and Paralegal/Female

As predicted, the first IAT, the Judge/Gender IAT, confirmed the hypothesis that law students hold implicit gender biases related to leadership positions in the legal profession. Participants displayed a significant association between Judge and Male (M=822.48) compared to Judge and Female (M=1035.18), producing a significant IAT effect (D=.23, t(49)=3.66, p=.001). The results support the conclusion that law students implicitly associate men with judges, and women with paralegals, and therefore harbor an "implicit male leader prototype" in the legal setting.

2.   Implicit Associations between Work/Male and Home/Female

As hypothesized, the second IAT, the Gender/Career IAT, confirmed the hypothesis that law students hold implicit gender biases connecting women with the home and family. Participants displayed a significant association between Male and Career (M=850.37) compared to Female and Career (M=1101.60), producing a significant IAT effect (D=.33, t(49)=6.87, p>.001). The results of this study support the conclusion that law students implicitly associate men with work and women with the home and family. These results replicated previous research outside of the legal profession.

3.   Relationship Between the Judge/Gender IAT and Gender/Career IAT

Because we created a new IAT, the Judge/Gender IAT, we were interested in whether it measured implicit constructs similar to the already established Career/Gender IAT. We thus conducted a correlational analysis. This analysis found that the two IAT scores (Judge/Gender, Career/Gender) were weakly, but significantly, correlated (R=.33, p=.02). This result suggests that while the two IATs tap into a similar general construct (gender bias), each IAT also measures a unique association.

4.   The IATs and the Modern Sexism Scale

We also tested whether the responses to either of the IATs would be related to responses on the Modern Sexism Scale, in which participants report explicit gender attitudes. As predicted, neither of the IATs were correlated with the Modern Sexism Scale (p>.1). This result is expected, first because implicit and explicit measures are intended to test different constructs, and second because the Modern Sexism Scale is designed to test responses to somewhat different societal issues than the IATs we implemented. The difference between the responses to the IATs and the Modern Sexism Scale demonstrates the importance of investigating both implicit gender biases and explicit gender attitudes.

5.   Judicial Appointments

For the judicial appointments measure, participants rated masculine and feminine judge attributes to be equally important (Mdiff=.5, t(49)=.47, p>.1). However, individuals' scores were not correlated (R=.162, p>.1), suggesting that there were individual differences in how attributes were rated. We thus were able to investigate whether implicit biases from the IATs predicted gender bias in the responses to the judicial appointments measure, as we hypothesized they would. A difference score was created by subtracting feminine judge attributes from male judge attributes, so that higher difference scores indicated a preference for masculine judge traits. A multiple regression analysis was run to determine if implicit scores (from both the Judge/Gender and the Gender/Career IATs) predicted an emphasis on feminine or masculine traits.

The overall regression model was significant (F=6.06, p>.001), and explains 41% of the variance of the dependent variable (R²=.41). The main effects of gender of participant (b=5.307, t=3.04, p<.05), Career/Gender IAT score (b=−18.42, t=−4.93, p<.05), and Judge/Gender IAT score (b=9.727, t=3.21, p<.05) all significantly predicted the difference between importance for masculine and feminine judge attributes. The interactions between participant gender and Career/Gender IAT (b=20.79, t=3.753, p<.05) and participant gender and Judge/Gender IAT (b=−10.686, t=−2.511, p<.05) were also significant predictors. Importantly, these interaction effects tell us that implicit bias predicted responses on the judicial appointments measure, but that the results differed depending on the gender of the participant. Therefore, we report the results separately for male and female participants.

For the male participant regression model, there were two interesting results demonstrating the IATs' predictive validity, but in different directions. First, as implicit associations between male and judge increased, ratings of masculine judge attributes increased as compared to female judge attributes (B=9.727). That is, the more implicit bias the participants displayed linking judges to males, the more they preferred masculine judge attributes. This finding supported our hypothesis that implicit gender bias would predict biased decision-making. Second, as implicit associations between home and female increased on the Career-Gender IAT, ratings of feminine judge attributes increased as compared to masculine judge attributes (B=−18.416). Put simply, the more implicit bias male participants displayed linking men to career, the more they preferred feminine judge attributes. The direction of this finding was thus not as we predicted.

For the female participant regression model, there were also two results demonstrating predictive validity, but similar to the male participant regression, the results were in different directions. First, as implicit associations between female and home increased on the Career/Gender IAT, the gap between ratings of masculine and feminine judge attributes increased (B=2.375). Put simply, the more implicit bias the participants displayed linking men to career, the more they preferred masculine judge attributes. The direction of this finding was as we predicted. Second, as implicit associations between male and judge increased on the Judge/Gender IAT, ratings of feminine judge attributes increased as compared to masculine judge attributes (B=-.959). That is, the more implicit bias female participants displayed linking men to career, the more they preferred feminine judge attributes. The direction of this finding was thus not as we predicted. These interesting predictive validity results deserve further exploration, a task we will consider in subsection D.

6.   Resume Study

Consistent with our hypothesis, participants hired the male and female job candidates at approximately the same rates, regardless of participant gender or the resume they saw (X^2=.00, p>.05; (X^2=2.35, p>.05). Ashley was hired slightly more (N=31) than David (N=19) for the summer position, although the difference was not statistically significant. The gender of the participants was also not a significant factor in determining which candidate was hired. However, there was a trend here as well: male participants hired Ashley more (N=17) than female participants (N=14), while female participants hired David more (N=12) than male participants (N=7). Male participants decided to hire Ashley more often when she was paired with an international resume (N=14) than with a business resume (N=4), suggesting that something about the female candidate with an international interest appeared to impress participants.

Ashley was rated higher than David on all ratings of the resume, though many of these differences were small. Paired t-tests demonstrated that participants rated Ashley as more likely to succeed as a summer associate (Mdiff=.18, t(49)=2.64, p>.05) and to receive an offer at the end of the summer (Mdiff=.12, t(49)=2.20, p>.05). Participants also gave Ashley a significantly higher overall rating (Mdiff=.180, t(49)=2.137, p>.05). These ratings demonstrate that law students do not penalize female entry-level law candidates, and in some cases prefer them. This was true, of course, despite the implicit biases displayed by the participants.

A logistic regression was run to determine if either implicit measure predicted hiring decisions. The model did not approach significance (all p's>.1). This result indicates that participants' implicit biases did not likely affect their choice of resume.

* * *

D. Interpreting the Empirical Results

The results of our empirical study paint a picture of implicit gender bias in the legal profession that is both concerning and hopeful. The concerning part is that the law student participants consistently held implicit gender biases, and they did so on both the Judge/Gender IAT and the Career/Gender IAT. Contextualized within legal scholarship on gender stereotypes, these results confirm that law students associate men with career and women with home and family, as well as hold implicit male prototypes for the position of judge. Considered within the broader social science discourse, these findings document the existence of implicit gender bias in the legal profession, and also show that the job specific associations people hold can be implicit in nature. The hopeful part of the results is that the participants were mostly able to resist their implicit biases and make decisions in non-biased ways. Namely, participants did not discriminate against women in the judicial appointments measure, the resume study, or the budget cut measure. In fact, in some instances, such as in the resume study, participants rated the female candidate more favorably than the male candidate. The remainder of this subsection interprets the results in more detail.

The results indicate that implicit gender bias affected the participants on both IAT measures. But what do these results mean? As social psychologists have surmised, implicit associations often predict the way people act and make important decisions. For example, one study found that participants who showed more implicit bias on a White/Black IAT acted differently towards blacks, and a subsequent study by different researchers found that it even predicted discriminatory behavior (such as making racial epithets). A study on medical decision-making and race found that doctors with high implicit racial bias were less likely to order certain medical procedures for their black patients. And, directly relevant to gender bias in the legal profession, a researcher found that employers in Sweden who harbored implicit biases related to Arabs were less likely to call Arab candidates for job interviews. If law students hold the implicit biases that were documented in this study, we must wonder whether they are truly able to navigate their professional lives without acting on those stereotypes. Studies of gender bias in law firm partnership decisions, for example, heighten this concern.

Building on the research linking implicit biases to discriminatory actions, we designed the non-implicit measures to test whether law student participants would act on their implicit biases or whether they might resist them. The majority of our results support the argument that our law student participants successfully resisted or compensated for the implicit biases we tested. First, they did not act in a discriminatory manner to women. And second, the results of their IATs did not predict their decisions on the non-implicit measures, other than the judicial appointments measure. And even for that particular measure, only some of the results indicated that the IATs predicted gender discrimination in the expected manner. Other results showed that participants sometimes acted in ways directly contrary to their implicit biases. There are several possibilities that might explain why the participants in our study harbored implicit biases but for the most part did not act on them. Here, we briefly consider these possibilities, focusing on the two strongest rationales.

First, participants may have been successful in resisting their implicit biases if they were implicitly motivated to control the influence of prejudicial stereotypes. Researchers have found that some participants can overcome their implicit biases either because they have high implicit motivations to avoid prejudice or they are temporarily influenced by their egalitarian surroundings. Jack Glaser and Eric Knowles, for example, had participants take unique IATs that were designed first to test people's implicit motivation to avoid prejudice, and second to test how much they implicitly considered themselves prejudiced. They also had participants complete a "shooter bias" task, which measures how people respond to visual images of black and white men with guns and non-gun objects in a video game-like setting, asking them either to shoot armed men as quickly as possible or to press a "safety" button when unarmed men appear. Glaser and Knowles found that the more the participants were implicitly motivated to avoid prejudice, the less bias they displayed on the shooter bias measure. Furthermore, they showed that the worst performers on the shooter bias measure were those who not only had low implicit motivation to control prejudice, but also did not implicitly consider themselves as prejudiced.

The researchers therefore demonstrated that it is possible for people to hold harmful implicit biases and simultaneously hold egalitarian implicit norms that allow them to resist these biases. Related research has supported the idea that people who hold implicit egalitarian norms (even if they are only temporarily activated) can resist stereotypic thought activation. Considered in the context of the results of our study, it is possible that a large part of our law student sample was implicitly motivated to resist gender bias. Although it might seem unlikely that the majority of our participants would hold such implicit views when the majority of the broader population likely does not, we might note that law students generally, and these law students in particular, could have higher than average levels of implicit motivation to control prejudice. After all, research has demonstrated that simply being in the presence of "egalitarian-minded others" can inhibit prejudice. Without having tested for implicit motivation to control bias, however, we cannot speculate further as to whether that might account for the some of the results. Future studies on law students could test this possibility.

A second possible explanation why our participants were able to control the effects of their implicit biases is that they may have suspected the purpose of the study.

* * *

V. Future Directions

A. The Next Generation of Research

Although our research provided detailed information about implicit gender biases of law school students, further empirical testing should continue to investigate implicit gender bias in the legal profession. Conducting additional empirical research would provide both an opportunity to test new hypotheses about implicit gender bias in the legal profession, as well as allow a chance to improve on the current study.

* * *

ALICE WOOLLEY AND ELYSA DARLING, *NASTY WOMEN AND THE RULE OF LAW*

51 UNIVERSITY OF SAN FRANCISCO LAW REVIEW 507 (2017)

Woolley (above) is a Justice on the Alberta Court of Queen's Bench. She previously was Professor of Law and former Dean-Academic at the University of Calgary Faculty of Law. Darling (below) is a graduate student at the University of Calgary Faculty of Law. She currently acts as a consultant, often advising private sector companies on working with Indigenous communities.

* * *

Introduction

No one enters the legal profession expecting social popularity—or, at least, no one should. But recent events create the impression that women lawyers face more than the generic suggestions of dishonesty, untrustworthiness, greed, and adversarialism that typify anti-lawyer criticisms. For women lawyers, attacks and criticisms are not only role-related (arising from her occupation in a professional role) but also personal, specific, and gendered. Lawyers in general are labeled as morally troubling; women lawyers risk being specifically and personally identified as morally transgressive, even when performing acts expected of a person in their role. Women who take on law firm leadership, advocate in notorious trials, lead teams in complex corporate transactions, demonstrate political ambitions or political leadership—that is, women who do things that lawyers might normally be expected to do—risk gendered and hostile forms of criticism. They risk being labeled unlikable, unattractive, unfeminine, unpleasant, and immoral—basically, a bitch. Such attacks are not certain to occur. They may be more likely for some women than for others and the form and tone that attacks take almost certainly vary with context. But a woman who chooses to enter the legal profession does not just risk generic unpopularity—she also risks being labeled a "nasty woman."

That is the premise of this paper. We do not prove that women lawyers risk being attacked in this way, although we note some examples of those who have. We also respond to some objections to this premise and discuss the extent to which gender equality has eluded the legal profession to this day, even in comparison to other professions. Primarily, we focus on why gendered and personal attacks on women might occur. Why did the criticisms of Marcia Clark's handling of the OJ Simpson Trial have an unpleasant sexist undercurrent? Why do commentators discussing the highly successful Canadian defense lawyer Marie Henein invariably focus on her high heels, clothes, and attractive appearance? Why was Hillary Clinton attacked in vicious and misogynist ways from the very beginning of her time in the public eye and throughout her final, unsuccessful run for the Presidency?

Our thesis is that attacks on women lawyers arise from the intersection between the normative structure of the lawyer's role and sexist stereotypes. The lawyer's function in achieving the social settlement of law, including maintaining the rule of law, requires lawyers to occupy positions of moral ambiguity and power. Lawyers have the privilege and responsibility to pursue the interests of their clients within the bounds of legality, even where doing so inflicts harm or violates valued norms of ordinary morality. That role makes all lawyers unpopular. However, when this is combined with prescriptive gender stereotypes about appropriate conduct for women, it makes women lawyers seem not merely morally dubious, but personally dangerous. The perceived danger presented by a woman lawyer connects to an individual woman where *she, specifically,* presents the danger, rather than simply being part of a group or category of dangerous people, and *she* invites the moral outrage. The dissatisfaction and criticism arising from a woman lawyer in her role will not be directed at lawyers, or even at women lawyers; it will be directed just at this one particular "nasty woman."

This paper sets out this thesis, and considers its ramifications for women, the legal profession, and the rule of law that the lawyer's role is designed in significant part to achieve. The paper simplifies the analysis insofar as it discusses the problem of attacks on women without separating out additional complexities and issues for women of color or LGBTQ women. It also does not consider the question of whether the issue and analysis here would apply to men of color. In our view, these additional questions merit consideration. Our analysis applies to women generally, but issues of race, gender and sexual orientation mean that the issue is more complex than our analysis reflects. We also suspect that men of color experience similar problems, as suggested by some of the racist attacks on President Obama. This paper starts the conversation, but does not conclude it.

* * *

Gender Diversity and Inequality in the Legal Profession

* * *

Women lawyers also appear to be subject to gendered forms of criticism as seen when they appear in public roles, particularly those roles that involve challenging norms or standards, like advocates or politicians, or when they involve seeking power. To illustrate, after shifting the focus of her attention to safer ground as First Lady, Michelle Obama has become a beloved public figure. However, during President Obama's 2008 campaign, when she criticized America's history on matters of race she "was labeled by her critics as angry, bitter and militant." Similarly, harsh criticism and media coverage of Marcia Clark during the trial of OJ Simpson has been recently critiqued as reflecting double standards and sexism, an assessment that a review of contemporaneous records makes difficult to refute.

* * *

Gloria Allred, a Los Angeles attorney specializing in notorious cases of women who allege mistreatment by famous men, is regularly labeled a "fame-whore." Googling "Gloria Allred bitch" generates an impressive list of blogs and commentaries stating the same. Janet Reno's recent death generated many admiring eulogistic articles, and during her time as Attorney General she enjoyed significant positive press. However, during the fall-out over the disastrous FBI assault on the Branch Davidian compound in Waco, Texas, the media criticized her personal demeanor, seeing her as "abrasive," "cool . . . to the point of iciness," and "testy under questioning."

The most remarkable criticisms have, however, been reserved for Hillary Clinton. Considering only her career up to 2008, it is not difficult to find comments and criticisms apt for a sexism playbook:

It's not that [Hillary Clinton]'s an accomplished modern woman. It's just that she's grating, abrasive and boastful. There's a certain familiar order of things, and the notion of a coequal couple in the White House is a little offensive to men and women.

[Hillary Clinton] is a bitch . . . [t]hat's the only thing [Newt] ever said about her.

Rush Limbaugh called Clinton the woman with the "testicle lock box" and MSNBC commentator Tucker Carlson stated that "[t]here's just something about her that feels castrating, overbearing and scary," and, on another article, he stated that "when she comes on television, I involuntarily cross my legs." Finally, radio talk show host Don Imus has often referred to Clinton as "that buck tooth witch Satan" and Bill Clinton's "fat, ugly wife, Satan."

After her 2007 victory in the New Hampshire primary, when she said "This is very personal for me. It's not just political. It's not just public," Senator Clinton was ridiculed by political commentators who argued that "[s]he pretended to cry, the women felt sorry for her . . . and asked whether Hillary [could] cry her way back to the White House."

Hillary Clinton has been subject to even more vitriolic descriptions: "power-hungry," "castrating," "Hitlerian," and "feminazi." During her presidential campaign [in 2008] she coped with sales of a Clinton nutcracker, charges that she reminded men of a scolding mother or first wife, and hecklers with signs demanding "Iron my shirt."

Those types of criticisms did not abate in the recent campaign. As Rebecca Solnit recently summarized:

Clinton was constantly berated for qualities rarely mentioned in male politicians, including ambition—something, it's safe to assume, she has in common with everyone who ever ran for elected office. It's possible, according to *Psychology Today's* headline, that she is 'pathologically ambitious.' She was criticized for having a voice. While Bernie Sanders railed and Trump screamed and snickered, the Fox commentator Brit Hume complained about Clinton's 'sharp, lecturing tone,' which, he said, was 'not so attractive,' while MSNBC's Lawrence O'Donnell gave her public instructions on how to use a microphone, Bob Woodward bitched that she was 'screaming' and Bob Cusack, the editor of the political newspaper *The Hill*, said: "When Hillary Clinton raises her voice, she loses."

* * *

Even women lawyers who receive relatively positive press are often described in highly gendered ways. Hannah Brenner and Renee Newman Knake observe in a media study that women nominees to the Supreme Court tend to have their appearance and family life commented on somewhat more than do male nominees. Well-known celebrity divorce lawyer Laura Wasser is noted for her clothes and appearance and was described in a 2016 Financial Times article as having "a ready smile and lustrous brown hair reaching down her back." The Financial Times noted TMZ's descriptions of her as "super hot" and "the hottest attorney chick I have ever seen." Coverage of whistleblower Jesselyn Radack routinely discusses her family and her appearance—her matching nail polish, her "unruly blonde hair" and her "calf-high leather boots." Media coverage of well-known Canadian criminal defense lawyer Marie Henein fixates on her clothes and looks, describing how she "sweep[s] past in a stunning black dress and designer jacket," with a "slash of scarlet lipstick" and "patent stilettos." Henein, however, has been criticized as "not a feminist" for her successful defense of accused rapists.

Implicit in the discussion of these examples are two claims. First, that these examples reflect sexism and misogyny, as opposed to being justified criticisms of problematic conduct. Second, that these examples relate to the fact that the women are lawyers, rather than simply being sexist attacks directed at women who achieve positions of prominence or power. Both of these claims can be challenged; for every 2016 article suggesting that Hillary Clinton faced sexism in her campaign for president is another article suggesting that her defeat was unrelated to sexism or misogyny. Many of the women we note could be legitimately criticized for aspects of their professional choices. Further, critics could quickly identify women outside of law and politics that have faced similar attacks, such as Megyn Kelly and the women of Gamergate. It is also possible to argue that the attacks on Hillary Clinton do not relate to the fact that she is a lawyer; that she is one is coincidental, not causative.

With respect to the first challenge, our claim is not that sexist criticism and attacks on women never reflect legitimate grounds of moral or political disagreement. Rather, our assertion is that the tone, intensity, certainty, and nature of the criticisms directed at these women go beyond any claimed substantive justification. In essence, if a woman behaved in exactly the same way as a man, any criticism leveled at her in tone and substance sounds very different—our criticisms of that woman can be characterized as sexist, and in some cases, misogynistic. We cannot prove that assertion; it flows from what we see when we consider the examples here and our personal experiences. To us, labeling Michelle Obama angry and bitter because she notes the existence of racism was both sexist and racist. Shifting attacks of Janet Reno from what she did in handling the Waco incident to emphasize her personal abrasiveness and coolness reflects traditional stereotypes employed against women in leadership roles. Critiquing Marcia Clark for her clothes, demeanor, and her "likability" reflects classic negative gender stereotypes. Gloria Allred's undoubted appreciation of media attention would be labeled differently if she were male—as suggested by comparing commentary about her to the discussion of lawyers such as Jim "The Hammer" Shapiro, one of the more notorious creators of aggressive lawyer advertising, who is criticized but not castigated.

The attacks on Hillary Clinton are in our view overtly and indefensibly misogynistic, and have been since she first entered public life. Even positive coverage of women lawyers that focuses on their appearance, clothes, and "hotness" belittles the professional capacity and accomplishments of those women and may set them up for future criticism. The woman who is sophisticated, well-dressed and attractive today, may become a self-promoting harlot if her legal work makes her more susceptible to criticism.

We believe that all women lawyers, whether famous or not, are susceptible to sexist attacks and criticisms of this type—even without the notoriety of the women we have used as examples here. If someone sees something different, we have no argument or tools to persuade him or her that our perception is the correct one. Our argument is, simply, if what we see is what is there, then why does that occur and what does it mean?

In relation to the second challenge, we acknowledge that women outside of law also experience sexist and misogynist attacks and criticism. We do not, however, think that means that the attacks and criticism of women in law are unrelated to their role. Professions other than law can be unpopular, but we still understand the unpopularity of lawyers in light of the work they do. Sexist attacks are inflicted on a range of women, but it is still worth considering why women lawyers experience them.

Importantly, women lawyers suffer such critiques due to the morally ambiguous and problematic nature of the lawyer's role—the role requires women to challenge or subvert accepted moral and social norms and, consequently, to violate prescriptive gendered stereotypes, making women lawyers susceptible to personal and sexist attacks. When women outside of law are attacked for challenging or subverting accepted moral and social norms, the criticisms support our thesis rather than challenge it—the reason for the attacks is in substance the same as the reason we suggest leads to such attacks on women lawyers. For example, Madonna is not a lawyer, but she has continually challenged conventional moral norms and standards, and exhibited ambition and agency over her own life. The "constant bullying and relentless abuse" inflicted on her as a consequence is, in our view, a different iteration of the phenomenon we describe here.

With respect to Hillary Clinton, we concede that she is an imperfect example of the phenomenon we discuss insofar as she has not been in active legal practice since the early 1990s. However, we believe that she remains relevant for our analysis. Notably, attacks on her have been directly connected to her professional work and status as a lawyer, both when she first came into the public eye and during the last presidential campaign. As noted earlier, her defense of a man accused of sexual assault was explicitly invoked as one of the reasons to view her with suspicion and distrust. Additionally, and more importantly, many of the arguments that we make apply to women in politics because law and politics are closely analogous.

As discussed below, the issues for women lawyers arise in significant part because of the role lawyers play in relation to achieving the social settlement of moral and political disagreements in law. Politicians also work to create that social settlement—indeed, politics is law's source; law is a product of politics.

To the extent that hostility towards women lawyers arises from their role, women politicians are likely to have similar problems. The attacks leveled at Hillary Clinton arise, therefore, from a position closely analogous to the lawyer's role and from her status as a lawyer. For that reason, we maintain her relevance to our analysis. Furthermore, considering Hillary Clinton's experiences is important, because it suggests how bad these sorts of attacks can get. Her experiences demonstrate just how vilified a woman lawyer can be.

Gender inequality in the legal profession is evidenced by generalized data indicating that women have decreased participation in the profession and lower levels of accomplishment than men, and by the common personal and sexist criticisms experiences by successful women lawyers. We are neither the first people to note this inequality nor the first people to consider explanations for it. Generally speaking, scholars observing and explaining gender inequality in the legal profession have emphasized the role of negative gender stereotypes and implicit bias, the absence of mentoring and networking opportunities for women, and the structure and function of law firms.

The issue with these general explanations of gender inequality in the legal profession, however, is that they largely tend to assume that law is like any other prestigious and male-dominated profession. Other than noting some issues related to private law firms, they do not identify whether, or why, the legal profession might present unique and more intractable issues for women. An absence of mentoring and networking opportunities for women would be an issue in any male dominated field. Stereotypes related to female incompetence, women's lack of commitment to professional life, and that women "are rated lower when they adopt authoritative, seemingly masculine styles" could inhibit the professional advancement of women accountants, doctors and engineers just as much as they could undermine women lawyers. That is not to say that those explanations are not important or relevant, and some of them will be useful to our analysis, but they do not account for the lag in equality experienced by the legal profession in particular.

In addition, scholars writing about women in the legal profession tend to focus primarily on opportunities for women's advancement in the profession and in legal organizations, rather than considering the hostility or criticism that women lawyers may face. Although this difference is not noted, these scholars tend to focus on descriptive stereotypes about women's capabilities, not prescriptive stereotypes about appropriate behavior for women. The criticism faced by women lawyers relates to issues of lawyer advancement, as we will note below, but it is a distinct question, and it requires consideration of prescriptive and descriptive gender stereotypes. If gender stereotyping accounts for the attacks directed at women, it seems likely to be because women have violated stereotypes about how they *ought* to behave, rather than because they have defied stereotypes about how they *will* behave.

Eli Wald addresses some of these gaps in his compelling assessment of the reasons for the failure of women to advance in large law firms. Wald argues that modern law firms have adopted a "hypercompetitive ideology" in which law firms emphasize total commitment to clients and client service, and the elite status of the firms depend on portraying "lawyers as near-heroic servants, zealous service providers who pursue the interests of their clients around the clock." Wald argues that the combination of hypercompetitive ideology with negative descriptive stereotypes about women as insufficiently committed to their professional lives, has made large law firms incompatible with the retention and success of women attorneys.

Wald's argument is compelling. While it relies on many of the insights of other scholars about the nature and significance of gender stereotyping, it illuminates the particular issues for women in large law firms. Women in large firms do not have problems simply because they are women in a male-dominated profession; they have problems because they are women working in a hypercompetitive law firm, where gender stereotypes about women create unique barriers to advancement. Wald focuses on descriptive gender stereotypes, but his explanation highlights the issues arising for women specific to an aspect of legal practice.

Further, Wald's thesis indicates the type of explanation likely to be useful to address the challenges faced generally by women in law, and the personal and sexist attacks that women lawyers may face. In his analysis of descriptive gender stereotypes about the nature of women's abilities and capacities, Wald demonstrates that the gendered issues for women in law firms arise at the intersection between the firm's norms and negative gender stereotypes. Assuming that issues for women in law arise in a manner similar to the issues Wald identifies for women in large law firms, their source is likely to be the intersection between norms and values of legal practice and negative gender stereotypes. Our analysis of the relevant gender stereotypes will include prescriptive gender stereotypes about what women *ought* to do or be, rather than descriptive gender stereotypes about what women are capable of doing or being. Wald's example takes us to the key question: How might the intersection of the norms underlying the practice of law with negative gender stereotypes give rise to personal, hostile, and sexist attacks on women lawyers?

* * *

The Problem with Women Lawyers

The Woman Problem

As discussed in Part III, the normative structure of the lawyer's role links to the complex attitude society has towards lawyers and the work that they do. People recognize the importance of the peaceful settlement of our disagreements, and the freedom of people to pursue their own conception of the good within that social settlement, and even recognize the importance of having lawyers to help enforce that settlement and the space for personal autonomy. Yet, at the same time, people see the costs that work imposes, and its preference for legality—for "technicalities"—over substantive moral values of importance. The importance of the work that lawyers do creates, rather than disrupts, the uncomfortable social position that they occupy.

Why, though, does that unpopularity and uncomfortable social position look different for women? Why do women struggle to achieve equality in the profession? Why do they risk personal gendered commentary and criticism that male lawyers generally do not? In our view, the most plausible explanation arises from the intersection between the requirements of the lawyer's role and prescriptive gendered stereotypes about how women ought to act. By virtue of her role—pursuing client interests within the bounds of legality—a lawyer is required to be competent, authoritative, and rational. She acts in the interests of her client, not in the interests of others, and will not be deferential, generally concerned with the interests of others or act with emotional sensitivity, except insofar as doing any of those things advances her client's interests within the bounds of legality. But by acting in this way, she not only violates our expectations of what women *can* do, she also violates our standards about what women *ought* to do.

Robust psychological literature demonstrates the existence of gender stereotypes, both descriptive—what we believe men and women can do and be—and prescriptive—what we believe men and women ought to do and be. In general, we believe that men ought to reflect agentic qualities, to be focused on achievement, to have an "inclination to take charge" and to be autonomous and rational. Simultaneously we believe that women ought to reflect communal qualities, to be concerned about others, to seek affiliation, and to be deferential and emotionally sensitive. These qualities can be articulated in more detail, and have been identified consistently over time and across cultures.

* * *

Prescriptive gender stereotypes are "oppositional"; women ought not to exhibit traditional male qualities, and men ought not to exhibit traditional female qualities. Women "are prohibited from demonstrating the self-assertion, dominance, and achievement orientation so celebrated in men," and are expected to be "communal, demonstrating socially sensitive and nurturing attributes reflecting their concern for others."

The literature also demonstrates that women who violate prescriptive gender stereotypes will experience "social censure and personally directed negativity," will be viewed as "less socially appealing," and will be "less liked and more personally derogated" in relation to men with similar qualities. Further, women will experience greater negative reactions for violations of expectations about appropriate female behavior. An absence of communal behavior may result in a woman being "characterized as the antithesis of the female nurturer—as the quintessential 'bitch' who is concerned not at all about others but only about herself." Women may also be especially subject to backlash or hostility when they demonstrate negative but masculine qualities, for example, being arrogant or aggressive as opposed to competent and assertive.

* * *

The evidence suggests that a woman in leadership may be able to alleviate some of these challenges if she adopts "participatory styles of leadership," or if she can exhibit communal qualities, either directly through her work or by virtue of her status as, for example, a mother. However, doing so may prevent a woman from being perceived as qualified to occupy a leadership position in the first place, since that position requires her to demonstrate that she possesses masculine qualities. Success without backlash requires the capacity and opportunity to combine the ideal masculine capacities, without demonstrating an absence of ideal female capacities: "[I]t is not easy to be competent and effective without offending anyone's sensibilities, nor to be warm and creative without taking one's eye off the instrumental goal."

The combination of these prescriptive gender stereotypes with the requirements of the lawyer's role explains the experience of women lawyers. It explains why women are more likely to be viewed as not up to the job. It explains why traditional narratives around lawyer conduct tend to evoke models of masculinity—whether Rambo or Atticus Finch. It explains the tendency to focus on women's feminine accomplishments—their looks, their clothes, their families, and their children. And it explains the harsh, derogatory, and sexist backlash that women lawyers sometimes experience.

Being a lawyer requires the prescribed masculine qualities, and much of the time it precludes the prescribed feminine ones. A lawyer representing the interests of a client within the bounds of legality has to focus on accomplishment of the client's goals. She has to be "assertive, dominant [and] forceful." She must be "independent, self-reliant, decisive . . . analytical, logical [and] objective." Further, she cannot consistently be "kind, caring, considerate . . . warm, friendly, collaborative . . . obedient, respectful, self-effacing . . . perceptive, intuitive, understanding." Those qualities may be helpful from time to time, particularly in advising a client or in negotiation, but they are simply inconsistent with much of the work that lawyers do, particularly when acting as zealous advocates in an adversarial trial. No lawyer cross-examining a hostile witness can realistically expect to be perceived as kind, caring, or considerate.

Given descriptive gender stereotypes, women can expect to be seen as less likely to be able to do the work that lawyers do. Further, women who receive favorable attention or media coverage can expect that coverage to focus on their counter-acting feminine qualities, particularly their beauty, compliance with norms of feminine dress and attire, or their commitment to their families and children. Coverage will not focus exclusively on their work, because if the coverage focused on their lawyerly conduct or abilities it would, in terms of prescriptive gender stereotyping, not *be* positive coverage. No feminine virtues can arise from doing the job itself. Finally, women risk being targets of gendered hostility, because being a good lawyer means being a bad woman. It means abandoning or acting contrary to the communal behavior women ought to exhibit, in favor of the agentic values men ought to exhibit. This is particularly so if the woman is an aggressive lawyer, exhibiting the kind of zeal and occasional incivility that the profession frowns upon, since doing so could be considered a violation of a "gender-intensified proscription."

The issues for women do not, however, arise simply because of the occasionally adversarial nature of lawyer's work. They rather arise because of the lawyer's role as understood through a modified positivist perspective.

The woman lawyer in that role will act to assert individual interests against communal values, whether of morality or—insofar as her client contests its meaning or application—of the law itself. The moral ambiguity of the lawyer's role that scholars identify as the source of lawyer unpopularity will hit women particularly hard because it is necessarily non-communal. The woman asserts her client's interests and needs even where it hurts others, even where doing so requires challenging current legal norms, and doing so violates accepted moral norms. She asserts rather than appeases, and she resists rather than conforms, even outside an adversarial trial. By doing so, she violates prescriptive gender stereotypes.

It also means that women lawyers cannot adopt the ameliorating strategies sometimes available to women in leadership, at least within the confines of traditional legal practice. The job itself does not permit the consistent exhibition of communal values, at least not where the lawyer pursues the interests of a client. Pursuing client interests necessarily conflicts with acting in an affiliative or deferential way in relation to others. A woman may be able to assert her compliance with gendered norms in other ways, through her dress or demeanor, but those factors are unlikely to counter-act the violation of gender prescriptions that the lawyer's role requires. They may simply become another basis for criticism, suggesting that the woman is hypocritical or sexually transgressive if she succeeds in communicating femininity, or as additional evidence of her lack of feminine virtue if she fails to do so.

Further, while the literature on the consequences for women who violate prescriptive gender stereotypes focuses on women who advance in their careers or occupy leadership roles, a woman lawyer may experience the consequences of violating prescriptive gender stereotypes at any point in her career. Since the issues arise by virtue of the role, a woman merely needs to occupy the role to violate gender norms; she does not need to have a leadership role or professional success. Although, women who do so have compounded risks of personal attacks, since they may be perceived as having further violated prescriptive gender stereotypes.

Some professional roles may cause less difficulty for women than others—a woman who advises behind the scenes will have greater opportunities for apparently communal behavior than a woman who goes to court. Ultimately, however, even the lawyer as advisor risks backlash. Her advice to her client may be contrary to the interests of others; it may assist the client to do things that the law permits but morality condemns. To the extent her participation in that conduct is known, she risks being perceived as violating prescriptive gender stereotypes.

Further, certain roles that women lawyers pursue or occupy, especially in politics, heighten the difficulties that the role creates. Holding political office arguably creates more opportunities for the expression of communal virtues, to be warm, sensitive, and to pursue communal interests and values. At the same time, however, politics is the point where the social settlement of law arises; politics exists to permit peaceful resolution of our disagreements. That means, therefore, that a woman lawyer in politics in a sense occupies ground zero of the problem of the lawyer's role. She participates in choosing some moral values over others, and by doing so again must necessarily demonstrate agentic virtues rather than communal ones. She may have greater opportunities to ameliorate the issue through also demonstrating communal virtues than are, say, available to a criminal defense lawyer, but she also has greater risks by virtue of her direct participation in the creation of the social settlement of law.

Further, a woman who seeks political office must necessarily have and demonstrate ambition. By definition you cannot seek something without actually *seeking* it, and doing so violates prescriptive norms about how women ought to behave. Indeed, insofar as it is conduct we find unappealing in men as well, women who engage in it may experience heightened risks of backlash, since it is women who demonstrate non-preferred masculine behavior or an absence of preferred feminine behavior who are most vulnerable.

* * *

CARLA PRATT, *SISTERS IN LAW: BLACK WOMEN LAWYER'S STRUGGLE FOR ADVANCEMENT*

2012 MICHIGAN STATE LAW REVIEW 1777 (2012)

Pratt is the Dean of Washburn University School of Law. She engages in scholarship examining racial diversity in law school and the legal profession. She served as Associate Justice for the Supreme Court of the Standing Rock Sioux Tribe in Fort Yates, North Dakota from 2012–2018.

Introduction

Many observers of the legal profession have noted that the number of women graduating from law school and entering the legal profession has increased significantly in the past two decades. Nonetheless, women still comprise a very small minority of lawyers in leadership positions in large corporate law firms, Fortune 500 companies, and law schools. So while the presence of women in law school and the legal profession has improved greatly, the uncomfortable reality is that women tend to occupy positions in the legal profession that subordinate them to men.

Commentators offer several explanations for the position of women in the legal profession. Some argue that women aspire to leadership positions in the profession at lower rates than men and this explains the low numbers of women in leadership positions. Others argue that structural barriers create a "glass ceiling" or a "leaky pipeline," which prevents many women from achieving positions of leadership in the profession. One example of a structural barrier is a profession that requires working in excess of 2,000 hours a year despite the awareness that many women simply cannot meet this requirement due to family responsibilities. Others point to gender stereotypes in the workplace that stigmatize women as less ambitious, less productive, or less competent, and prevent them from receiving the work opportunities that would allow them to showcase their skills and earn promotion.

When women lawyers are disaggregated into distinct racial groups, we see that the challenges confronting women lawyers, as a whole, are not always the same in nature or degree. There are common patterns to gender that unify women lawyers in their struggle for professional advancement, but not all women perform or experience gender in the same way. Many of the challenges confronting women lawyers of color are unique and different from the challenges confronting white female lawyers. For women of color, race is not merely an added layer that makes them subject to additional challenges, but rather a component of their identity that intersects with gender to expose them to unique challenges.

* * *

This Essay examines the experience of black women lawyers and argues that this group confronts unique challenges arising from the intersection of their race and gender. The racial identity of women lawyers matters because it creates a unique context in which a particular group of women experience the legal profession. This is not because each racial group possesses some essential characteristics that make all of its members the same. Rather it is because each racial group has a unique history that locates it within the law and the larger society and positions it relative to the dominant racial group. Moreover, each racialized and gendered group has a unique set of stereotypes assigned to it that influences how others view and interact with members of that particular group. The result of this is that black women have a different position and experience in the legal profession when compared not only to their white female peers, but also when compared to other women of color. In other words, the level of abstraction matters when attempting to identify challenges confronting women lawyers of color and the solutions that may aid in overcoming those challenges. This Essay explores some of the unique obstacles to professional advancement black women lawyers confront and suggests some modest measures for grappling with some of these obstacles.

I.   Not Merely a Problem of Numbers

* * *

Currently, black women in law school outnumber black men three to one. Yet given the declining numbers of black enrollment at U.S. law schools in recent years, the profession should be concerned with potential regression in the number of black women who are entering law school and becoming lawyers. Being mindful of and working to improve the number of black women entering the legal profession is still an important goal, but improving the professional experience and opportunities of black women who become lawyers is the focus of this Essay. Like women generally, the primary problem for black women has not been getting into law school and, subsequently, becoming a lawyer. The primary challenge for black women has been advancing within the profession and ascending to positions of power.

II.   The Struggle to Portray a Professional Image

Presenting and maintaining a professional image is important in the workplace, particularly the professional workplace. All persons in the workplace must contend with the appearance expectations of employers and society. People who are deemed unattractive have a more difficult time obtaining employment and are evaluated less favorably than their peers who are viewed as attractive. To state it bluntly, appearance matters. Since entering the workplace, black women have struggled to present the image of the ideal female worker in order to satisfy employers' desire for all female workers to approximate the normative image of the ideal female worker. The white woman's image with slender body type, European facial features, light skin, and straight flaxen hair has become the archetype of the ideal female worker, especially in the context of the professional workplace. While European beauty bias in the workplace affects black women in many ways, the primary challenge for black women in presenting and maintaining a professional image is hair. Because most black women have hair that grows up into an Afro naturally and does not hang down, black women have to go to greater lengths than their non-black female peers in order to conform to employers' expectations of straight or lightly curled hair that hangs down. The burden imposed on black women to satisfy white beauty standards is best articulated in Chris Rock's documentary film Good Hair, which chronicles how black women have to either chemically treat their hair to get it straight or have straight hair extensions sewn into their hair. Both processes are very expensive to maintain and chemical treatments can result in hair loss and unhealthy skin conditions.

When black women enter the legal profession, they are cognizant that law as a profession and corporate law firms, in particular, are conservative in their perception of what constitutes the image of the professional black woman. Black women lawyers are well aware of the bias held by employers against natural hairstyles for black women. They also know that employers can refuse to hire them or even terminate them once hired if they choose to wear their hair in styles that accommodate their natural hair texture. In the elite environments of law practice, the texture and length of a black woman's hair "becomes a proxy for legitimacy and determines the extent to which [she] can 'crossover' from the private world of segregation and colonization (and historically, in the case of black women, service in another's home) into the mainstream of American life." Unstraightened or "nappy" hair is viewed, perhaps subconsciously, as evidence of a black woman's inability or unwillingness to assimilate into the conservative profession of law. It tacitly signals to others in the profession that this woman does not really belong. Moreover, since appearance influences evaluations of competence and job performance, an inability or unwillingness to conform one's appearance to the professional ideal may call into question the professional judgment and competency of black women who opt to wear their hair in its non-conforming natural state. Ethnic hairstyles for unprocessed or natural kinky hair, such as braids, cornrows, or finger waves, often are viewed as unacceptable presentations of black women who desire to be viewed as professional. Accordingly, most black women are confronted with the dilemma of whether to straighten their hair or wear a hairstyle that will accommodate their natural hair. The choice to wear black hair in its natural state is a voluntary assumption of the risk of negative assessments by workplace supervisors and colleagues. Rather than risk having their hair become an impediment to career advancement, many black women cover their natural hair with a wig or chemically treat their hair so that it can be worn in styles that lay down and conform to society's definition of professional womanhood.

It should be noted that not all black women lawyers carry the same burden in presenting a professional image. Those with more Eurocentric facial features, hair texture, and skin color enjoy a degree of white privilege that enables them to more easily approximate the image of the ideal professional woman, and as a result they are less burdened by the bias in favor of European standards of beauty. The struggle to portray a professional image is not one contrived by black women. It is a struggle that all women confront. Yet black women lawyers confront unique challenges around appearance, especially when it comes to hair, and those who embrace their natural locks find little protection in the law and may suffer negative assessments of competency, thereby frustrating their advancement in the legal profession. As more black women with proven records of professional achievement embrace natural hairstyles, employer distaste for black women's natural hair will hopefully dissipate further.

III. Stereotypes in the Workplace

Appearance-based bias is closely connected to the practice of stereotyping because both incorporate assumptions about an individual based on the individual's physical appearance. While the ABA's study of women of color in law firms reveals that women lawyers of color are likely perceived differently by their professional peers, the professional identity of black women lawyers is shaped, in part, by the particular stereotypes applied to black womanhood. Regina Austin in her groundbreaking law review article entitled Sapphire Bound! used bell hooks's work to articulate and examine the stereotypes that are applied to black women. These stereotypes include the domineering and emasculating Sapphire, also known as the strong black woman, who Austin calls the "stereotypical black bitch." The other primary stereotype applied to black women is the hypersexual promiscuous Jezebel who uses her sexual prowess to seduce unsuspecting men, particularly white men, in a plot to extract some benefit from the man. The third primary stereotype applied to black womanhood is virtually the complete opposite of Sapphire and Jezebel. It is the desexualized, self-sacrificing and nurturing Mammy. Mammy historically is portrayed in media as overweight, dark skinned, with short kinky hair; she is always pleasant in her interactions with others, very patient and kind, and always puts the needs of others before her own.

Black women lawyers are well aware of the stereotypes that are ascribed to their black female bodies. The 2010 ABA study revealed that women of color often reported that they felt like they could not be themselves in the law firm environment—that they had to downplay their femininity and "mannify" themselves. This finding should not be surprising, especially when applied to the lived experience of black women. A recent study of African American women reported that 97% of black women acknowledged that they are aware of negative stereotypes applied to black women and 80% of those women surveyed acknowledged that they had been personally affected by these negative stereotypes. Black women who become lawyers are no exception; they too are aware of the stereotypes surrounding their gendered racial identity and they are constantly performing their professional identity as lawyers in ways that seek to avoid confirming these negative stereotypes. Black women cannot afford to lose their temper or even assert their positions too strongly because doing so could cause them to be viewed as Sapphire, the angry black woman. In a recent collection of interviews of women lawyers of color, one black female lawyer demonstrated that she was acutely aware of the Sapphire stereotype applied to her gendered racial identity when she stated, " 'Well, the choice I made early on was that I did not want to be stereotyped as sort of the "big, black, angry woman." That I am. [laughs] And so I think I made my natural personality—I made myself very, very reserved professionally.' " As revealed in this testimony, black women monitor and restrict their workplace conduct so as not to be viewed through the lens of a stereotype applied to their gendered racial identity.

Another stereotype that black women lawyers seek to rebut in the workplace is the hypersexual Jezebel stereotype. The behavior modification necessary to rebut this stereotype might include choosing clothing that does not accent the curves that black women tend to have and rebuffing lunch or other invitations from white male colleagues. Black women understandably want to avoid being cast as Jezebel because such an identity is inconsistent with the professional identity they want to create for themselves, but they may also seek to avoid the Jezebel label for fear that being viewed in this way might subject them to sexual harassment in the workplace. Such a concern is not necessarily misplaced. Psychologists argue that stereotypes fuel sexual harassment, and at least one psychologist posits that racial and gender stereotypes about black women may put them at risk for experiencing sexual harassment and greater negative outcomes associated with the harassment.

When black women lawyers do become the object of sexual harassment, they may be more likely to suffer in silence, and not file a complaint for fear that the offending male co-worker will successfully deploy the Jezebel stereotype against them and convince others that she welcomed or initiated the sexual advances. Another reason that black female lawyers may suffer sexual harassment in silence is that, for many, they are the primary or sole income earner in their household, which means they are more economically vulnerable and less able to suffer the negative career consequences that come with calling out a male colleague or supervisor for unlawful behavior. Half of married black women earn more annual income than their husbands. Moreover, nearly half of all black women in the workforce are not married and are the financial head of their household, making them solely responsible for their own financial welfare and that of their children if they have any. This status of black women as the primary financial support for black households renders them less able to suffer the loss of employment or the loss of income that may be associated with challenging unethical or illegal behavior in the workplace.

The Jezebel stereotype might also be harming black women lawyers' chances for advancement in large corporate law firms and other law practice settings because it discourages black women from trusting white men. When a white male lawyer takes an interest in mentoring a black female lawyer she has to ask herself—Why is he doing this? Where is this going to go? Does this man have a sexual agenda for me or is he genuinely and exclusively interested in helping me professionally? These questions are only magnified if the white male lawyer is from the South because black girls who are coming of age often receive a warning from their fathers and uncles to beware of the fascination southern white men have with black women. Rather than risk the relationship devolving toward sexual harassment, black women lawyers may shy away from white males who are willing to mentor them, when the reality is that white men are often the persons best positioned to help black women lawyers advance their careers. Testimonials from women of color who have achieved significant levels of success in law practice confirm the need for black women lawyers to embrace white men as mentors. Latina lawyer Carmen Toledo stated that her mentors in the law firm where she practices are white men "[b]ecause there's no [other] Puerto Rican woman, I'm the only one here. There are a few other women litigators but it's so unfair to them. They can't be expected to be everything to everyone. It's unfair to expect them to be mentors to everyone."

Of course, even if the more senior white male lawyer has no sexual agenda and truly wants to mentor the black female lawyer to help advance her career, there is always the perception of others in the workplace with which the black woman lawyer will need to contend. The Jezebel stereotype may provoke others to question the success of the black female lawyer and attribute her success to the fact that she is "sleeping her way to the top." This assumption, of course, is related to another stereotype about black women, which is that they are less intelligent and less hardworking than non-black lawyers. Unlike Asian American women lawyers who may be viewed through the model minority stereotype, which attributes hard work and strong intellect to people of Asian descent, blacks labor under the negative stereotypes of laziness and unintelligence. In her book discussing what it takes for women of color to thrive in the practice of law, Monica Parker shared that as an African American lawyer, she is "always worried about being perceived as lazy or not smart." Ms. Parker's worry of having these negative stereotypes assigned to her by others is not unusual. In a recent study of black lawyers seeking to ascertain the challenges they confronted in becoming lawyers, one common challenge identified by study participants was the recognition that others frequently viewed them as less capable of intellectual pursuits than their non-black peers.

If black women lawyers are viewed, perhaps subconsciously, as less hard working or less intelligent than their peers, any success they achieve is at risk of being viewed through a lens of doubt and suspicion. Accordingly, the success of the black female lawyer is continuously at risk of being attributed to being the sexually loose Jezebel or being a less qualified affirmative action beneficiary. While the additional identity work that black women lawyers perform in the workplace is aimed at rebutting negative stereotypes associated with the identity of black women, it may be a double-edged sword that operates to impede their opportunities for professional advancement. The fear of performing in a way that might confirm preexisting stereotypes applied to a particular identity, such as black womanhood, is what psychologists call "stereotype threat." Stereotype threat has been shown to undermine the performance of a group of people, including white men, when the group in question is an "ability stereotyped group" in relation to the task they are asked to perform. Black women are an ability stereotyped group when it comes to performing intellectually challenging tasks for long periods of time because they labor under both the stereotype of laziness and unintelligence. Because black female lawyers labor under these negative stereotypes about their ability, their fear of doing something that might confirm one of these negative stereotypes in the minds of their colleagues may frustrate their ability to perform. Likewise, a simple error such as a typographical error in a legal brief is at risk of being viewed by supervising lawyers as confirmation of the negative stereotypes attached to black womanhood—an oversight due to laziness or lack of attention to detail—rather than excusable human error that all lawyers make from time to time. With the extra identity work that black female lawyers have to contend with while performing their professional roles, it is not surprising that they are not advancing in the legal profession at an acceptable rate; nor is it surprising that many black women lawyers leave the white male dominated corporate law firms in search of more diverse work environments where accomplished black women are less of a novelty.

* * *

TONJA JACOBI & DYLAN SCHWEERS, *JUSTICE, INTERRUPTED: THE EFFECT OF GENDER, IDEOLOGY & SENIORITY AT SUPREME COURT ORAL ARGUMENTS*

103 VIRGINIA LAW REVIEW 1379 (2017)

Jacobi (left) is Professor of Law at Northwestern Pritzker School of Law. Jacobi specializes in judicial behavior and strategy in public law. Schweers (right) graduated cum laude from Northwestern Pritzker School of Law and is an associate at Goodwin in Boston.

INTRODUCTION

In a *New York Times* article discussing Senator Mitch McConnell's silencing of Senator Elizabeth Warren on the U.S. Senate floor, Susan Chira asked: "Was there a woman who didn't recognize herself in the specter of Elizabeth Warren silenced by a roomful of men?" Chira claimed this event "resonates with so many women precisely because they have been there, over and over again. At a meeting where you speak up, only to be cut off by a man. Where your ideas are ignored until a man repeats them and then they are pure genius—or, simply, acknowledged." Similarly, when

Senator Kamala Harris was repeatedly interrupted by her male colleagues when questioning Attorney General Jeff Sessions, the *Boston Globe* declared simply: "To be a woman is to be interrupted." These acts of men silencing women were performed on the Senate floor, confirming research that the legislative branch is not immune to the gender inequalities that exist in society generally. This Article shows that the highest court in our judicial branch suffers from the same disparate patterns of communication between men and women—regularly and predictably. By analyzing judicial behaviors during oral arguments, this Article determines which factors significantly affect the rate of interruptions between the Justices, finding that gender and ideology are highly predictive, and that seniority is relevant but less influential.

The effect of gender is striking when listening to recent oral arguments. For example, in *Bank Markazi v. Peterson*, Justice Ruth Bader Ginsburg began asking advocate Jeffrey A. Lamken a question, but only got as far as saying, "Is there—are there any—" before being interrupted by Justice Anthony Kennedy, who said, "Well, suppose there were three unrelated cases." Lamken responded, "Pardon?" and Kennedy restated his comment and then asked a question. He and the advocate had a back-and-forth exchange before Kennedy acknowledged, "I—I inadvertently interrupted Justice Ginsburg . . . ." But rather than ceding the floor to Ginsburg, Kennedy continued with his inquiry. This is just one of numerous examples from the 2015 Term where a male Justice interrupted a female Justice.

We find that male Justices have been interrupting female Justices in this manner for a long time. We examine the Roberts Court, using publicly available data, as well as earlier Terms, 1990 and 2002, using a secondary database we created by hand coding all interruptions in every case during those Terms. We also hand coded the 2015 Term, which allows us to compare the two databases to check that the coding is consistent. The hand-coded data allows us to study in depth three different periods of the Court when one, two, and three female Justices, respectively, sat on the previously exclusively male Bench. Together, the two databases allow us to comprehensively examine interruptions on the modern Supreme Court.

We find that interruptions do not always occur in a direct manner like the example above. In fact, the most unusual aspect of the *Markazi* example is that Kennedy acknowledged interrupting Ginsburg at all. We find numerous instances where male Justices acknowledge interrupting other men but very few occasions where a Justice acknowledges interrupting a woman.

Other gendered interruption behavior includes what is now the recognized phenomenon of "mansplaining," whereby a man either unnecessarily explains to a woman something that the woman is just as likely to know, or explains to a third party what the woman is trying to say. An example of the latter, from the 2002 Term, is seen in *Boeing Co. v. United States*:

> **Kent L. Jones**:—I'm sorry. I meant the reg. The 861–8 reg was . . . was formulated with the calculation of combined taxable income expressly in mind, and we know that both by the terms of the reg 861–8(f)—

> **Sandra Day O'Connor**: Well, how do we know that?

> **Anthony M. Kennedy**: Getting back to Justice Scalia's question, and I think it relates to what Justice O'Connor is asking too, is . . . is your answer to the last argument, that a transaction-by-transaction basis . . . we would . . . would clearly not have this problem . . . is we clearly would have this problem and we'd look at 861, and you'd lose there too?

This exchange illustrates two things. First, notwithstanding the recent attention given to "mansplaining," it has been occurring for decades. Second, even female Justices on the Supreme Court are subjected to this phenomenon, despite having reached the highest pinnacle possible in one of the highest-status professions.

Using a variety of statistical techniques, we find that even though female Justices speak less often and use fewer words than male Justices, they are nonetheless interrupted during oral arguments at a significantly higher rate. Men interrupt more than women, and they particularly interrupt women more than they interrupt other men. This effect is not limited to the male Justices, as our research shows the male advocates also regularly interrupt the female Justices. This is surprising, both because the Court's guidelines explicitly prohibit advocates from interrupting Justices, and because the Chief Justice manages the oral argument and is in a position to intervene when this occurs. We see a clear example of the Chief Justice intervening in *Wiggins v. Smith*:

> **Antonin Scalia:** No. He reached the conclusion because—

> **Donald B. Verrilli, Jr.:** And that's completely supported by the proffer.

> **Antonin Scalia:**—He reached the conclusion because he—

> **William H. Rehnquist:**—No two voices at the same time. Justice Scalia is asking you a question.

> **Donald B. Verrilli, Jr.:** Excuse me.

In contrast, in *American Insurance Ass'n v. Garamendi*, Chief Justice Rehnquist allowed the following exchange:

Ruth Bader Ginsburg: But when you take what the President undertook, which was just to use best efforts, that doesn't sound like—

Kenneth Steven Geller:—Under the Supremacy—

Ruth Bader Ginsburg:—this Court would have much to—

Kenneth Steven Geller:—Justice Ginsburg, I think it's the operation of the Supremacy Clause.

Whether direct interruptions, lack of acknowledgment of interruptions, or "mansplaining" interruptions, the differences in the behaviors among and between the male and female Justices and the advocates and the female Justices raise a question: are female Justices on the Supreme Court provided equal opportunity to question advocates during oral arguments? The example below, from *Fisher v. University of Texas*, provides some insight into that question, as Justice Antonin Scalia blatantly interrupts Justice Sonia Sotomayor in the middle of her question:

Bert W. Rein: His estimate was that a very small number, and it—it's in his opinion. It's—it's not only by percentage, but it's by number, and that number is insignificant relative—

Sonia Sotomayor: Do you think—do you think that change has to happen overnight? And do you think it's—

Antonin Scalia: Excuse me. Can I—can I hear what you were about to say? What are those numbers? I was really curious to hear those numbers.

Bert W. Rein: He assumed, at the outside, that any of the admits that were actually African-American or Hispanic outside the Top Ten, he said let me take that assumption and see what it would add.

Given that Justices are permitted to, and frequently do, interrupt advocates, Scalia's interruption was a breach of that norm, prioritizing both the advocate's response and his own interest above that of Sotomayor's inquiry. The effect of this breach was that Sotomayor's question went unaddressed, as Rein instead responded to Scalia's demands. One may look at the significant discrepancies in seniority and ideology between Scalia and Sotomayor, however, and surmise that the interruption could be the effect of such differences.

Seniority could be relevant to judicial interruptions either directly, as an application of the more general norm that one should not interrupt one's elders, or as an interaction with other factors, particularly gender and ideology. We know that there are some seniority-based norms on the Court. For example, Justices speak and cast votes in order of seniority at post-conference, and the most junior Justice has to open the door and take notes at the conference. This raises the expectation that other norms of seniority could apply, particularly an expectation of greater deference to more senior Justices. While scholars have looked at whether there is a "freshman effect" on interruption behavior, with Justices being more reticent when first appointed to the Court due to their inexperience, we anticipate a broader effect could apply, either because senior Justices are given more deference or because senior Justices are confident enough—or perhaps feel more entitled—to be more forceful in their questioning.

* * *

Nevertheless, seniority is important in a different way: longer tenure on the Court provides time and opportunity to learn. For this analysis, we are able to go even further back in time, to the entry onto the Court of the first female Justice, Justice Sandra Day O'Connor. We are able to pinpoint shifts in the way women ask questions on the Bench. We find evidence that all four female Justices have learned to change their speech patterns, transitioning from a less assertive questioning style to a more direct, aggressive style that men typically use to avoid being interrupted as regularly.

* * *

First, we explore whether the effect of ideology is categorical or continuous—that is, does the size of the ideological gap between Justices of opposing ideologies also matter? If not, then ideology on the Court looks a lot like partisanship, a dispute between two camps of ideologues. If true, then ideology on the Court looks more like outcome-based disputes between Justices with a variety of views who are not simply polarized along partisan lines. Second, we expect that interruptions, commonly recognized as assertions of dominance, occur more across party lines than within ideological camps, but will the effect be symmetrical? Whether there are innate differences between liberals and conservatives or not, Republicans have dominated the Court for the last half-century, both in terms of appointments and in terms of the ideological spectrum of the Court. As such, we may see differences between conservative and liberal judicial behavior. Third, the fact that interruptions of the advocates are increasing is no secret, but its cause is not clear. One possibility is that disruptive behavior on the Court reflects the broader political polarization in the nation, which accelerated after the Republican Revolution of 1994. Alternatively, some have pointed to the entrance of Justice Scalia in 1986 as being the catalyst for increasing disruption on the Court. With data going back to 1990, we are able to distinguish between these two theories by assessing whether there was an ideological divide in judicial interruptions after 1986 and prior to 1994.

* * *

I. THEORY AND LITERATURE OF INTERRUPTIONS

A. *First Impressions*

Anyone listening to Supreme Court oral arguments in the 2015 Term should have been struck by how frequently female Justices were interrupted by their male colleagues and by the advocates. As a professor and a student, respectively, in a law school class on Supreme Court oral arguments, we were each struck by the extent of this gendered series of faux pas. This is what a count of all interruptions in the 2015 Court Term looks like considered in terms of pairwise interruptions:

TABLE 1: ALL INTERRUPTIONS IN 2015, BY JUSTICE-PAIRS

Got Inter-rupted	WHO INTERRUPTED								
	Alito	Breyer	Ginsburg	Kagan	Kennedy	Roberts	Scalia	Sotomayor	Thomas
Alito		2	1	6	3	12	3	2	
Breyer	3		2	1	8	5	12	2	
Ginsburg	1	2		6	11	4	3	1	
Kagan	10	6	7		11	10	8	2	
Kennedy	1	9	2	3		3	3	6	
Roberts	4	3	5	3	7			5	
Scalia	1	4	4	6	2			2	
Sotomayor	14	3	4	7	15	12	5		
Thomas									

As seen in Table 1, women were interrupted far more often than men. For example, we observe only two instances of a male Justice being interrupted by another single Justice at a double-digit rate (ten or more times), but seven instances of a female Justice being so interrupted. Note that this disproportionate rate of the female Justices being interrupted occurred despite the fact that there were only three women, compared to six men, on the Court, and, if interruptions were gender-blind, we would expect twice as many interruptions of men at any given threshold. Also, note that no woman interrupted any man in such high numbers during the entire 2015 Term. We wondered how typical was this behavior. Was 2015 a particularly contentious year, or are female Justices, despite having reached the pinnacle of a high-status profession, still subject to being treated as conversational inferiors? We also noted similar discrepancies in interactions between Justices and advocates and wanted to explore that related phenomenon.

But of course, gender is not the only salient characteristic of a Supreme Court Justice. Any serious scholar of the Court knows that ideology is a significant predictor of various forms of judicial behavior, so we were alert to potential ideological causes of interruptions. Note from Table 1 that the two moderates on the Court, Kennedy, the median, and John Roberts, the Chief Justice, were not interrupted at these high rates by any other Justice on the Court. However, these two Justices are each responsible for double-digit interruptions of three of their colleagues, and Kennedy and Roberts alone account for six of the nine instances of frequent interruptions. We wanted to know if ideology predicts interruptions, either as an expression of cross-ideological disagreement or as a reflection of the power of the median or moderate Justices over their more extreme colleagues, since the extreme Justices are dependent on the central Justices to form majority coalitions.

Finally, we considered the possibility that seniority may be at play and that gender simply coincides with seniority. We recognized that two of the three female Justices, Justice Kagan and Justice Sotomayor, are more junior on the Court and that each is interrupted far more frequently than Justice Ginsburg. In addition, Table 1 provides some provisional support for the seniority hypothesis because of the most senior Justices—Ginsburg, Kennedy, Scalia, and Breyer—only Ginsburg and Breyer are interrupted at high rates. In contrast, the more junior Justices—Kagan, Sotomayor, and Alito—account for the other seven high interruption rates.

Thus, by examining interruption behavior just in the 2015 Court Term, we formed three key hypotheses: that gender, ideology, and seniority—or some combination of the three—explain the variation in rates of interruptions. The rest of this Part describes the relevant literature pertaining to each of these three hypotheses and develops in more detail the theory behind each.

* * *

1.   The Significance of Oral Arguments

The central debate concerning oral argument is whether and to what extent it matters at all. While some have found no indication that the procedure "regularly, or even infrequently, determines who wins and who loses," this is a minority view. The majority of researchers have found that oral arguments can "focus the minds of the [J]ustices and present the possibility for fresh perspectives on a case." Additionally, many studies have found that oral arguments help the Justices gather information, and one study found that the Justices often "seek new information during these proceedings" in an effort to reach decisions as close as possible to their desired outcomes. Professor Barry Sullivan and Megan Canty outline the myriad functions served by oral arguments for both advocates and Justices. For the advocates, oral argument allows counsel to better emphasize what is important, crystallize relevant issues, and provide a platform to explain the issues to the public. For the Justices, the process facilitates informed decision making and serves as an opportunity to communicate and persuade their colleagues.

A study by Professors Timothy Johnson, Paul Wahlbeck, and James Spriggs took the significance debate further by researching whether oral arguments can actually influence the Justices' votes. Their findings strongly suggest that oral argument is a critical component of judicial decision making. Controlling for compelling alternative explanations, such as a Justice's ideology, they found that the Justices do respond to the quality of oral argumentation. Specifically, "the relative quality of the competing attorneys' oral arguments influences the [J]ustices' votes on the merits." Of particular importance to our investigation, Johnson et al. found that "[J]ustices who are ideologically opposed to the position advocated by a lawyer have an increased probability of voting for that side of the case if the lawyer provides a higher quality oral argument than the opposing counsel." This shows that, to some extent, oral arguments can sway the Justices against their general ideological proclivities. Therefore, not only does the bulk of the research suggest that oral arguments have a purpose, it also supports the view that the proceedings can influence the outcome of the decision.

It should be noted, however, that even the Justices themselves are split on the issue. Former Chief Justice Rehnquist and Justices Brennan, Douglas, and Blackmun have all made comments highlighting the significance of oral arguments, while Justice O'Connor and former Chief Justice Warren have downplayed their impact. Rehnquist noted, "[I]f an oral advocate is effective, how he presents his position during oral argument *will* have something to do with how the case comes out." Brennan agreed: "I have had too many occasions when my judgment of a decision has turned on what happened in oral argument . . . ." Harlan said "there is no substitute" for oral arguments in "getting at the real heart of an issue and in finding out where the truth lies." Recently, Justice Kagan chimed in on the potential impact of oral arguments, saying, "You can sway people to your side or you can also lose a case in the oral arguments." The Johnson et al. study confirms that the majority of Justices behave in a way that comports with the Rehnquist-Brennan-Kagan view that oral arguments matter; overall, they found that "nearly all [J]ustices are influenced by the quality of oral arguments."

* * *

2. *Behavior at Oral Arguments*

If oral arguments serve multiple purposes and have the power to influence the Justices' voting, then it is essential that Justices are able to ask the questions they want to ask. The act of interrupting threatens that capacity. Due to the interactive nature of oral arguments, interruptions of the advocates by the Justices are commonplace. There is only limited research on interruptions among the Justices, but what there is suggests that it is also common and has been increasing in recent terms. Despite the increasing prevalence of Justice-to-Justice interruptions, there is minimal research devoted to the topic.

* * *

3. *Illustrations of Gendered Interruptions*

After reviewing the oral argument transcripts from the 1990, 2002, and 2015 Terms, we immediately noticed a behavioral pattern that could potentially be rooted in Ainsworth's "women's speech" theory. Not only are male Justices and advocates interrupting female Justices at higher rates, but female Justices appear to adopt an increasingly aggressive, direct style of questioning the longer they are on the Bench. It seems that the female Justices learn to ask questions directly so as not to be interrupted as often. For example, in the 1990 Term, a male Justice would often interrupt Justice O'Connor when she started her question with a frame, such as saying the advocate's name or using a qualifier, as seen in *Metropolitan Washington Airports Authority v. Citizens for the Abatement of Aircraft Noise*:

> **David L. Shapiro:** We don't think it can be answered in all of the hypotheticals that Justice O'Connor raises in her question, because we think that if Congress were to use this condition device as a way of putting Members of Congress into essentially executive roles in the playing out of Federal programs at the State level, that that would be a usurpation of executive authority and interference with the executive role.
>
> **Sandra Day O'Connor:** Well, Mr. Shapiro—
>
> **William H. Rehnquist:**—Does the Government take a position as to whether the Members of Congress who are appointed to this . . . these State, or State boards, or this board set up by the States, whether their term on the board survives their term on the committee in question?
>
> **David L. Shapiro:** Yes, Your Honor. We believe that the requirement that the members of the Board of Review be both Members of Congress and in most cases members of certain relevant committees do constitute solely qualifications for appointment.

Or, seen even more clearly in *Connecticut v. Doehr*:

> **Henry S. Cohn:** . . . Your Honors, this is a facial challenge to the statute, and I say this because it was noted in the opening paragraph of Judge Pratt's opinion for the Second Circuit and was so noted in all the papers and opinions below. It arose on summary judgment—

> **Sandra Day O'Connor:** I'm not sure I—

> **William H. Rehnquist:**—Mr. Cohn, what does that mean in the context of a case like this to say that it's a facial challenge? I mean, we're not dealing with a First Amendment situation here.

> **Henry S. Cohn:**—Yes, Your Honor, the evidence before the court was limited, and therefore matters such as the effect on the debtor and the length of time it takes to obtain a hearing, the post . . . the immediate post-seizure hearing, things of that nature, were not developed in the district court.

In these examples, O'Connor does not directly ask her question, but rather starts with a frame, a kind of throat clearing that indicates to the listener that she is about to ask a meaningful question. It is during this framing period, however, that she is often interrupted. Notably, twenty years after she joined the Bench, O'Connor is interrupted less frequently and utilizes a more direct approach, which allows her to fight through interruptions, as seen in *Kentucky Ass'n of Health Plans v. Miller*:

> **Sandra Day O'Connor:** Have we ever—

> **Antonin Scalia:**—Have you—

> **Sandra Day O'Connor:**—analyzed a case that way in solving these problems? Have we ever relied on that difference in language, Mr. Feldman?

> **James A. Feldman:** Well, in the . . . I think the Court in the Pireno case, for . . . oh, the difference in language?

Here, O'Connor starts with a more direct, assertive style of questioning and overcomes Scalia's attempt to interrupt. In contrast, Ginsburg in the 2002 Term utilized the polite framing technique, and she was interrupted at a very high rate. For example, in *State Farm Mutual Automobile Insurance Co. v. Campbell* (2002):

> **Laurence H. Tribe:** . . . Now, the Double Jeopardy Clause—

> **Ruth Bader Ginsburg:** Mr. Tribe, I thought you answered—

> **John Paul Stevens:**—What's the authority for that proposition?

> **Laurence H. Tribe:**—I would . . . I just made it up.

* * *

Both Sotomayor and Kagan start with "sorry," which is an example of Ainsworth's "women's speech." O'Connor and Ginsburg appear to have transitioned, or changed, their ways of asking questions so as to not be interrupted as much. There are numerous examples of Kagan and Sotomayor framing their questions by asking if they may interrupt the advocate, only to get interrupted themselves, as seen in *Fisher*:

Sonia Sotomayor: May I ask—

John G. Roberts, Jr.: Could you associate a number with "the very small?" I guess it would be the number of students who were admitted with the consideration of race who were not also—

Bert W Rein: Correct.

Kagan and Sotomayor often frame their questions with a question, such as "may I ask," or "could I ask," rather than just asking the question. This indirectness is exactly what Ainsworth was referring to when she described "women's speech" as more polite. These framing words provide the opportunity for an interruption to occur before the Justice even gets to the heart of the question. There is evidence, however, that the style of questioning is not the *cause* of the interruptions but just one means of *opportunity*, because the interruption does not always occur within the first few words, as seen here in *Dollar General Corp. v. Mississippi Band of Choctaw Indians*:

Sonia Sotomayor: Mr. Kneedler, I don't know that you've answered—I'm going to assume everything you said and accept it. I think it was very clear from the committee report here, every word you've said, and some of us do believe that since a bill is sent with the committee report and Congress is voting on both, if a member hasn't read it, they've abused their official responsibility.

Antonin Scalia: Does Congress vote on the committee report, Mr. Kneedler?

Edwin S. Kneedler: Sometimes.

Here, Sotomayor is setting up her question, albeit indirectly, and Scalia interrupts before she can finish and form her question.

Additionally, women are interrupted even when they begin their question more directly, as seen here in *Roell v. Withrow*:

Lisa R. Eskow: . . . You also had in this instance a district judge who referred the case to the magistrate before the defendants had even been served, much less had an opportunity to consent, and the magistrate judge did not comply with local practice of confirming on the record all parties' consent—

Ruth Bader Ginsburg: But she was . . . she—

William H. Rehnquist:—Well, can . . . can local rules in one district produce a different result than another district which didn't have that local review with respect to this sort of consent?

Lisa R. Eskow: Absolutely not, Mr. Chief Justice.

* * *

II.   EMPIRICAL ANALYSIS 1: THE ROBERTS COURT

In the next two Parts, we go beyond examples and use various empirical techniques to comprehensively determine the effect that gender, ideology, and seniority play in the interruption of Justices during oral arguments. In this Part, we focus primarily on the Roberts Court, partly because the transcript of every oral argument from 2004 through 2015 is available on the Supreme Court's website. The Roberts Court begins with the 2005 Term; however, we also have data from the 2004 Term, which includes Justice O'Connor and Chief Justice Rehnquist. Our regression analysis of the Roberts Court data yields strong evidence for all three of our hypotheses—i.e., that interruptions are gendered, ideological, and affected, albeit to a lesser extent, by seniority. We show, however, that there is a problem studying only the Roberts Court—a problem that is difficult to overcome: all of the female Justices on the Roberts Court are liberal. The ideological proximity of the three female Justices in the Roberts Court makes it hard to confidently parse between the effect of gender and the effect of ideology for that time period. We resolve the dilemma in this Part by including 2004 and in the next Part by looking at earlier Terms, providing in-depth analysis of the 1990, 2002, and 2015 Court Terms.

* * *

CONCLUSION: IMPLICATIONS AND RECOMMENDATIONS

Our findings clearly establish that women on the Supreme Court are interrupted at a markedly higher rate during oral arguments than men. Additionally, both male Justices and male advocates interrupt women more frequently than they interrupt other men. In other words, women are more likely to be the interruptee, while men are more likely to be the interrupter. While gender is certainly a significant factor affecting these interruptions, it is not the only one influencing interruptions. Our findings indicate that ideology and seniority also play a role in the interruptions between the Justices. Much like gender, ideology was a significant variable, while seniority was less significant. Interruptions are more likely to occur across ideological lines, and, in particular, conservatives are more likely to interrupt liberals than vice versa. Furthermore, ideology has an effect not just categorically but also as a continuum, supporting the view that Justices are not simply partisans but rather disagree over substantive outcomes. A more senior Justice is slightly more likely to interrupt a junior Justice than the reverse, but the effect is small. The most significant effect of a lengthy tenure on the Court is that, with time, female Justices learn to stop using the female register, in particular framing words such as "may I ask," which primarily operate to give men an opportunity to interrupt.

These three variables do not operate in isolation, but rather compound, such that senior male conservative Justices are far more likely to interrupt junior female liberal justices. All of our results were consistent throughout the Roberts Court and further back in time, all the way to the 1990 Term. The fact that gender, ideology, and seniority all influence interruptions among the Justices is extremely significant because interruptions of this kind constitute a breach of norms of equality (gendered interruptions) and neutrality (ideologically driven interruptions), and show that traditional power dynamics (seniority effect) still have some impact.

It is essential that women have an equal opportunity to question advocates, for many reasons. This Article does not directly examine the outcome effects of these interruptions, but given that others have shown that oral arguments can shape case outcomes, it follows from this pattern of interruptions that there is a marked difference in the relative degree of influence of the women and the men on the Court. As others have noted, the discussions at oral arguments serve many purposes, including: focusing the Justices' minds, helping them gather information to reach decisions as close as possible to their desired outcomes, helping them make informed decisions, and providing an opportunity to communicate and persuade their colleagues. When a Justice is interrupted during her questioning, her point is often left unaddressed. Without being able to ask her question, and without receiving an answer, the interruptee may be inhibited from using this point to persuade her colleagues. Because women, liberals, and junior Justices are all interrupted at significantly higher rates than the other members of the Court, this could ultimately lead to more conservative coalitions, and, potentially, more conservative decisions and reduction in the influence of women and younger Justices. It could make it much harder for women to make arguments and win votes during the post-conference process. At the very least, a woman's unequal opportunity to ask questions and complete statements during oral arguments could make it far more difficult for women to gather their thoughts, engage with the advocates, and clarify points that were disputed in the briefs.

Our findings, however, do not just reveal potential implications for the Court, but also for our society. After all, the oral argument process is the only opportunity for outsiders to directly witness the behavior of the Justices of the highest court. The Justices not only interpret our nation's laws; they are also role models. While these interruptions occur during *arguments*, one should still expect to find reasonable discourse conducted in civil fashion at this elite level. Our findings that female Justices are consistently interrupted more than their male counterparts in this setting show that gender dynamics are robust enough to persist even in the face of high levels of power achieved by women. Furthermore, our findings that there is a gender disparity on our nation's highest Bench add strength to Zimmerman and West's theory that microlevel interactions between the genders are microcosms for a much larger issue—society's apparent gender-based hierarchy. The same applies to our findings on ideology—the dominance of conservative appointees to the Court in recent decades has translated to liberals being regularly interrupted at much higher rates than their conservative counterparts. The fact that both of these behaviors are mirrored by advocates is particularly problematic.

* * *

PAULA SCHAEFER, *ON BALANCE: LEADING BY LEAVING*
83 TENNESSEE LAW REVIEW 931 (2016)

Schaefer is Associate Dean for Academic Affairs and Professor of Law at the University of Tennessee College of Law. Her scholarship considers issues of attorney ethics, fiduciary duty, and behavioral legal ethics.

Introduction

Even though women make up half of law school classes in the United States, hold half of elite judicial clerkships, and accept almost half of the jobs in large law firms, only a small number of women make partner or serve in leadership roles in those firms. Much has been written about barriers to gender equality in elite law firms, yet misconceptions persist about why time demands of "big law" disproportionately impact women.

This Article highlights evidence contrary to those misconceptions, and argues that the women-and men-who leave large firms in search of balance are exhibiting leadership. Contrary to Sheryl Sandberg's advice that they should "lean in" if they hope to lead, these former big law attorneys are leading by leaving.

* * *

II. Misconceptions about How Time Demands Create a Gender Disparity in Large Law Firms

Attorneys in large law firms are expected to have little life and few obligations outside of the firm. Time-particularly, the amount of time billed-is everything in big law; as Anne-Marie Slaughter put it, "Nothing captures the belief that more time equals more value better than the cult of billable hours afflicting large law firms across the country." More specifically, law firms value "continuous and full time work" and expect lawyers to be available on demand-twenty-four hours a day, seven days a week. Eli Wald has described the ideology of the modern elite law firm as "hypercompetitive," characterized by well-credentialed lawyers working around the clock in pursuit of their clients' interests. The ideal candidates for big law are those who can meet the firms' "merit credentials," and who are "willing to sacrifice personal lives, indeed to allow their professional identity to overtake and consume their personal identity."

In a large U.S. law firm, the minimum billable hours for an associate is roughly 2,000 per year. If an attorney works five days a week, for fifty weeks of the year, the math works out to a minimum requirement of eight billable hours a day. Anyone who has billed time, however, knows that it takes far more than eight hours in the office to bill eight hours of time. A typical attorney will work ten to twelve hours a day-including many weekends-to bill the minimum 2,000 hours a year. Unfortunately, attractive flexible and part-time options are not available to attorneys who practice in most of these firms.

These time demands contribute to women leaving large law firms before they achieve partnership and leadership positions. But why do time demands impact women at a higher rate than men?

A. Lack of Ambition

Facebook COO Sheryl Sandberg famously urged women to "lean in" to gain leadership roles in corporate America. In her book by the same name, she describes an "ambition gap" between men and women that results in women choosing not to participate fully or lead in the workplace. A recent study reveals that professionals widely share the belief that women value career less than men. The conventional wisdom is that "a woman's primary career obstacle is herself" through her choices to "forgo opportunities, projects, and jobs."

But there is reason to doubt that professional women who leave large law firms lack ambition. Women who join these firms are ambitious; they attended the best law schools, received the best grades, and participated in key extracurricular activities, such as law review. In U.S. law schools, women hold just over half of leadership positions on law reviews, and just under half of editor-in-chief positions. Further, many women who join large law firms held prestigious judicial clerkships after graduation. During the time they practice in large law firms, women continue to demonstrate their ambition; for example, men and women have similar levels of billing in these firms.

Further, if a lack of ambition were the problem, then the standard "off track" part-time and flexible time programs would be a solution. But that has not been the case. Many lawyers who transition to part-time complain that the work they receive is uninteresting and does not utilize the full range of their skills. Beyond that, many firms attach a stigma to part-time lawyers and provide no real opportunity for advancement. This new work environment can be particularly frustrating for women who have always succeeded academically and professionally. Unsurprisingly, many women would rather leave big law than work in these second-class positions.

B.   Motherhood and the Primary Caregiver Burden

Another popular explanation for the male-female imbalance in big firm partnership and leadership is that it is a consequence of motherhood and the desire to be the family's "primary caregiver." When female professionals become mothers, they typically assume the role of primary caregiver and try to "do it all." Often, they will not ask or expect a spouse to share equally in parenting tasks (or if they do, they are likely disappointed). As a result, female lawyers are overwhelmed working as both full-time lawyers and mothers. Eventually, something has to give, and it is usually career. Lynne Hermle, an employment litigation partner at Orrick, Herrington & Sutcliffe, a global law firm, has described the issue as this: "We lose [women] to families . . . . The issue is the roles we play as mothers and caregivers and how difficult that is in the work that we do." Other commentators advise women that instead of leaving their professional careers to deal with the time demands of motherhood, they should expect more from their partners.

But the "primary caregiver" explanation for gender imbalance in large firms does not align with reality. All lawyers who become parents-men and women alike-face a dilemma. Even when a child is in daycare or school for ten to twelve hours a day, the child still requires care the other twelve to fourteen hours each day. But, based on the time demands of big firm lawyers, they can reliably play-at best-a small supporting caregiver role. In other words, the problem is not that the big law attorney needs a life partner willing to split the parenting enterprise fifty-fifty. Rather, she or he needs a spouse willing to handle all (or at least the vast majority) of the parenting.

The parents most likely to leave big law are those whose spouses are also trying to maintain a career (i.e., the reason the spouse cannot do the vast majority of the parenting). The parents most likely to remain in big law are those whose spouses are willing to forego a career to become a primary caregiver for the family, including the lawyer. Statistically speaking, male attorneys are much more likely than female attorneys to have spouses willing to do so. It then follows that many more male than female parents remain in partnership or partnership-track positions.

Ultimately, when big firm lawyers are confronted with division of parenting duties, some male lawyers stay, some male lawyers leave, and most female lawyers leave. This is a reality driven by the lawyers' spouses or partners (and their respective careers) as much as by the lawyers themselves. When Sheryl Sandberg and others tell women that they need "a real partner," they miss the point. Women (and men) do not just need a fifty-fifty parenting partner in order to "lean in" to big law; they need a stay-at-home spouse or a live-in nanny to handle most of the caregiving. However, having a stay-at-home spouse is not a feasible option for most professional women with children, or for men whose partners value their own careers. Additionally, full-time help is not a palatable option for many of these parents.

III. On Balance: Leading by Leaving

As long as large law firms demand that their lawyers have no lives outside of the law, many women and men will leave. But that does not mean that they are failures. When lawyers leave big law in search of more balanced lives-whether they seek time to parent or to pursue other personal interests-they are demonstrating leadership. This Part considers what individuals leaving big law are seeking and where they are finding it. This discussion concludes with thoughts on the leadership qualities demonstrated by lawyers making the choice to leave big law.

Balance can be a loaded word. Professionals often hear that there is no such thing as "balance." Because it is elusive, it should not be a goal. But that misses the point; lawyers in other workplaces can have a more balanced life than those in big law. A career that does not leave time for personal errands, attending children's activities, or having interests or hobbies outside of work is not balanced. And this is the life of most associates and partners in large law firms.

Many high-performing professionals leave large law firms (and other sacrifice-everything-for-work careers) to seek personal fulfillment on other fronts. They want a life outside of work and a meaningful career. Outside of big law, many lawyers are finding balance.

Significantly, lawyers leaving big law are not leaving law entirely. Most of these departing lawyers continue practicing in a different setting. Opportunities include positions in government, non-profits, and companies as in-house counsel. Unlike jobs in large law firms, lawyers report that these positions provide a "clearer path to advancement" and more predictable schedules. Others find solo practice or academia to be attractive alternatives to big law. In both of these career paths, attorneys largely control their schedules, and can continue to use their lawyering skills in an area of the law that they enjoy. Alternatively, other departing big firm lawyers join boutique firms, an attractive option for well-credentialed attorneys who want to continue doing interesting work in a setting that may require less face time in the office.

In sum, former big firm lawyers can find fulfillment in new workplaces that allow them to continue to perform at a high level. Lawyers want to keep using the skills they developed in big law, and continue (or start) working on issues that are interesting or meaningful to them. Finding a career that involves meaningful work and allows the development of mastery contributes to professional motivation and happiness. Even though they are making less money, lawyers are fulfilled in these positions, in part, because of they continue to use their talents and handle work that matters.

Perhaps even more importantly, lawyers gain autonomy when they make such a move. When attorneys control their time, they stand to gain both personally and professionally. On the professional front, autonomy is third in the trifecta of factors that shape workplace motivation. On the personal front, autonomy means the ability to juggle priorities between work and home. Indeed, studies recognize that shared parenting and financial responsibility benefits men, women, and families alike.

Attorneys leaving elite firms to find balance are not failures. Seeking balance demonstrates self-awareness and vision-key qualities associated with leadership. For an over-achiever to leave the money and prestige of practicing law at a large firm in order to obtain balance and fulfillment in their lives demonstrates leadership. While these lawyers could have sacrificed balance for career advancement, they made a different choice. Because of that choice, they can serve as role models for the next generation of lawyers, as they plan to strike the right balance of personal and professional success.

Further, these balance-seeking lawyers are leaders because they can influence structural change in large law firms. Eventually, the continuing exodus of talented attorneys should cause large firms to adapt. The following section considers how leadership education can introduce these lessons to students of both genders.

IV. Leadership Education: Work-Life Balance and Gender Diversity in the Profession as "Attorneys' Issues" and not "Women's Issues"

We do our students a disservice if we frame issues of work-life balance and gender disparity as "women's issues." Male lawyers have a stake in addressing these issues, too. As highlighted throughout this Article, these problems impact both genders. Moreover, gender equality impacts the legal profession as a whole. A diverse law firm is a better law firm. It is illogical to think that one gender can address these issues, irrespective of the actions of the other. Law school is the ideal time to start a discussion about how to address these issues.

Law students should explore why working toward balance is a worthy and necessary goal for both career success and personal happiness. They should be encouraged to explore and identify their values to determine the balance that makes sense in their lives. Stories of lawyers who left big law provide important insight for law students to consider when charting out their future paths. We should also encourage students to forge new paths. In a changing market for legal services, entrepreneurial lawyers will find success by developing innovative (and less time-consuming, hourly-billing-focused) ways to serve clients.

Law school is an ideal time for this planning and reflection. It may be easier for a law student to be rational before his or her perspective is skewed by life, and rewards, inside a large firm. While, theoretically, attorneys may like the idea of work-life balance, it is easy for competitive individuals to shift their focus in order to succeed in the firm environment. Before being immersed in that world, it is useful for students to make a plan to achieve the things that are important to them.

Law students should also explore the consequences of imbalance. Beyond personal sacrifices of health, happiness, and family, a lack of balance can impact the profession as a whole. Lawyers who devote all of their time to a demanding workplace perpetuate a system without room for those who need to have a life outside of the law. If the firm norm is an attorney who spends 3,000 hours a year in the office, and is supported by a fulltime, at-home caregiver, then attorneys with any responsibilities or interests outside of the firm will not be able to keep up. Attorneys should understand that devoting everything to the firm makes it harder for other attorneys to have balance, and ultimately makes it more difficult for firms to achieve gender diversity.

Students considering a career in big law should recognize their potential for changing an environment that currently makes gender equality difficult to achieve. Workplace norms and structures can evolve. While most baby boomers (those occupying management positions today) do not have full-time working spouses, the vast majority of millennials are part of dual income partnerships, and many seek work-life balance. While millennials will face resistance, they may have sufficient numbers to effect change in the legal workplace.

To achieve that culture shift within big law, however, lawyers of both genders must seek more reasonable (i.e. "part-time" or "flexible" by current big firm standards) schedules. Men and women alike must demand positions that allow them to use their full skillset while maintaining a measure of control over their schedules. As Deborah Rhode has explained, "Gender hierarchies will persist until concerns about the quality of life become more central professional priorities . . . ."

While these options will not be as lucrative, the other attributes of such positions are more important to many people. Further, these flexible and part-time options should not exclude a person from partnership. Again, law firm partners working fewer hours will not enjoy the same compensation as full-time partners, but the partnership designation need not be solely about money. It signifies recognition of the lawyer's contribution to the firm, and gives the lawyer a seat at the table for decision-making and future leadership positions. While certain leadership positions cannot be held by part-time attorneys, keeping those attorneys in the firm, and elevating them to partner while working reduced schedules, ensures leadership is an option in the future.

Lawyers, and firms, that make flexible and part-time work possible will have success keeping talented women and men who would otherwise leave big law. Accordingly, legal educators should prepare lawyers for the roles that they can play in seeking balance and leading their firms to accept new models for the practice of law.

SAURABH VISHNUBHAKAT, *GENDER DIVERSITY IN THE PATENT BAR*

14 JOHN MARSHALL REVIEW OF INTELLECTUAL PROPERTY LAW 67 (2014)

Vishnubhakat is an Associate Professor of law at Texas A&M School of Law. His scholarship focuses on innovation and intellectual property, including patents, and how they affect administrative agencies, federal courts, and the marketplace. Much of Vishnubhakat's research is empirical in nature and draws from institutional economics, including transaction and cost analysis and principal-agent theory.

I.   INTRODUCTION

This article describes the first public dataset gender-matching the attorneys and agents who are registered to practice before the United States Patent and Trademark Office. Significantly, all the underlying sources and methodologies used in developing this dataset are also from public sources. As a result, the contribution of this study is not merely a new and useful dataset to support empirical research into diversity within the U.S. patent system, but also a mechanism for ensuring that the dataset may be readily updated and more easily tailored to fit particular research needs.

Much current research on the participation of women in the intellectual property system has been doctrinal, focusing on the intersections of feminist theory with patent and copyright law and with intellectual property law more generally. While this literature advances a conceptual framework and normative proposals, empirical work in this area has been sparse.

This article invites quantitative research to fill this gap by gender-identifying USPTO practitioners generally and practitioners of record on granted patents specifically, publishing the dataset as well as the methodology, and drawing more detailed comparisons across geography and technology. By examination of these dimensions in particular, discussions of gender diversity in the patent bar will be more fully connected with the broader economic discourse on the geographical and technological specificity of innovation and entrepreneurship.

II. RELEVANT DIMENSIONS OF GENDER DIVERSITY

In describing gender diversity in the intellectual property system, the relevance of geography and technology is apparent in the broader empirical literature on diversity. Moreover, the importance of these dimensions to the patent bar proceeds from several upstream arenas of knowledge and skills development including undergraduate and graduate education in science and engineering disciplines as well as legal education.

In the case of geography, scholarly discussion of diversity has often treated geography as a subject of diversification on par with characteristics of race, ethnicity, socioeconomic class, age, and gender—and done so across a range of legally salient contexts such as democratic participation, administrative decision-making, and corporate governance. A geography of gender itself is of somewhat recent vintage, particularly with respect to regional geography. Professor Townsend's seminal paper arguing for such a literature placed it within the school of "new regional geography" to which studies of gender had already contributed.

Quantitative detailed scholarship on legal institutions and the legal profession, however, has been sparse in response to this call for geographically segmented examinations of gender diversity. More common have been qualitative discussions of gender equity in a variety of settings such as within law firms and in-house legal departments, on corporate boards, and at law schools both among faculty and students.

A principal concern of this literature is the so-called "pipeline problem" that limits the diversity of populations of interest according to the diversity of available candidates. Thus, for example, large corporations recruit laterally from large law firms and consequently tend to inherit the relative gender homogeneity of those law firms. Moreover, similar to concerns of diversity in the contents of a pipeline are the mechanisms by which such future constituencies may prepare themselves for entry into the profession, positions of leadership, and other indicia of meaningful diversity.

A related strain in this literature has also argued for a reframing of gender diversity from an end in itself to an instrumental mechanism for otherwise desired ends such as profit-maximization and cross-cultural competence. It is perhaps not surprising then, that the shift away from gender diversity as a metric of primary interest inviting further geographic cross-tabulation has led instead to separate examination of gender and geography (among other traits of interest) in service of metrics that are themselves more complex and difficult to estimate, such as institutional influence and professional satisfaction.

The problem thus reframed, however, has received some empirical attention with regard to gender diversity in the legal profession generally. Studies in this literature include the emergence of gendered outcomes such as two-tiered partnership tracks, the gendered role of personal priorities in advancement, and the antecedent prevalence of gender bias that such other findings suggest.

The dimension of technology, for its part, has received even less empirical attention with regard to gender diversity than has geography. A notable exception is Annette Kahler's 2011 article on trends in education and downstream invention and patenting by women. Professor Kahler's empirical analysis focused primarily on female inventors, as have two subsequent reports published in 2012 by the National Women's Business Council.

Congress, too, has expressed interest in studying with greater empirical detail the participation of minorities, including women, in the patent system, requiring in the Leahy Smith America Invents Act that the USPTO "establish methods for studying the diversity of patent applicants, including those applicants who are minorities, women, or veterans." The USPTO duly published its methodology in March, 2012, and is currently implementing it.

This initial focus on inventors is appropriate, and points to existing investigations of gender diversity in education geared toward science, technology, engineering, and math disciplines as a whole as well as toward particular disciplines such as clinical medicine, mechanical engineering and materials science, computer science and information technology, and biomedical engineering.

Moreover, the empirical interest in inventors as a link between science and engineering education on the one hand and the patent system on the other also invites complementary research on issues including the diversity of the patent bar. Indeed, Professor Kahler's article briefly addressed this question with a gender-identified dataset of registered USPTO practitioners as of 2008 and, for a subsample of practitioners, drawing comparisons across region, law firm type, and educational background.

To build on this work, the dataset presented here provides an updated gender-identified USPTO practitioner roster and provides the first gender-identified data on that subset of patent attorneys and agents who have successfully prosecuted patents to issuance during the last five years. The result is a comprehensive empirical platform for exploring gender diversity across geography and technology and enabling a wide range of policy and market analyses.

III. THE PATENT BAE GENDER DATA FILE

A. *Data and Methodology*

Source data on practitioners registered to practice before the USPTO was matched with gender data on the frequencies with which given names occur among women and men. The result is a new dataset that estimates the genders of registered practitioners. The new dataset is matched to locational information, allowing for geographic analysis. Also used is the USPTO public full text data on patent grants, available until recently through Google and going forward from Reed Technology and Information Services.

* * *

IV. DISCUSSION

As of December, 2012, the USPTO roster listed 41,833 actively registered practitioners. Of these, 40,640 had a U.S. address of record. Of these 40,640 U.S.-based practitioners, a gender match was possible for 35,562. The gender of another 5,078 remains indeterminate. The following preliminary findings are limited to U.S.-based practitioners, as the dictionaries used for gender-matching are themselves derived from U.S. census data.

The disparity between women and men is higher among registered attorneys than among registered agents (Table 2 and Figure 1). Conversely, while more registered practitioners in general tend to be attorneys than agents, among registered practitioners, men tend to be attorneys rather than agents by a higher margin than women do (Table 3 and Figure 2).

Among government-employed practitioners, the disparity between women and men is higher among attorneys than among agents (Table 4 and Figure 3). However, while more government-employed practitioners in general tend to be attorneys than agents, there is no statistically significant difference between women and men as to attorney status versus agent status (Table 5 and Figure 4).

From the different geographic levels of abstraction at which gender disparity may be estimated, findings confirm expectations regarding sample size and statistical precision.

The proportion of gender-matched practitioners who are female is consistently lower than the proportion who are male, whether aggregated by state (Figure 5), by city of record (Figure 6), by zip code (Figure 7), or by metropolitan and micropolitan statistical area (Figure 8). These gender gaps are also robust to the disaggregation by attorney or agent status, both at the state level (Figure 9) and the MSA/μSA (Figure 10).

Moreover, at each geographic level, variation among the gender proportions of similarly sized practitioner populations is sensitive to practitioner population. As Figure 5 shows, e.g., variation is greatest among states with small gender-matched practitioner populations. As that population increases, variation diminishes. This variation appears to be distributed normally around the gender proportion of the most practitioner-populous state, California. The same is also true of gender proportions at the level of city of record, zip code, and metropolitan and micropolitan statistical area (Figures 6–8).

Similarly, comparing across technologies reveals marked differences among the levels of gender diversity in subsets of the patent bar. As shown in Figure 11, for patents granted during the five-year period of 2008–2012, the proportions of gender-matched attorneys and agents of record for granted patents were highest for Drugs and Medical inventions, at over 25% women and at times nearly 30%. Second-highest were for Chemical inventions, starting at just over 25% women, but generally declining toward 20% over the five-year observation window (Figure 12). The remaining categories were almost entirely below 15% in the representation of women among attorneys and agents of record, with Mechanical inventions the lowest at under 10% for most of the observation window (Figure 16).

Figures 12–17 show in further detail the gender gaps across subcategories in the Hall-Jaffe-Trajtenberg scheme. Among Drugs and Medical inventions, the higher representation of women was due primarily to Biotechnology inventions and Drug inventions (Figure 14). The trend among Chemical inventions was a wider spread in the degree of representation among subcategories as well as greater volatility in the gender gaps of the leading subcategories: Resins; Organic Compounds; and Agriculture, Food, and Textiles (Figure 12).

For the relatively gender-disparate Electrical and Electronic inventions, female attorneys and agents were better represented in Electrical Device inventions at 20–30% (Figure 15) while the other subcategories were largely below 15%. The remaining technology categories generally reflect low representation and appear to vary only with respect to the variation among subcategories. Such variation was broader for Other inventions, with proportions at 0–20% (Figure 17), than for Computers & Communications inventions (Figure 13) and Mechanical inventions (Figure 16), both below 15%.

V. CONCLUSION

The descriptive relationships between these rates of gender diversity and related trends over time, across geography, and among technologies invites considerable further study. Of particular value may be event studies comparing gender disparity before and after changes in policy, whether in legal or regulatory regimes pertaining to gender, or in private initiatives aimed at greater inclusion of women in historically or persistently underrepresented segments of industry and academia.

To these ends, the dataset described here is amenable both to methodological refinements and to matching with related data. The principal methodological refinement already available would be to abstain from estimating gender at the level of the individual practitioner, as is currently done. In place of this simple estimated count, the count may instead be assigned the probability itself. For example, in the given sample calculation where there is a 98.1% likelihood that a practitioner named Ryan is male, and a 1.90% likelihood that such a practitioner is female, the data would show 0.981 men named Ryan and 0.190 women named Ryan. Though counterintuitive with respect to individuals, in the aggregate this probabilistic estimation would yield a truer estimate of gender distributions and the gender gaps that result.

Beyond methodology, related data of interest to which this dataset may be matched includes the USPTO study in progress on the diversity of USPTO applicants, not only with respect to gender diversity between applicants on one hand and practitioners on the other, but also with respect to gender as one indicium of diversity among others.

Other relevant data includes gender diversity information about state bars generally, of which registered patent attorneys may be considered a subset. Such analysis, taken together with examination and admission statistics to state bars around the country, would shed valuable comparative light on the general pipeline from legal education into practice and the specific pipeline from scientific and intellectual property education into patent practice.

Not least, USPTO data on examiners of record for patent grants is already available through the same public full text data from which attorney and agent information was extracted for the present dataset. Detailed analysis on interactions between practitioners and examiners, as well as between practitioners and inventors, holds rich potential for studying whether and how returns from innovation are appropriated in a gendered way.

It is hoped that descriptive studies, as well as the normative arguments and recommendations that they support for crafting diversity policy in government, industry, and academia, will proceed with quantitative precision on the basis of data such as this article presents.

CHAPTER 6

POLITICAL LEADERSHIP

■ ■ ■

INTRODUCTION

Although the United States has never had a female president (at least as of late 2019), other nations have more longstanding traditions of female leaders in their top political positions. Even in countries where it is more common for women to be in key leadership roles, gendered dynamics play out in the media and other commentary about their work. For example, the Prime Minister of New Zealand, Jacinda Ardern, shocked the world in 2018 with her revelation that she was unmarried, pregnant . . . and planned to stay in office. She continued to stun onlookers by bringing baby Neve Te Aroha to official events including a speech she gave before the General Assembly at the United Nations. Arden was only the second female head of a country to give birth while in office, following Pakistan's Prime Minister Benzir Bhutto, who was removed from her position seven months after her daughter was born in 1990. The focus of this chapter is on political leadership in the United States, but it is important to keep in mind that we can learn from international experiences. While some countries have allowed women to hold the highest offices for decades (consider that Margaret Thatcher became Prime Minister of the United Kingdom in 1979. . .and centuries before women like Queen Elizabeth I, reigned from 1533–1603), most nations have not embraced women in this way. The Zambian Minister of Gender, Elizabeth Phiri, speaking at the 63rd United Nations Commission on the Status of Women in 2019, encouraged women to pursue political leadership even though many decline to do so because the male-dominated field is unwelcoming.

The statistics for other leadership positions highlighted in the previous chapters hold true for political leadership and elected offices—white men have been the overwhelming majority to hold these positions and, indeed, at the founding of the U.S. were the only ones allowed to hold them. As the case of Merrie Abbott reveals in the opinion excerpted below, capable and qualified women were routinely barred from elected office simply because they were women—even if they were elected by the public!

Studies show that when women run for office, they win. This begs the question: why don't more women run? Part of the reason lies in the institutional norms and history of the country, which excluded women entirely from this aspect of public life for more than a century. This also may be due, in part, to the reality that it is difficult to imagine ourselves in a position of leadership or power if we do not see others with whom we can identify in the role. As Madeline Albright noted in more than one speech, "I never imagined that I would one day become secretary of state. It's not that I lacked ambition. It is just that I had never seen a secretary of state in a skirt." Professors Jennifer Lawless and Richard Fox have shown with "clear and compelling evidence that women, even in the highest tiers of professional accomplishment, are substantially less likely than men to demonstrate ambition to seek elected office."[1] The readings included in this chapter offer additional explanations.

The 2018 midterm elections in the wake of President Donald Trump's ascendance into the White House seem to suggest that the number of women in elected office may be increasing. Over 270 women ran for Congressional seats and governor's offices, and hundreds more ran for state and local positions. A lot of these women won. Congress welcomed 127 new women, with more than 100 female members serving in the U.S. House of Representatives, a first in U.S. history. Other firsts were also achieved. Among the newly elected members of the House were the first Muslim women (Rashida Tlaib and Ilhan Omar) and the first Native American women (Sharice Davids and Deb Haaland). Tennessee and Arizona elected their first female Senators to Congress, Marsha Blackburn and Krysten Sinema. Sinema is also the first openly bisexual Congress member. Michigan elected an entire slate of women to lead: Governor Gretchen Whitmer, Attorney General Dana Nessel (also the first openly lesbian attorney general in the nation), Chief Justice Bridget McCormack and Secretary of State Jocelyn Benson.[2] They joined a number of other women representing Michigan in Congress: U.S. Senator Debbie Stabenow and U.S. Representatives Elissa Slotkin, Haley Stevens, and Rashida Tlaib. Harris County, Texas, elected nineteen black, female judges along with a 27-year-old immigrant from Colombia, Lina Hidalgo, as Harris County's chief executive, which is essentially the governor of Houston. Nevada became the first state with a majority-female legislature.

Are the results of the 2018 elections a sign of progress for gender and racial diversity, or merely a symptom of dissatisfaction with President Trump? Only time will tell. But, even with wins like these, the make-up of political leaders is a long way from reflecting the diversity of the public. Political scientists and legal scholars have explored the dynamics that prevent women from running for office, as well as the impact of women's presence across sectors of government. The readings included in this

---

[1]   Jennifer L. Lawless and Richard Fox, *Why are Women Still Not Running for Public Office?*, BROOKINGS, May 19, 2008. The full study is available at https://www.brookings.edu/research/why-are-women-still-not-running-for-public-office/.

[2]   Notably, every woman holding the highest offices in Michigan have law degrees—Whitmer (Michigan State University College of Law), Nessel (Wayne State University Law School), McCormack (New York University School of Law) and Benson (Harvard Law School).

chapter draw from this literature to explore the history of women's political leadership and consider the impact of women in political leadership roles.

Hillary Rodham Clinton, a lawyer and former First Lady, U.S. Senator, and Secretary of State, was the first female to receive a major party nomination when she ran for president in 2016. **Shirley Chisholm** was the first African-American woman elected to the U.S. House of Representatives, elected in 1968. She was later the first African-American candidate for a major party's nomination and the first woman to run for the Democratic party's nomination for president.

Credit: Gage Skidmore (left) and public domain (right)

Neither was the first woman to run for presidential office, however. That distinction belongs to **Victoria Woodhull**, a leader in the suffrage movement, who ran in 1872, though she would have been too young to accept the role had she won at age 34. The U.S. Constitution mandates an age of 35 years.

THOUGHT QUESTIONS

As you read the materials excerpted below, consider the following questions:

1. As noted in the Michigan Supreme Court opinion *Attorney General v. Abbott*, women were historically barred from holding elected office. That decision is over 100 years old, and women are no longer explicitly banned from elections. Even so, are there aspects of the opinion that endure today? What do you think about the 2018 election results in Michigan (described above) in light of this court opinion?

2. Are there special leadership qualities required for success in politics? Does it make a difference that political officials are elected by the public, rather than appointed or selected by a private individual or group? How are pipelines to elected office shaped by influences beyond the candidate? Are the traits and experiences that win elections the same ones needed to lead a government body?

3.   Have you ever considered running for elected office? Why or why not? Have you ever encouraged a friend or colleague to consider doing so? Identify a political leader you admire and conduct some research about his/her beginnings, including whether a political career was always an aspiration.

4.   As you read the article excerpts below, consider the Madeline Albright quote listed above in the introduction. Does it matter if elected officials reflect the diversity of the public they represent and serve? Should quotas be implemented to ensure that a certain percentage of political office holders are women or minorities or members of other under-represented groups? What other efforts might be made to expand the diversity of elected officials?

5.   Some of the political leaders mentioned in the introduction and the readings have law degrees. Is there something special about a legal education that prepares one for political leadership?

ATTORNEY GENERAL V. ABBOTT

Supreme Court of Michigan
121 Mich. 540 (1899)

Michigan Supreme Court Justice Charles D. Long Credit: public domain

After graduating from the University of Michigan Law School, Merrie Abbott was elected to hold the office of Prosecuting Attorney in Ogemaw County on November 8, 1898. The Michigan Attorney General filed a legal action known as an "information in the nature of a quo warranto" in the Supreme Court of Michigan challenging her right to hold the office because she was a woman. According to the dissent, there was "no question in the minds of any one who heard the very able oral argument made by her in this case about the entire competency of Mrs. Abbott to discharge the duties of this office." But, the majority opinion sided with the Attorney General and Abbott was not permitted to remain in office.

Opinion

LONG, J.

Merrie H. Abbott, the respondent, a woman of the age of 21 years and upwards, was elected to the office of prosecuting attorney of Ogemaw county at the general election held on the 8th day of November, 1898. She duly qualified, and is now in the discharge of the duties of that office. An information in the nature of a quo warranto is filed in this court by the attorney general, in which it is claimed that the respondent unlawfully holds and exercises the duties of that office. The only question raised is whether a woman is eligible under the constitution and laws of this state to hold such office. Section 3, art. 10, of the constitution of this state, reads as follows: 'In each organized county, there shall be a sheriff, a county clerk, a county treasurer, a register of deeds and a prosecuting attorney, chosen by the electors thereof, once in two years, and as often as vacancies shall happen, whose duties and powers shall be prescribed by law.' It is the contention of the attorney general that the office of prosecuting attorney is a constitutional office, created by the constitution of this state, which expressly provides that such official shall be chosen by the electors of the respective counties, and that such electors have no authority under the constitution and laws to elect other than one of their own number to such office. On the other hand, it is contended by the respondent that the constitution and laws do not expressly require that the prosecuting attorney shall be an elector, while for some other officers named in the constitution this qualification is distinctly required, and that this would indicate that as to those officers in regard to which the instrument is silent to such qualification is necessary; for, if the qualification of an elector is needed in order to hold the office of prosecuting attorney, then every other officer elected by the people and named in the constitution must also be an elector. It is also contended by the respondent that the common law of the state does not forbid a woman to hold the office of prosecuting attorney.

There being no express provision of the constitution or the laws of the state conferring upon the respondent the right to hold this office, the question must be determined by the principles of the common law, and the manner in which those principles have been construed in this state for the past years. It is conceded that the respondent is not an elector, and that she could not vote for a candidate for this office. Section 1, art. 7, of the constitution provides who shall be electors. There can be no question of the common-law rule that a woman cannot hold a general public office in the absence of express constitutional or statutory authority conferring upon her such right. If she is eligible to this office, then she is eligible to any constitutional office within the state. Judge Cooley, in his work on Principles of Constitutional Law (page 266), in discussing the question of eligibility to office, says, 'When the law is silent qualifications to office, it must be understood that electors are eligible, but no others.' For more than 60 years his has been regarded as the settled law of this state. It commenced when this state was admitted into the Union, and during all the time since no one, to our knowledge, has ever insisted that women are eligible to those offices which must be filled by the votes of the qualified electors of the state or other municipalities.

* * *

In Robinson's Case, 131 Mass. 376, the right of a woman to vote or hold office was fully discussed; and the common-law rule, that in the absence of express authority a woman has no legal right to hold office, was fully sustained.

* * *

It necessarily follows, it seems to us, that when women are excluded from the right to vote when these officers are to be elected, they are also excluded from the right to hold the offices voted for.' Whatever may be said of some of the decisions of other states which counsel contend are at variance with the cases above cited and quoted from, it is difficult to get away from the proposition laid down by Judge Cooley, above quoted, that, 'when the law is silent respecting qualifications to office, it must be understood that electors are eligible, but no others.' Cooley, Const. Law, p. 266. Judge Cooley undoubtedly wrote that with the full understanding of its significance. He had in mind, without doubt, that that had been the uniform practice in this state for nearly 60 years at that time, and that such was the common law of the state. It follows that a judgment of ouster must be entered.

HOOKER, J. (concurring).

The record in this case raises the question of the eligibility of a married woman to the office of prosecuting attorney. The respondent, having received a plurality of the votes cast for that office in her county at the election held in November, 1898, and entered upon the discharge of its duties, responds to a writ questioning her right thereto.

* * *

That the legislature, and it only, has power to do this, is obvious. Certainly the courts are not authorized to do so, and a growing public sentiment favoring an enlargement of the rights of women should not have such effect. Laws are not repealed by a neglect to enforce them, and the legal status of woman rests on a more stable foundation than a varying or advancing public opinion of what that status should be.

It is argued that, inasmuch as the constitution is silent upon the subject of the qualifications requisite to this office, we must recognize the right of any one to hold it. Aside from the fact that we find few authorities supporting this claim, we think that it is fallacious. The constitution does not say that aliens may not hold many of the highest public offices. Neither does it say that infants may not, nor that persons non compos mentis may not. Nor does it say that a man shall be compelled to support his wife, nor that she may pledge his credit for necessaries, nor that she cannot make a valid contract, nor that the presumption of coercion by her husband shall not attach when she is charged with crime. Nor did the earlier constitution declare that only attorneys at law could be prosecuting attorneys. Yet the court so held in the case of People v. May, 3 Mich. 610, and all of the other legal principles mentioned were unchanged by the adoption of the constitution. It must be evidence that when a new constitution is adopted the legislative blackboard is not washed clean. On the contrary, existing laws and rights under them remain, except as clearly inconsistent with the terms of the constitution. There are many cases which hold that aliens are ineligible to public office.

* * *

We are confronted by the fact that women have held offices, and by cases which sustain some of their claims upon them. Some of the cases cited hold that minors may be deputies under certain officers, and that they are capable of discharging ministerial duties, while they deny the right of holding public offices generally. See Railroad Co. v. Fisher (N. C.) 13 Lawy. Rep. Ann. 721, and note (s. c. 13 S. E. 698). Authorities are not wanting in England that decide that women may hold offices which they inherit (but can get in no other way), and may perform the duties through deputies. There are also instances where it has been held that they could hold local offices of little importance, where the duties were wholly ministerial. But, while these cases support the claim that women might hold some offices, they reinforce the authorities which deny the general right contended for here. It is undeniable that many women have held office under state and federal governments, such as postmasters, pension agents, notaries public, deputy clerks, school officers, attorneys at law, etc.

* * *

Again, it may be said that the reason for the common-law rule no longer exists, and that the rule should fall with the reason for it; that Michigan by legislation has in recent years recognized the capacity of women to do many things that she was not permitted to do at common law, one of which is to hold the position of attorney at law, and therefore there is no longer any reason for denying her eligibility to any office, and consequently there is no law prohibiting it. This, in short, amounts to saying that, when the legislature made a change in the status of woman by making her eligible to one office, it removed all of her political disabilities, except that relating to the ballot, which was beyond legislative power. If this is so, why did it not have the effect of removing all other disabilities? Why is she not now free to contract, and sign notes with others as surety? Why is she not drawn as juror and talesman in our courts of justice?

* * *

We have attempted to discuss this from a purely legal standpoint. An endeavor has been made to show that, in adhering to the doctrine here enunciated, 'courts are not putting prohibitions into constitutions, upon some supposed understanding of the people at the time of their adoption.' They are refusing to assert the implication of a repeal of laws which the constitution expressly says shall continue in force. Taking that view of the question, we have no occasion to discuss the progress of the age, or the injustice of law to women. As we have said, the legislative branch of government is the proper one to consider the advisability of a change. I concur in the conclusion reached by Mr. Justice LONG.

GRANT, C. J., and MONTGOMERY, J., concurred.

MOORE, J. (dissenting).

I do not reach the same conclusion in this case as Mr. Justice LONG. It is doubtless true the authorities cited by him tend to sustain the conclusion reached by him, but a careful examination of them shows that the question involved here was not directly involved in the cases cited, while reason, as it seems to me, sustained by a very respectable weight of authority, reaches a conclusion more in keeping with the trend of modern thought.

* * *

The disqualification imposed upon woman at the common law was incident to the prevailing order of society, whose theory it was that the functions of womanhood were limited to the domestic sphere, and that she could have no legal existence apart from her husband. She could not engage in business on her own account, nor make a binding contract without his consent. Her time and her earnings belonged to him, and it was said, because of the delicacy of her nature, she was unfitted for the activities pursued by men. Under the common law an unmarried woman had no redress for wrongs against her purity. She could be slandered without a right to bring an action for slander. Upon marriage her person as well as her property was given over to her husband. He might beat her, and she could not complain. She was the victim of his will, and had such rights only as he chose to give her. Under the chapter headed 'Legislative Assemblies,' Cush. Law & Prac. Leg. Assem. 24, it is said: 'The same descriptions of persons, namely, minors, idiots and lunatics, women, and aliens, who have already been mentioned as excluded from the right of suffrage by the common political law, are also prohibited, and for the same reasons, from being elected to any political office whatever. Such persons consequently cannot be members of a legislative assembly.' The reasons assigned for these disqualifications are, in the case of infants, the same general ground on which they are prohibited from doing any other legal act, namely, their presumed want of capacity. When they attain their majority the incapacity ceases and the disqualification ends. Idiots and lunatics are also excluded for the same reason,—want of capacity. As to the former the disability is perpetual, because the want of capacity is perpetual. As to lunatics, the disqualification ceases during lucid intervals. Aliens are disqualified because they are not supposed to have knowledge of our institutions. But when they become naturalized the disqualification ends. But it is now said that though woman is no longer disqualified, for want of intelligence or ability, to make contracts or to intelligently perform all the duties of citizenship, 'they, being designed by the law of their sex for a state of existence purely domestic, are therefore incapable of deciding upon those interests which are involved in questions of political suffrage' (Cush. Law & Prac. Leg. Assem. 15); and so she is to continue to be classed with children, idiots, lunatics, and aliens. As the reason stated is so contrary to what we see daily in our contact with pure, refined, intelligent, and capable womanhood, the rule of the disqualification ought to pass with the reason of the rule, unless the law is so firmly established that it remains for the people to act by an expression of their will in the written organic law. As we shall see later, they have so expressed themselves upon the question of suffrage, but, as I shall endeavor to show, they have not precluded woman from holding certain of the offices at their bestowal.

* * *

With all its harshness towards woman, it is doubtful if the common law ever went to the extent of saying that when an office, the duties of which she was fitted to perform, was offered to a woman, she could not hold it, simply because she was a woman. England has had many rulers who were women. All history does not record a more brilliant reign of any sovereign than the intelligent and capable Queen Victoria. Women have held almost all the offices of the kingdom. 3 Camp. Ch. Just. 108. Anne, countess of Pembroke, held the office of sheriff of Westmoreland, and exercised the duties thereof in person, at a time when the sheriffs held court and exercised judicial power. Co. Litt. 326; 8 Bac. Abr. 661; 41 Alb. Law J. 244.41 Alb. Law J. 244. Eleanor was appointed lord keeper of England, and performed the duties of lord chancellor in person. She sat as judge, performing the duties of lord chancellor, judicial as well as ministerial, for nearly a year. . . . Woman was allowed to be the keeper of a castle. Lady Russell's Case, Cro. Jac. 18. So, an overseer of the poor (Rex v. Stubbs, 2 Term R. 395); governor of a workhouse (2 Ld. Raym. 1014); keeper of a prison (Lady Braughton's Case, 3 Keb. 32, 151); commissioner of sewers (countess of Warwick's Case, Callis, Sew. [4th Ed.] marg. p. 250); and marshal of a court (41 Alb. Law J. 245). Women have been appointed to, and successfully filled, the positions of postmasters, pension agents, and other positions under the federal government, though the constitution and statutes did not in express terms authorize her appointment to any of these positions. No one has suggested that because of the common law she was disqualified. The validity of these appointments, so far as we know, has never been questioned.

* * *

Up to this point the discussion does not directly determine the question involved in this case, to wit, may the people elect to a constitutional office one who possesses all the requisite qualifications (when no qualifications for the office named are mentioned either in the constitution or the statutes), except that she is a woman?

* * *

It is urged that at the time the constitution of the state was adopted no one supposed woman would want to hold an office, and the constitutional provision must be construed in the light of that supposition.

* * *

The statutes of this state confer upon woman the right to practice law. She may represent her client in the most important litigation in all the courts of the state, and no one can dispute her right. She may defend a person charged with murder. Can she not prosecute one charged with the larceny of a whip? To say she cannot seems illogical. The state, by granting her a certificate to practice law, has held her out to all individuals as a person competent to do so. Individuals may employ her, and the courts must recognize her employment. If the people see fit, by electing her to an office the duties of which almost wholly pertain to the practice of the law, to employ her to represent them in their litigation, why should not the courts recognize the employment? I confess I can see no reason why they should not.

* * *

I think I have shown by the great weight of authority that, where the constitution and the statutes are silent as to the qualifications for a given office, the people may elect whom they will, if the person so elected is competent to discharge the duties of the office. The duties of the office of prosecuting attorney are prescribed by statute. Those duties are such as can, in the main, be performed only by a person learned in the law. None of them are of such a character as to preclude one from their performance simply because of sex. Mrs. Abbott is a citizen of the state, upward of 21 years of age. She is a graduate of the law department of the University of Michigan. She is duly authorized to practice law in all the courts of this state. There can be no question in the minds of any one who heard the very able oral argument made by her in this case about the entire competency of Mrs. Abbott to discharge the duties of this office. I think the respondent is eligible to hold the office, and that the information in the nature of a quo warranto of the attorney general should be dismissed.

CARRIE SHARLOW, *MICHIGAN LAWYERS IN HISTORY: MERRIE HOOVER ABBOTT*

97 MICHIGAN BAR JOURNAL 40 (MAY 2018)

Sharlow has worked at the State Bar of Michigan since 2007. She studied English at Hope College and English Literature at the University of Sheffield, and pursues history as a hobby.

Emelia Schaub is generally claimed as Michigan's first female prosecutor. It would be more precise to say that Schaub was the state's first female prosecutor who was allowed to keep her elected office. Let me introduce you to Merrie Hoover Abbott. Merrie (or Marie or Mary) Hoover was born in Clinton County in the 1870s to Jacob and Cynthia Hoover. The Hoovers were a pioneer family and produced 14 children, 12 of whom survived to adulthood. Merrie was somewhere in the middle of the bunch. After graduating from the St. Johns public schools, she attended school in Ypsilanti, where she received training for secretarial work.

By 1891, she was working as a stenographer at Marshall Field & Company in Chicago, where she met her husband, Charles Stewart Abbott. The couple married in 1894 and settled in West Branch. Initially, the Abbotts ran a mercantile business, but Merrie talked her husband into attending law school and she accompanied him. Charles graduated from the University of Michigan Law School in 1897 and Merrie finished up a year later.

The Abbotts returned to West Branch, where Merrie was considered an oddity around town. Her status as a "lady practitioner" was viewed as a handicap, and she didn't attend events held by the "social set of West Branch."

She was also considered a joke, and her nomination to run for county prosecutor of Ogemaw County was supposed to be seen as one. After all, what was more amusing than a female officer of the court? The 1898 election was only three weeks away when Merrie was nominated; certainly, no one would vote for a woman. Besides, the area was staunchly Republican, and the Democrats didn't expect to win any seats.

Everyone underestimated Merrie. She didn't see the handicap or the joke, and over the next three weeks, she campaigned in good weather and bad, showing the community that she was "bright, witty and forceful." Even so, everyone—except Merrie—was surprised when she won. There was apparently a recount, but Merrie won by four or six votes. Her successful election made headlines across the country and was viewed as a huge victory for the women's suffrage movement; if women could be elected to office, surely the right to vote was right around the corner.

The patriarchy was less pleased. The incumbent, William T. Yeo, refused to yield the office to Merrie, who threatened to "incarcerate [him] in the county jail unless he complie[d] with her demand." Lame duck state attorney general Fred A. Maynard said she couldn't take office without a ruling by the Supreme Court, and even the dean at her alma mater flatly stated that "Mrs. Abbott is clearly ineligible."

Of course, no one questioned the validity of Horace Oren's election to the office of state attorney general that same year. Once he was sworn into office, he filed "an application for a writ of quo warranto" to remove Merrie from her elected seat.

On June 22—when she could have been doing her job prosecuting cases in Ogemaw County—Merrie went before the state Supreme Court to argue her right to hold office. She spoke "for three-quarters of an hour, and created the impression that she [was] a good advocate." Her argument was logical: she had graduated from law school, been admitted to the bar by this exact Court, been nominated for the office, and "received the votes necessary for her election." Granted, women weren't allowed to vote, but there were other examples in the state of women holding office. Judge Allen

Morse and Thomas A. E. Weadock, both legends in the Detroit circuit, argued for Merrie as well.

Oren's argument was the opposite of the suffrage movement's victory: if a woman couldn't vote, she couldn't hold office. The attorney general argued that "in the absence of express constitutional authority, women were not entitled to hold office." It made absolutely no sense to "permit one who was precluded from voting for a candidate for a certain office to hold the office itself."

The judgment was rendered in October and Merrie was removed from office. That, too, made headlines across the country, as the Michigan Supreme Court proclaimed that "women cannot hold office." Despite earning a degree from the University of Michigan Law School and being older than 21, Merrie was viewed by the law as having a "want of capacity," and classed with "children, idiots, lunatics, and aliens."

The Court's decision notwithstanding, Merrie had practiced as Michigan's first female county prosecutor for 10 months. Later references note that she tried 156 cases, losing only once.

Merrie continued on in private practice. The Abbotts moved to Detroit and formed the firm of Abbott & Abbott, and eventually Merrie became more famous for her vigorous defense of poisoner Rose Barron and less for her ouster. Of course, it helped when the Nineteenth Amendment was ratified and any question of women not being electors was nullified.

About a decade before Merrie's death, another female Michigan attorney ran for county prosecutor and won, and this time was allowed to keep her seat. When Emelia Schaub was touted as "Michigan's first woman prosecutor" in 1936, a newspaper sought to set the record straight and interviewed Merrie, who was fairly modest about her experience some 38 years earlier.

Michigan's first female prosecutor, Merrie Hoover Abbott, died in October 1946. Every woman lawyer who has come after her carries her legacy.

* * *

ROBERT YABLON, *CAMPAIGNS, INC.*
103 MINNESOTA LAW REVIEW 151 (2018)

Yablon is an Assistant Professor of Law at the University of Wisconsin Law School. Prior to becoming a professor, he served as a law clerk for Judge William Fletcher of the U.S. Court of Appeals for the Ninth Circuit and for U.S. Supreme Court Justices Ruth Bader Ginsburg and Sonia Sotomayor.

Politics has always been theater. Today, it is also business. The billions of dollars that flow into modern U.S. election campaigns sustain a thriving ecosystem of political service providers who develop strategy and execute operations in virtually every major race. This is not news to historians who have charted the evolution of campaigning or to political scientists who study the activities of campaign professionals. Leading scholars in these fields have described the emergence of the campaign industry as a singularly important development in our nation's politics. Yet, remarkably, the campaign industry is almost entirely absent from election law discourse.

* * *

Having emerged from a particular legal milieu, the campaign industry has proceeded to reshape the democratic process in its own distinctive image. The industry's impact has been transformative both for individual campaigns and for the political system writ large. Consider first the campaign-level perspective. Candidates and other campaigners rely on the campaign industry to convert a particular input—namely, dollars—into electioneering activities that ultimately aim to produce a particular output—namely, votes. The industry can offer these political actors valuable expertise and operational capabilities, but it does not always serve them well. Rather than scrupulously promoting their clients' interests, campaign professionals may seek to aggrandize themselves or maximize their own financial returns instead. While such agency problems can arise in a host of contexts, particular features of campaigns and the campaign industry may make them especially prevalent and acute. For example, Super PACs and similar entities, which reap a substantial share of campaign dollars, allow campaign professionals to operate with minimal oversight, inviting self-dealing and other abuses. For campaigners and their funders, the pertinent question is how to ensure that campaign professionals faithfully and effectively advance their electoral interests.

A campaign-level vantage point, however, offers only a glimpse of the campaign industry's import. A broader, system-level perspective reveals the industry's impact on our politics as a whole. For starters, campaign professionals affect the complexion of those who seek office. In particular, they tilt the playing field toward candidates who, by virtue of their fundraising potential and perhaps their perceived pliability, are attractive clients to campaign professionals. Second, the campaign industry and its economic incentives affect the nature of electioneering. Among other things, professionals overemphasize capital-intensive campaign activities that they can monetize, such as mass media advertisements, which offer a lucrative source of commissions. In contrast, they underemphasize activities, such as grassroots outreach, that may foster deeper democratic engagement. The industry may thus contribute to the rising tide of political cynicism and disenchantment. Third, the campaign industry's dominance affects policy positions and priorities. Willfully or not, campaign professionals may nudge candidates and officials toward positions that accord with the interests of actual or prospective non-campaign clients, including corporations, trade associations, and foreign governments and officials.

* * *

Initially, campaign professionals play an important gate-keeping role. They often choose candidates as much as candidates choose them. This not only means deciding whether to take on or seek out particular candidates as clients; it can also mean actively working to identify and recruit candidates. Even at the presidential level, professionals routinely play an instrumental role in grooming potential candidates and persuading them to run.

These early judgments by professionals can significantly affect who seeks and wins elective office. This is partly because professional services directly help candidates mount viable campaigns, but also because professionals—and especially highly regarded ones—can serve to validate candidates by choosing to affiliate with them. A top professional's decision to work with a particular candidate can help that candidate draw early interest and funds. For political elites and the media, a candidate's success in building an all-star professional team signals the candidate's strength. Conversely, failing to attract top-tier staff and consultants can derail a candidacy from the outset.

As campaign professionals select their candidate clients, they tend to prioritize several key criteria. These criteria differ from the ones that most citizens will later use to make their voting decisions. They also diverge in part from the selection criteria that would prevail if parties or the media exerted relatively greater electoral influence. Party organizations would presumably favor candidates with a record of loyalty and service to the party and perhaps also candidates perceived to be especially capable of advancing the party's substantive agenda. Media-dominated campaigns, meanwhile, would presumably favor effective communicators with big personalities and perhaps also advantage candidates with preexisting public profiles. Such candidate attributes may be relevant to campaign professionals, but they typically take a backseat to other considerations.

First, because campaign professionals want to get paid, and preferably more rather than less, professionals consider a candidate's fundraising potential. In a survey of 200 political consultants, ninety-eight percent reported that "a candidate's ability to raise money and pay the bills was either very or somewhat important." Other research has indicated "that more consultants cared about whether their clients could pay their bills than whether they were capable of governing." The market for professional campaign services thus amplifies the electoral system's tendency to favor "candidates who are themselves wealthy or have networks of wealthy friends . . . relative to candidates with other kinds of political skills." Commentators sometimes discuss the phenomenon of the "money primary," in which candidates compete to attract early momentum-generating funds. But potential candidates may not even enter the money primary if they fare poorly in the consultant beauty pageant.

Second, campaign professionals assess a candidate's likelihood of electoral success. Professionals are sometimes willing to work with long-shot candidates, especially ones with deep pockets. After all, professionals can distinguish themselves by guiding long shots to victory, while explaining away losses as inevitable. But, on the whole, professionals generally prefer to have more winning races on their resume than losing ones. For better or for worse, this may make professionals—at least the most well-established and reputable ones—risk-averse in their choice of candidates, potentially giving conventional candidates a boost over unconventional ones and incumbents a boost over challengers.

Both of these considerations have implications for candidate diversity. If professionals prefer candidates who are connected to wealthy donor networks—networks that are disproportionately Caucasian and male— and who resemble candidates who have succeeded in the past, then minorities and women may find themselves at a particular disadvantage. The campaign industry's own demographics may reinforce this dynamic. Women and minorities are significantly underrepresented among campaign service providers. According to one study, less than two percent of payments the National Democratic campaign committees made to consultants during the 2010 and 2012 cycles went to minority-run firms. And women comprise just thirty-two percent of the membership of the American Association of Political Consultants. Perhaps unsurprisingly, studies indicate that political insiders encourage women to run for office less often than they encourage men, even though women are equally responsive to such suggestions when asked.

* * *

ORI ARONSON, *THE NEXT FORTY PRESIDENTS*

24 WILLIAM AND MARY JOURNAL OF WOMEN AND THE LAW 235 (2018)

Aronson is an Associate Professor of Law at Bar-Ilan University and Deputy Director of the Center for Jewish and Democratic Law. Prior to becoming a professor, he clerked for Chief Justice of the Israel Supreme Court, Aharon Barak, and Second Circuit U.S. Court of Appeals Judge, Jon Newman.

* * *

The defeat of Hillary Rodham Clinton in the 2016 presidential election ended a historic run, being the first time a major party had slated a woman as its candidate for President of the United States. While other, nonmajor, parties have done so before, and while each of the two major parties has already once selected a female vice-presidential nominee, 2016 was seen by many as the closest a woman has ever realistically gotten to becoming president. A woman president would have been a glass-shattering moment in American political history, bending the arc of the moral universe a little closer to justice. As such, the fact of its political feasibility should be a cause for celebration to all Americans, regardless of gender or party affiliation. Clinton did not win though, the glass ceiling remains intact, and the future of feminist political mobilization is again up for grabs.

With Donald J. Trump in the White House, we are left wondering what exactly it would have meant, in terms of gender relations and identities, to have a woman as the forty-fifth president, and, *ipso facto*, what it means for the first ever real woman candidate to have lost the election. It is arguable whether Clinton's loss should be viewed as a defeat to all American women, or to the totality of feminist causes. Had she won, it is debatable whether such a victory would have been considered a victory to all American women, regardless of race, creed, age, ideology, or party affiliation. The first woman to be elected president—if this ever happens—will not be "any woman," just as the first African American president was not representative of all African Americans, nor necessarily the best proponent of causes related to their interests. Hillary Clinton, for example, was a white, sixty-nine-year-old, former First Lady, Democrat, with a very certain set of values, ideologies, policy preferences, life experiences, affiliations, and character traits. In the age of intersectional identity politics, many people who might have thought that it is time for the United States to elect a female president could still reasonably believe—and apparently did in fact believe—that she was not the one they would have liked as president. In other words, other considerations that figure into a citizen's choice of leader in a democracy, such as ideology, competence, and character, can reasonably outweigh one's preference to electing the first woman president.

* * *

Perhaps an actual feminist reform of the presidency is needed. We might imagine a gendered modification to the institution of the President of the United States that would go beyond the historical significance of the fact that a woman had a chance to hold the office at one time or another. One way to do this is to look back in time, before looking forward again into the future. The U.S. presidency has been occupied by very different persons over the nearly two and a half centuries since the establishment of the office, each with distinct positions and affiliations. People of different beliefs and expectations celebrated some and decried others, and most have felt a little bit of both toward all. One obvious thing however that was *not* exceptional about any of the presidents to have so far held the office was the fact that they were all men. The reason, of course, was that only men were ever seriously up for election to the presidency in the history of the U.S., up to the 2016 election.

Think of the richness of male leadership this fact has enabled the U.S. polity to experience over the generations: while not nearly representative of the diverse identities and communities that comprise it, the U.S. constituency did get to be governed by Democrats and Republicans, conservatives, liberals, and centrists, Northerners and Southerners, highbrow intellectuals and down-to-earth populists, Episcopalians, Unitarians, Presbyterians, Methodists, Baptists, Quakers, and a Catholic, whites and an African American, lawyers, soldiers, farmers, teachers, businessmen, journalists, governors, senators, congressmen, an engineer, an actor, an athlete, men in their 40s, 50s, 60s, and 70s, healthy and disabled, and so forth.

Clearly, the first woman president, when she arrives, will not be all of that. She will only present a sliver of what female political leadership to the extent that such a thing exists—is like, and she will only represent a sliver of what the U.S. body politic is made of. Clearly, to get an idea of the potential that a "female presidency" holds for the U.S., comparable to the one we have about male leadership, a single such presidency cannot do. Indeed, it would seem that to level the proverbial playing field, in terms of both corrective justice and prolific and pluralist experiences, we would need to have some forty women presidents in a row—from hereon and for the next several generations. This Article suggests such a thought experiment and seeks to show that there are several good reasons to consider a new constitutional norm that would require all candidates for the next forty U.S. presidencies to be women, while no men would be allowed on major party tickets.

This sounds like a radical reform, and in the context of the U.S. constitutional system its political feasibility indeed seems farfetched. But the purpose of this Article is to illustrate that if you think about this long enough and consider the main arguments, it is in fact difficult to fully and rationally oppose this view. A rule that would ensure that the next forty presidents are women turns out to be an attractively just policy, with few social drawbacks, and with a capacity to transcend ideological and sectorial divides in its favor (in this it also differs from comparable reforms that would secure representation for other minorities in the presidency, as I elaborate below). This does not mean the reform is on its way, but starting to imagine reform is certainly a good point of departure. Perhaps more accessibly, the Article can be read as a thought experiment locating feminist constitutionalism in the realm of intergenerational justice. It explores the contours of a sequential model of corrective justice, applying a heightened version of affirmative action to a unitary institution of governance, usually considered the most important in the country, that has also been purely restricted to men for the entirety of its existence. This context presents a unique analytical challenge for normative theory, and the discussion of what I term *the forty female presidents rule* reveals that there is room for innovation in tackling such problems of gender inequality in the intergenerational sphere.

* * *

I. THE IDEA OF THE FEMALE PRESIDENCY

The defeat of Hillary Clinton in the 2016 presidential election was a sour end to what may be considered a "good year" for women in political leadership in post-industrialized democracies. It came four months after the selection of Theresa May as Prime Minister of the United Kingdom, one of Europe's two largest economies, the other being Germany, led since 2005 by Angela Merkel. In the United Nations, outgoing Secretary General Ban Ki-moon publicly called for the member states to elect a woman to succeed him, for the first time ever; although another man—António Guterres— was eventually selected. Other noteworthy international institutions are already led by women, including the International Monetary Fund (Christine Lagarde) and the World Health Organization (Margaret Chan). Few would disagree that a leaders' summit involving these countries and institutions would be a unique and notable sight, reflecting an undeniable cumulative shift in gender politics and in equality of political opportunity in the twenty-first century. Though if it would also signify a shift in the nature and quality of leadership is unclear. In other words, beyond symbolics, we must still consider whether the gender of our leaders in fact matters.

There is ample evidence today to support the belief that it does, even if we do not exactly know how or why.

* * *

If women in politics are not a mere replication of men in politics, then we have been missing *something* by never electing a woman as our leader. This might be a different style of leadership or management, a different set of beliefs, attitudes, or understandings, a different vocabulary or analytical perspective, a different collection of life experiences or outlooks. This is of course a richly developed—if contested—element of feminist literature. As cultural feminists have demonstrated extensively, women can be shown to share a distinct set of ethical and conceptual categories and sensibilities that have been missing from public life for too long. Although espousing a competing narrative of women's liberation, power ("radical") feminism has also insisted as much, in its claim that the subordination of women has effectively precluded the elocution of an independently female voice in public (and private) life. Even those critical of the idea of a distinct female "voice," seeing in it an anachronistic reification of gender roles and stereotypes, cannot deny the liberating (to liberal feminists) or destabilizing (to postmodern feminists) force of having women hold "men's" positions and make "male" choices, including ones detrimental to women, such as going to war or cutting welfare payments.

Whatever feminist (or nonfeminist) position one takes, the fact is that we do not know what a "female presidency" means in the U.S. since it has never been tried. It might be distinguishable in consistent, impactful ways from a "male presidency," and it might turn out to be significant in diverse and contradictory ways. We have good reasons to believe that such a thing exists though, and therefore it ought to become part of a nation's collective life story as a republican democracy, if it is to finally fulfill its egalitarian and pluralist ideals of membership and leadership. Some people would surely learn to value and appreciate the political possibilities revealed by female presidents; just as others are likely to prefer the male alternative after all. The current Article takes no stake in that question—it just accepts as its premise that it is a question we ought to finally explore through politics.

II. THE NEXT FORTY PRESIDENTS

A. *The Model*

Under the "forty female presidents rule," no men would be allowed on the ballot for the next forty presidencies, from hereon and for several generations—basically replicating the status of women in presidential elections since independence to the very near past, *de jure* or *de facto*.

* * *

The idea of reserving certain seats or positions, even in democratically elected bodies, for members of specific identity groups, is not new. Other countries have done so openly, usually for one of two reasons: to secure some degree of representation for women (and sometimes other minorities), notably in developing countries with traditionally patriarchal political cultures (e.g., Afghanistan, Algeria, Bangladesh, China, Iraq, Jordan, Kenya, Morocco, Niger, Pakistan, Saudi Arabia, Uganda); or to preserve an intergroup balance of power in a multicultural setting, from token assurances of representation (e.g., Croatia, Slovenia) to structured arrangements of consociationalism power-sharing (e.g., Belgium, Bosnia and Herzegovina, Burundi, Lebanon). Informally, this has become a consistently followed practice in the U.S. and other countries in such areas as judicial and ministerial positions, some of which are reserved to appointees of specific group affiliations, more or less explicitly: it is, for example, difficult today to seriously imagine an all-white, let alone an all-male, appointed court or cabinet.

What is unique about the forty female presidents model, however, is that it is not about representation within a collegial body or a class of public officials. Rather, it is directed at occupying a single elected office which *cannot be shared*, at least not contemporaneously. If the reform is adopted, therefore, and assuming no other change is made in the relevant constitutional (and biological) fabric, this would mean that for the next 160–320 years (depending on single-or double-term tenures), the U.S. will only have women presidents.

* * *

Why Presidents?

What makes the presidency a position that uniquely fits the suggested reform? Exclusion from political participation has been part of all levels and functions of government for generations. In the branches of the federal government, Congress suffers from underrepresentation of women to this very day, and so does the Supreme Court, with the three current female justices constituting an all-time record. Why not create mandatory gender quotas for other institutions as well? What is the reason to stop with the presidency, or indeed to start with the presidency?

The answer is that, ironically, the presidency is not about representation. A political position held at any time by a single individual, the presidency, by definition, is *in*capable of providing all members of the constituency the sense of presence, belonging, and shared participation that is regularly used to legitimize the coercive power of law in a democracy. Unlike the collegial institution of democratic government—Congress—the presidency is not intended, and is structurally unable, to reflect in its makeup, decision-making process, modes of reasoning, or ultimate actions the diversity of membership and ideology exhibited in the population that elected it. The legitimacy of presidential power derives from its function in promoting the democratic values enshrined in the Constitution, not from popular accountability (especially so in the second term) or representativeness. The Court similarly does not rely on popular acceptance, but it is a collegial institution whose makeup and behavior is susceptible to evaluation and critique along identitarian lines; and it seems to matter to many people whether there are on the Court women, members of racial minorities, and the like.

What this means is that imposing gender exclusions on the access to such collegial institutions does real harm to the notion of representative democracy; while no such harm takes place if the presidency is limited to women alone. In the presidency, a man is no less "represented" than a woman by a female president, since, by definition, only one or the other could serve at any given time. If only women were allowed to run for Congress, then men would have a real claim of under-representation, since Congress can be made up to represent both men and women; unitary positions like the presidency cannot. Put more accurately, the only relevant sense in which we can talk of "representation" in single-person institutions is diachronic: along a temporal line of successive office-holders that, over time, should come to reflect the full diversity of the constituency. As we know, however, the promise of such diachronic representation in the presidency has completely failed women (and other classes) over the generations, hence invoking the corrective measure of the forty female presidents model.

In this sense, the logic of the reform suggested here can extend to other unitary elected positions from which women have been systematically excluded—governors, mayors, and the like. Such extensions of the argument, however, should be treated with care. Establishing a comprehensive "forty female executives" norm across the board would entail the marginalization of men from a broad stretch of political agency, and the accompanying social costs of such an exclusion in terms of civic engagement and public commitment are likely to outweigh the gender-equality-related benefits of the reform. Again somewhat ironically, one of the attractive features of the forty female presidents rule lies in its limited applicability to a single position nationwide, a position that is extraordinarily difficult to attain or even to plan or prepare for in any practical way: few people are likely to change their life choices and behavior following its adoption. In addition, unlike many other executive positions in the states, the president in fact is not elected popularly, but rather through the mechanism of the Electoral College, which presents another buffer between the representation of popular will and the eventual selection.

Given that access to the presidency is so exceptional, and because presidential selection and tenure bely assumptions of representation anyhow, the offense to democratic expectations implied by the forty female presidents rule is relatively less pronounced than possible parallel reforms in other branches or levels of government. Sometimes, initiating reform at the top can be more readily just than starting from below.

CONCLUSION

The forty female presidents rule is not likely to materialize in the foreseeable future; less provocative constitutional reforms have been failing the demanding obstacles of the Constitution's amendment process for decades. This does not mean it is not worth considering seriously, as such an exercise can be valuable in helping us recognize our institutional blind spots, as well as our normative fixations. Imagining a truly radical reform, especially one that rests on essentially unassailable moral grounds—here, the clear injustice in the gendered formation of the presidency for centuries—is a useful way to begin discussing real, or more feasible, reforms, but this time with a much broader normative pool of institutional possibilities from which to draw.

* * *

CHAPTER 7

CORPORATE LEADERSHIP

■ ■ ■

INTRODUCTION

Despite research that suggests that the presence of women in leadership roles can increase the financial success of corporations, women remain significantly underrepresented in all areas of corporate leadership including boards of directors, CEOs, and general counsels.

According the *2019 General Counsel Landscape*, women make up 30 percent of general counsels in the Fortune 500, with male general counsels were paid an average of 39 percent more than their female counterparts.[1] Research from Catalyst reveals a pyramid shape representing the position of women in the Fortune 500.[2] At the bottom, 44.7 percent of the corporate workforce is made up of women. This is similar to the women entering the legal profession, where the numbers suggest relative equality. One step up from the bottom of the corporate hierarchy, women are among 36.9 percent among first/mid-level managers, and at the higher executive/senior manager level, women make up 26.5 percent. Women consist of 21.2 percent of directors on corporate boards, while 5 percent of CEOs are women.[3]

> **As of January 2019, the 5% of female CEOs include 25 women:**
>
> Mary T. Barra, General Motors Company (GM)
> Gail Boudreaux, Anthem, Inc.
> Heather Bresch, Mylan N.V.
> Michele Buck, Hershey Company
> Debra A. Cafaro, Ventas, Inc.
> Safra A. Catz, Oracle Corporation (co-CEO)
> Mary Dillon, Ulta Beauty, Inc.

---

[1] Sue Reisinger, *ACC Survey Finds Most GCs Come From In-House, Earn an Average of $400,000+, Corporate Counsel*, CORPORATE COUNSEL (Nov. 27, 2018), https://www.law.com/corpcounsel/2018/11/27/acc-survey-finds-most-gcs-come-from-in-house-earn-an-average-400000/?slreturn=20190406232549. When it comes to compensation in the corporate hierarchy, only 11 percent of the top earners are women. *Pyramid: Women in S&P 500 Companies*, CATALYST, May 1, 2019, https://www.catalyst.org/research/women-in-sp-500-companies/.

[2] *Pyramid: Women in S&P 500 Companies*, CATALYST, May 1, 2019, https://www.catalyst.org/research/women-in-sp-500-companies/.

[3] *Id.*

Adena Friedman, Nasdaq, Inc.

Michelle Gass, Kohl's Corporation

Lynn J. Good, Duke Energy Corporation

Tricia Griffith, The Progressive Corporation

Marillyn A. Hewson, Lockheed Martin Corporation

Vicki Hollub, Occidental Petroleum Corporation

Patricia Kampling, Alliant Energy Corporation

Margaret Keane, Synchrony Financial

Beth E. Mooney, KeyBank

Phebe N. Novakovic, General Dynamics Corporation

Patricia K. Poppe, CMS Energy Corporation

Barbara Rentler, Ross Stores, Inc.

Virginia M. Rometty, IBM Corporation

Lori Ryerkerk, Celanese Corporation

Susan N. Story, American Water Works Company, Inc.

Lisa Su, Advanced Micro Devices, Inc.

Jayshree Ullal, Arista Networks, Inc.

Kathy Warden, Northrop Grumman Corp.

To address the low representation of women on corporate boards of directors, the California legislature took affirmative steps by passing a law that required companies to increase diversity by including at least one woman on the board of directors by the end of 2019.[4] By the end of 2021, for five person boards, at least two directors must be women and for boards with six or more directors, three must be women. In April of 2019, the Illinois legislature also took up this issue but went a step further by requiring not just the presence of a woman on corporate boards in that state—but also an African American. The bill passed in the Illinois House and was considered by the Senate but ultimately the legislation that passed only required companies to report information about diversity such as the gender and race/ethnicity of board members and demographic diversity efforts. It is widely thought that the California law will be challenged in court on constitutional grounds.[5]

With the increased number of women serving in corporate and other leadership roles, researchers have started paying attention to the dynamics surrounding their promotion. There is a common perception that once a corporation has hired a woman as its CEO, this might open the door for subsequent hiring of women leaders into that role. However, among

---

[4] *California Becomes First State to Require Women on Corporate Boards*, NBC NEWS, September 30, 2018, https://www.nbcnews.com.

[5] Emily Stewart, *California Just Passed a Law Requiring More Women on Boards. It Matters, Even if it Fails*, VOX (October 3, 2018), https://www.vox.com/2018/10/3/17924014/california-women-corporate-boards-jerry-brown; Alexandra Silets, *Controversial Proposal Would Require Corporate Board Diversity*, WTTW, April 29, 2019, https://news.wttw.com/2019/04/29/controversial-proposal-would-require-corporate-board-diversity.

Fortune 500 companies, women have directly succeeded other women as CEO only three times. Anne Mulcahy was the CEO of Xerox between 2001 and 2009, followed by the appointment of Ursula Burns, who served from 2009 until 2017. Andrea Jung was CEO of Avon between 1999 and 2011, and Sheri McCoy followed in the role from 2012 until 2017. Susan Cameron was CEO of Reynolds American on two separate occasions. She returned from retirement in 2014 and served until the beginning of 2017, at which time Debra Crew succeeded her, serving only one year. There is also evidence to suggest that sometimes women's ascendance into positions of leadership occurs at a time when the organization is struggling, thus setting the leaders up for failure. Researchers Michelle Ryan and Alexander Haslam famously coined the term the "glass cliff" to describe these circumstances; we explored the "glass cliff" in greater detail, and especially how it can also extend into the legal profession, in Chapter 4.

Inequality exists in places not previously considered and manifests in sometimes unusual ways. Legal scholars Ann McGinley and Benjamin Edwards explore gender in the context of venture capitalism, a sector of the business world that often escapes attention when it comes to diversity. The scholars note: "When venture capitalists fund business development, they direct disproportionate amounts toward male entrepreneurs. In 2016, all-male firms raised $58.2 billion in venture capital funding. In contrast, all female firms raised only $1.46 billion. Although these numbers do not reveal funding disparities per founder, other research has revealed stark contrast for individuals seeking capital: " 'Black-female-founded start-ups raised an average of $36,000, while the white-male-led startups that failed raised an average of $1.3 million.' "[6] This reality has led to an overwhelming performance by women who embrace a masculine identity. "Massive funding for men means that Silicon Valley has an established, self-perpetuating, pattern-matching preference for a masculinized founder archetype. As a founder's identity approaches that archetype, investors view the opportunity more favorably."[7]

Many of the kinds of inequality described in this chapter and throughout the book, do not rise to the level of being legally actionable (at least not yet. . .). The last part of this chapter focuses on the notion of gender sidelining and how it functions specifically in the corporate context.

---

[6] Benjamin P. Edwards & Ann C. McGinley, *Venture Bearding,* 52 UNIVERSITY OF CALIFORNIA DAVIS L. REV. 1873 (2019) (citation omitted).

[7] Ann C. McGinley & Benjamin P. Edwards, *'Venture Bearding' Masks Silicon Valley's Big Gender Problem,* THE HILL (November 6, 2018), https://thehill.com/opinion/finance/415165-venture-bearding-masks-silicon-valleys-big-gender-problem.

Credit: Andy Mettler, World Economic Forum

Indra Nooyi served as CEO of PepsiCo from 2001–2018. The number of female CEOs in the Fortune 500 dropped by six in the year prior to her departure. Nooyi is lauded for turning PepsiCo into one of the most successful food and beverage companies in the world. Following her departure, Nooyi joined the board of directors of Amazon and will be teaching at West Point. Despite overwhelming career success, after stepping down from PepsiCo, Nooyi publicly disclosed the challenges of balancing professional ambitions with her children and family.

THOUGHT QUESTIONS

As you read the articles excerpted below, consider the following questions:

1.   How does inequality in the corporate context impact women and minorities? Why are there so many women in entry level positions but not in positions of leadership? What will it take to shift this dynamic?

2.   Do you understand the roles and responsibilities of various corporate actors like boards of directors, CEOs, and general counsels? What are their functions in a corporation? Have you contemplated who is at the helm of the corporations whose products, goods, or services you use? Take moment to research the identity of CEOs and board members or general counsels of companies whose products you use every day. Are these leaders diverse?

3.   Explore the background of several of the 25 women CEOs in the Fortune 500. How did they navigate the pipeline to power? What kinds of professional experience did they have before they assumed their role? What about academic credentials? What distinguishing characteristics or similarities exist among the women do you observe?

4.   What is gender sidelining? How is it different from legally actionable discrimination? How does gender sidelining impact women's advancement in the corporate world?

DOUGLAS BRANSON, *PATHWAYS FOR WOMEN TO SENIOR MANAGEMENT POSITIONS AND BOARD SEATS: AN A TO Z LIST*
2012 MICHIGAN STATE LAW REVIEW 1555 (2012)

Branson is the W. Edward Sell Professor of Business Law and Professor Emeritus of Law at the University of Pittsburgh. He is the author of numerous books and articles dealing with corporate law, corporate governance and securities regulation. His most recent book, THE FUTURE OF TECH IS FEMALE, explores the pervasive issue of inequality in the technology sector and offers innovations for reform.

* * *

The expectations for the emergence of women in the corporate sphere have been high, justifiably so, for thirty-five years now, but the numbers are lackluster and the reality lags even behind the reported numbers. If a pipeline to power exists, there are a lot of leaks in it. A robust stream enters at the intake end; a barely discernible trickle emerges.

Pathway may be a better description than pipeline in corporate governance, an area still dominated by the "good ole boys' club." Even pathway may be too strong a word for it connotes a relatively straightforward journey to the destination. The sojourn women must undertake often is a circuitous one, especially compared to the similarly situated male.

For example, in order to reach the prestigious position of corporate director, a woman may have to leave business, make her way upward in academe, the not-for-profit profit sphere, government or consulting, or smaller corporations, areas in which women fare far better, and then re-emerge in the business world's main arena as a director. Approximately 67.3% of women directors have reached the corporate board of directors by "side stepping" in this fashion, sometimes with two or three sidesteps, rather than ascending vertically in business organizations. A woman's best chance of becoming a corporate director may be to be a tenured professor in business, engineering, or the health sciences at a prestige university rather than having patiently worked her way up through corporate organizations. By contrast, in business, the male's ascent seems to be a decidedly more linear one.

* * *

The subject of diversity in corporate governance is a broad one, one in which I have been involved since 1999. I dare not attempt to cover the waterfront on the subject in this, a symposium piece. On the other hand, judging from the content I have seen at other women's studies or feminist jurisprudence conferences, diversity in governance is a subject that receives short shrift, as opposed to women as judges, or as law firm partners, or as elected officials. Women in corporate governance often is limited to no more than ten to fifteen minutes, in a two day meeting, consigned to the smallest meeting room, in the most distant corner of the hotel, or not discussed at all. The subject begs for exposition because I strongly believe that women's increased participation in the upper echelons of Corporate America is the most promising pipeline to power existent.

The compromise I have decided upon involves compiling an A to Z list of sub-topics on diversity. The list will by no means cover the waterfront, but it should give the reader an introduction to this all-important subject.

* * *

VI. An A to Z List on Women and Corporate Governance

Aggressiveness/Assertiveness. The advice books (the how-to books) for women who aspire to succeed in corporate settings are uniform, and universally wrong. They are anecdotal: "I did this," or "my friend did that." Universally, they counsel unrelenting aggressiveness, a variety of which Hillary Clinton refers to as "shoulder-pad feminism." Many advice book authors use sports metaphors: "Be the quarterback," "Score the touchdown," "Throw a knockout punch," "Hit a home run," "Be the team leader."

Publication of management and advice books for women has been a land office business. Titles include:

Susan Adams, The New Success Rules for Women (2000).

Esther Wachs Book, Why the Best Man for the Job Is a Woman (2000).

Donna Brooks & Lynn Brooks, Seven Secrets of Successful Women (1997).

Catalyst, Inc., Advancing Women in Business (1998).

Nina DiSesa, Seducing the Boys Club (2008).

Gail Evans, Play Like a Man, Win Like a Woman (2000).

Carol Gallagher, Going to the Top (2000).

Pamela B. Gilberd, The Eleven Commandments of Wildly Successful Women (1996).

Sylvia A. Hewlett, Off Ramps and On Ramps (2007).

Pat Heim & Susan Golant, Hardball for Women (1992, rev. ed. 2005).

Pat Heim & Susan Golant, Smashing the Glass Ceiling (1993).

Linda Hirshman, Get to Work (2006).

Kelly L. Johnson, Skirt! Rules: For the Workplace (2008).

Ann Morrison et al., Breaking the Glass Ceiling (1987; rev. ed. 1992).

Anthony Stith, Breaking the Glass Ceiling (1998).

Sheila Wellington, Be Your Own Mentor (2002).

Certain of these advice books suggest women take up golf, or watch Monday Night Football with male co-workers. Others counsel the "iron maiden" approach, which involves pinstriped pant suits and a severe appearance coupled with heavy doses of assertiveness.

The latest generation of advice books actually espouses use of feminine wiles with co-workers and superiors:

I play on [men's] masculine pride and natural instincts to protect the "weaker" sex.

"I can't figure this out, and I'm exhausted," I will say, "[I]f it's not done by tomorrow, I'm dead.'"

"I'll do it," he'll invariably say.

But his rescue mission won't be truly satisfying to him unless I show appreciation for the sacrifice he is making. . . .

"No, no, you're swamped, too," I'll say.

"I'll make the time for it."

"Thank you. I love you."

"I know. You're welcome."

It's like great sex. Everyone walks away fulfilled.

An examination of the careers of women who actually have succeeded in business demonstrates, conclusively so, that while aggressiveness may aid a woman in obtaining her initial promotion, thereafter the most likely outcome will be to sidetrack or derail a career altogether.

B

Bully Broad. In fact, organizational psychologist Jean Hollands has coined the somewhat infelicitous term "bully broad" to describe the overly aggressive woman manager. She has consulted with Cisco, Intel, Wells Fargo, Oracle, and a number of other major corporations. She finds that invariably the Bully Broad reputation dead ends a woman's career.

The Women's National Basketball Association (WNBA) started out in the 1990s with women coaches. Quickly, owners and general managers weeded out women coaches, replacing them with men. One of the principal reasons, Hollands reports, is that the first generation coaches were Bully Broads. What had caused those women to succeed in their careers as players and in coaching in the lower ranks of the game, did them in when they reached coaching's upper echelons. "Why have women washed out as coaches? For the same reason they have washed out in the corporate world[ ] Women can't get away with the harsh and command-and-control style that many male coaches and [managers] can." Although it is doubtful that anyone, man or woman, can succeed today with such a management style, it certainly holds true for women.

C

Comply or Explain. Foreign stock exchanges, such as those in London and in Sydney, have corporate governance regimes but they are not mandatory. Instead, in their annual disclosures, listed companies need only elaborate on those governance attributes or recommendations with which they are not in compliance. They must further state why the company is out of step.

The UK Corporate Governance Code elaborates:

The "comply or explain" approach [has been] the trademark of corporate governance in the UK. It has been in operation since the Code's beginnings It is strongly supported by both companies and shareholders and has been widely admired and imitated internationally.

In the UK, in 2010, the Council included within the new Governance Code a diversity statement: "The search for board candidates should be conducted, and appointments made, on merit, against objective criteria and due regard for the benefits of diversity on the board, including gender."

In 2010, similarly the Australian Stock Exchange (ASX) sharpened its pencil with regard to addition of women on corporate boards. Effective January 1, 2012, Australian public corporations must "comply or explain." "Companies should establish a policy concerning diversity and disclose the policy or a summary of that policy." Further, "The policy should include requirements for the board to establish measurable objectives for achieving gender diversity for the board to assess annually both the objectives and progress in achieving them." The Australian guidelines even reach beyond corporate governance to recommend disclosures on the proportion of women in the company's work force overall and in the ranks of senior management. Despite grumbling about the unprecedented reach of the ASX regulations, and the increase in workload compliance entails, most Australian corporations will comply and disclose what steps they have taken, adding to the pressure both to enlarge the pool from which women candidates to the board may be chosen and to name additional women to the board.

The ASX and the business press term the requirement the "if not, why not rule" perhaps as code that the rule contains more of an imperative than the other "comply or explain" ASX rules which exist. In the last several years, Australia has seen a sea change on the subject of women on corporate boards, evidenced by the "if not, why not rule" of the stock exchange. " 'My impression is that in many of these [corporate] boardrooms the conversation has changed, and the conversation is not "should we do it?" but how best to do it.' "

In the United States, neither the New York Stock Exchange nor the NASDAQ has either a regulation or a proposal for a regulation regarding diversity and board composition.

D

Disclosure Regimes. Since February 28, 2010, however, the U.S. Securities and Exchange Commission (SEC) has had in place a mandatory rather than comply or explain diversity disclosure requirement for the approximately 16,500 corporations who file periodic reports with it. With little fanfare, the U.S. SEC's "Proxy Rule Disclosure and Solicitation Enhancements" amendments took effect, amending SEC omnibus disclosure Regulation SK. Regulation SK is the umbrella disclosure regulation which dictates what material public companies must disclose and sometimes in what format they must disclose it, across the breadth of documents corporations file with the SEC (registration statements, tender offer documents, proxy statements, periodic disclosure documents (8Ks, 10Qs and 10Ks)).

With regard to diversity on their boards, U.S. publicly held companies must disclose:

(1.) Whether diversity is a factor in considering candidates for the company's board of directors;

(2.) How diversity is considered in the process of selecting board candidates;

(3.) How the company assesses the effectiveness of whatever policy and process it has chosen to adopt.

Appraisal thus far has been that corporate compliance with the new disclosure regulation has been spotty at best.

Viewed charitably, many corporate draftspersons may not have developed a feeling for what the SEC and Regulation SK now require. As the years progress, additional corporations will improve their disclosures. As a result, many reporting companies will enhance the processes on which they are reporting, with a resulting increase in diversity on boards of directors.

By contrast, viewed less charitably, early reports are that a significant number of companies opt out of the diversity disclosure process altogether by means of a simple one-line disclosure, "The Company has no fixed policy dealing with the diversity of candidates for election to the board of directors," or no disclosure at all. Wal-Mart, America's largest corporation by revenue, remained silent in both its 2010 and 2011 proxy statements. Brazen corporations such as Wal-Mart may short-circuit the SEC mandated disclosure requirements, negating altogether the intended effect, or any effect, of the disclosure requirement. The "no policy" alternative seems to be what our English colleagues would term "the coach and horses" exception to the board diversity disclosure requirement.

E

Elevator (Glass). Most women and many men are familiar with the term "glass ceiling," a term commonly used to describe that impenetrable but transparent barrier that allows women to see but not to climb the highest rungs of the corporate promotion ladder. Even lower on the ladder, however, women complain of obstacles which prevent even horizontal movement within corporate organizations. One common phenomenon is that women tend to be shunted toward what are called (again, infelicitously) "pink collar jobs," such as human resources, staff marketing positions, or jobs with the corporate foundation.

But women complain that once in such positions they encounter insuperable obstacles to re-joining the upward promotion march. Thus, they see male counterparts ascending the promotion ladder, but those males seem to be ascending in a transparent elevator, rising in a transparent elevator shaft. The women in the HR or staff jobs remain "stuck." Other women complain that when they seek to move laterally, say, to obtain a "line position" (one with bottom line revenue, cost and profit responsibilities), they run smack dab into a glass wall. The glass wall allows them to see but not to obtain the varied experience thought necessary to reach the higher heights.

F

Financial Literacy. After Jill Barad became the first female CEO in the Fortune 500, at Mattel Toy in 1997, she did not last long. She had made her way upward as a marketing whiz, responsible for the record setting sales of Barbie dolls. As CEO, though, she made overly optimistic projections of sales, revenues, and profits. Seemingly, she had no feel for how important financial analysts and investors regard making your numbers, or how those numbers had been complied, or how much confidence should be placed, or not placed, in them. The story of Carleton Fiorina at Hewlett-Packard is similar, although she remained in office for six rather than two years. The paradox is that Fiorina had MBAs, two of them, from the University of Maryland and MIT. Perhaps she just did not know when to duck.

Women who aspire in business need not major in accounting or finance. Often specialists cannot see the forest for the trees, making them not the best candidates for the top-most positions. Managers uppermost in the hierarchy too will have lawyers, accountants, and financial people around them who can help answer the questions, or seek out responses and answers. But the top dogs need to evaluate what underlings are saying as well as have a certain feel for and confidence in their understanding of markets, share prices, accounting numbers, projections, and the like.

Of what does financial literacy consist? For women who actually have become CEOs, the bar has been high. Of twenty female CEOs analyzed in 2010, twelve had MBAs, one an MSEE (Ursula Burns at Xerox), and one a JD (Angela Braley at Wellpoint). But immersion need not be that deep.

I tell aspirants that they should at least have a course in a managerial accounting (not debits and credits but what are financial statements, what do they demonstrate and, more importantly what do they not tell you); a course in finance (corporate, not personal—leave that to Susie Orman); economics 101 (to develop a feel for supply and demand, for markets, and for how they work); and perhaps a course in stocks, commodities, and investments (useful as well for managing personal finances). After that, major in French (Laura Sen, CEO at BJ's Wholesale Club did, as well as did Mary Sammons, CEO at Rite Aid), or geography (Christina Gold at Western Union), or psychology (Irene Rosenfeld at Kraft Foods). Literacy and feel, not necessarily deep expertise, are the goals.

* * *

H

Harvard/Hewlett Packard. As I stated previously, your best chance of becoming a female director at a Fortune 500 company may be to side step from a position as professor or dean at a university. The leader in that regard, at least in 2001, was Harvard University. "Thirteen women professors from Harvard held twenty-one Fortune 500 board seats. . . ."

Hewlett Packard (H-P) is a legendary Silicon Valley pioneer, a corporation about which several books have been written. Bill Hewlett and Dave Packard espoused "management by walking around," whereby each company founder spent time walking the shop floor and visiting with engineers and other workers. In a sense, H-P was a bottom-up organization in which all managers who had company cars, from the lowest to the highest, had the same model—a Ford Taurus. But by the mid-1990s, H-P had stagnated. Pundits described it as the company that would sell sushi as "cold dead fish."

The H-P directors then reached out to name a female CEO, only the third (after Jill Barad at Mattel and Andrea Jung at Avon Products) in the current era and of the 17th largest company in the U.S. She was Carleton Fiorina, daughter of a highly regarded federal court of appeals judge. Suddenly, H-P became a top-down organization. Armani Carl, as she was known, appeared on forty-plus magazine covers in her first year as CEO alone. She caused the company to buy a top of the line Gulfstream jet, which we used to fly around the world, making eighteen stops, in one week. Chainsaw Carly, as she also was known, laid off tens of thousands of H-P workers. "The H-P Way had become an excuse for all sorts of bad habits, particularly slowness and risk-aversion. . . ." "Preserve the best, reinvent the rest," she told reporters and H-P employees. Rank-and-file H-P did not appreciate her disdain for the vaunted H-P Way.

Under Fiorina, H-P's share price fell drastically, to less than half the price when she took office. She adamantly refused to hire a "number two" (chief operating officer or COO) despite director requests that she do so. The H-P board then removed her from office in February 2005.

Hewlett-Packard is noteworthy not only for hiring a female CEO once but also for naming a second, and accomplished woman, to the top post. In January 2012, the H-P board named Meg Whitman, former CEO of eBay and unsuccessful 2010 candidate for governor of California, to the top position of what now is the world's largest information technology company. It is too soon to evaluate Ms. Whitman's tenure at H-P but, by virtue of its chief executive selections, the company deserves a place in the A to Z list.

I

Iron Maiden/Ice Queen. Previous entries on this list have described the iron maiden and ice queen stereotypes. Recollection of those identifiers as well as others (mother figure, mascot, clown, queen bee) can segue into a discussion of stereotypes generally. Some women in business seek out a role which, more likely than not, will carry with it a stereotype. Role playing (the mother figure, the clown) may lead to a sanctuary, putting a safety net under the woman or other minority person. For example, co-workers, whether peers or superiors, may regard the mother figure as different, less vulnerable to the vicissitudes that buffet others, or not subject to the criticisms they launch against one another.

Other women, however, do not retreat to stereotypes, dreading application to them by others. The reason is that a stereotype, while perceived as providing a safety net of sorts, also is perceived as lessening, or masking altogether, achievement. Many capable women feel that they do not need a safety net. They further feel that they can and will produce, for which production they want, a full measure of recognition, undiluted by application of a stereotype. Stereotypes and analyses of them are vital to an understanding of diversity issues. On balance, or even without it, generally speaking they are not good or desirable things.

J

Japan (Portugal Too). Among developed nations, these two nations (one facing the Atlantic, the other facing the Pacific) are the cabooses, the last on the Boo Lists for their respective hemispheres. In Japan, women hold 1.4% of the available board seats, compared with 13.8% in Australia, 10% in New Zealand, and 8.9% in Hong Kong. The comparable number for Portugal has been as low as. . . .6%. European numbers (not necessarily European Union) include Norway at 40%+, 28.2% in Sweden, 26% in Finland, and over 20% in the Netherlands and France.

K

Keep Humble. Arrogance and high-handedness, just as excessive assertiveness or aggressiveness, can derail a woman's career even before her progress has reached full stride. Australia is an egalitarian country. One manifestation of that egalitarian spirit is the tendency to cut down anyone who has become a "tall poppy." Americans do much the same, taking down a notch or two those who "have become too big for their britches." It behooves a woman who seeks to rise to the higher heights of an organization to avoid accumulating a reputation as a tall poppy, or "too big for her britches."

Hewlett-Packard CEO Carly Fiorina avoided it, just barely, in her ascent to the CEO suite, but she did very much become a tall poppy CEO once she got there. In the end it contributed to her downfall. She traveled too much, as explained in her biography, describing travel to Korea, Belgium, France, Switzerland, the Netherlands, Brazil, and China for her previous employer, Lucent, alone. As has been seen, the "Fiorina Palooza" jetted to eighteen H-P and customer sites on three continents in one week.

In her autobiography, written after H-P fired her:

Ms. Fiorina is disingenuous. She talks of the media invitations she turned down but never about all those she accepted, the countless feature stories about her, the magazine covers which featured her, the sixty or more off-campus speeches she gave each year, her monthly telecasts to all H-P employees, and more. At times her ego knew no bounds. She set herself up for a comeuppance.

Women managers who do similar things will find themselves vulnerable as well.

L

The Labyrinth of Leadership. In 2007, Alice H. Eagly and Linda L. Carli, professors at Wellesley College and Northwestern University, respectively, published an apologia for Corporate America of the type one sees from time to time. The co-authors previewed the book, Through the Labyrinth: The Truth About How Women Become Leaders, in a lead article in the Harvard Business Review. Their thesis was that because women had achieved promotion, including advancement to the highest positions, in the not-for-profit and political spheres; no glass ceiling exists. The routes toward the top thus are in all probability free and clear in the business world as well.

Of course, the Eagly-Carli expositions beg the question, which is given that fewer barriers to advancement exist in the not-for-profit and political fields, why do those barriers persist in the business world? We also have wondered about women's progress in the political sphere: women seem to have stalled at 17% in both the U.S. Senate and the House of Representatives for some years now.

Along similar apologia lines, three-fourths of male CEOs of large corporations aver that no such thing as the glass ceiling exists. According to Catalyst, over 80% of the CEOs they interviewed had an alternative explanation about why women have not advanced to the very top in their organizations, namely women's lack of line experience and of profit-and-loss responsibilities.

Conservative economists, who have spawned a "human capital" literature, assert similar propositions. One proposition is that women have disadvantageous positions because they "self-select" into jobs that require less education or less skill. The second proposition is that labor markets, including the market for managers, are efficient. Gender discrimination, and the glass ceiling that is a component of it, does not exist because they could not survive in a market that is competitive. It is inefficient to exclude managers from promotion on the basis of sex. Firms that did so would not survive in the Darwinian product markets and business worlds generally. Instead women do not rise to the top for a variety of reasons: they self-select; lack line experience; allow themselves to get "stuck" in dead-end positions; prefer to go onto the "mummy track" to raise children; and so on.

* * *

M

Mentoring. Women should have almost as many mentors as stocks in their investment portfolio. They should not only have female as well as male mentors, but they should also have them inside and outside the company, even at a competitor company, and in finance, engineering, marketing, accountancy, and so on. Certain recipes for advancement by women ascribe the paucity or lack of mentors as a principal reason why women have not advanced in the numbers and to the extent one would expect.

One can easily conjure up three negatives, or more, about mentoring that the how-to books never discuss. One is that mentoring, by and large a good thing, may disguise a "star system," generally a bad thing. In a star system, stars of the first magnitude, which directly report to the CEO, have trailing behind them stars of the third, fourth, and fifth magnitude. When and if the star of the first magnitude falls from grace, stars of the lower orders may never be seen or heard from again. Inside, with their star systems, some corporate hierarchies still function as did medieval satrapies.

Second is that a mentor may morph into an overly protective "office uncle." Rather than conferring with a mentee about how to approach and work through problems, the office uncle tries to steer his mentees, females especially, away from problems. At the extreme, the office uncle may attempt to steer the mentee into a pink-collar or dead-end, but placid, position. "Plastic bubble" is another name for the phenomenon derived from the cocoon-like placement that the office uncle may attempt to procure for his mentee.

Third is that recent criticisms have complained that mentoring is less of a benefit than many of the advice-givers maintain. These critics point out that it is mentoring plus some form of sponsorship, rather than mentoring alone, that will produce the desired results.

O

Opting Out. One of the principal leaks farther along the pipeline is that educated women, with law, MBA, or engineering degrees, win managerial positions followed by promotions. In doing so, they have postponed childbearing until their early or mid-thirties. When they do bear children then, they do not return to the workplace. Or alternatively, if they do return, they do not return after giving birth to a second child. Lisa Belkin wrote a celebrated piece discussing these issues for the New York Times Magazine titled simply The Opt-Out Revolution.

The reasons for opting out are varied and many. Many accomplished women want to work but the emphasis on 24/7 availability, maximum face time in the office, travel on short or no notice, and other features of turbo capitalism turn them off. Women know that if they take any more time off than a single minimum maternity leave, say to have a second child, to see their children off to school for the first time, go part time, or seek flex time employment, at age forty they will earn 60% or so of what a comparable male makes. Knowing that such an outsized discount to their worth may be in their future many accomplished women opt out in early middle age.

Enlightened corporations realize that the loss of institutional memory, specialized expertise, customer relationships, and so on when women opt out are significant costs. Moreover, the difference between a male who works thirty-seven years and a female who works thirty-five years is statistically insignificant. With alumnae and welcome back programs, those corporations are attempting to take away the more permanent aspects of opting out.

P

Plastic Bubble/Plow Horse. I have already talked of the plastic bubble phenomenon that gives some women misgivings about some mentors. The "plow horse" designation comes from the business best seller Good to Great by Jim Collins. Collins found that the CEOs of what he and his staff, after extensive research, found to be exceptional companies, were all plow horses: not flashy, emotionally intelligent, good people managers, adept at listening, and the like. He also coined the term "show horse" for the type of CEO who is flashy, listens to no one else (indeed, ignores everyone), pursues his own personal vision for the company at all costs, and so on.

About the time Collins published his book, a psychologist, Michael Macoby, published another best seller, The Productive Narcissist: The Promise and Peril of Visionary Leadership. Although he did not use the term show horse, Macoby's viewpoint was the exact opposite of Collins's: the best CEO candidates are productive narcissists, or in other words, show horses.

I cannot answer the question of who makes the best CEO. But in his book, Macoby uses one hundred past and present CEOs as examples of his paradigm. Not one, save perhaps Carleton Fiorina, CEO at Hewlett-Packard 1999–2005, is female. Of the twenty-two women CEOs I chronicle in my book, every one, save perhaps Fiorina, is a plow horse. None fits either the show horse or the productive narcissist specification.

Q

Quota Laws/Queen Bee Stereotype. The literature labels as a "queen bee" the woman who relishes her status as the only woman in a work group, at a certain management level (e.g., regional sales directors, or vice presidents) or otherwise among her peers. The Queen Bee thus makes it difficult, sometimes extremely so, for any woman who would fain attempt to follow in the Queen Bee's footsteps. Once she is safely on her perch, the Queen Bee pulls up the rope ladder she used to get there.

In 2003, Norway enacted a quota law, which stated that as many as 40% of a public corporation's directors had to be of the opposite sex of the other directors. The deadline for achievement of that goal, which public companies in Norway by and large reached, was 2008.

Several EU member nations (Belgium, France, Italy, the Netherlands, and Spain) have followed Norway, a non-EU member, in adopting quota laws, as have Iceland, Israel, Switzerland, and Malaysia, among non-member states. Impatience with the continued male dominance of seats on corporate boards is growing.

Parliaments in Italy, the Netherlands, and Belgium have followed Norway, enacting gender-based director laws. Spain, the second nation to act, ordered achievement of the 40% level by 2016, a significant jump from the 5% level that prevailed in Spain at the time of the law's adoption. The Spanish statute, though, is largely aspirational while the Norwegian law has severe penalties. Norwegian companies that do not comply are not only subject to delisting on the stock exchange or monetary penalties, but to outright dissolution as well.

France, the third nation to act, adopted a 40% quota law early in 2011. Looking northward to Norway, a deputy of the l'Assemblée Nationale introduced a 20% quota bill in 2006. Thereafter the notion of gender parity, at least in French corporate governance, had to negotiate a twisting route. In 2009, besides looking northward towards Norway, and adding to the momentum for adoption of a quota statute, the French quota measure's supporters found that only 8% of directors in France's largest one hundred corporations were women. Further, they bemoaned that in that year French public companies added only six new women directors to corporate boards.

The recently enacted French quota mandate is staged. Public companies' boards must have 20% women directors within three years of the enactment and 40% within six years (2017). Thus far, large French corporations are out in front of the 2014 objective, having passed women on 24% of directors on boards by early 2012.

Sweden, Finland, Germany, and the UK have all come out in opposition to quota laws, for various reasons. Sweden (28.2%) and Finland (26%) already have meaningful representation of women on their boards. On the other hand, Germany and the UK have middling to poor and so-so records, respectively, on the issue. Both countries have long traditions of bucking trends and becoming recalcitrant when told what to do. Outside of the European Union, besides Norway, Israel, Iceland, and Switzerland have adopted quota laws.

Quota laws have unintended as well as intended consequences. In the rush to name females to directorships, for instance, Norwegian companies named one—no doubt very capable—woman to eleven corporate boards. No one, not even Superwoman, can serve adequately on more than three or perhaps four boards, especially in the current era with its emphasis on proactive, hands-on directors. Quota laws produce a surfeit of women trophy directors, which may help produce unqualified, figurehead (token) female directors.

Quota laws also may result in a surfeit of celebrity directors, who also may be regarded as tokens. Allegedly that has happened in France where board seats have gone to former first lady Bernadette Chirac (luxury goods retailer LVMH); Nicole Dassault, wife of the controlling shareholder

(Dassault Aviation); Florence Woerth, spouse of the former Minister for Labor (Hermes); Brigitte Longuet, wife of the former Minister of Defence (broadcaster Canal Plus); and Amélie Oudéa-Casteras, former tennis professional and wife of Société Générale CEO (media group Lagardere).

Other consequences thought due to the enactment of a quota law include companies downsizing their boards of directors so as to reduce the number of women candidates necessary, and thus, search costs. An extreme consequence is that some companies may go private in order to evade a quota law's requirements altogether.

Opposition to enactment of a quota law is strong in nations such as New Zealand, a country in which women make up 59% of the work force and which recently was governed by a female prime minister, yet in which many corporate executives oppose mandatory or other guidelines. The New Zealand Stock Exchange has publicly stated that it will not even follow its Australian counterpart, the Australia Stock Exchange (ASX), which has a requirement for companies to set and meet voluntary quotas for increasing the number of women at the top. In the United Kingdom, a recent government reports urges a voluntary quota of 25% by 2015 but pointedly stops short of any recommendation that the UK adopt a compulsory quota, as France, Spain, Belgium, the Netherlands, Norway and other states have done. By contrast, the Malaysian government has imposed a quota that publicly held companies there have 30% women directors by 2016.

R

Rubber Floors/The Rooney Rule/Risk Taking. The entry above about glass elevators and elevator shafts discusses the rubber floor as well.

A discussion of the Rooney Rule might begin with discussion of the Dutch 2008 "Talent to the Top" pledge, which requires public corporations to add women to their board if they voluntarily subscribe to the pledge. The 110 largest Dutch companies have done so, including many very large household name corporations such as Shell, Phillips, Heineken, Reed Elsevier, and Unilever. These actions, and the follow through which succeeds the pledges, have played a part in raising Dutch corporate boards from approximately 7% women in 2006 to 20.9% in 2010.

The U.S. has its advocates of a pledge program. In two luncheon speeches, in November 2010, Securities and Exchange Commission (SEC) Commissioner Luis Aguilar commended the U.S. National Football League's (NFL's) Rooney Rule as a model for corporate pledges in the board composition area. Board Diversity: Why It Matters and How to Improve It was his principal address on the subject; Changing the Dialogue on Diversity to Achieve Results preceded it by several weeks. Dan Rooney, a principal owner of the Pittsburgh Steelers Professional Football Club, chaired the NFL Committee on Diversity. The committee drafted and the National Football League adopted the Rooney Rule, which requires each professional team to pledge to include a minority candidate among the finalists for each coaching vacancy and general manager position, and to conduct an on-site interview with that finalist. Since the rule was adopted in 2003, the number of black head coaches in the NFL increased from 6% to 22%. Commissioner Aguilar stated that "[t]he NFL moved from lip service to action and the results are self-explanatory. Let's face it—many corporate boards need their own Rooney Rule."

But not all certificate or pledge programs have met with success. The European Union followed the Netherlands example when it requested large publicly held companies in Europe to pledge voluntarily to achieve the 30% level by 2015. The program failed miserably. After a year, only twenty-four companies in the EU had signed the pledge. Calling for quota laws, EU Justice Commissioner Viviane Reding explained: "One year ago, I asked companies to voluntarily increase women's presence on corporate boards I regret to see that despite our calls, self-regulation so far has not brought about satisfactory results."

Recent interviews with female CEOs highlight the necessity of an aspiring woman taking risks in mid-career and thereafter. "I have stepped up to many 'ugly' assignments that others didn't want," remembers Beth Mooney, CEO at KeyCorp. " 'The most important factor in determining whether you will succeed [is to] [b]e open to opportunity and take risks. In fact, take the most challenging assignment you can find, and then take control.' "

S

Star Systems/Stereotypes/Shoulder Pad Feminism. These all are topics germane to the subject of this Article, but they have been addressed in various of the headings *supra*.

T

Trophy Directors. Many male CEOs' boards limit them to one outside directorship, or to none at all. By contrast, large publicly held corporations in the U.S. have a penchant for naming the same women over and over. In fact, the largest growth sector among female directors is of trophy directors, those who serve on more than four public companies' boards of directors, growing from thirty in 2001 to seventy-nine in 2005. Thus one woman, whose husband happened to be a U.S. Senator at the time, served on eight boards of directors while a number of other women served on five, six, or seven boards.

It is doubtful that any person can do an adequate job serving on more than three boards. In my book, No Seat at the Table, I term anyone who serves on four or more boards a "trophy director." What is wrong with trophy directors, besides perhaps an inability to do the job expected of a corporate director? One argument against trophy directors is that the practice of naming the same women over and over crowds out more deserving and younger women. The penchant for trophy directors also deprives other deserving women of the opportunity to "show their stuff" and to gain the boardroom experience, which may help propel them to other companies and other boards.

U

Urgency. At present rates of inclusion, Lord Mervyn Davies calculates that it will take at least until 2080 for women to achieve a measure of parity in the boardroom, and that is without any stumbles or steps backward. The latter are bound to occur. The glacial pace toward a respectable percentage of women among the directors of public companies (not parity but perhaps 30% or 35%) adds to the sense of urgency many feel in discussing the issue.

V

Verbal Hedges. Many men in positions of power (CEOs, board chairs, directors) downplay the contribution any woman could make to corporate success, terming women "too emotional," "intuitive rather than analytical," and the like. Linguists, such as Robin Lakoff at the University of California Berkeley, or Deborah Tannen at Georgetown University, have studied and written about the phenomenon. In our society, as in many other societies, women tend to act and speak differently than men ("in a different register"). Women tend to avoid the use of imperatives while men do not. Women tend to have a rising intonation in their sentences while men do that only in asking questions. Women use modal verbs ("might," "should," "ought") while men use imperatives, as stated ("do," "run the numbers," "make that sale," etc.). Women tend to end sentences with verbal hedges ("maybe," "I suppose," "perhaps," "kind of," "about," or "around").

Professors Lakoff and Tannen demonstrate that acting or speaking "in a different register," means little. The different speech patterns do not bear any correlation to the behaviors that men in power tend to recite. Women are not necessarily less analytical or emotional because they speak differently.

Nonetheless, the how-to books advise women who aspire to succeed in business to lower and deepen their voices. Women, they are told, never should remain quiet or acquiesce in the face of arguments or directions. They should respond even if no response is necessary. Evidently, the authors of these advice books have neither read nor examined the conclusions reached by Professors Lakoff and Tannen.

W

Work/Life Issues. The whole panoply of issues, including child bearing, child rearing, household work, cooking, and the like is subsumed under the umbrella of work/life issues. The necessity of women giving birth to and to a great extent caring for children, at least in their early years, is an inescapable biological fact. That fact is accompanied by the uneven breakdowns of stereotypes, which leave women still with the bulk of household responsibilities. The combination of inescapable biological fact and uneven assumption of household burdens holds many, but not all, women back from achievement in business careers. Centers exist for the discussion and analysis of these issues. Women who have succeeded in business universally describe how they compartmentalize their lives rather than continuing to be all things to many people. Other women who have succeeded testify as to how, earlier in their careers, they reached understandings with their spouses about whose career had the most upward trajectory and to which they would devote the most resources.

There are, however, no silver bullets. " 'The myth,' [says] Ms. Braly [CEO of Wellpoint] 'is that women and their families don't have to make tradeoffs to have an "extreme career"; they absolutely do.' " "The myth, continues Deanna Mulligan, CEO of Guardian Life Insurance, is 'that you can have a "balanced" life at all times.' " Those reservations made, "Ms. Wilderotter of Frontier [Communications] believes women are better at multitasking than men. 'We do it naturally.' "

X

XEROX. From the 1970s until Ann Mulcahy took office as CEO in 2002, Xerox's market share fell from 90% to 13%. The stock fell from $63.69 to $4.93 in one year (2000) alone. The Xerox board plucked Mulcahy from a supposed dead-end, pink-collar job. She was the head of human resources. But, by most accounts, she fixed Xerox, to paraphrase the title of the BusinessWeek article heralding her ascension. She oversaw the company's return to profitability and the stock's rise back to some level of respectability.

When Mulcahy left office in 2009, Xerox became noteworthy, at least for purposes of this subject, because the Xerox board chose a second female as CEO, just as Hewlett-Packard later did when its board hired Meg Whitman. Xerox does H-P one better, though, at least in terms of diversity. Xerox became the first Fortune 500 company to choose an African-American female CEO. She is Ursula Burns, an engineer who holds an MSEE from Columbia University.

* * *

Z

Zenith. The zenith is "the point of the celestial sphere that is vertically above the observer and directly opposite the nadir." If the nadir is zero, as in no female directors, would the zenith be 50%, or would it be 100%, women directors of large publicly held companies? I believe either answer to be academic, as I do not believe that the proportion of directors who are women will ever reach either height.

When an alternative definition of zenith is sought, the denotation is "the upper region of the heavens." I take that to mean that the zenith for which we should aim is 35%, perhaps 40%. That would satisfy my sense of social justice and remedy promises not kept, that male executives and Corporate America have for decades made: "it is only a matter of time," or "next year," "or next decade." The point for which we aim should be high but need not necessarily be "vertically above" and "directly opposite the nadir."

That is my A to Z list on the subject of gender and diversity in corporate governance.

ALEXANDER M. NOURAFSHAN, *FROM THE CLOSET TO THE BOARDROOM: REGULATING LGBT DIVERSITY ON CORPORATE BOARDS*

81 ALBANY LAW REVIEW 439 (2018)

Nourafshan is a Fintech associate at Goodwin Procter LLP in San Francisco. His practice focuses on payments, lending, data privacy, banking and emerging financial services regulatory issues. Mr. Nourafshan's scholarship on LGBT rights issues and intersectionality has been published in the Duke Journal of Gender Law and Policy, Albany Law Review, and FSU Law Review.

I. INTRODUCTION

In corporate America, diversity is the new black. It is no secret that corporations have aggressively prioritized diversity in recent years, attempting to remedy a history of underrepresentation for various minority groups. Major corporations have established offices of diversity and inclusion, hired chief diversity officers, implemented diversity hiring programs, offered diversity-oriented mentorship programs, enacted inclusive nondiscrimination policies, and hosted extensive diversity trainings in the workplace. In some regards, the modern workplace is beginning to reflect the diverse demography of the county. Diversity, it seems, is succeeding at taking hold in corporate culture—at least in terms of professed values. However, these values are not always reflected at the highest levels of a company, no matter how much a company touts a commitment to diversity.

A disjuncture remains between increased emphasis on diversity and meaningful representations of diversity in the C-Suite and on corporate boards. Ninety-seven percent of senior management teams of U.S.-based corporations fail to reflect the racial demography of the overall workforce. White men remain overrepresented in management and executive levels of corporations. The financial services industry provides a compelling example of the stark division in representation. In this industry, white men constitute thirty-one percent of the labor force, yet hold sixty-four percent of leadership positions. Women, on the other hand, make up fifty-nine percent of the total workforce in the financial services industry, but comprise only twenty-nine percent of executive and senior level positions. Similarly, racial minorities make up approximately thirty-percent of the workforce, but hold a mere ten percent of executive and senior level positions. Approximately eight percent of the American financial services workforce is Latino, however, only three percent of corporate executives are Latino. And while twelve percent of the workforce is black, only 2.5 percent of executive positions are held by black men and women.

Fortune 500 companies present a similar picture. White men hold roughly seventy percent of board seats among Fortune 500 companies. Tim Cook, the CEO of Apple, is the only openly homosexual CEO in the Fortune 500. There are no openly transgender executives or board members in the Fortune 500. Some industries reflect particularly significant deficiencies in diverse representation. As shown, the financial services industry "shows a severe underrepresentation" of women and racial minorities at senior and executive positions.

This is also the case with diversity on corporate boards. As former SEC chair Mary Jo White has observed, "[t]he low level of board diversity in the United States is unacceptable." Diversity on corporate boards is low by any measure. Women, racial minorities, and LGBT individuals are all underrepresented in the boardroom. The phenomenon of underrepresentation of racial minorities, women, and LGBT individuals on corporate boards is not unique to the United States, but is observable in corporations around the world. Data suggests that women and racial minorities are also underrepresented on nonprofit and private foundation boards.

Recognizing the stagnant progress for various underrepresented groups in the boardroom, the SEC introduced a diversity disclosure rule for public reporting companies in 2009. While the SEC's diversity disclosure rule was significant in the sense that the rule formalized the SEC's recognition of minority underrepresentation on corporate boards, this rule has not been successful, either in terms of eliciting meaningful information from disclosures, or impacting the demography of corporate boards. Even former SEC chair, Mary Jo White, acknowledged that the SEC's diversity disclosure regime has been unsuccessful to this point. This article proposes reforms to the SEC's diversity disclosure rule to generate more substantive disclosures about diversity on corporate boards, and to indirectly encourage companies to diversify at the board level.

This article examines two questions in depth: First, should LGBT diversity be considered coextensive with racial and gender diversity in the context of corporate boards? While scholars and practitioners have extensively addressed gender and racial diversity in the corporate board context, LGBT representation on corporate boards has been relatively unexplored in legal scholarship. This article argues that LGBT status is an important form of diversity in the corporate context for many of the same reasons that other forms of demographic diversity, like race and gender, are important. This article imports a framework from the critical race theory context, which posits that transformative change for marginalized groups requires addressing multiple forms of subordination, supporting the position of this article that efforts to increase demographic diversity should include LGBT diversity along with racial and gender diversity. Like women and racial minorities, LGBT individuals are significantly underrepresented on corporate boards, warranting explicit inclusion in reform efforts.

Second, this article considers mechanisms for achieving greater demographic diversity on corporate boards, including gender identity and sexual orientation diversity. This article ultimately argues that the SEC should amend its diversity disclosure rule by defining diversity to include LGBT status and mandating demographic disclosures. This paper argues that including LGBT diversity as part-and-parcel of demographic diversity is consistent with the explicitly pro-LGBT stance that many corporations, consumers, and shareholders have already embraced. This article addresses the unique issues implicated by disclosing LGBT status as context for discussing possible regulatory reforms to diversify corporate boards.

* * *

II. DIVERSITY IN CORPORATE AMERICA

A. *Current State of Diversity in Corporate America*

* * *

1. **Efforts—Corporations "Talk the Talk"**

Corporate boards and executives recognize diversity as an important priority area, and have articulated a general commitment to increasing diversity in the workplace. As described above, corporations have adopted a variety of policies and programs intended to diversify the workforce, and to consecrate inclusion as a central tenet of corporate culture. From diversity recruitment programs to inclusion-oriented training, many companies have formal policies that reflect a corporate commitment to diversity.

Some companies have "put their money where their mouth is" to achieve these goals. For example, Apple has committed $50 million to recruiting and retaining larger numbers of women, racial minorities, and veterans. Similarly, Intel has committed $300 million to diversity initiatives, and set a goal of increasing diversity of underrepresented groups by fourteen percent by 2020. On a more day-to-day level, "many managers are [increasingly] tasked with the complex goal of 'managing diversity'—which can mean anything from ensuring equal employment opportunity compliance, to instituting cultural sensitivity training programs, to focusing on the recruitment and retention of minorities and women." There are several organizations dedicated to improving corporate diversity, including the DirectWomen Initiative, the Alliance for Board Diversity, Catalyst and the InterOrganization Network ("ION").

Government agencies have also made concerted efforts to increase diversity. For example, the Dodd-Frank Wall Street Reform and Consumer Protection Act of 2010 required nine agencies to establish Offices of Minority and Women Inclusion ("OMWI"). OMWIs are tasked with promoting diversity within the nine subject regulatory agencies and among regulated institutions. Among other responsibilities, OMWI is required to "develop standards for assessing the diversity policies and practices of entities regulated by that Agency."

Many corporations have earnestly endeavored to promote diversity internally. Some of these companies deserve an A for effort. But are these efforts having any real impact? The following subsection attempts to answer that question, noting the ongoing underrepresentation of various minority groups at the highest rungs of the corporate ladder.

2. Outcomes

As this paper highlights, many companies are aggressively prioritizing diversity initiatives to recruit and retain diverse employees, and to foster a working environment of inclusivity. The success of these efforts, however, is underwhelming. As this section will emphasize, corporate boards are still not diverse. By every metric, corporate boards have failed to embody the model of diversity touted in aspirational diversity statements and inclusion-oriented policies and practices. The following subsections discuss representation of women, racial minorities, and LGBT minorities respectively, reflecting a common underrepresentation across and among these groups.

Although the following subsections separately address race, gender, and LGBT minorities, and this paper often refers to these groups in isolated terms, intersectional diversity must be considered as part of increasing diverse representations on corporate boards. Intersectionality refers to membership in more than one minority group. Thus, a black woman (racial minority-gender minority), Latino homosexual (sexual orientation minority-racial minority), or transgender bisexual (sexual orientation minority-gender identity minority) would all be considered intersectional. As I have written elsewhere, failure to consider intersectionality, particularly in the employment context, is an underinclusive view of diversity.

A concept from the critical race theory context suggests that transformative change for subordinated groups requires addressing interlocking social hierarchies such as race, gender and sexual orientation. If only some forms of bias and discrimination are addressed, then marginalization for minority subclasses will persist. For example, if gender discrimination is addressed without addressing racial discrimination, white women will be the primary, and possibly only, beneficiaries of these efforts. That is because the intersection of gender and race results in a lived experience for women of color that is often different from the lived experience of white women. Narrowly addressing the subjugation of one minority group without addressing others will yield incomplete progress, and leave certain social hierarchies intact. This insight both supports including LGBT diversity as part of efforts to diversify corporate boards, and underscores the need to consider intersectional diversity. Although this paper discusses gender, race, and LGBT status as separate traits, this is largely necessitated by previous scholarship and available statistics.

i. *Gender Representation on Corporate Boards*

* * *

While women have made gains in the workforce, scholars describe women's progress at the highest levels of corporations as "stalled." "Women, especially those seeking positions on corporate boards, continue to face challenges that men do not." Without achieving not only diversity, but critical mass of gender diversity, female board members may have limited efficacy on the board. If progress continues at the current pace, it will be approximately seventy years before there is gender parity on Fortune 500 boards.

ii. *Racial Representation on Corporate Boards*

With respect to racial minority representation on corporate boards, the pace of progress has been slow. Although studies vary slightly in the numbers and proportions of racial minority representation on corporate boards, studies consistently find a severe underrepresentation. In 2010, men and women of color occupied 9.8 percent of board seats in the Fortune 500. By 2016, another survey found that "fewer than fifteen percent of all board seats in the Fortune 500" were occupied by racial minorities. Black representation on corporate boards has increased the most rapidly of any racial minority group. African American women, in particular, have increased representation on Fortune 500 boards by 18.4 percent.

It is also worth noting that some minority board members serve on multiple boards, meaning that aggregated statistics count a few minority individuals multiple times for serving on multiple boards. For example, two black directors each serve as directors on eight corporate boards. As one source notes, these directors serving on eight boards are serving on "more [boards] than any other individual, black or white. This overlap not only means that diversity on corporate boards is overstated but also suggests that many directors of color are mere figureheads who are too overextended to play a significant role in corporate management." Thus, statistics reflecting demographic diversity may overestimate the already small proportion of racial minorities represented on corporate boards.

Latino board representation is even lower than black representation. Latino men and women occupy 3.5 percent of Fortune 500 board seats. Since 2012, Latino board members gained only six board seats among the Fortune 500. Asian/Pacific Islanders currently hold 3.1 percent of Fortune 500 board seats. Interestingly, women and racial minorities are both better represented in the Fortune 100, as opposed to Fortune 500. While some companies have expressed a commitment to reaching certain racial diversity targets, it remains to be seen whether these targets will be reached.

iii. LGBT Representation on Corporate Boards

There are no reliable statistics measuring LGBT diversity on corporate boards, "which makes it impossible to know just how poorly represented LGBT people are." It is particularly difficult to measure LGBT representation on corporate boards because individuals must choose to self-identify as LGBT in order to be included in a tally of LGBT board members. Quorum, an organization dedicated to placing LGBT individuals on corporate boards, has observed "[t]he boardroom is one of the last areas in which LGBT+ individuals continue to have almost no representation or visibility."

While the LGBT community has made meaningful advances toward both formal legal equality and social acceptance in recent years, these gains are not reflected on corporate boards, which arguably represent the pinnacle of American industry. According to available statistics, less than 0.3 percent of the Directors of Fortune 500 companies are openly LGBT. Moreover, while the majority of Fortune 500 companies have nondiscrimination policies that include sexual orientation and / or gender identity, only two Fortune 500 companies explicitly include LGBT status as part of diversity for purposes of recruiting new board members. Corporations have tended to overlook LGBT recruitment in looking to fill board seats, which partially explains the disproportionately low LGBT board representation.

3.　Discussing Disparate Outcomes

There are numerous factors that account for the lack of diversity in the boardroom. From a recruitment perspective, the lack of diversity among existing senior officers may limit the pool of potential directors. Corporate boardrooms have been characterized as "boys clubs," limited to a predominantly white, heterosexual, male subset. As some have noted, "[i]t is unrealistic to expect boards to see the light and diversify themselves. Homogeneous institutions tend to replicate themselves with homogeneous successors."

While board turnover could theoretically create opportunities for diverse directors, diverse board members are elected at disproportionately low rates. For example, women composed thirty-four percent of all board members elected in the first quarter 2011, which was lower than the thirty-eight percent of women elected to board seats in the previous quarter. While on one hand, the rate of election for new female directors outpaces women's current representation on boards, white men still hold nearly two-thirds of all board seats and continue to be elected at similar rates. Regardless of term length, existing board members tend to be reflexively re-nominated, limiting opportunities to meaningfully shift the homogenous demographic composition of corporate boards.

Various rationales have been offered to explain or justify the lack of diversity on corporate boards. Some factors include "the desire to maintain social comfort levels and board cohesion, narrow search criteria and procedures for selecting new directors, skepticism about the so-called 'business case' in favor of appointing women to corporate boards, and plain old-fashioned sex discrimination." It is shocking that "social comfort levels" and "board cohesion" are cited as serious concerns justifying the exclusion of various groups from the boardroom in 2018. In weighing the need to diversify boards against the "comfort" levels of existing directors, "comfort" that is rooted in excluding various groups from representation should not be given any credence. The suggestion that heterogeneity inherently produces discomfort is problematic for many reasons. This is similar to the modern concept of corporate "culture fit," which has been used as a proxy for comfort and has been characterized as a pretext for discrimination in some cases.

* * *

These problems are already in operation, given that very few companies have multiple minority directors or senior-level officers. Moreover, in addition to overt discrimination, minority directors and senior executives often face ingrained or implicit biases, potentially undermining the efficacy of these directors on corporate boards. The outcomes of corporate diversity efforts leave much to be desired. However, an explicit commitment to diversity is a significant first step, which should be applauded and further pursued, particularly in the context of corporate boards.

B. The Business Case for Corporate Diversity

This article has extensively documented the underrepresentation of women, racial minorities and LGBT directors on corporate boards. This section takes a step back and asks a more fundamental question: Why is diversity on corporate boards an important policy or governance consideration? While this may be a rhetorical question in the fields of feminist legal studies, critical race theory, or LGBT legal studies, which are rooted in the premise that equality for marginalized groups is an inherently good thing, this article bridges these disciplines with corporate governance scholarship, requiring an exploration of this threshold question. A number of rationales have been advanced for addressing corporate diversity, ranging from moral appeals to economic arguments. Because the viewpoint of this article implicitly embraces the equality-based focus of feminist legal studies, critical race theory, and LGBT legal studies, this article explicitly addresses the business case for diversity.

The business case for corporate diversity posits that increased corporate diversity leads to positive financial performance. Research suggests that corporate diversity "increases the overall effectiveness of the board and hence the corporation, [and] also enhances the corporation's profitability." Specific economic benefits of board diversity include "an increase in firm value, improved corporate governance, an increase in the return on equity, and a higher return on invested capital."

* * *

More generally, scholars recognize the need to encourage diversity in both for-profit and non-profit sectors to improve decision-making informed by diversity of experience and perspective. It is in a company's interest to include and encourage diverse viewpoints to contribute to discussions and decision-making. Among other things, diversity in the context of corporate boards can help to challenge the status quo and prevent group think. This is significant because, among other things, "[c]orporations are powerful entities and decisions made by boards of directors can impact employees, shareholders, consumers, and the community.

Diversity on corporate boards also serves an important signaling function. Both employees and consumers have demonstrated positive reactions to signaling that a company embraces diversity. A company may improve its standing with consumers, in terms of, for example, brand loyalty, given that consumers have increasingly embraced and come to expect a pro-diversity posture from corporations. As an additional potential benefit in terms of improved corporate governance, the SEC has suggested that diversifying boards can increase director independence, because boards may need to conduct broader-reaching searches outside the current board's immediate network to find diverse candidates.

Scholars have advanced specific arguments regarding the benefits of various minority groups on corporate boards. Although the need to consider intersectionality remains, as discussed above, scholarship and statistics tend to measure demographic diversity on a single-axis basis, eliding the overlap between minority subclasses. The following subsections address specific arguments that have been advanced in the gender, race, and LGBT contexts, respectively. These arguments are similar across demographic groups.

1. The Business Case for Gender Diversity

There is an emerging consensus that the business case for diversity applies in the context of gender, meaning that gender diversity improves the financial performance of a company. Companies with three or more female directors perform better than companies with no female board members "at rather astonishing rates." One study by Credit Suisse found that companies with more women on the board had "higher returns on equity, lower leverage, better growth, and higher price/book value multiples." Moreover, strong female representation in the boardroom is necessary to represent the perspectives of female consumers, who make the majority of consumer decisions in America. Because women do not operate from a singular perspective, it is crucial to include as many women on the board as possible to represent the spectrum of diversity among women.

Several business benefits of increasing female representation on corporate boards have been identified. These benefits include representing different perspectives, improving recruiting efforts with broader sets of candidates, signaling inclusiveness to current and prospective employees, consumers, and the market, improving decision-making, and serving as a source of new ideas. Among the reasons that it is particularly important to have female representation on boards is to have female influence on important policy issues, such as the pay gap that adversely affects the vast majority of women. Women earn approximately eighty-one percent of what men earn, variable by race, according to the Bureau of Labor Statistics, irrespective of qualifications, such as educational attainment, and type of work performed.

It is particularly important to have multiple women on the board because not all women will feel strongly about using a board seat to advocate for policies that might be viewed as "women's issues." Nor should there be an expectation that any woman do so. With more women represented, those women with an interest in pursuing certain issues traditionally framed as "women's issues" can do so, without imposing pressure or an unspoken expectation that all women actively address such issues.

Finally, greater female representation on the board can benefit other minority groups. For example, one study demonstrated that increased gender diversity on corporate boards leads to greater support for LGBT-protective corporate policies, demonstrating that gender diversity benefits not only women, but other minorities as well. Thus, greater representation of women on corporate boards yields a wide-range of positive results.

2.   The Business Case for Racial Diversity

With respect to racial diversity, studies have demonstrated a positive relationship between a racially diverse board and strong financial performance. "Companies in the top quartile for racial and ethnic diversity are 35 percent more likely to have financial returns above their respective national industry medians." Similar to gender diversity on corporate boards, there are recruitment, retention and signaling-based benefits to increased racial diversity. Moreover, the reputations and perceptions of companies with strong racial diversity are higher than those companies that do not have similar levels of racial diversity. Some scholars have hypothesized that "[r]acial and ethnic diversity has a stronger impact on financial performance in the United States than gender diversity, perhaps because earlier efforts to increase women's representation in the top levels of business have already yielded positive results." Increasing the proportion of racial minorities, including intersectional racial minorities, has shown to have a positive relationship with a corporation's financial performance.

3.   The Business Case for LGBT Diversity

The business case for diversity has been addressed primarily in the context of race and gender, and less comprehensively with respect to sexual orientation and gender identity. However, available evidence suggests that the general business rationale for corporate diversity applies equally to LGBT diversity. This article identifies several compelling business-focused rationales for increasing LGBT representation in corporations, generally, and on corporate boards, specifically.

First and foremost, consistent with the business case for diversity, having LGBT perspectives included at the highest levels of a company can help the company maximize financial performance. Among other things, diversity of thought may facilitate a company's expansion into the LGBT market. According to Quorum, "the global LGBT+ market opportunity is estimated at $3.7 trillion." One study demonstrated that corporations that had high corporate equality scores from the Human Rights Campaign, which measures the corporate commitment to diversity, had stock prices that over-performed similarly situated companies without high scores from HRC.

A second, business-related, reason that it is important to have openly LGBT board members and executives is because having LGBT representation at these high levels of an organization can facilitate the recruitment and retention of top talent. This, in turn, should have positive impacts on a company's financial performance.

* * *

Third, having openly LGBT board members sends positive signals to both employees of an organization, and to consumers that a company has adopted a pro-LGBT inclusive stance. As Marian Wright Edelman once observed, "you can't be what you can't see." This is true in politics as well as corporate America. A visible LGBT presence at the top of an organization can signal to other employees that it is okay to be "out," or open about LGBT status at work. According to Quorum, eighty percent of LGBT+ employees are more likely to be out at work when senior executives in the company are also out. Not coming out can have material consequences for LGBT employees. LGBT employees that are "in the closet" often have to perform extra work in order to minimize the visibility of LGBT traits. Often, this involves "covering," or seeking to minimize traits associated with LGBT status. For gay men, for example, this may mean changing one's clothes or modulating voice pitch to downplay characteristics associated with homosexuality. Eighty-three percent of LGBT employees in one survey report covering in some form or another. Researchers have noted "that there are no differences between LGBT and heterosexual workers on job performance. However, the performance of the LGBT employees might be impaired when their cognition is undermined by the energy expended on concealing or fear of disclosing their sexual orientation." Although covering occurs with most frequency among LGBT individuals, pressure to cover identity traits impact various historically underrepresented groups. Beyond creating a positive environment for LGBT employees, a pro-LGBT corporate posture also has positive signaling implications for consumers. "Firms may attempt to employ board diversity as a signal that the firm has considered the needs of certain demographic groups in product development and service." Studies have suggested that "consumers are keenly aware of companies' use of LGBT-friendly signals (e.g., using gay themes in advertising or supporting gay causes). LGBT consumers use these signals to develop positive brand attitudes and are willing to pay a premium price for goods and services LGBT-friendly companies produce." Additionally, there is little risk of anti-gay backlash from most advertising at this point. Even where a potential for backlash exists, companies are still embracing social issues, such as LGBT rights. In 2018, lacking diversity or opposing equality may pose more of a reputational risk than foster a diversity-supportive image.

To reap the benefits of LGBT diversity, LGBT-supportive, company-wide policies are particularly important. Research suggests that LGBT-supportive policies could be a source of competitive advantage, and have a positive relationship with firm performance. There is evidence "that LGBT employees experience less discrimination when their employer[s have] a nondiscrimination policy" covering sexual orientation and/or gender identity. Employees are more likely to be out at work if they believe that their employer is supportive of LGBT issues. This in turn leads to psychological and productivity benefits for the company when employees are openly LGBT. Thus, a board that is supportive of LGBT-inclusive nondiscrimination policies will reap numerous direct and tangential benefits beyond the amorphous concept of inclusion.

It is important to have LGBT perspectives in the boardroom to ensure that the interests of LGBT employees are protected. For example, LGBT corporate board members can advocate for broad, LGBT-inclusive nondiscrimination policies. Because LGBT individuals are not uniformly covered under federal employment discrimination laws, these policies have even more importance to LGBT employees. Many employers have voluntarily enacted LGBT-supportive policies, reflecting an implicit conclusion that doing so is a sound business practice. There are additional benefits for employers with nondiscrimination policies, such as increased employee loyalty.

Corporations have been leaders in promoting LGBT rights. Corporations have historically outpaced law and regulation when it comes to promoting and protecting LGBT rights. Given that LGBT employees and citizens lack many legal protections, corporations have been important institutions for promoting equality, even before companies are legally required to do so. Many companies have enacted nondiscrimination policies, thereby voluntarily exceeding legal requirements when operating in states that still permit discrimination on the basis of sexual orientation or gender identity.

Many corporations appear to have already concluded that adopting a pro-LGBT posture is good for business. For example, numerous businesses and organizations, from Fintech giant PayPal to the NCAA, diverted planned business from the state of North Carolina after North Carolina enacted an anti-transgender bathroom law. Additionally, companies appear to be attuned to diversity ratings' metrics. For example, many companies seek to have a strong rating from the Human Rights Campaign's Corporate Equality Index. This score is based on policies and efforts directed at recruiting, retaining and welcoming LGBT employees, which requires concerted effort. However, this score is, in many regards, a theoretical exercise. It does not measure outcomes, such as the proportion of LGBT employees in the workplace. Of relevance to businesses, these metrics appear to have positive financial implications for companies that receive high marks. Based on available statistics, there is more work to be done, yet these policies evince a commitment to the long fight for equality.

Beyond individual corporate policies, corporations have engaged in political activism on behalf of LGBT causes at all levels, from local to national, further demonstrating a commitment to LGBT rights. Yet, in spite of this recognition that LGBT diversity is important as a business matter and matter of principle, corporations are not embracing this belief at the top of the ladder by proactively recruiting LGBT board members, even when doing so would be good for business.

4.   Critiques of the Business Case for Corporate Diversity

Although the business case for diversity is widely touted as a sound rationale for promoting policies to increase diversity, the business case for diversity has been the subject of critique. The primary argument marshaled against the business case for diversity is that studies demonstrating strong financial performance related to corporate diversity merely demonstrate correlation, rather than causation, leaving open the possibility that factors other than diversity account for the positive financial results observed. Other scholars argue that there is simply not enough empirical evidence to conclude whether diversity has a positive impact, if any, on corporate diversity. One scholar explains the cyclical issue with empirically verifying the business case for diversity, which is that "it may not be possible to engage in meaningful empirical studies until board diversity increases and this increase may not take place in the absence of stronger evidence of the business case."

In spite of these critiques, the business case for diversity continues to have currency. "While correlation does not equal causation (greater gender and ethnic diversity in corporate leadership doesn't automatically translate into more profit), the correlation does indicate that when companies commit themselves to diverse leadership, they are more successful." Additionally, there are numerous meritorious equality-based rationales for addressing diversity. For example, some argue that irrespective of the business rationale for corporate diversity, corporations can and should act in the interest of social responsibility, which requires diversifying corporate boards.

In practice, the business case has been unsuccessful in persuading corporate boards to increase diversity, given the persistent underrepresentation of all historically underrepresented groups. Thus, even if the business case is empirically sound, it is not altering behavior in a way that suggests that corporations fully believe the business rationale. However, given increased shareholder and consumer activism related to diversity, and the positive correlation between diversity and strong financial performance, corporations may be ignoring diversity at their own peril.

III.   REGULATING DIVERSITY

In recent years, there has been an increased interest in regulating corporate diversity generally, and corporate board diversity, specifically. This section first discusses the history of regulating diversity, both in general, and with respect to corporate boards. The second section addresses international approaches to regulating diversity on corporate boards. The third section discusses the SEC's diversity disclosure rule in depth, including criticisms of the rule in its current form. The fourth section addresses additional approaches to regulating diversity on corporate boards.

A.   History of Regulation

Workplace diversity cannot be addressed through a single law or regulatory regime. Laws addressing diversity generally take the form of remedial antidiscrimination statutes, rather than affirmative requirements to incorporate diversity. For example, Title VII of the Civil Rights Act of 1964 is the bedrock federal employment discrimination statute. Along with the Americans with Disabilities Act, the Age Discrimination in Employment Act and the Pregnancy Discrimination Act, which are federal laws that prohibit discrimination on the basis of disabilities, age, and pregnancy, respectively, these statutes form the basis of federal employment discrimination law. Although sexual orientation and gender identity are protected under many state employment discrimination statutes, and some courts, scholars, and agencies construe Title VII to cover gender identity and/or sexual orientation under a broad interpretation of Title VII's prohibition on sex discrimination, these categories are not explicitly recognized under federal law. Moreover, while the spirit of the Civil Rights Act may support equality and diversity on corporate boards, the composition of corporate boards are not subject to challenges under Title VII or other antidiscrimination statutes.

While antidiscrimination laws have been somewhat successful in facilitating the diversification of the workforce, there is no analogous regulatory regime that applies to corporate boards. Elections of corporate directors are generally within the province of state corporate laws, which provide procedures by which shareholders to elect directors. State corporate laws generally do not address diversity in the corporate board context. However, the SEC indirectly regulates diversity issues in connection with its regulation of public companies, which is generally achieved by mandating certain disclosures to investors. The SEC's regulatory philosophy is that "[s]unlight is said to be the best of disinfectants; electric light the most efficient policeman." This is generally interpreted to mean that so long as information is disclosed to the public, investors will have sufficient information to make informed investment decisions.

Until 2010, there were no laws that directly addressed diversity on corporate boards. The SEC took the first step to addressing the lack of diversity on corporate boards by enacting the diversity disclosure rule in 2010. Prior to the SEC's adoption of a diversity disclosure rule, corporate board diversity was primarily addressed in the context of the SEC's shareholder proposal rule, Rule 14a–8. This rule has been effective in raising awareness, if not affecting policy, regarding social issues, including diversity.

* * *

B. *International Regulation of Board Diversity*

There have been varied approaches to regulating corporate board diversity internationally. Many other western democracies have taken aggressive, affirmative approaches to increasing diversity on corporate boards. While these approaches may not be appropriate models for regulation in the United States, it is important to recognize that corporate diversity is an international issue. Moreover, it is interesting to consider whether international approaches to regulation are more effective than approaches adopted in the United States, which have been fairly feckless to this point.

Quota systems are one popular regulatory approach to increase board diversity abroad. For example, some countries have adopted quotas to increase gender diversity on corporate boards. The first, and most aggressive, quota requiring gender diversity on corporate boards was adopted in Norway in 2005, which required publicly traded companies to increase female board representation to forty percent by 2008, or face severe consequences, including possible delisting from securities exchanges. As of 2016, women held 40.1 percent of board seats in Norway. France enacted a similar quota in 2010, requiring forty percent of board seats to be held by women by 2017. Spain enacted a forty percent gender diversity quota in 2016, however, this quota did not include an enforcement mechanism, leading scholars to characterize Spain's quota as voluntary. The Justice Commissioner of the European Union has urged all member states to adopt quotas to increase boardroom diversity. Other European countries are considering establishing similar quotas.

Quotas have clearly been effective abroad. However, such quotas may be vulnerable to legal challenges if mandated in the United States at federal or state levels. This type of quota system would also be extremely controversial, and, politically infeasible. Beyond the constitutional implications, mandating diversity on corporate boards is problematic for a number of reasons. First, corporate law in the U.S. is generally the province of state law, and state corporate law does not generally impose such heavy-handed requirements on corporate governance. This could also lead to inconsistency among states if liberal states enact diversity requirements, while conservative states decline to do so. Second, mandating diversity targets may diminish some of the economic and competitive benefits of diversity. Third, requiring diversity in such a top-down manner may cause backlash from some corporations and consumers. Fourth, adopting a mandatory approach may unfairly stigmatize minority directors. Finally, insofar as this paper correctly identifies the SEC as the proper entity to address corporate diversity through regulation, adopting quotas is inconsistent with the SEC's disclosure-based approach to diversity. Although effective, for the reasons identified herein, adopting a quota system is an impracticable solution for United States-based corporations.

The enhanced mandatory disclosure regime advocated in this paper is much less severe than the approaches to diversity adopted abroad. Moreover, this disclosure-based approach would be consistent with the SEC's general regulatory philosophy, favoring mandatory disclosure over more direct intervention.

C. SEC Disclosure Rule

In 2009, the SEC announced a modest step toward addressing diversity on corporate boards. The SEC's diversity disclosure requires public reporting companies to

> [d]escribe the nominating committee's process for identifying and evaluating nominees for director, including nominees recommended by security holders, and any differences in the manner in which the nominating committee evaluates nominees for director based on whether the nominee is recommended by a security holder, and whether, and if so how, the nominating committee (or the board) considers diversity in identifying nominees for director. If the nominating committee (or the board) has a policy with regard to the consideration of diversity in identifying director nominees, describe how this policy is implemented, as well as how the nominating committee (or the board) assesses the effectiveness of its policy.

Thus, under this rule, boards are not required to disclose the actual demography of the board of directors, but instead, boards must self-report whether efforts to increase diversity are in place, and how the efficacy of such efforts are measured. Additionally, "companies that lack diversity policies and/or do not consider diversity when choosing director candidates must still disclose this information in their proxies." Notably, the term "diversity" was not defined by the SEC, leaving many companies free to define diversity without reference to demographic characteristics, which was the intent behind the rule. Many companies missed the mark in terms of the information disclosed, by defining diversity to include "diversity of backgrounds, skills, experiences, and perspectives," rather than demographic traits like gender or race.

Prior to enacting this rule, the SEC solicited comments about whether diversity was important for investors. Many commentators agreed that demographic diversity was important information for investors to consider.

In terms of outcomes, it does not appear that the SEC's disclosure rule has successfully elicited meaningful information about board diversity from corporate disclosures, and has not been successful in terms of diversifying boards. Many companies simply ignored what was required by the SEC's diversity disclosure rule. Data has demonstrated that disclosures of many companies "remain largely superficial and uninformative," in addition to being incomplete in a majority of cases.

Not only has the SEC's diversity disclosure rule failed to elicit meaningful information, it has also not been successful in terms of impacting the demography of corporate boards. Although the SEC claims that it did not intend for diversity disclosure policies to directly steer behavior, many had hoped that board diversification might be a byproduct of this rule. As one source explains, "[n]ominating committees might, for example, conduct broader searches that would improve director quality or result in directors with fewer ties to the board or management and greater independence." This optimistic forecast has generally not come to fruition.

Scholars, regulators, and practitioners have been critical of the SEC's diversity disclosure rule. Former SEC chair Mary Jo White concluded that the "rules have failed to draw out meaningful information," and failed to impact demography, given that "the share of minority directors for the largest public companies has 'stagnated' at 15% for the past several years." Part of the problem is that the SEC failed to define diversity, and instead left it to companies to define diversity. Moreover, some companies appear to have misunderstood the information the SEC is seeking through this rule. "Many companies have parsed the rule's language and view consideration of diversity in nominating directors as different and distinct from having a formal diversity policy . . . [t]herefore they do not trigger the rule's requirements of discussing implementation of the policy and how the company assesses the effectiveness of the policy.

While the SEC's diversity disclosure rule appropriately recognizes the need for a regulatory response to minority underrepresentation on corporate boards, this rule requires significant changes. Specific recommendations will be discussed in Section IV, *infra*.

* * *

IV. PROPOSALS FOR REFORM

Scholars have suggested a number of approaches for increasing demographic diversity on corporate boards in the U.S. This article adds to this canon of scholarship by echoing calls for the SEC to take a greater role in regulating corporate diversity under an expanded version of the current diversity disclosure rule. The SEC's disclosure-based approach to regulating diversity strikes the appropriate balance between providing investors with meaningful information about diversity on corporate boards, while also providing proper deference to corporate decision-making. Insofar as consumers value diversity on corporate boards, this approach may yield positive financial results for corporations that disclose high-levels of demographic diversity.

This section argues that the SEC should maintain existing requirements of the diversity disclosure rule, but should amend the diversity disclosure rule to define the term 'diversity' to include specific demographic traits, including race, gender, sexual orientation and gender identity. This section further argues that the SEC should expand the scope of the existing diversity disclosure rule by mandating disclosure of board diversity, as defined by the amended rule. This section also argues that the SEC should create an enforcement mechanism by imposing penalties or other punitive measures for companies that fail to comply with the revised disclosure rule.

Because this article argues that the SEC's disclosure rule should include LGBT status as part of demographic diversity, this section addresses the unique concerns implicated by mandatory "outing" of LGBT board members, and suggests protective measures that could strike a balance between eliciting meaningful information about LGBT representation and protecting the privacy interests of individual LGBT board members. Finally, this section argues that consumer and investor activism, in conjunction with more transparent corporate disclosures, can help move the needle in the direction of greater diversity on corporate boards.

* * *

JESSICA FINK, *GENDER SIDELINING AND THE PROBLEM OF UNACTIONABLE DISCRIMINATION*
29 STANFORD LAW & POLICY REVIEW 57 (2018)

Fink is the Clara Shortridge Foltz Professor of Law at California Western School of Law. Professor Fink's research focuses on how traditional employment law doctrines have been complicated by developments in the modern workplace and examines how those tensions have played out in civil litigation.

INTRODUCTION

On a summer night during the 2016 Summer Olympics in Rio de Janeiro, thousands watched as Team USA swimmer Katie Ledecky smashed her own world record in the 800-meter freestyle, beating her previous record time by an astonishing two seconds. Finishing more than eleven seconds ahead of the closest runner up, Ledecky not only captured the gold medal with her incredible performance, but also became the first woman in almost fifty years to win a gold medal in the 200-, 400-, and 800-meter freestyle races, as well as one of only two swimmers in the history of the games to win a gold medal in consecutive Olympics as a teenager. That same night, celebrated American swimmer Michael Phelps failed to capture a gold medal in what promised to be his last individual Olympic race, the 100-meter butterfly, ultimately becoming part of a three-way tie for second place.

While most media outlets across the nation praised Ms. Ledecky's stunning achievement, one previously obscure newspaper, the *Bryan-College Station Eagle,* attracted significant attention for its coverage of these two races. Reporting on the outcome of the day's swim meets, the *Eagle* ran a headline in large, bold font that said, "Phelps ties for silver in 100 fly." Beneath the headline, in smaller and less prominent print, the paper wrote, "Ledecky sets world record in women's 800 freestyle." Almost immediately, a backlash ensued, with members of the public condemning the *Eagle* for its biased coverage that seemed to downplay Ledecky's achievement. University of Denver Law Professor Nancy Leong referred to the headline as "a metaphor for basically the entire world," with 34,000 people re-tweeting her comment, and another commentator observed that the paper's framing of these events "made it seem like even the most historic achievements of a woman are less important than a pretty good performance from a man."

One readily might attribute this incident to a simple case of sloppy editing by a small newspaper with minimal distribution or impact. Yet while this newspaper's coverage diverged from the norm in this particular situation, this type of incident is far from isolated; Ms. Ledecky is not alone in having her momentous achievement brushed aside when compared with the accomplishments of a male peer. To the contrary, in a wide variety of workplaces both nontraditional (i.e., an Olympic swimming pool) and more generic, women continue to face an uphill battle in their quest for recognition, respect and reward. Female employees from the athletic field to the boardroom to the science lab often find that their male counterparts garner more of the limelight, attracting more attention and recognition. Likewise, female workers frequently confront media portrayals and/or public perceptions that belittle or minimize their contributions. Women often find their workplace accomplishments described using a different vocabulary than that applied to their male peers—one that fails accurately to portray their achievements. Female workers lack access to important opportunities, encounter barriers to mentorship, or feel subjected to greater scrutiny than their male peers.

None of these slights, in isolation, likely would give rise to a viable gender discrimination claim. Indeed, whatever the workplace—the athletic field, the stage, or the corporate boardroom—these types of obstacles often blend into the background of the broader employment setting, seen as annoying and persistent but not particularly surprising—no more significant than the copying machine that habitually jams or the staff meeting that inevitably runs too long. Yet collectively, these incidents—which constitute what this article refers to as "gender sidelining"—accumulate to create very real obstacles for women at work.

This article examines the many ways in which women across a wide range of employment settings face obstacles that inhibit their advancement at work through policies and practices not reached by traditional antidiscrimination laws.

* * *

I. THE LIMITS OF TITLE VII

Despite the existence of comprehensive federal, state and local legislation designed to redress gender discrimination in the workplace, these laws generally will fail to provide relief for most examples of gender sidelining. For most female workers, the ability to sue an employer for gender discrimination begins and ends with Title VII, or with a comparable state law antidiscrimination provision. In proving their case under such a law, most employees—absent any direct evidence of discrimination—rely upon circumstantial evidence, using the well-established framework set forth by the U.S. Supreme Court in *McDonnell Douglas Corp. v. Green*. Under this framework, a plaintiff must establish, *inter alia,* that she suffered an adverse employment action, and must show that this adverse action was *because* of her gender, and not because of any legitimate reason that might be set forth by the employer.

Courts have adopted a fairly narrow view in interpreting what constitutes an "adverse action" for purposes of Title VII. Specifically, courts have held that "[a]n adverse employment action in the context of a Title VII discrimination claim is a 'materially adverse change in the terms and conditions of employment because of the employer's actions.' " Accordingly, adverse actions generally have been deemed to include harms related to hiring, firing, failures to promote, reassignments with significantly different responsibilities, or decisions that cause a significant change in benefits. Courts have made clear in this context that "a bruised ego is not enough." Thus, calling an African-American plaintiff ignorant and berating him in front of his coworkers has been held not to rise to the level of an adverse action for purposes of a Title VII race discrimination claim. A confrontation between an African-American employee and her supervisor in which the supervisor "rudely interrupted" a meeting that the employee was attending and then made inquiries of the employee "in a very aggressive tone" likewise was deemed not to satisfy this requirement in the context of a race discrimination suit. Even examples of a supervisor's animus-laden language (telling an African-American employee that "he was lazy like the rest of his people and that is why they are all in prison") or placing a black employee under constant observation when white employees were not monitored in the same way was deemed not to result in a "materially adverse" change in the employee's employment status or in the terms and conditions of his employment.

Further examples of this limited view of adverse action abound: In one case, a court declined to find a "hostile work environment" under Title VII, despite recognizing that the plaintiff's work atmosphere resembled a "men's locker room environment." In another case, a court held that a superior's refusal to greet or speak to the plaintiff were "trivial matters that do not rise to the level of actionable retaliation," observing, "not everything that makes an employee unhappy is an actionable adverse action." Yet another plaintiff's claims that a supervisor "gave her the 'cold shoulder,' sat far away from her at meetings, became too busy to answer her questions, and generally tried to avoid her" likewise were not found to constitute adverse actions, with the court observing that such "alleged 'snubs,' though surely unpleasant and disturbing, are insufficient to support a claim of retaliation under our caselaw . . . ." In this respect, the courts have made clear that "Title VII . . . does not set forth a general civility code for the American workplace," nor does it prohibit "genuine but innocuous differences in the ways men and women routinely interact with members of the same sex and of the opposite sex." According to at least one court, this might include tolerating "an unpleasant, harsh, combative or difficult work environment," or "the sporadic use of abusive language, gender-related jokes and occasional teasing."

This narrow view of the "adverse action" requirement arises in a context of a narrowing view of antidiscrimination claims generally. In her book *Discrimination Laundering: The Rise of Organizational Innocence and the Crisis of Equal Opportunity Law,* Professor Tristin Green discusses the proliferation of limits that have been imposed upon antidiscrimination law. Green discusses the various doctrinal and evidentiary rules (including the courts' interpretation of the adverse action requirement) that have developed in antidiscrimination cases. According to Green, these developments are "aimed at reigning in judge and juror discretion . . . at focusing the legal inquiry on key employment decisions, those that indicate material job success, like pay and promotion, hiring, discipline, and discharge." Green also highlights the constrained view of Title VII's "because of sex" requirement that many courts seem to adopt, observing that "[s]ome judges openly resist using the law for work culture change in all-male work environments . . . . They see the cultures that develop in these workplaces as personal and private and beyond the purview of Title

VII." Through all of these mechanisms, according to Green, antidiscrimination law has shifted its focus away from broader, structural concerns and instead has allowed courts to focus on isolated, concrete examples of bias, such as an executive making a biased comment or ordering lower-level decision makers to discriminate.

Thus, Green argues, "[t]he law misses entirely discrimination that accrues over time or is otherwise difficult to identify in a precise moment . . . ."—precisely the kind of systemic bias that often confronts women in the workplace. As discussed in greater detail below, not all bias appears in the form of a missed promotion, a cut in pay, or a seemingly groundless termination. Rather, for many women, the obstacles that they face at work are more difficult to pin down—a lack of access to certain opportunities, the diversion of credit for an idea, a nagging sense of being held to a higher standard than their male peers. In this sense, and as highlighted below, discrimination can creep its way into the workplace, not in the form of "specific, observable employment decisions" but rather "build[ing] subtly over time so that an identified moment of decision making—such as the manager's decision not to promote—may appear perfectly natural even when it is in fact the product of biased perceptions, judgments, and behaviors of the manager and also of others." For these plaintiffs who complain about this type of subtle discrimination at work, the courts' existing jurisprudence under Title VII means that obtaining legal relief may be an uphill battle.

While some might lament the inability of existing antidiscrimination law to reach these less obvious examples of bias in the workplace, extending Title VII or other statutes to cover these types of behaviors in fact would constitute a grave error. Title VII is not and never has been intended to reach every possible slight that an employee might experience in the workplace; employees are not encouraged or expected to turn to the courts to deal with every workplace complaint. In the harassment context, for example, renowned Judge Richard Posner has observed that the courts apply a standard of mere negligence, and not strict liability, to an employer's vicarious liability for harassment claims because of the "infeasibility of an employer's stamping out this sort of harassment without going to extreme expense and curtailing the privacy of its employees, by putting them under constant video surveillance." Given the nuance that pervades much of what constitutes gender sidelining, it would be nearly impossible to expect employers to detect and deal with every incident of such gender bias at work. Employers would be forced to monitor daily minutiae in the workplace, examining workplace interactions both formal and spontaneous in an effort to prevent even subtle slights against female workers—something that a litany of cases makes clear is far beyond what Title VII was intended to require.

* * *

II. GENDER SIDELINING ACROSS WORKPLACES

At the same time that the law fails to reach this type of subtle discrimination at work, the instances of gender sidelining appear to be proliferating. In all sorts of workplaces, women frequently feel brushed to the side: Their ideas are undermined, their efforts are upstaged, and their contributions are ignored. For employees in nontraditional workplaces, like Ms. Ledecky in her "workplace" of a swimming pool, this sidelining may be sporadic and evanescent, encapsulated in episodic anecdotes or media coverage. In more conventional employment settings, this sidelining may be more entrenched, embedded in a host of policies, procedures and practices that function (perhaps unintentionally) to inhibit female employees' ability to succeed. Yet across all of these workplaces—whether the athletic field, the stage, the laboratory, or the boardroom—gender sidelining functions to undermine achievement.

* * *

E. *In the Boardroom: Sidelined Corporate Executives and Employees*

Perhaps nowhere is the sidelining of women more notable than in the corporate world. From the manner in which men and women conduct themselves in meetings, to the manner in which they receive mentoring and guidance, to the manner in which they receive credit (or not) for their workplace contributions, men and women tend to experience the workplace in profoundly different ways.

In one respect, the demographic makeup of the modern workplace creates a perfect storm for women to run into barriers. Despite decades of efforts at expanding the percentage of women at work, women remain drastically underrepresented at every level of the corporate ladder, from entry level to management to vice president roles to C-suite positions. A 2016 report by McKinsey & Company ("McKinsey Report" or "Report") found that women are both hired and promoted at lower rates than men, leading to far fewer women occupying senior roles. While existing antidiscrimination law is rife with precedent that could be used to vindicate an alleged gender-based failure to hire or to promote, the law likely would fail to redress many of the more subtle obstacles that women frequently face in the corporate world.

1. *Gender Sidelining Manifests In Female Corporate Employees' Access To Leaders And Opportunities For Growth*

One subtle yet pernicious obstacle encountered by female workers is a lack of access and opportunity that they receive in comparison to that provided to their male peers. The McKinsey Report found that only 67% of women (compared to 74% of men) believe that they are able to participate meaningfully in workplace meetings, and that only 62% of women (compared to 68% of men) claim to recently have received a challenging work assignment. The Report noted that "[w]omen get less access to the people and opportunities that advance careers and are disadvantaged in many of their daily interactions," and observed that while both men and women view sponsorship by senior leaders to be a key component of ultimate success, women reported fewer substantive interactions with senior leaders as compared to their male colleagues—a gap that seemed to widen as men and women advanced up through the corporate hierarchy.

Gender Sidelining Manifests In Female Corporate Employees Being Held To A Higher Standard Than Their Male Peers

In addition to concerns regarding lack of access and opportunity, many female executives and lower-level corporate employees also cite the sense that they are held to a different (higher) standard than their male peers. Reviewers, evaluators and peers simply seem to require more of women than they do of men. Female CEO's in particular seem to experience such scrutiny, with everything from their management decisions to their strategic plans to their personal lives often being subject to rigorous public examination. As a result of this scrutiny, many female executives shy away from entering into transactions unless they are confident that they will come out on top, because failure can have devastating consequences. Professor Joan C. Williams has referred to this higher standard imposed on female employees as the "Prove It Again" bias, in which women must prove themselves again and again in order to get selected for managerial positions. According to Williams, because the public has an easier time visualizing men (rather than women) as CEO's, government leaders, or as others in positions or power, they see female leaders as more of a risk, forcing them "to prove themselves over and over again." While men find themselves judged according to their *potential,* women find themselves judged according to their *performance,* making even small failures seem critical. Accordingly, women's mistakes tend to be noticed with greater frequency and are remembered for longer; they tend to be judged more rigorously than men by their superiors; and they tend to receive more polarized evaluations.

A recent study co-authored by Professor Williams highlights the extra scrutiny imposed on female employees, focusing on the treatment of female junior attorneys at a Wall Street law firm. Examining the performance evaluations received by both male and female junior attorneys— evaluations that included both a numerical rating and a narrative component—the study found that male attorneys received more favorable numerical ratings than their female peers, even when compared to women who were described in the narrative section of the review as having high levels of perceived technical competence. In other words, female attorneys who were described very positively in the narrative portion of their evaluations received numerical scores that did not match those of seemingly "comparable" men.

This differential treatment and heightened scrutiny for female employees may emerge in less formal ways as well. In a telling experiment conducted by two employees of a movie reviewing website, a male writer and a female writer switched email signatures for two weeks, ultimately highlighting the different manner in which clients treated men and women within their company. When the male writer responded to emails under his female colleague's email signature, he described the experience as "hell," with clients questioning "everything he asked or suggested," and treating him in a condescending manner—despite the fact that he had had easy interactions with those same contacts in the past, when he dealt with them as a male. In contrast, his female colleague, who previously had been experiencing problems with her productivity, suddenly "had the most productive week of her career." The male writer concluded that he "wasn't any better at the job" than his female colleague; he "just [had] had this invisible advantage." He previously had been able to accomplish more than his colleague not because of any innate greater skill, but rather because she had had to spend time "convinc[ing] clients to respect her."

3. *Gender Sidelining Manifests In Female Corporate Employees' Ideas Being Overlooked, Ignored And Usurped*

When female workers in the corporate world are not searching for opportunities and access that seem out of reach, or navigating standards and expectations that seem to apply more strictly to women, they must grapple with an even more daunting obstacle to success—the fact that their ideas and contributions often are overlooked, ignored, or in some cases misappropriated. The same McKinsey Report that decried the lack of opportunities available to women at work found that only 49% of women (compared to 54% of men) believe that their workplace contributions are valued appropriately. Moreover, only 56% of women (compared to 63% of men) believe that they are turned to for input regarding important workplace decisions. Behind these statistics lie troubling examples of why women adhere to these views.

Much already has been written upon the tendency of female workers to remain quiet at work, withholding contributions for fear of the "backlash" that speaking up might create. In one recent study that focused of the speaking patterns of chief executives (among others), researchers found that male executives who spoke more than their peers received 10% higher competency ratings from colleagues, while female executives who spoke more than their peers were rated (by both men and women) to be 14% *less* competent. Women in a professional setting must worry about what tone to adopt when they do speak, fearing the consequences if they are either too passive or too aggressive. Many feel that they must "walk[ ] a tightrope" when speaking at work, balancing between being "barely heard" or being seen as unpalatably forceful.

Related to this often-self-imposed silence, many women find that when they do speak up, their ideas are commandeered by their (usually male) colleagues. Numerous columnists and commentators have written about the tendency for women to be "manterrupted" at work, and about women finding their ideas "bropropriated" or "bro-opted" by male colleagues. A cartoon by Riana Duncan, originally published in *Punch Magazine,* poked fun at this phenomenon, showing an image of a boardroom populated by one woman and five men, with the caption "That's an excellent suggestion, Miss Trigs. Perhaps one of the men here would like to make it." More serious scholars have observed this phenomenon as well. In her thesis, *Perceived Muted Voice and Its Impact on Female Communication Techniques in the Workplace,* Masters candidate Rachel Lepchitz studied the communication patterns of women who already perceived their voices as being "muted" in the workplace. Lepchitz's interviews with these women exposed their feeling that "their ideas [were] being ignored yet when a male or other counterpart repeats the same idea, they run with it." The women interviewed noted "times when their ideas were not heard, but when a male counterpart said something similar it was acknowledged." In a separate report—this time, a journalistic examination of women working in Silicon Valley—one veteran software engineer described an interview in which a male job applicant ignored both her and one of her female colleagues, only responding favorably when a male employee was sent to interview him. Another female Silicon Valley employee summed up the atmosphere in her workplace by saying "[i]t wasn't overt sexism; it was more like being dismissed and disrespected, not feeling like we were good enough to be there—even though, objectively speaking, we were."

Of course, all of these potential slights exist alongside more overt examples of gender bias in the business world—examples that likely *could* support a cognizable discrimination claim. Women continue to receive unequal pay for arguably comparable work. They continue to be denied promotions for reasons that often seem tied to nothing other than their gender. And of course, women continue to face severe and pervasive sexual harassment in many workplaces. Such actionable examples of gender bias, however, are beyond the scope of this paper. The more subtle instances of upstaging, ignoring, or otherwise disadvantaging women, without more, remain more difficult to fit into a Title VII mold. Simply providing female workers with less access to leaders or not greeting women's ideas with appropriate recognition likely would not, in isolation, violate the law. Even the notion of holding a female worker to a higher standard than her male colleague—something that seems more concrete and easily provable—often won't suffice on its own, due to the inherently subjective nature of most evaluation processes. So long as the workplace permits, fosters and replicates these more subtle gender-based distinctions, women will continue to feel sidelined in the corporate world.

III. WHY GENDER SIDELINING MATTERS

Understanding the range of workplaces in which gender sidelining occurs and the various forms that this sidelining takes undoubtedly is an important endeavor. Equally important, however, is recognizing why gender sidelining matters. Far from some theoretical, obscure problem that simply makes us feel not-very-good about one aspect of society, the policies and practices that lead to gender sidelining have a host of significant ramifications in the workplace and beyond, silencing female voices at work, undermining women's productivity and job satisfaction, and hindering their advancement and perceived value. As discussed in greater detail below, the harms that flow out of gender sidelining not only create negative ramifications for *women* in their respective workplaces, but also work to the great detriment of society as a whole.

A. *Gender Sidelining Silences Female Voices*

Perhaps the most insidious impact of Gender Sidelining is the silencing of female voices in the workplace. As women feel less valued with respect to their contributions, they may choose to refrain from speaking out with their thoughts and ideas. Notably, the idea that female voices are silenced in the workplace actually runs counter to some of common assumptions about how men and women interact, both inside the workplace and beyond. While many in society adhere to the stereotype of the "chatty female," statistics show that men speak much more frequently than women (at least within professional settings). In fact, many women report not only feeling as if they must keep their ideas to themselves at work rather than speak out, but also cite concerns that when they do speak out, their ideas often are discounted or ignored. Facebook COO Sheryl Sandberg described this experience in an editorial that she wrote for the *New York Times,* along with co-author and Wharton Professor Adam Grant. Sandberg and Grant described the careful balance that women must strike when they choose to speak in a professional setting, noting that a woman "either [is] barely heard or she's judged as too aggressive." As a result, Sandberg and Grant noted that women often conclude that "saying less is more."

Much has been written about this pressure upon women to remain passive at work. In some cases, this deference may be tied to broader notions of a woman's femininity. In an article compellingly titled, *Do Women Lack Ambition,* psychiatrist and Cornell University medical professor Anna Fels wrote about "the unspoken mandate that [women] subordinate needs for recognition to those of others—particularly men." In Professor Fels' view, one of the significant forms of discrimination faced by women is "the expectation that 'feminine' women will forfeit opportunities for recognition at home and at work." She observes that "[w]omen tend to feel foolish asking for appropriate acknowledgement of their contributions. They find it difficult to demand appropriate support—in the form of time, money, or promotion—to pursue their own goals. They feel selfish when they do not subordinate their needs to those of others." Thus, according to Professor Fels, "[w]hen women speak as much as men in a work situation or compete for high-visibility positions, their femininity is routinely assailed. They are caricatured as either asexual and unattractive or promiscuous and seductive . . . ."

* * *

This silencing of female voices at work not only arises due to women's tendency to self-censor, but also may result from a more unconscious downgrading of women's ideas. Research has shown that the manner in which listeners break down information when both a male and female speaker are saying the same thing may differ significantly according to the gender of the speaker. Indeed, it turns out that "the voice itself is the source of unconscious bias for the listener, and women are interpreted differently as a result." For example, a listener who hears a male speaker say the word "academy" might assume that he is speaking about a school, but listeners who hear a woman say the word "academy" more likely will presume that she is discussing an awards show. In addition, gender can impact the extent to which others find a speaker to be dependable, intelligent or reliable. Research indicates that even when a female voice generally is deemed trustworthy, clear, and comprehensible, her voice still will receive lower ratings when compared with a man's voice. In fact, even if a man's voice is deemed not-so-reliable, or not very intelligent on its own, his voice will benefit from a boost in ratings when it is compared to a woman's voice. In this way, women may find themselves silenced not by the content of their comments, but rather but inherent assumptions associated with their gender as a speaker.

Finally, and perhaps most unfortunately, this silencing that women experience in the workplace often becomes part of a vicious circle: The more women feel silenced or "man-terrupted" or as if their ideas have been "bro-opted" by male peers, the more they may doubt their real value in the workplace. They "shut down, become less creative, less engaged . . . revert into [them]selves, wondering if it's actually [their] fault." It is in this vein that various scholars have studied the "imposter phenomenon" among women, where women—despite garnering objective indicators of achievement (degrees, honors, professional recognition)—"do not experience an *internal* sense of success." Indeed, as at least one author has observed, the presence of sex and gender stereotypes "are not only prevalent, but sometimes also self-fulfilling," noting the extent to which men and women are trained from a young age to buy into biased and gender-based views. Thus, the more that women disengage and doubt their value, the less likely they are to speak up in the face of further interruptions or appropriations. Silence begets further silence; disempowerment begets disempowerment. Without any positive reinforcement to encourage women to push back against marginalizing behavior in the workplace, women may continue to tolerate (or even grudgingly expect) such sidelining, writing it off as simply another cost of doing business in the predominantly-male working world.

B. *Gender Sidelining Robs the Workplace of Female Input and Perspectives*

Closely related to the notion that gender sidelining silences women in the workplaces is the idea that those in the workplace inevitably will lose access to female input and perspectives. In other words, it is not only the silenced female speakers who suffer when women's ideas are crowded out; those of both genders who could have benefited from those ideas also lose out.

In their *New York Times* article, Sheryl Sandberg and Adam Grant noted an experiment conducted by University of Texas researcher Ethan Burris in which he asked teams of individuals to make strategic decisions for a bookstore. Burris surreptitiously informed one random member of each team of helpful data related to the bookstore. According to Sandberg and Grant, Burris's subsequent analysis showed that when a female team member received this information and used it to suggest changes to the bookstore's operations, team leaders viewed them as less loyal and were less likely to act upon their suggestions. In fact, even when all of the team members were told that one team member possessed inside information that could be helpful to running the bookstore, the suggestions from female team members with this inside information still were discounted. This disregard for female voices on the team deprived the team of valuable information that could have benefitted the larger group.

Other benefits tend to emerge from female leadership—benefits that may be lost if women are crowded out of the environment. Women frequently drive innovation in the workplace, adopting novel approaches to addressing challenges. They tackle problems with a perspective that often fundamentally differs from that of their male colleagues, and therefore can see solutions that might not appear to men in the workplace. Women also tend to foster greater collaboration than their male peers. A study by Harvard Graduate School of Education lecturer Catherine Krupnick, which examined a year's worth of recorded classes conducted by twenty-four instructors at Harvard College, not only found that male students spoke more frequently than female students (a conclusion that even the researchers noted was "scarcely news"), but also confirmed previous research that highlighted the impact of gender on discussion patterns within a group. According to Krupnick's study, groups composed entirely of women tended to have a "rotating" participatory discussion style, in which women took turns speaking and contributed to the discussion on more or less equal parts during the class period, while male discussion groups tend to be more contest-like, with very uneven amounts of talking per male participant and an establishment of hierarchy. For those who believe that collaborative discussions tend to lead to higher quality outcomes than those in which a few select speakers dominate, these findings shed further light on a risk inherent in blocking out female voices in the workplace.

If women are shoved aside in the workplace or made to feel that their efforts lack importance, many women may make the logical choice to remain silent and withhold their valuable contributions. They won't offer their novel insights; they won't try to collaborate with their male colleagues. In this way, the sidelining of women at work leads to a significant detriment within an organization itself, as that organization loses out on the valuable feedback and ideas that women otherwise could offer to improve overall operations.

C. *Gender Sidelining Undermines Employee Morale and Productivity*

This sense that women have about being silenced in the workplace not only affects their ability to share their ideas with their fellow workers, but also may have the additional consequence of undermining workplace morale and hindering productivity. In her article, *Do Women Lack Ambition,* discussed above, Professor Fels observed that "multiple areas of research have demonstrated that recognition is one of the motivational engines that drives the development of almost any type of skill. Far from being a pleasant but largely inessential response, it is one of the most basic of human requirements." Citing research by renowned psychologist Jerome Kagan and his co-author Howard Moss, Professor Fels noted that the authors found a "high positive correlation between mastery and recognition" and that they observed that "it may be impossible to measure the desire to improve a skill independent of the individual's desire for recognition." According to these researchers, acquiring expertise in any area often *requires* recognition. In other words, Professor Fels observes, "[t]o attempt to master a skill, particularly one that requires prolonged effort, you must believe you are likely to succeed."

Others have reached similar conclusions about the impact that a lack of recognition and appreciation has on a woman's level of productivity and drive to succeed. Rachel Lepchitz's research, discussed above, found that an individual's "level of perceived muteness can impact productivity," leading employees to become frustrated, angrily disengaged, or in some cases resigned and apathetic. A recent study conducted by researchers at the Wharton School at the University of Pennsylvania similarly found a clear relationship between gratitude and work engagement, noting that university fundraisers who received a pep talk from their supervisor expressing gratitude for their services made 50% more phone calls than their peers who had not received such recognition. As one workplace consultant has observed, "[w]hen you're feeling challenged and interested at work . . . you're more likely to stay at a company and advance at that company." At bottom, therefore, the extent to which women's efforts and accomplishments are (or are not) recognized in the workplace can create a self-fulfilling prophesy, either reinforcing achievement or worthlessness. Women who repeatedly are praised and recognized in the workplace will be motivated to try even harder, while women who feel overlooked and ignored may see their drive and ambition diminish.

Thus, it's not just that Gender Sidelining leaves women feeling ignored or slighted, with their tender feelings hurt due to the absence of an appropriate pat on the back. This lack of recognition—this "sidelining"— has a concrete impact on women's desire and ability to excel, muting their drive and ambition. They move through their chosen professions receiving recognition that is "quantitatively poorer, qualitatively more ambivalent, and . . . less predictable," and as a result, become increasingly demoralized regarding the prospects for their own success.

D. *Gender Sidelining Fuels Existing Biases that Hinder Women's Advancement at Work*

In addition to all of the aforementioned ramifications of women experiencing sidelining at work—women's voices being silenced, their ideas and input being excluded from workplace discussions, their drive and productivity being muted—gender sidelining also produces another more concrete negative impact for women in that it actively hinders women's advancement up the workplace hierarchy. Abundant research confirms that, as a general rule, it simply takes longer for women to reach the top of their relevant work environment. One recent study examined the career paths of twenty-four women who head Fortune 500 companies, finding, *inter alia,* that the median "long stint" for these female CEO's was twenty-three years spent at a single company in one stretch before being elevated to CEO. When the authors compared this result to a random sampling of male Fortune 500 CEO's, they found that for men in that sample, the median "long stint" at a company was just fifteen years. In other words, the climb to the top for these female CEO's was over 50% longer than that of their male peers.

So how does this relate to gender sidelining? Other research shows that having a woman fill a top executive position can provide support for other female executives, because it allows that female leader to serve as a mentor or role model—even without creating an explicit mentoring relationship. Moreover, the presence of female leadership within an organization "can also be a proxy for the organization's unobserved cultural and institutional characteristics, such as female-friendliness, affirmative action policies, or an egalitarian culture." In this way, the appointment of a women into a position of power can provide legitimacy for other women to step into leadership positions, both by diluting existing stereotypical views of women and by contributing to a more favorable view of women as leaders. In this respect, there is a symbiotic relationship between the tendency to sideline women at work and the ability of women to emerge as leaders, with each of these dynamics feeding off of the other: The more women are undermined, ignored, or upstaged at work, the fewer women who will emerge as leaders within the organization. But the more women are able to claw their way to the top and capture leadership positions, the less tolerance there will be—*across the organization as a whole*—for policies and practices that disempower women.

Sadly, significant evidence points to this vicious circle operating in a negative direction for many women, with increased sidelining undermining female advancement instead of female advancement decreasing sidelining. The manner in which companies approach the (still somewhat rare) appointment of women into leadership positions exemplifies this depressing and regressive result. As a recent study by Kellogg School of Management Professor Edward Smith and his colleagues revealed, many companies face great uncertainty in announcing the appointment of a new CEO when that new CEO happens to be female. On the one hand, ample evidence supports the many advantages associated with female leadership, such as greater collaboration in the workplace and increased innovation, indicating that investors should respond favorably to the appointment of a female CEO. On the other hand, separate research indicates that when a company announces the appointment of a female CEO, many investors react negatively.

When Professor Smith tried to interpret these seemingly conflicting conclusions, he determined that much depended on the manner in which the *media* covered the female CEO's appointment: He found that when companies appointed female CEO's and received significant media attention for those appointments, they were more likely to experience negative market reactions. Conversely, companies whose female-CEO announcements received less media attention were more likely to experience positive market reactions. Thus, in Professor Smith's view, "investors can reward the appointment of a female CEO, but *only* if Ms. Chief Executive Officer does not get too much press."

Hence, women continue to fall into a cycle of disempowerment and diminishment. The more that companies remain wary of publicizing their decisions to advance women up the corporate ladder, the more idiosyncratic those promotions will continue to seem. Rather than fostering a *norm* whereby women are viewed as being as naturally capable of leadership as their male peers, these policies feed into stereotypes that inhibit advancement. Women assume that they are not capable of achieving greater power because they have no example upon which to base such an ambitious path. Without adequate role models to serve as a guide for the value that female leaders bring to the workplace, and for what can be accomplished by placing women in leadership roles, future generations of female workers may have an even more difficult time envisioning themselves in such positions—and future generations of employers may be more reluctant to place them in such roles.

E. *Gender Sidelining Encourages Women to Opt Out of Professional Opportunities*

On top of all of these other ramifications of gender sidelining, perhaps the least surprising but most unfortunate result is that it leads women entirely to opt out of professional opportunities. Women who feel unappreciated and marginalized in the workplace not only may experience lower productivity and morale, but also might determine that their current field (or, sadly, any field) simply holds no room for female contributions.

Much has been written about the low representation of women throughout various sectors of the workforce. Women hold only roughly one quarter of the computing and math-related jobs in the United States, a fraction that actually has decreased over the past fifteen years. They remain underrepresented at every level within the corporate pipeline, from entry-level positions, to managerial and director roles, to Vice President and C-Suite positions. While women enter careers in law, medicine and business at rates approaching those of their male peers, they represent a mere minority of the workforce in those professions within just a few years. Theories abound as to *why* so many sectors of the U.S. labor market suffer from this shortage of women—from the lack of adequate paid maternity leave, to workplace policies that do not sufficiently accommodate a reasonable work-life balance, to overtly discriminatory and/or harassing behavior that drives women from the workforce. Without a doubt, however, gender sidelining plays a role here as well. Perhaps one additional reason why many women choose to leave the workforce is that they no longer wish to feel like second-class citizens in their own workplace.

In some fields, this "dropping-out-due-to-not-belonging" seems prevalent and obvious. In the tech field, for example, women not only are hired in lower numbers than men, but they also leave the field at a rate more than twice that of their male peers. Significantly, these women frequently are not leaving their positions for the often-assumed "family reasons," or because they dislike the work. Rather, they tend to leave due to "workplace conditions, a lack of access to key creative roles, and a sense of feeling stalled in one's career," with "[u]ndermining behavior from managers" also playing a major role. Women similarly drop out at higher rates than men in the legal field, including women who already have reached high-level partnership positions. Again, while family obligations drive many women to leave, women also cite many other obstacles to their success, including gender stereotypes, a lack of mentoring, inflexible work structures, and receiving less desirable "grunt work" assignments. Women seem to fare no better in medicine, leaving the medical field at notably higher rates than their male peers. Among the reasons cited for this departure is "burnout," which is more common for female doctors than for male doctors and which can increase if a women does not feel well respected.

Even in cases where women do not drop out of the workforce altogether, many forego significant opportunities for advancement due to feeling marginalized or overlooked. One intriguing finding in the McKinsey Report involved the extent to which working women reported being significantly less interested in achieving top executive status within an organization, with only 40% of women surveyed expressing an interest in such a position, compared to 56% of men surveyed. Again, while it is tempting to chalk up this distinction to different views regarding family obligations and/or work-life balance, this conventional wisdom seems not to tell the whole story here. The McKinsey Report observed that both women and men worry equally about balancing work and family, with this being the main concern cited by both groups for their reluctance to promote. Moreover, women with *and without* children disclaimed wanting the pressures associated with this type of promotion. Thus, there seems to be more to this avoidance of advancement than a simple desire to spend more time with one's family; even women without significant family obligations shied away from promotion opportunities, perhaps because of such feelings of muted disempowerment.

* * *

MELINDA S. MOLINA, *ADDRESSING THE LACK OF DIVERSITY ON CORPORATE BOARDS: BUILDING RESPONSIVE LAW SCHOOL PEDAGOGY AND CURRICULUM*
49 LOYOLA UNIVERSITY CHICAGO LAW REVIEW 669 (2018)

Molina is Associate Dean for Academic Affairs and an Associate Professor at Capital University Law School. Her scholarship focuses on how the law impacts subordinate and marginalized groups in the United States. She has co-authored two national studies on Latina lawyers.

Corporations hold incredible power over many aspects of American life. Their power and influence are felt in our economic, political, and educational systems. Recent corporate scandals demonstrate the havoc that corporations can wreak on housing markets, job markets, and the global marketplace. Scholars have long posited that greater corporate board diversity will lead to better strategic decisionmaking, organizational behavior, and financial performance. Yet, the underrepresentation of women and people of color serving on corporate boards and the barriers to achieving greater diversity persist. Common barriers include stereotypes about aptitude and capabilities, the scarcity of mentors and role models, and the lack of access to informal networks. Another obstacle to gaining greater corporate board diversity is the overreliance on traditional recruitment practices.

Given these barriers, can law schools build responsive pedagogy and curriculum that help? Maybe. The goal of this Essay is to explore and propose modest curriculum changes that can be used to address some of these barriers.

* * *

I.   CORPORATE BOARD DIVERSITY

Corporations often tout the benefits of diversity. Advocates and academics posit that board diversity is essential to better governance and decisionmaking, which leads to greater corporate profitability, and/or that board diversity should be sought out of fairness and equity concerns. Yet, the racio-ethnic and gender composition of corporate boards remains predominantly white and male. Almost three-quarters of Fortune 500 board seats are held by white men. While modest gains have been made, progress is slow. Collectively, women and people of color hold 30.8 percent of Fortune 500 board seats.

Women have excelled in educational attainment. They also participate in the labor force at almost an equal rate to men. This should set the expectation that women are equally represented on corporate boards and in leadership positions. However, women held only 20.2 percent of the seats on Fortune 500 boards in 2016. This represents modest gains from previous years, with women holding 16.6 percent of Fortune 500 board seats in 2012 and 15.7 percent in 2010. Women are also underrepresented in leadership positions in Fortune 500 companies, representing 5.2 percent of CEOs, 26.5 percent of senior executive officer positions, and 36.9 percent of mid-level manager positions. These percentages are far below the percentage of women participating in the labor force. The percentages also run counter to the fact that women surpass men in obtaining advanced degrees.

For people of color, the underrepresentation on corporate boards is striking. In 2016, people of color held fewer than 15 percent of Fortune 500 board seats. More specifically, African Americans, Hispanics, and Asians/Pacific Islanders accounted for 7.9 percent, 3.5 percent, and 3.1 percent of Fortune 500 board seats, respectively. Of all board seats in the Fortune 500 in 2016, women of color held 3.8 percent. Black women held 2.4 percent, Hispanic women held 0.8 percent, and Asian women held 1.0 percent of those board seats.

II.　BARRIERS TO ACHIEVING GREATER DIVERSITY

Why has progress toward greater board diversity stalled? One obstacle is that corporate leaders and board members do not believe that board diversity will enhance corporate profits. Studies examining the relationship between board diversity and enhanced corporate performance are mixed. While some studies have found positive correlations, others found negative correlations or no significant relationship. Increased corporate earning rationale tends to dominate the diversity debate because it "appeals to a culture steeped" in maximizing shareholder value. It could be that the focus on corporate earnings is misguided. Greater emphasis should be placed on the fact that board diversity may lead to better decisionmaking, greater access to a broader talent pool, and enhanced corporate reputation among shareholders and consumers.

Common barriers also include stereotypes about aptitude and capabilities, the scarcity of mentors and role models, and lack of access to informal networks. These barriers are due in part to "in-group" bias, which is the preference that individuals feel for those who share similar backgrounds "such as race, ethnicity, and gender." These preferences affect both favorable and unfavorable assessments of an individual's intelligence, accomplishments, and aptitude. In-group members will favorably assess the credentials and accomplishments of their own members, ascribing them to "intelligence, drive, and commitment." Meanwhile, the credentials and achievements of out-group members are seen as unmerited, and due to a fluke or preferential treatment.

These barriers are reinforced with affinity bias, which is the tendency to align ourselves with people who share similar identities, interests, and backgrounds. This leads people to invest in and allocate resources to those who are in their affinity group, while excluding others. These biases can affect whom an organization hires, promotes, and develops, which leads to barriers to opportunity.

Another obstacle to gaining entry to the boardroom is the over-reliance on traditional recruitment practices. The selection process relies significantly on existing director or personal networks. Corporate directors are often selected from the senior officer ranks of corporations. Because women and people of color hold few senior-level positions, they are less likely than white men to be selected to join corporate boards. This leads to the appointment of directors that share similar backgrounds. The few diverse board directors that are selected tend to serve on multiple boards. They are also more likely than white men to do so. This shows that companies would rather draw from the same pool of diverse candidates than cast a wider net. In other words, in order to serve on a board, diverse candidates need to already be on a board.

III. MODEST CURRICULUM PROPOSALS

Given these obstacles and barriers, can law schools build responsive pedagogy and curriculum that help? Maybe. Law schools may do so by augmenting their business curriculum to better prepare students to become business lawyers and eventual board members. The first step would be to do extensive outreach to business leaders and communities to understand: (1) the attributes that are important to both business and legal hires; and (2) their short-term and long-term business needs. The outreach should include alumni to gauge their level of preparedness when entering the workforce and their ability to complete job responsibilities. Alumni outreach could also seek feedback on what courses best prepared them for the workforce and where improvements in the curriculum can be made.

Based on this outreach, law schools can then recast their business curriculum as a tiered model. The first tier could include course(s) on business and financial literacy and concepts including, but not limited to: understanding financial statements and instruments, basic accounting principles, and valuation techniques. The second tier could allow students to take more advanced business courses. Law schools could offer simulation-based business law courses that provide students with an opportunity to see a transaction unfold while identifying possible risks, proposing solutions, and defending their proposals based on facts, data, and legal and regulatory constraints.

Advanced business courses could follow a traditional law school and/or cross-disciplinary course model. A cross-disciplinary approach may broaden the scope and add to the depth of a school's business curriculum by enhancing faculty resources and expertise. Throughout their careers, lawyers and business professionals will work together and learn from one another, so it may make sense to bring them together sooner as students. Cross-disciplinary education can also help students develop connections and relationships within local business and legal communities, which will broaden their professional and personal networks. The third tier could move students into various field placements where they could explore potential career opportunities while enhancing their resumes.

How might these curriculum proposals address the obstacles and barriers to achieving greater boardroom diversity? Law schools can integrate critical scholarship throughout their business law curriculum. Critical scholarship can be used to challenge the status quo of corporate leadership and board homogeneity. It can provide the theoretical framework that will help students understand the role that historical and present-day discrimination and implicit bias plays in reinforcing negative stereotypes about the qualifications and capabilities of women and people of color. Students can then use this framework as future practitioners and academics to develop and improve upon existing diversity initiatives and programming.

As mentioned earlier, directors are still found primarily through personal networks. Law schools could invite business leaders—including board members—into the classroom as either guest speakers or adjuncts. This might create and strengthen relationships between the law school and business leaders, which could benefit students by improving their understanding of corporate boards and raising the law school's visibility. While immediate corporate board diversity gains will not be realized, it may serve as a catalyst for future opportunities. It may also provide a competitive advantage for students for field placements or entry-level positions.

In order to provide these opportunities to diverse students, law schools must take steps to generate interest among diverse students in taking business law courses. Diverse students may not enroll in these courses because of lack of familiarity or exposure to the corporate law profession. Steps may include programming or episodic mentoring/networking opportunities with business faculty and alumni. These opportunities should be geared toward building and developing relationships so students gain familiarity and exposure to business law.

* * *

CHAPTER 8

LEADERSHIP IN OTHER CONTEXTS: ATHLETICS, HIGHER EDUCATION, MEDICINE, MILITARY, SCIENCE AND MORE

■ ■ ■

INTRODUCTION

Many of the same kinds of biases and aspects of discrimination covered in previous chapters are present in other professional contexts beyond the legal profession, but differences do exist. Chapter 8 explores the ways in which gender and leadership intersect in other fields, focusing specifically on examples from athletics, higher education, medicine, the military, the sciences, and more. The readings underscore how all professions face similar and nuanced gender issues, especially in leadership roles. Internationally, the challenges for some women are even greater.

Consider other areas beyond the legal profession where reports about sexual discrimination and harassment have made the headlines. In the months before this casebook went to press, news coverage about sexual misconduct included industries like film and media, financial services, higher education, performing arts, race car driving, restaurant and food service, and more. Much of this attention is due to the #MeToo Movement, which Chapter 9 covers in greater detail as we turn to solutions. For now, it is important to realize that the issues facing the legal profession are not entirely unique, and to reflect upon what we might learn from others. We also recognize that for women in other countries, legal and cultural impediments present even greater challenges in the pursuit of leadership roles.

Credit: Creative Commons Attribution 4.0 International License, author Emna Mizouni

Until 2018, women in Saudi Arabi were banned from driving cars, among other inequalities. **Loujain Al-Hathloul** challenged this ban by posting public videos of herself driving at age 24, landing in jail for more than two months. She also called out other restrictions, for example joining a petition signed by more than 14,000 who sought the end of the requirement that a male guardian permit marriage or travel out of the country. A graduate of the University of British Columbia, she has received international recognition for her work in human rights. Among these awards, Time Magazine named her to its list of 100 most influential people in 2019. As this casebook went to press, she remained imprisoned for her activism.

THOUGHT QUESTIONS

As you read the articles excerpted below, consider the following questions:

1.   Prior to reading this casebook, had you considered the impact of gender inequality in positions of leadership and power in the legal profession? Had you considered it among any other professions? How does law compare with other professions like athletics, education, health care, the military or science?

2.   In the past decade, significant emphasis has been placed upon encouraging more women and minorities to choose jobs in STEM fields—science, technology, engineering and mathematics. Have you been part of a program or experience that promoted these areas as you considered your future career path? What is your reaction to efforts like this? How might these initiatives be helpful or unhelpful?

3.   The readings highlight inequities among professions other than law in the United States. Do other countries face similar diversity challenges? Conduct some independent research about professions from other countries and try to find one or two examples of professions outside the United States that are working to address gender disparity among their leadership. How do limitations on basic aspects of public and personal life, like the ability to drive a car or travel abroad or decide whom to marry, impact one's leadership trajectory?

4.   Are there lessons or guides from other professions that you believe the legal profession should consider for addressing gender inequality in leadership?

DOMINIQUE POTVIN, *A NEW, DATA-BASED CHECKLIST TO HELP BOOST WOMEN IN SCIENCE LEADERSHIP*

THECONVERSATION.COM, MAY 30, 2018

Potvin is a Lecturer in Animal Ecology specializing in behavior and evolution at the University of the Sunshine Coast, Australia.

Gender equity in academic science may seem like a pipe dream, with the percentage of scientific leadership positions held by women in institutions a mere 5–20%.

However, new data from science societies—the professional associations that bring researchers of a particular specialty together—tell a different story.

Published today, research from my colleagues and I shows that globally, women make up about 33% of zoological society boards, and about 25% of executive positions (presidents, vice presidents, treasurers and secretaries).

While still short of equality, this represents a trend in the right direction. And we can take some lessons from some of the finer points of our analysis to address gender equity in science leadership more broadly.

To that end, we've created a Gender Equality Checklist for scientists to apply in their own professional operations. A few easy examples:

- outline a mission statement in your constitution or on your website regarding inclusion, diversity and/or anti-discrimination

- have written and enforceable grievance policies and procedures for harassment

- commit to blind objective reviewing for conference papers, grants, scholarships and awards.

Visible statements of diversity matter

Scientific societies are organisations with a goal of advancing scientific knowledge through grants, conferences, and journal publications. They also help to unite geographically distant researchers within a field, and provide mentors or role models for early-career academics. Perhaps most importantly, societies provide opportunities for networking, both formally and informally.

Using quantitative models, we tried to pinpoint potential predictors of gender ratios across more than 200 societies in the field of zoology. We found that older, larger societies were more male-biased.

But we also saw one of the most important factors in predicting whether women held leadership positions in a society was simply a visible statement of diversity, inclusivity or anti-discrimination.

While it may make intuitive sense that a society that states its valuation of equality does have a more balanced representation of men and women, it's nice to see this idea supported by empirical data.

A Gender Equality Checklist

There are no lack of studies bemoaning the state of women in science. Not many, however, allow insight into positive or negative factors that contribute to equality (especially quantitatively, with the data and numbers that scientists love to see).

In this study, we wanted not only to report on the state of affairs, but also to increase our understanding about the characteristics of societies that promote women in science, and identify actionable steps that societies can take to help reach equality.

Published in the paper, our Gender Equality Checklist does just that: it can be brought to any Annual General Meeting (AGM) to help societies evaluate their own values and courses of action to help promote diversity and equality within their own field.

Along with other actions such as keeping demographic data and offering mentorship opportunities, these steps forward can help create a much more inclusive, safe and thus productive and efficient scientific network or body.

The importance of gender equality in science

I'm a behavioural ecologist, with the benefit of having amazing female (and feminist male) mentors—both past and present—throughout my career.

One thing I am asked (more often than I should be, I think) is: why do we care about gender equality in science?

If the intrinsic values of equality, removal of subconscious bias or simply the human right to educational opportunity isn't enough, consider the evidence.

Various studies have shown that more diverse and gender-balanced organisations (in science and elsewhere) are more innovative, productive, efficient and personally satisfying to members or employees. It seems like a no-brainer that we should be aiming for this kind of culture in science.

Scientific societies may, at first glance, appear to play a small role in the life of an academic: we pay our membership fees, attend a conference or two, and encourage our students to apply for small societal grants.

However, the role of the scientific society in the pursuit of gender equality in science and related fields is likely bigger than we have previously thought (if we have thought about it at all).

These boards make publishing and funding decisions, contribute to advocacy, and provide a platform for mentoring and networking across generations and nationalities. Their importance should not be underestimated.

The seemingly sluggish rate of improvement for women in science can tend to inspire hopelessness. This is symptomatic of institutional culture, with staff turnovers and bureaucracy in general being slow processes, some taking decades to visibly change.

However, scientific societies give us hope. The young membership, frequency of elections and more relaxed networks that used to contribute to a reputation of an "old boys' club" feel of societies may now be positive influences on female promotion.

Here, behind the scenes, we may find more opportunity for rapid change in the right cultural environment.

ERIN E. BUZUVIS, *SIDELINED: TITLE IX RETALIATION CASES AND WOMEN'S LEADERSHIP IN COLLEGE ATHLETICS*

17 DUKE JOURNAL OF GENDER LAW AND POLICY 1 (2019)

Buzuvis is a Professor of Law and Director of the Center for Gender & Sexuality Studies at Western New England School of Law. Her research focuses on gender and discrimination in education and athletics, including the intersection of sexual orientation and race discrimination in collegiate women's athletics, retaliation and related discrimination against female college coaches, and participation policies for transgender and intersex athletes.

Introduction

For fourteen years, Lindy Vivas was the head volleyball coach at California State University at Fresno (Fresno State). In that position, she transformed a program that had never had a winning season into one that regularly produced successful and highly competitive teams. In fact, under Vivas, Fresno State women's volleyball teams had an overall win-loss record of 263–167 and received more invitations to post-season tournaments—including national and NCAA tournaments—than all teams in the history of the program, and the Western Athletic Conference named her coach of the year three times. Her success notwithstanding, Vivas was informed in December 2004 that her contract would not be renewed, ostensibly because she had failed to meet her performance objectives.

Vivas was more than a successful and winning coach. She was an advocate for gender equity at a university with a long history of discrimination against women's athletics in violation of Title IX. Along with other female coaches and administrators, several of whom also lost their jobs, Vivas had complained about discrimination to university officials and government regulators responsible for enforcing Title IX. Specifically, she alleged that Fresno State paid lower salaries and awarded shorter contracts to female coaches and allocated fewer resources, less support, and unequal access to facilities for the women's volleyball team.

Vivas filed suit against Fresno State, alleging that although the athletic director cited performance reasons for her termination, she was actually fired for her gender, her marital status, her perceived sexual orientation, and her whistleblowing on gender discrimination within the department. In July 2007, jurors in the Fresno County Superior Court agreed, except as to the marital status claim, and awarded her $5.85 million in damages—at the time, the largest jury award in a Title IX case. Later that year, Fresno State announced a multi-million dollar settlement with Diane Milutinovich, an athletic department official who also claimed she was fired in retaliation for her efforts to ensure the department's compliance with Title IX. Fresno State then lost another high-profile trial involving similar claims of retaliation. This time, the damages award to the plaintiff, former women's basketball coach Stacy Johnson-Klein, was a staggering $19.1 million.

Due to the record-setting jury awards and multiple separate plaintiffs, the Fresno State cases are the most visible examples of Title IX retaliation cases in the wake of the Supreme Court's 2005 decision, Jackson v. Birmingham Board of Education, which recognized a private right of action for retaliatory discrimination under Title IX. In the short time since the decision was released, it has already been invoked in a number of retaliation cases involving college athletics. Coaches, administrators, and other university officials from California to Florida—both male and female, but mostly female—have filed suit against their institutions, complaining that their contracts were terminated or not renewed, or that they were harassed or otherwise mistreated, because they raised concerns about gender equity on behalf of students, other coaches, or themselves. These cases, some of which have also resulted in significant verdicts and settlements, provide insight into athletic department culture and reveal obstacles women face in reaching positions of leadership in college athletics. These cultural considerations are particularly relevant in light of the enormous gender gap among college head coaches and athletic administrators. Women fill less than a quarter of head coach and athletic director positions in college athletics, and are even minorities among coaches of women's teams.

Discrimination against women seeking or serving in leadership positions in sport is worthy of analysis, not only for the sake of individual women who desire to self-actualize as a head coach or athletic administrator, but because the unique role of sport in society gives underrepresentation of women in leadership positions additional significance. Due to its high visibility and widespread appeal—its veritable iconic status—sport is a salient site of cultural production. That is, sport operates on a symbolic level, reflecting and transmitting shared cultural values. Among these values, sport helps define the attributes associated with leadership, and thus, derivatively, power. By remaining, in the words of Carole Oglesby, "uniquely impervious to the inclusion of women," sport operates to ensure women's exclusion from powerful social roles more generally, as both men and women exposed to the male-dominated realm of sport "internalize . . . the dominant vision" of power as a masculine trait. Put another way, when women serve in head coaching positions, "the visibility and responsibility associated with coaching implies [sic] that women are capable in leadership positions of any kind."

The current spate of retaliation cases is, therefore, a relevant source of information about an important social problem. Moreover, the fact that plaintiffs in Title IX retaliation cases against college athletic departments are enjoying new levels of success provides an opportunity to speculate optimistically about the power of law to effect positive change in the culture of college athletics. Following the Supreme Court's recent validation of a private right of action to challenge retaliation in Jackson, coaches and athletic administrators have never before had more legal remedies with which to tackle sex discrimination in college athletics. Together with the recent high-profile multi-million dollar jury verdicts and settlements, these legal remedies create a strong incentive for athletic departments seeking to avoid liability to monitor for and address institutional practices that drive and deter women from coaching.

* * *

B. Florida Gulf Coast University

Florida Gulf Coast University is, like Fresno State, paying several million dollars to settle Title IX retaliation cases filed by two female coaches and the former university counsel who advocated on their behalf. The dispute giving rise to this litigation began in May 2007, when two female head coaches, Jaye Flood (volleyball) and Holly Vaughn (golf), along with two female assistant coaches, had a meeting with FGCU's former athletic director (the director emerita), Merrily Dean Baker, and enlisted her support in efforts to address discriminatory treatment against female coaches and student-athletes. Soon after the meeting, Baker wrote a letter to the university's interim president, Richard Pegnetter, summarizing the coaches' concerns. Baker's letter characterized the athletic department's workplace culture as one of "intimidation," "isolation," "intolerance," and "insensitivity." Baker criticized the athletic director for failing to hire female coaches, failing to support female coaches, using closed searches to make hiring decisions in the department, paying female coaches lower salaries under shorter employment contracts, and directing hostility toward a coach because of her sexual orientation. The letter also detailed disparities in the resources allocated to the men's and women's programs.

In their eventual lawsuit, the coaches alleged that soon after Baker's letter was delivered, they were presumed to be the source of the information it contained and were targeted for retaliation as a result. Specifically, soon after the letter was delivered, both head coaches received negative performance evaluations for the first time ever and Flood was placed on administrative leave for what FGCU publically described as "issues involving student welfare." The basis for this action was revealed to be a claim that Flood had inappropriately tugged at a player's shirt during practice.

FGCU's response to the substance of Baker's letter was also controversial. In January 2008, an outside law firm hired by FGCU to conduct an external review of the athletic department's Title IX compliance concluded that the specific grievances Baker alleged did not constitute actual Title IX violations. However, the report does not address a major theme in Baker's letter: the hostile, intimidating atmosphere for female coaches. The external investigation did, however, discredit the negative performance evaluations that Flood and Vaughn had received and failed to substantiate the "shirt tugging incident" as grounds for disciplinary action. Moreover, the law firm's investigation uncovered evidence suggesting that the Athletic Director and another athletic department official likely created the negative performance evaluations as pretextual grounds to fire the coaches in the future.

The external investigation report contained one final twist. It revealed that FGCU was concerned about more than just the shirt tugging incident: there were also charges that Flood had inappropriate sexual contact with a female person not associated with the University while on a volleyball road trip and that she had been in an inappropriate, "amorous" relationship with a female student intern. The report concluded that this latter charge was substantiated by evidentiary support, and this conclusion provided the basis for FGCU's decision to terminate Flood four days later.

While Flood publically denied that she had had an affair with a student, her lawsuit challenging her termination focused on the reason for

FGCU's investigation in the first place. Flood maintained that the investigations into her personal life were, like the negative performance evaluations, part of the athletic department's efforts to "manufacture grounds for her removal" because she had participated in efforts to expose gender disparities which she reasonably believed to constitute sex discrimination in violation of Title IX.

Holly Vaughn joined Flood's lawsuit as a second plaintiff in May 2008. Vaughn had resigned at the beginning of her fall 2007 season in response to the hostility and pressure directed at her following the release of the Baker letter. Vaughn maintained that her negative performance evaluation was retaliation for her presumed role in the Baker meeting as well as her past efforts to challenge the athletic department's discriminatory employment practices.

FGCU's former general counsel, Wendy Morris, was the third plaintiff to bring a retaliation case against the university in the wake of the Baker letter. According to Morris's complaint, filed in April 2008, the former interim president, Richard Pegnetter, targeted her for retaliation because she had urged him to investigate and take seriously the charges of sex discrimination raised in the Baker letter. Pegnetter refused to let Morris's office participate in the internal investigation. She was suspended, then fired, soon after she reported to the Board of Trustees her suspicions that Pegnetter was attempting to cover up Title IX violations.

In October 2008, Flood and Vaughn agreed to drop their case against FGCU in exchange for a combined total payment of $3.4 million and FGCU's agreement to submit to an independent review of its Title IX compliance. FGCU also settled with Wendy Morris for $800,000. Most recently, a fourth plaintiff, former provost Bonnie Yegidis, has come forward alleging that her resignation was requested in response to her efforts to support Morris and the female coaches. Her suit is pending [as of early 2019].

* * *

Retaliation Cases and Barriers to Women's Leadership in College Athletics

As noted in the Introduction, women are the minority among college coaches, constituting less than a quarter of head coaches overall and less than half of coaches of women's teams. Similarly, less than a quarter of all athletic directors are women; this percentage drops to below 10% among colleges and universities belonging to NCAA Division I. In contrast, before Title IX was passed in 1972, women's sports were coached and administered almost entirely by women, causing some to describe today's dearth of female coaches as an "unintended consequence" of Title IX. [Casebook authors' note: This is one of many examples of unintended consequences that may occur when reforms are implemented to help women. In Chapter 9, we return to this dilemma and reflect on how, if at all, it can be avoided.] It is argued that the legislation elevated the profile and status of women's sports, with different impacts on men and women regarding leadership positions: greater prestige and compensation make such positions increasingly attractive to men, while simultaneously generating additional pressure, time, and travel demands that make those positions less attractive to women. Accordingly, a popular explanation for the gender gap in college coaching and administration is that women leave or avoid careers in college athletics as a matter of personal preference for jobs that are more family-friendly; indeed, there is empirical evidence to support this theory. Unfortunately, the predominance of this explanation for the gender gap in college coaching creates the perception that college athletics departments are limited in their ability to address the problem because head coach and upper-level administration positions are, due to long hours and travel requirements, family-unfriendly by their very nature. Yet what these retaliation cases reveal is that other gendered dynamics of college athletic department culture are also operating as obstacles to women's participation and advancement in leadership positions in college athletics.

* * *

A. Predicate Discrimination Relating to Employment Conditions and Discrimination Against Female Student Athletes

* * *

[T]he centrality of employment and programmatic discrimination to the narrative of these retaliation cases complements existing empirical research on the dearth of women coaches, which demonstrates a correlation between their perceptions of discrimination on the one hand, with lower job satisfaction and higher turnover on the other. For instance, one qualitative study of female American and Canadian intercollegiate coaches suggests that the coaches' perceptions of gender discrimination in athletic departments in terms of "salary, job security, workload, historic pension contributions, team facilities and operating budgets (e.g., travel, recruitment, scholarship monies)," contributes to the higher rates of job turnover among female coaches compared to male coaches.

Another study found that while both male and female coaches were likely to report high levels of job satisfaction, and thus lower turnover intent, when they perceived their athletic department to be distributing resources equitably among men's and women's teams in compliance with Title IX, the perception of equality was more predictive of female coaches' job satisfaction than it was for male coaches of women's teams. This difference could be due to female coaches' heightened awareness of inequities that affect all women's teams, regardless of the coaches' sex, or it could reflect a greater incidence of discrimination against those women's teams with female coaches. Either way, this study underscores the relationship between employment and programmatic discrimination, as revealed in the narratives of the retaliation plaintiffs examined in this Article. In addition, it sheds light on the career choices of women as they relate to leadership in women's sports.

B. Retaliation Against Coaches and Administrators Challenging Inequalities in Athletics

* * *

It is common for employees who challenge discrimination to experience retaliation because those who challenge discrimination are "transgressing the social order." To those who benefit from privilege bestowed on the basis of race or sex, retaliation is an effective, and thus attractive, mechanism for sustaining the social order that creates that privilege.

Retaliation operates to this end by raising the cost of speaking out against discrimination relative to the benefit of doing so. Especially in small professions like college athletics, the risk of losing one's job is a particularly high cost because positions are competitive. Moreover, the insularity of college athletics adds to the cost of challenging discrimination because it creates the possibility that the negative reputation as a troublemaker that a coach or administrator earns by whistleblowing could hinder her future job prospects.

Another important characteristic of retaliation is that it is more likely to target individuals who are not part of the dominant class. Women and persons of color, historically marginalized from athletics, are thus particularly susceptible to reprisals when they challenge athletic departments' discriminatory practices. This is not to say that men do not object to sex discrimination or experience retaliation for doing so. Coach Roderick Jackson's case serves as a primary example of this point, as does Paul Thein's case against Feather River College. Another example is a case which recently settled against University of California at Davis that was filed by former wrestling coach Michael Burch. Burch was fired after—and arguably because—he advocated for the rights of women who wanted to continue to wrestle for the team after the university terminated female wrestling opportunities. And Kevin Wilson was not renewed to his position as head women's basketball coach at Southern Oregon University after he protested discriminatory distribution of budget resources, access to facilities, office space, and other inequities; his Title IX retaliation claim also settled. Despite these cases in which men were the plaintiffs, the fact that female plaintiffs have dominated the trend of retaliation cases post-Jackson (even though technically, the legal significance of the Jackson decision is to secure protection for those who are not also direct victims of sex discrimination) is consistent with the view that members of the non-dominant group are more vulnerable to retaliation.

Because retaliation works in the service of discrimination itself, and operates to the same end to secure the hierarchy of privilege, retaliation is "more likely to occur in organizations with a high tolerance for, and incidence of, discrimination." The existing entitlement and privilege that inures to men's sport, as well as its significant contribution to the gender order more generally, could explain an athletic department's decision to favor males in the distribution of athletic opportunities to students, men's teams in the distribution of resources, and male coaches in compensation, job security, and other benefits of employment. For example, it is not surprising that the culture of Fresno State's athletic department allowed for widespread Title IX violations in the form of inequities between men's and women's sports, backsliding on obligations to ameliorate the same, and reprisals against women in the athletic department who called that backsliding into question. The correlative desire to retain sport as a male preserve and sustain that hegemonic privilege, and the high cultural stakes of doing so, suggests why an athletic department's leadership would be threatened by, and thus retaliate, against women who seek to challenge it.

C. The Retaliation/Job Performance Double Bind

Having examined generally the nature of the predicate discrimination and the cultural context for the retaliation, this section examines how aspects of both operate simultaneously to pose obstacles to women's success. The relationship between these two mechanisms for discrimination consists of a double bind, in which coaches are punished not only for challenging discrimination in the allocation of resources to their programs, but also for failing to produce successful programs in a short time period, despite a discriminatory allocation of resources.

This bind is exacerbated by discrimination in the length of contract terms, discussed in the previous section. Hiring and renewing coaches on a one- or two-year basis provides athletic departments with more frequent opportunities to replace coaches who are not living up to their expectations, which may include expectations to produce winning records or nationally ranked, highly competitive programs. For coaches without the job security of a longer-term contract, one bad season may be the difference between losing and keeping one's job.

A double bind is thus created when, in addition to the job pressure created by high expectations and a short-term contract, a coach is hamstrung by limited resources and support, insufficient access to training and practice facilities, an inadequate number of assistant coaches, insufficient access to scholarship dollars, and inadequate opportunity to attract recruits by competing in the school's premier facility. As the Fresno

State and FGCU cases demonstrate, a coach who complains about either the length of her contract or the lack of support for her program puts her job at risk by appearing uncooperative, selfish, and difficult. On the other hand, her job is rendered vulnerable by the fact that discrimination in the allocation of resources and support is itself a barrier to her team's success. This vulnerability is exacerbated by a short period of contractual employment, which limits her opportunity to recover from isolated poor performance. This double bind is perfectly illustrated in the lawsuit filed by Deena Deardurff Schmidt, who was expected to produce a successful swim team even in the absence of a pool. San Diego State denied her the support she needed to achieve the benchmarks of success upon which she was being evaluated, and then fired her either because she advocated for more support (her allegation) or because she did not succeed (SDSU's defense). Amy Draper's case against Tennessee-Martin also reflects this theme, as she alleges that she was fired for lobbying for her team's fair share of resources, and the university defends that she was in fact fired for "poor performance" after having a losing season.

In sum, these cases suggest a tendency in athletic departments to essentially handicap female coaches by failing to provide their teams comparable resources and support, but holding them to the same or higher expectation to produce winning seasons. Thus, a double bind is created when coaches risk being fired in retaliation for complaining about the resources they lack, when this dearth of resources or support undermines their teams' performances and therefore negatively impacts their job evaluations. This double bind, which seems to affect female coaches, may be seen as a barrier to women's leadership in athletics and could even help explain women's underrepresentation in this field.

D.   The Gender Conformity/Nonconformity Double Bind

A second thematic double bind also emerges from the retaliation cases described in this Article: female coaches are exploited for gender conforming behavior and punished for gender nonconforming behavior. Robin Potera-Haskins, for example, alleged that she was hired with the expectation that she produce a winning team. Though she succeeded in doing exactly that, she may have ultimately been punished for having an intense and competitive personality and the athletic director's discomfort with her "abrasive" style. These characteristics are typical and acceptable among male coaches and administrators, but in Potera-Haskins's case, may have been seen as gender nonconforming. Similarly, Karen Moe Humphreys reported that her male supervisors at Berkeley criticized her for being "intimidating" and "too strong for a woman." Had either of these women adopted a friendlier, more easy-going style, however, they might have earned personality points with their bosses, but would have jeopardized their continued employment in athletics, a field that places a premium on strength and competitive spirit.

The Fresno State plaintiffs also faced a version of this double bind. Milutinovich, Vivas, and Wright all demonstrated gender nonconforming behavior by challenging the male leadership of the athletic department through their advocacy for gender equity. As a result of speaking out, Milutinovich and Wright were marginalized as "the other team" and received punishment in the form of inferior salaries and contract terms; ultimately, job termination befell Milutinovich and Vivas for their actions. In contrast, Stacy Johnson-Klein was hired for her gender conforming and heterosexy appearance, which she likely felt pressure to retain due to the homophobic sentiments directed at gender nonconforming coaches. But this approach did not protect Johnson-Klein from the subordination she, too, experienced in the form of sexual harassment and exploitation. These examples show how social expectations and stereotypes hamstring women in athletics. For the coaches mentioned here, the operation of the gender nonconformity/conformity double bind resulted in negative employment consequences. By creating additional obstacles for female coaches to maneuver, creating job dissatisfaction, and decreasing the amount of mental energy coaches have available to devote to other aspects of their jobs, the double bind may function as a barrier to women's leadership in athletics.

E. Homophobia and Discrimination on the Basis of Sexual Orientation

Several cases involving the intersection of sex discrimination and sexual orientation discrimination demonstrate how gay-baiting and homophobia continue to be deployed as weapons against female coaches. The litigation against Fresno State is rife with examples. The jury in Lindy Vivas's case validated her claim that she was discriminated against for her perceived sexual orientation after hearing testimony that the athletic director insisted female coaches play on the "home team" instead of the "other team," a reference to the female coaches he apparently suspected were gay. According to witnesses, the athletic director had also said, "we need to get rid of the lesbians," and that he had a "lesbian hit list" of coaches he wanted to terminate. He also tolerated a climate wherein it was acceptable for staff to "blar[e]" a talk radio program critical of Vivas and softball coach Margie Wright, a program in which the host made homophobic comments about them. This climate was such that the staff felt comfortable declaring "Ugly women's athletes day" while symbolically reproducing the stereotype of the mannish (lesbian) athlete by juxtaposing men's faces on female athletes' bodies.

Jaye Flood's case against FGCU also presents elements of homophobic undertones. After it became known that she had participated in the drafting of Merrily Dean Baker's letter about gender discrimination in the athletic department, Flood was charged with having a relationship with a woman on a road trip and inappropriately touching a student by tugging on her shirt. The charge that ultimately resulted in her termination (which she denied and claimed was part of the retaliation against her) was that she had an "amorous" relationship with a female student. The lawsuits against San Diego Mesa College and Feather River College both contain allegations that the college officials were concerned about the image of athletic programs led by lesbian coaches, and the Mesa College plaintiffs allege that they were fired in part because the newspaper mentioned their lesbian relationship.

In 1991, sport scholar Helen Lenskyj described the climate of college athletics as "so anti-woman, anti-lesbian and anti-feminist that most lesbians, whether athletes, coaches, administrators or faculty, remain invisible for reasons of simple survival." Later, in 1998, Pat Griffin's Strong Women, Deep Closets described the homophobic climate of athletic departments as either actively hostile toward lesbians (or those perceived to be lesbians) or "conditionally tolerant" of those who agree to cover their lesbianism and to adopt indicia of heterosexuality. The examples of homophobia presented in the contemporary retaliation cases discussed here suggest that, despite increasing public acceptance of gays and lesbians, elements of that same climate described by Lenskyj and Griffin still exist today. The examples also provide support to the theoretical basis for the existence of homophobia in sport.

One explanation for the persistence of homophobia in sport contexts including college athletics is that its primary purpose is not exclusion of gays and lesbians per se. Rather, similar to the discrimination and double binds discussed above, it is a weapon in the service of sex discrimination. Society is deeply invested in gender differentiation and hierarchy, and to that end, relies on sport as the context for creating and valorizing a hegemonic masculinity. Women's sport in general is acceptable and accepted only to the extent it does not pose a challenge to the association of sport with masculinity. Women whose appearance evokes feminine stereotypes of weakness, passivity, and lack of aggression or competitiveness do not threaten the hegemonic masculinity in sports, while also allowing women's athletics to be constructed as distinct and "other." This explains athletic departments' hiring preferences for coaches who convey normative femininity, including heterosexuality, and intolerance for coaches whose lesbianism is known or perceived. The Fresno State athletic director's comments on the hiring of Stacey Johnson-Klein, Feather River College's failure to hire Laurel Wartluft, and Mesa College's termination of coaches who were out in the newspaper, serve as examples of these tendencies and is consistent with other qualitative research along these same lines.

It has also been suggested that the sporting world's intolerance for lesbians allows the lesbian label to remain stigmatized and, thus, deployed as a powerful derogatory to intimidate women and control their experience in sport. As Griffin explains, the threat of the lesbian stigma can be used, for example, "to discourage the bonding that occurs among women in athletics" in order to "keep women from discovering their own power." Thus, it is no surprise that anti-lesbian sentiment was present in two athletic departments—those of Florida Gulf Coast University and Fresno State—where female coaches and administrators were cooperating with each other and acted with the support of a high-ranking woman. At FGCU, the female coaches and athletic director emerita Merrily Dean Baker worked together to present their concerns to the university administration. Fresno State coaches Vivas and Wright, and eventually Johnson-Klein, received support and advocacy from Milutinovich while she was associate athletic director and even after she had been transferred out of the athletic department. The labeling of the Fresno State coaches and Milutinovich as the "other team" was likely intended to discourage other women from joining their efforts by threatening that the lesbian stigma would attach to them by association. FGCU's investigation of Flood on charges having to do with lesbianism could also be seen as an effort to make an example of her in order to threaten, control, and divide the group of women who sought to collectively surmount their powerlessness in the department.

F. Double Standards

Another theme that emerges from the retaliation cases is gender-based double standards for job performance. Surina Dixon's case against Texas Southern is particularly emblematic of this theme. Dixon alleges that, despite being more qualified than a male coach hired at the same time, she was offered a lower salary and a shorter contract term than that male coach because she (but not he) had to "prove herself" to the athletic director. Similarly, Amy Draper complained that Tennessee-Martin held female coaches to a higher standard in two ways: first, by requiring only female coaches to have playing experience in the sports they coached, and second, by requiring female coaches, but not male coaches, to consistently have winning seasons. Karen Moe Humphreys's case against U.C. Berkeley suggested that she and other women were passed over for promotions and subjected to layoffs despite seniority and experience, while men who lacked both were retained and promoted.

Scholars have documented similar double standards in the hiring and retention of coaches. For example, studies have found that female coaches are more likely than male coaches to have majored in physical education and to have intercollegiate playing experience. The hiring of men due to their work experience, despite women's educational background and playing experience, demonstrates a double standard. Along that vein, female coaches, particularly younger ones, reported to focus group interviewers that they perceived having to work "twice as hard" as male counterparts in order to be taken seriously in their jobs. Such double standards contribute to a climate where female coaches are devalued and demeaned, which in turn creates job dissatisfaction and turnover.

G. Women Participating in Discrimination

The cases against Fresno State and FGCU both suggest that women are more likely to be successful in their efforts to challenge sex discrimination in athletics when they cooperate with each other to this end. The Fresno State plaintiffs, for example, worked together by testifying at each others' trials, and collaborated with the Senior Woman Administrator, Assistant Athletic Director Diane Milutinovich, as they advocated for equal treatment for themselves and their teams. At FGCU, the female coaches and assistant coaches worked with the athletic director emerita, Merrily Dean Baker, to present their concerns about gender equity to the department and university administration. But women in athletics are not always allies in disputes about sex discrimination. Many of the cases highlighted in this Article involve evidence or charges of women in positions of power actively perpetuating the retaliation alleged. For example, it appears that it was a female athletic department administrator at FGCU who laid the groundwork for Vaughn and Flood's termination by putting falsified negative performance evaluations in their files. Coach Draper of Tennessee-Martin claims the Senior Woman Administrator was instrumental in the discriminatory treatment she and her team received. The female college president at Feather River College was accused both of firing her male athletic director and a female basketball coach who were trying to bring the athletic department into compliance with Title IX and of making homophobic statements about the coach. And a female athletic director was a named defendant in Terri Patraw's suit against University of Nevada, Reno.

While it is impossible to speculate on the specific motivations of individuals involved in the cases described, allegations of women perpetuating or supporting discrimination against other women provide an opportunity to consider how male privilege operates to entrench discrimination against women in athletics. Women, too, may capitalize on male privilege by offering support to the existing gender hierarchy. Moreover, they may have reason to believe that doing so is necessary for retention or consideration for promotion to positions of power (or at least, token positions of power). Because Title IX issues are often perceived as pitting the interests of women's sports against those of men's sports, women in positions of power in athletics may be motivated to establish their loyalty to men with power over them (athletic directors, university presidents, powerful alumni and donors) or even to men subordinate to them whose support and favor they wish to cultivate, by rebuffing female coaches' demands for parity in pay and equality for female athletes. Feminist theorists describe such practices as complicity in one's own oppression. As the retaliation claims themselves make clear, such complicity cannot be considered without the context of the gender hierarchy that exists in sport: a hierarchy in which actions that sustain that hierarchy are rewarded while efforts to dismantle it are punished. Thus, the fact that women themselves participate in discrimination against other women suggests that another barrier to women's leadership, power, and equality is the effectiveness of the dominant culture at fracturing women's loyalties and rendering them less effective as a group.

In sum, the themes exposed by recently-filed retaliation cases reveal and underscore existing obstacles to women's leadership in athletics. In addition to exposing the fact and manner of retaliation coaches often face for speaking out against sex discrimination in athletics, such cases raise judicial and public awareness of themes inherent in the predicate discrimination itself. Such themes include discrimination against women's sports programs, employment discrimination, discrimination on the basis of gender nonconformity and sexual orientation, and pressure for female administrators and others to support and participate in such practices. However, it is possible such exposure enables a remedy. Thus, the remedial potential of the retaliation trend is examined in the next Part.

Part IV

Legal Significance of Retaliation Cases

To those who study sport and gender, the obstacles to women's leadership in athletics described in Part III are neither surprising nor new. What is significant, however, is that these issues are increasingly factoring into litigation and that several of those cases have produced verdicts and settlements favorable to plaintiffs. The retaliation complaints filed in the wake of Jackson v. Birmingham Board of Education are exposing judges and juries to double binds, double standards, homophobia, and other nuances of discrimination that sustain athletics leadership as a predominantly male enterprise. For both legal and practical reasons to be addressed in this Part, many of these situations would be difficult to remediate directly. For issues involving compensation discrimination, sexual orientation discrimination, and programmatic discrimination, for example, the retaliation cause of action is helping expose and indirectly make schools accountable for conduct that might otherwise not be litigated because it is marginal, difficult to prove, or outweighed by the financial (and other) costs of bringing a legal challenge. Thus, the right of action for retaliation operates to fill existing gaps in enforcement of Title IX and challenges to sex discrimination in athletics more broadly.

A.   Retaliation Claims and Pay Discrimination

The increased profile of retaliation cases may give plaintiffs greater leverage to address disparities in compensation. While salary disparities between coaches of women's and men's teams and between female and male coaches are widespread and well-known, they have proven difficult to remediate in court. Female coaches have sought to challenge salary disparities as sex discrimination under the Equal Pay Act and Title VII with mixed results. Both statutes prohibit employers from paying employees differently for similar work, but in the context of athletics, it can be difficult to compare head coach positions across sports or across teams. It is lawful for universities to offer higher salaries to coaches with greater job responsibilities due to larger rosters, bigger budgets, or greater travel obligations stemming from region of competition and recruiting. Moreover, differences in experience levels and the market value of the coach's services may also justify a decision to compensate some coaches more than others. Though regulatory guidance suggests that differences between head coach positions that derive from sex discrimination do not justify unequal pay, it may be difficult to identify, parse out, and prove such discrimination. Moreover, courts can avoid considering the possibility that such discrimination exists by relying on other differences between the coaches or their positions to justify the disparity in pay.

The difficulty and uncertainty surrounding pay discrimination cases likely deters plaintiffs from litigating them in many instances. But because a retaliation case does not depend on whether the challenged practice constitutes actionable discrimination, a coach may be more likely to file suit when she can bring a retaliation claim as well. The potential cause of action for retaliation also provides additional leverage that plaintiffs can use to negotiate for a favorable settlement.

In addition, the availability of a remedy for retaliation deters universities from engaging in unlawful reprisal and therefore makes it safer for a coach to challenge her salary and employment conditions internally. The potential for plaintiffs to win large jury verdicts and settlements in retaliation claims predicated on salary discrimination compels universities to contemplate the public, external costs of disparate salaries. On a societal level, litigation challenging retaliation raises both judicial and public awareness of the underlying problem of unequal pay, which may help pressure universities to distribute salaries more evenly. Given the relationship between salary and job satisfaction, the potential for retaliation cases to influence higher compensation for women coaches may in turn contribute to a solution to the gender gap in college coaching.

B. Retaliation Claims and Homophobia and Sexual Orientation Discrimination

Retaliation claims hold similar promise to address and mitigate homophobia and discrimination on the basis of sexual orientation in athletics. While women in athletics, including coaches, have been disproportionately subjected to scrutiny for gender nonconformity and stigmatized by suspicions of lesbianism, litigation on this issue is exceedingly rare. A likely explanation is that homophobia manifests itself in subtle ways that are difficult to bolster with concrete evidence. Without such proof, a plaintiff may assume the chances of victory are slim and decide not to bring suit.

Another explanation for the absence of litigation in this realm is that the law affords very little reliable protection against discrimination on the basis of sexual orientation. Sexual orientation discrimination generally receives the lowest level of constitutional protection and is not categorically prohibited by federal employment discrimination law or the antidiscrimination laws of many states. Courts may construe sex discrimination laws like Title VII and Title IX to prohibit discrimination on the basis of gender nonconformity—a potentially useful theory in the athletic context given the overlap between homophobia and sex stereotyping. But the fact that courts sometimes reject this theory or construe it narrowly likely affects plaintiffs' confidence in the potential to remediate sexual orientation discrimination through litigation.

Finally, the lesbian stigma itself likely causes coaches to be particularly risk averse in deciding to challenge homophobia in sport. By bringing such a claim, a coach associates herself publicly with lesbianism, which, so long as this is a stigmatized association in the field of athletics, compromises her future employability. With so much to lose, a coach could easily be dissuaded from filing suit by the legal and factual obstacles that a lawsuit would face. But when she can bolster her sexual orientation discrimination claim with a retaliation claim imbued in the confidence that flows from multimillion dollar verdicts and settlements, she is more likely to do so. Moreover, the fact that a jury validated Coach Sulpizio's retaliation claim but not her sexual orientation discrimination claim illustrates the relative difficulty in prevailing on sexual orientation discrimination claims and the value to plaintiffs in coupling them with retaliation claims. As in the context of pay discrimination discussed above, retaliation claims operate to deter discrimination in this context as well. This deterrence occurs by increasing the potential for litigation, which in turn raises the costs to universities of allowing athletic departments to maintain homophobic climates.

C. Retaliation Claims and Equal Treatment Claims

Retaliation claims also raise the potential for litigation about discrimination in the resources and support allocated to men's and women's athletics. While women's collegiate teams receive only about a third of the operating and recruiting funds allocated to men's teams, the inequities resulting from such disparate funding, in such areas as facilities, equipment, publicity and promotion, and recruiting budgets, have yet to receive much attention from private litigants. Most cases raising Title IX's application to college athletic departments have challenged an inequitable distribution of athletic opportunities to men and women (so-called "equal access" claims), either due to a university's decision to cut or demote an existing team or its failure to add new teams for which there is abundant interest. While OCR's attention is increasingly drawn to issues related to the relative quality of those opportunities (so-called "equal treatment" claims), it is usually the monetary damages—or threat thereof—that come from private enforcement that are credited with motivating universities to comply with Title IX and its implementing regulations. Equal treatment claims, however, have not been on the forefront of litigation seeking enforcement of Title IX, which has so far prioritized the lack of opportunity over inequities related to facilities, equipment, uniforms, promotion and publicity, and the like. Moreover, the cases in which student plaintiffs have raised equal treatment claims demonstrate such cases are vulnerable to early dismissal due to lack of standing, mootness, or failure to comply with the statute of limitations.

Retaliation cases predicated on complaints about unequal treatment have the potential to bolster enforcement of this aspect of Title IX as well. The availability of a remedy for retaliation predicated on such discrimination ensures that coaches can safely raise internal and external challenges to such disparities. Thus, after Jackson and in the wake of multi-million dollar jury verdicts and settlements awarded to coaches who experienced retaliation, a coach may feel more confident to speak freely about inequities to her Athletic Director, Title IX coordinator, or other appropriate university officials. Such protection may also bolster coaches' participation in the self-study about gender equity (among other issues) that the NCAA requires of its member institutions, and it may give coaches more confidence to file a complaint with the Office for Civil Rights. And while internal and external complaints may originate with others, such as students and parents, it is particularly important that coaches avail themselves of those procedures without fear of reprisal. Coaches are uniquely situated to perceive whether the resources their teams receive are adequate and fair and to present evidence of disparities. Coaches also have greater incentive than students or parents to address inequities that require a longer time horizon to redress, such as those related to facilities. Thus, ensuring that coaches can speak freely about programmatic disparities increases the likelihood that those disparities will be redressed.

Conclusion

The retaliation cases that have been litigated and filed in the wake of Jackson v. Birmingham Board of Education are valuable for what they reveal about obstacles to women's leadership in athletics. Their early success provides grounds for cautious optimism in the potential for these cases to destabilize those institutionalized impediments. With the momentum of multimillion dollar verdicts and settlements on their side, coaches are better situated now than ever before to seek remedies that will help ensure that the values college athletic departments are exercising and modeling include equal opportunity for the leadership of women.

DENISE CUTHBERT AND FIONA ZAMMIT, *UNIVERSITIES NEED TO RETHINK POLICIES ON STUDENT-STAFF RELATIONSHIPS*

THECONVERSATION.COM, NOV. 19, 2017

Cuthbert (above) is a Professor of Sociology and Associate Deputy Vice Chancellor for Research Training and Development and Zammit (below) is the Principal Advisor Policy and Strategy in the School of Graduate Research at RMIT University, Melbourne. The two have worked together both at RMIT and on the Australian Council for Graduate Research, the national peak body for Deans and Directors of research education in Australia. In 2017, they proposed a new approach to the management of staff-student relationships at RMIT. After a year of work, a new policy reflecting the principles articulated in this paper was approved by the Academic Board of the university in late 2018.

The Human Rights Commission report, Change the Course: National Report on Sexual Assault and Sexual Harassment at Australian Universities, was published in August 2017.

In response, Australian universities have taken various actions to address sexual assault and harassment on their campuses. Most are directed at making universities safer places to study and live. Measures include introducing mandatory responding to disclosure and training for all staff, teaching students about consent, and increasing the number of specialist counselling staff.

Framing staff-student relationships

Universities should also review policy governing staff-student relationships. Across the sector, these relationships are framed as consensual and are couched in unhelpful, ambiguous language. We conducted a review of staff-student relationship policies in Australian universities and international policies. We found the following similarities across most institutions.

Staff are generally discouraged from entering into sexual relationships with students. Discouragement aside, universities recognise that these relationships may occur. Many universities express reluctance to interfere in the "personal" lives of staff and students. Most set out some conditions that should apply when the discouraged but inevitable relationships form.

Conditions may include the staff member disclosing the relationship to the university. This may lead to adjustments to the duties of that staff member, which are then outlined in varying degrees of detail. Where specified, these may include removing the staff member from any assessment of the student's work. They may also not be able to make decisions regarding the award of scholarships or other distinctions. In the case of graduate research candidates, it may involve removing the staff member as senior or main supervisor. However, they may still be able to serve on the supervision team.

Many Australian universities then link this policy with their Conflict of Interest policy. This signals that the biggest concern about staff-student sexual relationships is the possibility of conflicts of interest emerging for the staff member. This does little to address the potentially damaging impact of these relationships on students, and on the learning and research environment for other students.

We need better professional standards

The health care sector has much clearer professional standards. For health care practitioners, professional boundaries are recognised as integral to good practitioner-client relationships. Accordingly, professional standards prohibit sexual relationships entirely. This lasts either for the duration of the professional association or for some period (up to two years in some cases) after the professional relationship has ended.

The Medical Board of Australia states:

A doctor should not enter into a sexual relationship with a patient even with the patient's consent.

For psychologists and counsellors, this prohibition extends to former clients and anyone closely related to the client.

The code of professional conduct set out by the Nursing and Midwifery Board of Australia notes the vulnerability of clients under their care, and their relative powerlessness, must be recognised and managed. Sexual relationships between these professionals and current or previous patients are deemed inappropriate and unprofessional.

In comparison, universities have a relatively relaxed stance on these types of relationships. The ethical standards applied to other professions are explicit that the power imbalance is one where free consent can't be assumed on the part of the client/patient. It is up to the practitioner to make sure professional boundaries are maintained at all times. Seeking sexual partners among their clients/patients puts their professional registration and their ability to practice at risk.

What would happen if we applied the same standards to university staff? If it is accepted that the imbalance of power between staff and students compromises the capacity of a student to provide free consent for sexual activity, and sexual activity without free consent is harassment or assault (as defined by law), then the current framing of staff-student "consensual" relationships by Australian universities is inappropriate. It is also inconsistent with the sector's stated aim to focus on the interests and needs of students.

Universities should consider adopting professional standards like those in the health care profession. Their stated aim is to prioritise the welfare of students and their entitlement to learn and undertake research in a safe, respectful environment. If we are really to "change the course", we need to do more than address student sexual conduct. We need to raise the bar for professional and ethical standards for all who work in this sector as well.

CHRISTY HARRIS LEMAK, *WHEN WOMEN ADVANCE IN HEALTH CARE LEADERSHIP THE PATIENT WINS*

AL.COM, MARCH 19, 2019

Lemak is a Professor and Chair of the Department of Health Services Administration at the University of Alabama-Birmingham. She teaches and researches in the areas of health care management and leadership development, with an emphasis on how leadership and organizational factors are associated with high performance.

New models of care, delivery and reimbursement are causing healthcare executives to reassess the competencies their leaders must possess for success.

Today's healthcare leaders must be deeply familiar with the patient population they serve. Leadership teams that are reflective of the patient population in terms of gender and race make much better patient-centered decisions.

When we provide care to patients and families, we must acknowledge the cultural values and beliefs of that family. Only then can we be efficient, effective, and safe in the care we provide. When our leadership is lacking in female and minority voices, healthcare systems will consistently miss opportunities to provide culturally inclusive care.

Nearly 78 percent of the healthcare labor force is composed of women. 70 percent of medical and health services mid-level managers are women. More than half of the graduating class of graduate programs in healthcare management have been women for over two decades. According to McKinsey & Co., women in healthcare are 25 percent less likely than men to be promoted to senior manager or director even though they ask for promotions as often as men. Across the country and here in Alabama, women are poorly represented in the executive ranks. Recent data suggests only about 20 percent of US hospitals have female CEOs, and the numbers are far smaller for Alabama.

Women are known to be the major purchasers of healthcare for their families. For example, 85% of women choose their children's physicians and 84 percent take children to their physicians' appointments. Additionally, females of all ages accounted for over half of all expenses incurred at doctors' offices. Women are the customers, the decision makers, and the workers in the healthcare field. Having more women in decision-making executive roles will ensure the organization's policies and services are in alignment with demographics that drive their business.

The time has come for health care organizations to pursue the intentional cultivation and strategic inclusion of diverse leaders in management and governance. Fortunately, we know what works: inclusive recruiting practices, intentional selection and promotion, rooting out implicit biases, inclusivity training, formal sponsorship programs, mentoring, access to informal networks, and a host of other activities proven effective in a variety of industries. To meet the needs of our communities, we must first create and sustain hospitals and health systems where all leaders can thrive.

ABIGAIL PERDUE, *MAN UP OR GO HOME: EXPLORING PERCEPTIONS OF WOMEN IN LEADERSHIP*
100 MARQUETTE LAW REVIEW 1233 (2017)

Perdue is a Professor of Legal Analysis, Writing, and Research at Wake Forest University School of Law.

* * *

Throughout history, women in positions of authority have often been perceived as violating well-established gender norms. Perhaps as a result, female leadership has often been viewed as a threat to male power and privilege and thus provoked resistance. Female leaders challenge longstanding sex stereotypes and patriarchal structures, subverting the identities of androcentric institutions and the people who comprise them. In so doing, they redefine notions of what it means to be a leader as well as what it means to be a woman. Cisgender male subordinates in particular may feel that their masculinity is under assault when they are placed under female supervision. This power struggle can be readily observed at the Virginia Military Institute (VMI), which enrolled women for the first time in 1997 after the United States Supreme Court declared VMI's all-male admissions policy unconstitutional. To explore the impact of coeducation at VMI, I collaborated with a sociologist and psychologist to anonymously survey VMI's student body. This Article relies upon the empirical data we collected to explore perceptions of women in leadership at VMI. Our findings reveal that like many female politicians, CEOs, and other women working in male-dominated spheres, female cadets at VMI are often perceived as unworthy intruders ill-suited for leadership who attain rank primarily because of their sex, not their merit. The prevalence of these attitudes among VMI cadets likely exacerbates tension between the sexes at VMI and undermines institutional efforts to foster leadership, solidarity, and mutual respect.

* * *

In conclusion, women leaders evoke resistance because they challenge traditional notions of what it means to be both a leader and a man. Thus, despite their uniquely masculine environment, female cadets in leadership often experience the same obstacles faced by women leaders in other male-dominated spheres throughout history. Cadet attitudes toward women in leadership likely reflect the longstanding gender bias, stereotyping, androcentrism, and gender polarization so deeply engrained in our sociocultural experience that, unwittingly or not, they have become a part of who we are and thus, impact how we view of ourselves and each other. Until we can understand *how* these phenomena influence our perceptions, they will continue to taint our notions of what it means to be a leader and a woman, causing history to repeat itself. Gendered notions of leadership, which are harmful and limiting, will endure.

* * *

CHAPTER 9

A GUIDE FOR RESTRUCTURING
THE PIPELINE TO POWER

■ ■ ■

INTRODUCTION

The first eight chapters of this book focused on understanding the various dynamics impacting women and minorities when pursuing leadership roles, with a particular emphasis on the legal profession. Unlike popular culture books on leadership that tell you how to lead, our emphasis has been on understanding the historical, institutional, and individual barriers that keep women—and especially minority women—from having the opportunity to lead in the first place. This is not to say that the material you have studied here will not help you develop as a leader. To the contrary, we believe the content of this casebook will serve as an important building block in the foundation of knowledge necessary for your leadership development. However, no amount of leadership development or training will produce equality for women if structural impediments keep them from being considered or selected for leadership roles.

Chapter 9 now turns to strategies to mitigate and remove barriers that impede women's advancement. Many of the readings from earlier chapters touch upon proposals for change. Here, you will revisit some of these ideas in greater depth and consider others drawn from new perspectives that challenge many of the common solutions promulgated over the past decades. We seek to bridge the ever-present divide between identification of the problem and creating practical solutions that actually work to break through barriers and transcend the pervasive inequality that persists in leadership roles. The readings highlighted below are intended help you critically analyze and evaluate reforms as well as formulate your own solutions.

Our focus is on creating structural changes in laws and policies to improve the leadership landscape for women—effectively redesigning the pipeline—rather than relying on individual women to conform their appearance or behaviors to fit the dominant leadership norms. As for inspiration to guide your own personal leadership development, we recommend reading autobiographies and biographies of transformational leaders. You will find a list of books to use as a starting point in the Appendix to this casebook.

*Credit: Steve Petteway,
photographer for the Supreme
Court of the United States
(public domain)*

Perhaps no other living figure has done more than **Ruth Bader Ginsburg** to further structural changes for women to enter professional life and pursue positions of leadership and power. In the 1970s she argued several cases before the Supreme Court that were instrumental in establishing equal rights for women and men. She was the second woman nominated to the Court, appointed by President Bill Clinton in 1993. She is by far the most-recognized jurist in the United States, if not the world, as a pop culture icon nick-named Notorious RBG with action figures, t-shirts, and even closet air fresheners made in her likeness. **Elena Kagan** is the most recent female to join the Court, appointed by President Barack Obama in 2010. Prior to joining the bench, she taught at the University of Chicago Law School, served in the Clinton administration, led Harvard Law School as dean, and also argued before the Court as the solicitor general. President Obama asked Justice Ginsburg at Justice Kagan's swearing in if she was happy that he had brought her a second woman. (Justice Sotomayor was nominated in 2009.) "Yes," she replied, "Yes, but I'll be happier when you bring me five more."

THOUGHT QUESTIONS

As you read the articles excerpted below, consider the following questions:

1. Many of the readings excerpted below as well as in previous chapters offer recommendations for addressing the pervasive gender imbalance that exists in leadership roles. Many of these ideas require changes in laws or institutional policies (*e.g.* mandatory quotas), and some are a mix of institutional changes and individual choices (*e.g.* leadership education for lawyers). Create two lists, one for the recommendations you believe are most likely to improve gender diversity in leadership roles and a second for the recommendations you find least likely to succeed. Do the items on your lists share common characteristics?

2. Based upon your own experiences leading up to law school, as a law student, and now reading the final chapter of this book, do you have additional recommendations beyond what appears in this text for navigating the climb to leadership, whether at the individual or institutional level? The article by Professor Rhode suggests law schools have a special obligation to provide leadership training. Do you agree or disagree?

3.   When advocating for reforms, some of the readings rely upon personal stories and anecdotes while others rely upon data, research, and statistics. Which do you find most compelling? Why?

4.   Fast-forward two decades—write a letter as yourself 5 years from now offering guidance and wisdom for navigating your way to a position of leadership and power. For example, if you're currently 25 years old, what would your 30-year-old self say to you now? (Here is a start: "You've got this! You're already off to a great start, learning how to improve leadership diversity by reading books like GENDER, POWER, LAW & LEADERSHIP. Now here's the next step. . .")

DEBORAH L. RHODE, *LAWYERS AND LEADERSHIP*
THE PROFESSIONAL LAWYER, 2010

Rhode is the Ernest W. McFarland Professor of Law at Stanford Law School. She was the second tenure-track female professor hired at Stanford Law School, after clerking for U.S. Supreme Court Justice Thurgood Marshall. Among her many leadership roles, she has served as President of the Association of American Law Schools and the President of the International Association of Legal Ethics.

Most lawyers come to the subject of leadership with well-founded skepticism. On first glance, the field seems a backwater of vacuous rhetoric and slick marketing. Retired CEOs peddle complacent memoirs, and consultants churn out endless variations of "management by fad." "Leadership lite" includes classics such as *If Aristotle Ran General Motors,* and *Leadership Secrets* from sources as varied as *Attila the Hun, The Toys You Loved as a Child,* and *Star Trek.* Why should lawyers squander time on that?

An equally interesting and possibly more important question is why we generally don't. Why don't we address the topic of leadership and in a more serious way than pop publications provide? After all, no other occupation accounts for such a large proportion of leaders. The legal profession has supplied a majority of American presidents, and in recent decades, almost half of Congress, and 10 percent of S&P 500 companies' CEOs. Lawyers occupy leadership roles as governors, state legislators, judges, prosecutors, general counsel, law firm managing partners, and heads of government and nonprofit organizations. In advising influential clients, or chairing community and charitable boards, lawyers are also "leaders of leaders."

Even members of the bar who do not land in top positions frequently play leadership roles in teams, committees, campaigns, and other group efforts. Moreover, many of the decision making, organizational, interpersonal, and ethical skills that are critical for leadership positions are important for professionals at all levels. Yet most lawyers never receive formal education in such leadership skills. Nor do they generally perceive that to be a problem, which is itself problematic, particularly considering the leadership deficit facing our profession and our world.

* * *

Today's leaders face challenges of unprecedented scale and complexity. In representing clients, shaping public policy, and leading corporate, government, and non-profit organizations, lawyers confront society's most urgent unsolved issues. On many of these issues, effective leadership is lacking. Corporate governance, environmental protection, human rights, national security, civil liberties, and entrenched poverty all demand leaders with broad skills and deep ethical commitments. So too, lawyers who head law firms, bar associations, and other legal organizations must cope with increased pressure, including intense competition and growing needs for legal assistance among those who cannot afford it.

Public confidence in many of these leaders is distressingly low. For example, only about a fifth of Americans have a great deal of confidence in the integrity of lawyers; only 11 percent have "a great deal of confidence . . . in people in charge of running law firms" and almost a third have "hardly any." Trust in business leaders is at its lowest ebb since polls started measuring it a half century ago, and they are now the least trusted group in American society. Less than a quarter of surveyed Americans trust the government in Washington "almost always" or even "most of the time," one of the lowest measures in the last fifty years.

* * *

Education in Ethics and Education in Leadership: Obstacles and Overlap

Legal Ethics in Legal Education

Ethics in legal education was traditionally notable for its absence. Most faculty treated the subject as "beneath our notice or . . . [beyond] our capacities." Early courses amounted to little more than "platitudinous exhortation;" "general piffle" was the general assessment. The prevailing assumption was that the "right kind of law student already knows what constitutes moral and ethical conduct and . . . a formal course in Legal Ethics will not supply the proper sort of character training for students who are not the right kind." American bar examiners took a similar view. Questions were infrequent and typically invited undemanding reflection on topics like "what the [state's] Code of Professional Responsibility mean[s] to me." It is not clear anyone read the answers.

Over the last several decades, much has changed but too much has remained the same. In the United States, law schools must offer instruction in the legal profession and its responsibilities as a condition of accreditation, and state bars generally include a separate examination on the rules of professional conduct. In other countries, the subject is often relegated to post-graduate practical training, and is still fighting for an academic toehold. But even where legal ethics is required, it generally remains at the curricular periphery, confined to a single required course and discounted by many as "mushy pap." Some of these courses offer little more than preparation for the law of lawyering on the bar exam; they are, in effect, legal ethics without the ethics. Like most research in the field, a recent influential report by the Carnegie Foundation indicted legal education for its inadequate attention to the moral dimensions of professional life. Although ethical questions arise in every substantive area of law, faculty tend to treat professional responsibility as someone else's responsibility. Many remain skeptical about the mission. Federal judge and law professor Richard Posner put still common views with uncommon candor: "as for the task of instilling ethics in law students . . . I can think of few things more futile than teaching people to be good."

I doubt that many of us in the field see that as our mission, or labor under the illusion that we could do much to advance it. Rather, our goals are more modest and have been defended with sufficient regularity that they don't need extensive treatment here. One is to build students' understanding of the rules of conduct before they are at risk of inadvertently violating one. A second is to encourage future leaders of the profession to consider where the lines *should* be and whether bar governance structures effectively serve the public's interest. It makes sense to address those issues in law school before individuals have a vested interest in coming out one way or another.

From that perspective, the task of ethics education looks far less hopeless. Most research suggests that significant changes occur during early adulthood in people's strategies for dealing with moral issues, and that well-designed curricula can assist the developmental process.

Leadership Education

Similar points are applicable to leadership education. Although most academic institutions consider preparing leaders as central to their mission, the creation of leadership curricula and texts has lagged behind. The traditional assumption has been, as management expert Peter Drucker once famously put it, that "leadership cannot be taught or learned."

Yet contemporary research is to the contrary, and Drucker ultimately revised his view. Studies of twins suggest that about 70 percent of leadership skills are acquired, not genetically based, and decades of experience with leadership development indicates that its major capabilities can be learned. Indeed, as a prominent expert notes, "it would be strange if leadership were the one skill that could not be enhanced through understanding and practice."

It is, of course, true that for thousands of years, leaders have developed without formal education in the qualities that made them effective. But informal methods of learning have been common, and many leaders have learned from history, for example, and experts in related fields. Martin Luther King, Jr. studied communication and nonviolent techniques of conflict resolution. John F. Kennedy worked hard on developing the personal magnetism he observed among Hollywood actors. Barack Obama looked for guidance in historical accounts of Franklin Roosevelt's first 100 days as president.

Yet for many lawyers, informal education often falls short. Large law firms, in-house counsel offices, government agencies, and public interest organizations are run by individuals who generally have had no management training, and whose skills as lawyers do not necessarily meet the demands of leadership.

* * *

Attention to ethical issues in leadership is in particularly short supply. In surveys by the Aspen Institute, graduates of MBA programs report that confidence in their ability to manage value conflicts actually falls during their time as students. Only about two fifths of surveyed students believed that business schools were doing enough to enable them to address such ethical issues.

Law schools cannot afford to replicate this neglect, yet most give leadership even less attention. Society, as well as the profession, has a large stake in addressing that oversight. As Robert Gordon has noted, in any democracy, the legal profession plays pivotal roles both in amplifying and constraining authority. In the public sector, lawyers shape and enforce law. In the private sector, they orchestrate responses to law through compliance, evasion, resistance, and reform. Moreover, because law is to large extent a self-regulating occupation, its leaders have special responsibility to act for the public, not just the profession, when its own governance is at issue. If, as experts have long argued, the organized bar has not always lived up to that responsibility, then legal education is part of both the problem and the solution.

Learning Leadership

Defining Leadership

How then can we teach lawyers to lead? A threshold question is what we mean by leadership, and what core competencies are central to its exercise. This issue has generated a cottage industry of commentary, and by some researchers' accounts, over 1,500 definitions and forty distinctive theories.

Although popular usage sometime equates leadership with power or position, most experts draw a distinction. They view leadership in terms of traits, processes, skills, and relationships. John Gardner, founder of Common Cause, famously noted that heads of public and private organizations often mistakenly assume that their status "has given them a body of followers. And of course it has not. They have been given subordinates. Whether the subordinates become followers depends on whether the executives act like leaders." Moreover, just as many high officials are not leaders, many leaders do not hold formal office. Mahatma Gandhi and Martin Luther King, Jr. led from the outside. In essence, "leadership requires a relationship, not simply a title. Leaders must be able to inspire, not just compel or direct their followers."

* * *

Certain attributes consistently emerge in research on effective leadership. Most characteristics cluster in five categories:

- values (integrity, honesty, trust, an ethic of service);

- personal skills (self-awareness, self-control, self-direction);

- interpersonal skills (social awareness, empathy, persuasion, conflict management);

- vision (forward looking, inspirational);

- technical competence (knowledge, preparation, judgment).

Although legal education can only do so much to develop or reinforce these qualities, it should do what it can, which is far more than it currently attempts.

Learning to Lead

How then can individuals learn to lead? Theories about learning abound, but on one point there is virtual agreement. Leaders need the capacity to learn from experience—both their own and others'. As Mark Twain famously observed, a cat that sits on a hot stove will not sit on a hot stove again, but it won't sit on a cold one either. What distinguishes effective leaders is the ability to draw appropriate lessons from the successes and failures that they experience and observe. In an apt, if possibly apocryphal exchange, a young lawyer asked a leader in his field how he came to acquire such a reputation. "People respect my judgment" was the response. "Why?" the associate wanted to know. "Well I guess I've made the right decisions." "How did you know what decisions were right?," the associate asked. "Experience" said the partner. The associate wouldn't give up. He was probably in training as a law professor. "What was the experience based on?" The answer: "Wrong decisions."

That is, no doubt, how most lawyers acquire leadership skills. But other ways are available through legal education. An effective curriculum should begin from the premise that individuals vary in how they learn best, and the ideal strategy is to incorporate multiple approaches such as interdisciplinary research and theory, problems, case studies, role simulations, group interaction, literature, and film. Three goals should be paramount. One is to enhance students' capacities to achieve and exercise leadership, and to understand the cognitive biases, interpersonal responses, and organizational dynamics that can sabotage effectiveness. A second objective is to help students become lifetime learners, and to manage their own leadership development. A third objective, and the one most relevant to legal ethics, is to reinforce a sense of responsibility to use leadership for the public good. Ben Heineman, former General Counsel of General Electric, now a lecturer at Harvard, puts it this way: the decisions of "the lawyer as leader" should seek "to make our national or global society a 'better place' however difficult that goal is to define, much less achieve." The point is not, of course, for faculty to use the podium as a pulpit to advance their own personal conceptions of the public good. It is rather to encourage students to develop their own views, and to see leadership not only as a way station to power and status, but also as an exercise of social responsibility.

With those objectives in view, law schools should both offer a course focused on leadership and integrate leadership issues throughout the curricula. Not all students will be comfortable self-selecting for a course labeled "leadership," so it is important to ensure some basic coverage of its core competencies in other offerings. For example, the leadership failures underpinning the recent financial crisis could become topics in corporate law and securities regulation.

Lawyers' role in the forefront of social change movements could figure in courses on civil rights, human rights, sex discrimination, poverty, environmental law, and public interest practice. Clinical courses could provide skills training in conflict management, team work, and problem solving.

Professional responsibility classes could address a wide range of leadership issues, such as the importance of diversity, the relationship between supervisory and subordinate lawyers, the role of moral counseling, the management of law firms, the special obligations of government attorneys, and the structure of pro bono programs. Leadership can be an ideal lens for exploring how the "good go bad" in circumstances where it matters most. A key determinant of ethical behavior in organizations is the "tone at the top." Students who will someday occupy those positions can benefit from analyzing the personal and institutional dynamics that sabotage moral judgment.

Among those dynamics is the disconnect between the qualities that often enable individuals to achieve leadership positions and the qualities that are necessary to perform effectively once they get there. What makes individuals willing to accept the pressure, hours, scrutiny, and risks that accompany leadership? For many lawyers, it is not only commitment to a cause, an organization, or a client. It is also power, prestige, and money. Successful leadership requires subordinating these personal interests to a greater good. The result is what some psychologists label the "leadership paradox." Individuals reach top positions because of their high needs for personal achievement. Yet to perform effectively once there, they need to focus on creating the conditions for achievement by others.

One mission of leadership education is to help future lawyers anticipate and avoid the consequences of unchecked ambition. Case histories of failed law firms and failed causes can illustrate how the self-centeredness that may propel individuals to leadership positions may sabotage their subsequent performance. The risk is exacerbated by leaders' reluctance to learn about their weaknesses. James Kouzes and Barry Posner put it bluntly: "most leaders don't want honest feedback, don't ask for honest feedback, and don't get much of it unless it's forced on them." Only about 40 percent of law firms offer associates opportunities to evaluate supervisors, and of those who engage in the process, only about 5 percent report changes for the better.

Of course, lawyer leaders are scarcely unique in their tendency towards self-protection. But the understandable human aversion to criticism is particularly problematic for leaders, because of both the power they hold and the understandable unwillingness of many subordinates to volunteer unwelcome messages. In Kouzes and Posner's survey of some 70,000 individuals, the statement that ranked the lowest in a list of thirty leadership behaviors was that the leader "asks for feedback on how his/her actions affect others' performance."

Yet without such information, lawyers may fail to identify problems in their own performance. Harvard economist John Kenneth Galbraith once noted that "[f]aced with the alternatives between changing one's mind and proving it unnecessary, just about everybody gets busy on the proof." Defensiveness and denial are particularly apparent when individuals' own self-evaluations are at issue. Leadership education can explore the cognitive biases that compromise not only performance but also learning from performance failures. One such bias is the "fundamental attribution error:" a tendency to attribute personal successes to competence and character, and failures to external circumstances. A related problem stems from confirmation and assimilation biases. People tend to seek out evidence that confirms their preexisting, typically favorable vision of themselves, and to avoid evidence that contradicts it. They also assimilate evidence in ways that favor their preexisting beliefs and self-image. In one random sample of adult men, 70 percent rated themselves in the top quarter of the population in leadership capabilities; 98 percent rated themselves above average.

The problem is compounded by the power and perks of position, which can inflate leaders' sense of self-importance and self-confidence. Being constantly surrounded by those with less ability or less opportunity to display their ability can foster what psychologists label the "uniqueness bias:" people's sense that they are special and superior. The result is to reinforce narcissism and a sense of entitlement; leaders may feel free to disregard legal or ethical rules, and standards of respect that are applicable to others. Yet by thinking that they are "better than those . . . little people," leaders "cut themselves off from [followers'] good ideas and good graces" and run the risk of scandal. Perceptions of entitlement concerning sex and money have marred the careers of many prominent lawyer leaders; students can benefit from exploring these cautionary tales.

One final pathology worth flagging in leadership education arises from leaders' high needs for approval and disdain for "soft" skills that may be essential to obtaining it. As one consultant notes, leaders' desire "to *look* good [often] displaces the intention to *be* good" and to pay attention to others' needs that don't translate into immediate payoffs. A related problem is the assumption that education in inter-personal dynamics and conflict management is a "touchy feely process," unworthy of attention from intellectually sophisticated individuals. Yet research makes clear that for many professionals, "the soft stuff is the hard stuff." Effective leadership requires more than analytic skills, and high achievers in intellectual domains may not have developed corresponding emotional intelligence.

* * *

Almost two decades ago, John Gardner noted that "we have barely scratched the surface in our feeble efforts toward leadership development." For lawyers, that remains true today. Legal education prides itself on teaching future practitioners to think like lawyers but does little to teach them to think like leaders. Many challenges they will face involve questions of values, so those of us who specialize in professional responsibility have a special opportunity and obligation to address them. We are, in effect, leaders of those who will become leaders. We owe it to our students, to our profession, and to our world to prepare them for that role.

JANET STANTON, *GENDER DIVERSITY IN LAW LAND: REASON FOR HOPE?*

ADAMSMITHESQ.COM, APRIL 22, 2019

Stanton is a consultant who helps law firms address the increasingly challenging business environments. She previously was Director, Client Relationship Program at Orrick, Herrington & Sutcliffe.

The reason we've never written about gender diversity before is that there was frankly not much to say; regurgitating dispiriting statistics without offering credible remedy is not what we do. But things seem to be changing for the better with more effective remedies—and we hear more are in the works.

A little background on why gender diversity matters beyond the worthy aspects of social tolerance and equal opportunity; there are hard-headed business reasons to support the tangible value of diversity.

From Corporate Land, there is ample evidence that a diverse workforce leads to increases in profitability. And, on this dimension why would law firms be different? Among many other reports, *Delivering through diversity*, a study published by McKinsey in January 2018 found a statistically significant relationship between a more diverse leadership team and better financial performance. Companies in the top quartile of gender diversity were 21% more likely to achieve above-average levels of profitability.

There's also a mounting body of support that diverse groups *make better decisions.* Most recently from Steven Johnston, author of *Farsighted: How We Make Decisions That Matter the Most* (a truly great read), "Diverse groups tend to make more nuanced and original decisions than homogeneous ones do. So, it's not just that we want more women in Congress, it's also that we want them there because the group will be collectively smarter.

How bad is it in Law Land?

In the most recent (2018) report from the National Association of Women Lawyers (NAWL) the average percent of female equity partners in AmLaw 200 firms (that responded to the survey) has just inched up to 20% (up from 15% in 2006). The report on their 11th annual survey speaks of a "relatively undisturbed pattern showing the absence of women in the upper echelon of law firm leadership."

As we know, averages can be misleading; ALM reported the highest percent at a firm was 44.4% female equity partners and the lowest an embarrassing 5.7%.

This is despite actions virtually all law firms have taken to address gender diversity. In fact, as reported in McKinsey's 2017 "Women in Law" report, Law Land is ahead of Corporate Land in implementing programs and policies to reduce bias in recruiting and promotions; 83% of participating law firms have level-specific initiatives to improve promotion rates for women versus 56% for participating corporations in the overall sample. Even so, Corporate Land has been (somewhat) more successful in increasing the percent of women in their senior ranks.

Clearly what law firms have been doing has not made a dent and if the status quo continues there's little likelihood of significant improvement. Which brings to mind the definition of insanity attributed to Einstein, "doing the same thing over and over again and expecting different results."

<u>What gives?</u>

It seems as if we (and others, in fairness) have been going about this all the wrong way. A revelatory piece in the *Harvard Business Review* points in an entirely new direction. I'm referring to "What Most People Get Wrong about Men and Women," by Catherine H. Tinsley and Robin J. Ely. The sub-head neatly encapsulates the findings and thesis of their piece; "research shows the sexes aren't so different."

Supported by rigorous, multi-sourced research, they contend "the sexes are far more similar in their inclinations, attitudes, and skills than popular opinion would have us believe." The problem is that organizations, acting on foundational, but incorrect stereotypes of gender differences, have instituted policies, company practices and patterns of interaction that create entirely different workplace experiences for men and women. Again, to quote the article, "When facing dissimilar circumstances, people respond differently—not because of their sex but because of their situations."

The solution is not to "fix" the women, but rather to change the workplace dynamics that produce different experiences for the genders. (Read that sentence again.)

Virtually all of the discourse or "advice" on increasing gender diversity—as far back as I can remember (bow ties for women—really?) and as recently as *Lean In*—has focused on changes women need to make to better align with corporate culture.

In clear, highly readable prose, Professors Tinsley and Ely debunk some of the most stubborn and commonly-held stereotypes about gender differences using meta-analyses and real-world examples. They also offer plausible remedies to avoid succumbing to the stereotypes. The stereotypes addressed in their piece include that women lack the stomach or skill to negotiate effectively, they lack confidence and are less likely to be risk takers. In all cases, the research unequivocally upends these commonly held assumptions.

They continue that in any organization individual success is partly driven by how they are treated and the opportunities available to them. To expand on this point, again quoting from the piece, "people are more likely to behave in ways that undermine their chances for success when they are disconnected from information networks, when they are judged or penalized disproportionately harshly for mistakes or failures, and when they lack feedback."

Again supported by rigorous research, it's an unfortunate fact that women are more likely to experience these dynamics. Therefore, since women experience a higher degree of scrutiny and are penalized more harshly for even small mistakes (than men are), not speaking up in meetings is a perfectly rational response. The result? They appear to lack confidence in their ideas. Voilà! Stereotype confirmed.

So, what about gender differences in Law Land?

For this we turn to the ever-charming Dr. Larry Richard, the leading expert on lawyer psychology who, using the rigorous Caliper instrument has gathered and analyzed personality data on thousands of lawyers (as well as other white-collar professionals). As Dr. Richard reports, "In the general population, women score slightly higher than men in Empathy and in Sociability on the Caliper. A more recent study shows that women leaders are also higher on a number of the 'persuasive' traits. But within the legal profession, *these differences largely disappear.*" (Emphasis mine.)

What doesn't work?

Hmmm. Where to start? Sadly, many of the well-intentioned "women's initiatives" at firms have actually been counterproductive (obviously some have had a positive impact—but not enough to move the needle industry-wide). Caren Ulrich Stacy, Founder & CEO of the Diversity Lab notes, "Gender diversity is not a woman-only problem, therefore, initiatives such as women's retreats without the other half of the population working in collaboration often undermine the very people they're trying to help." Further, the additional, non-billing time required to participate in women's initiatives is often viewed as an extra burden by younger female attorneys.

Certainly exhortations to become more diverse, without plausible remedies are pretty much a waste of time. NAWL issued its first "NAWL Challenge" in 2006, which called for a goal to increase women equity partners at law firms to at least 30%. That was so successful (not) that they issued another "challenge" in 2016: "The One-Third by 2020 Challenge," like changing the wording will have an effect. They further acknowledged the widespread adoption of women's initiatives has not really made a difference.

Not to be outdone, in 2016 the ABA issued Resolution 113 that "urges all providers of legal services, particularly law firms, to expand and create opportunities at all levels of responsibility for diverse attorneys." Their "remedy" seems to boil down to measuring everything in sight, implementing "bias interrupters" and ratcheting these up if goals are not met. "The top line takeaway is you need to analyze with metrics so there can be little question about what is currently happening in a given workplace," said the chair of the ABA Women's Commission. She added, "If you don't see change, use an iterative process until your metrics improve." Huh? If at first you don't succeed. . . Frankly, this approach could take millennia. (Einstein, anyone?)

What are the specific challenges for Law Land?

It is an understatement that Law Land operates in ways vastly different from Corporate Land. On a macro basis. Law firms have much less of a business mindset which impacts virtually every function at a firm, and, as it turns out, hobbles their efforts to increase diversity. Professor William Henderson rigorously lays out the argument for greater intentionality in all phases of a lawyer's development—from selection, through development, training and coaching in *Solving the Legal Profession's Diversity Problem*.

He posits, "the profession's lack of progress on diversity is a systems problem." The systems he refers to are those for recruitment, selection, development, feedback, evaluation and promotion. Systems that take green law school graduates and, over time (and a great deal of effort on their part) builds them into experienced partners. He adds, "the system is driven more by tradition and past practice than science." Moreover, the "systems" are sabotaged by a virtual absence of truly helpful data. He notes, "To the extent the system relies on measurement, the quality of the data is uneven and under-analyzed." One of many examples is the industry's heavy reliance on relative academic achievement in the selection stage which does not correlate positively with success.

Henderson, then goes through each of the aspects discussed above (recruitment, selection, development, feedback, evaluation and promotion) and provides evidence-based remedies.

His approach would certainly deliver on the premise outlined in Professors Tinsley's and Ely's piece; everyone would experience more similar experiences (with better data, to boot). In this, Henderson is absolutely right. That said, based on the peculiarities of Law Land (which he acknowledges and is keenly aware of), I fear his remedies are overly ambitious for the far majority of law firms; the patients' antibodies would likely reject the graft.

What's working in Law Land?

There are some basics that most firms have undertaken and, should certainly continue—such as firm-wide implicit-bias training, return-to-work programs, etc.

And, recently, there have been some new developments that hold promise for approaches that might actually work.

The "Mansfield Rule" requires law firms to include 30% diverse candidates (women and minorities) in slates for significant leadership roles. This was first piloted in 2017 under the guidance of Stacy's Diversity Lab with 50 law firms participating. It was reported that a total of 41 firms completed the one-year program, with 40% reporting increased diversity in their leadership ranks and 38% reported increases in partner promotions for women and diverse candidates. Angela Quinn, Chief Client Officer at Husch Blackwell, one of the participating firms, said, "We were focused on diversity before, but now it is more intentional—a way of life."

Generally speaking, I'm not a fan of quotas, but this may be a valid mechanism to jumpstart institutionalizing consideration of similarly-qualified diverse and non-diverse candidates for a given position—diversity "training wheels," so to speak. Moreover, we don't know what might have transpired at these firms *had they not* adopted the Mansfield Rule. That said, I have to believe once it becomes SOP to consider diverse candidates alongside their non-diverse peers, diverse candidates will be less likely to be viewed as "other" and, therefore be on more equal footing.

"Male Allies" is another great idea. I like this for its very simplicity and the fact that it happens in the trenches (NB: this technique is not Law Land-focused; many corporations also employ it.). We have recently heard many well-regarded MPs and Chairs speak convincingly, even passionately about their mandate to increase diversity at their firms—and they mean it. That said, it is farther down in their organizations where the day-to-day decisions reside—regarding clients, assignments, who's "at the table," etc. Contemporaneous "interventions" at the grass roots level can raise awareness and begin to change a firm's culture from the ground up.

Thomson Reuters supports an intensive program for a select group of "up-and-coming," newly-minted female partners at AmLaw 50 firms. Called Transforming Women's Leadership in the Law (TWLL), it provides, among other things, access to powerful GCs, insights into the business of law and business development opportunities. (Full disclosure, I've spoken at TWLL events.) Natalie Runyon, program strategist for TWLL who is hardly starry-eyed about the current state of diversity but does see progress. She noted, "Firms are heading in the right direction." She added, "I'd be more confident that true change will result when there's more action and tactics at the practice group-level."

Again, I'm not a fan of women-only initiatives (and, as discussed, they often backfire). That said, this program evinces a level of gravitas I've rarely seen. (Compared to, say, the bone-headed firm who brought in representatives from Ann Taylor to provide their female associates with wardrobe advice.)

Professors Tinsley and Ely have effectively re-framed the issue; it's not what's lacking in women—it's how organizations are failing them. Addressing this will require, first, a clear-eyed assessment of what's *actually* happening at your firm and developing remedies to address issues impeding women's progress. Obviously, tailor your remedies to be relevant to the issues at your firm. ("Industry best practices" oftentimes aren't) The good news is that you can scrap some of the more ineffective or counterproductive programs, so changing courses won't necessarily over-burden the firm or incur entirely incremental expenses (and some initiatives, such as Male Allies, cost virtually nothing). The benefits of a more productive, diverse workplace will redound throughout the firm—well into the future.

PAULA MONOPOLI, *PARITY AND THE UNITED STATES SUPREME COURT*

8 GEORGETOWN JOURNAL OF GENDER AND THE LAW 43 (2007)

Monopoli is the Sol & Carlyn Hubert Professor of Law and Founding Director, Women Leadership & Equality Program at the University of Maryland Francis King Carey School of Law.

* * *

There are more women than men in the United States and, thus, one might define our democracy as having a "dual nature." In order to better reflect this dual nature, the majority of the [United States Supreme Court] should arguably consist of female justices.

How can such a majority be achieved when the progress through the traditional nomination process has been so slow? In a number of other countries, voluntary or involuntary parity provisions have been used to achieve gender balance in the legislature when the rate of women elected to legislatures and parliaments has been seen as too slow. There are fewer examples of parity provisions with regard to the judiciary. South Africa is the dominant example. Its Constitution provides a conceptual foundation for a just balance on its courts. Americans are generally opposed to mandatory parity provisions or quotas because they violate basic notions of neutrality, i.e., that all citizens are equal and no one citizen should be given preference over another in a democracy. However, the time has come to consider such action to break through the social, structural and political barriers that keep women from fair representation at the pinnacle of the third branch of government. The justification for such action rests, in part, on the nature of the Court. The United States Supreme Court engages in significant policy-making and therefore it has an implicitly representative function.

While mandatory parity provisions may be justifiably characterized as quotas, which can be anathema to liberals and conservatives alike, the fact that there are so few seats on the Court militates for quotas to achieve a representative balance on the Court. There is no adequate "market solution" to this issue since there are so few vacancies. Even when a President nominates a woman, it has become clear that interest groups can defeat such a nomination before it has even been considered by the Senate. Such interest groups have been effective in derailing recent presidential nominations in this regard. Without a more proactive approach, the United States Supreme Court may well be an all-male bench in the year 2050. This is especially true given the longer life spans Americans now enjoy, a fact the Framers could have hardly envisioned when they conferred life tenure on justices.

This essay proposes a conceptual framework for achieving parity on the Court through statutory reform or, in the alternative, by constitutional amendment. This would ensure that this important power center of government becomes gender balanced over the next generation. My normative argument for parity is grounded in the historic views of the Framers and the early leaders of the Republic, the significant value of symbolic representation, the instrumental value of women judges, and a political theory that embraces the dual nature of society and rejects a "monosexual democracy" as inconsistent with our values as a nation. One can look to historic evidence in favor of geographic diversity, empirical evidence as to the effect of women judges on decision-making, affirmative action jurisprudence and an expansive reading of the Nineteenth Amendment as the bases for a statutory parity provision.

* * *

II. A PROPOSED PARITY PROVISION FOR THE COURT

The Constitution provides that the "judicial Power of the United States . . . be vested in one supreme Court, and in such inferior Courts as the Congress may from time to time ordain and establish." The Constitution further provides that the President may appoint Supreme Court justices only with the "Advice and Consent" of the Senate. Admittedly, amending the Constitution itself to require gender parity would be a difficult process. Seeking a constitutional amendment guaranteeing parity on the United States Supreme Court would be slow and painstaking. The chance of passage and ratification would be slim, at best. However, an amendment may well be the only mechanism that does not raise constitutional concerns.

A more efficient vehicle for parity would be a statutory amendment. The statute that establishes the size of the Court is 28 U.S.C. Section 1, which states that "the Supreme Court of the United States shall consist of a Chief Justice of the United States and eight associate justices, any six of whom shall constitute a quorum." Consider the implications of amending 28 U.S.C. Section 1 to read "The Supreme Court of the United States shall consist of a Chief Justice of the United States and eight associate justices, five of whom shall be female, and any six of whom shall constitute a quorum." Such a legislative enactment would guarantee gender parity on the court, reflecting the greater number of women than men in the population. Five out of nine seats would be reserved for well-qualified women from the state or lower federal courts or elsewhere. However, if there were constitutional concerns with Congress altering the qualifications for a national office, then a constitutional amendment that achieves a similar result would be the alternate means of achieving such parity.

Neither the Constitution nor 28 U.S.C. Section 1 say very much about the qualifications of Supreme Court justices, other than that they must act with "good behavior." The process the Framers finally decided upon, appointment by the president with the advice and consent of the Senate, was the means by which the country would be assured competent justices. The attributes associated with being a well-qualified judicial candidate, as articulated by Alexander Hamilton, included "firmness," "intellectual vigor," "judicial discretion," "independent spirit," and "moderation." People tend to also associate "consensus" with judges. While the ability to achieve consensus is often associated with women, many of the other attributes touted by Hamilton, like intellectual vigor and independent spirit, have masculine or agentic associations.

In practice, the Constitutional and statutory silence on qualifications has left a vacuum that has been filled by de facto requirements that implicate cognitive biases and their resulting gender schemas. In recent nominations, the public discourse has revolved around two de facto requirements in particular. The process now seems to require that the candidate be: (1) a "brilliant" graduate of an elite law school and (2) a sitting judge on a United States Circuit Court of Appeals. Of course, neither of these requirements was envisioned by the Framers as essential to a seat on the Court.

Both of these criteria pose structural problems for women ascending the Court in significant numbers since women are rarely described as "brilliant" and they hold few seats on United States Courts of Appeal. As de facto prerequisites for the Court, both the masculine attribute of "brilliance" and a Court of Appeals seat have a disparate impact on the likelihood that women will be nominated for the Court. Thus, in evaluating whether a parity provision (either by statute or constitutional amendment) is justified, one must first look to the views of the Framers and early leaders of the Republic about the value of diversity on the Court.

III. THE HISTORIC ARGUMENT FOR PARITY ON THE COURT

Historically, geographic diversity was clearly deemed important for the court. * * * The early leaders of the young nation understood the value of diversity of life experience and political interests on the bench. That understanding expressed itself in the adherence to geographic diversity in presidential appointments.

* * *

This view with regard to the representative aspect of state courts is even stronger when applied to the United States Supreme Court, given that its opinions have significant policy implications for all Americans. The early leaders of the Republic understood that for the Court's decisions to retain their legitimacy among the American people, the people must feel fully represented in that institution of government. These values, promoted by the informal system of nominating justices with geography in mind, can and should extend to gender balance on the Court.

It would have been inconceivable for a woman to have been nominated to the United States Supreme Court in the late eighteenth and early nineteenth century. They would have been deemed ineligible to participate in civil governance in any branch and women did not have the right to vote. However, most Americans would agree that the qualifications for the Court should evolve to reflect changing norms. This is particularly true given the recent understanding that subtle, cognitive bias is a significant barrier to women ascending to leadership positions in government as well as the private sector. If the original appointment process crafted by the Framers was intentionally fluid, one might argue that they contemplated that changing norms could be reflected in the process in future generations. Thus, providing for gender as a criterion is consistent with the approach of the Framers and their genius in allowing for changing norms to guide nominations. It is also consistent with the view of the early leaders of the republic that diversity on the Court was an important value.

The presence of women on the bench provides the kind of diversity of thought and experience that is essential to a well-balanced Court. In addition to bringing a wealth of different experience to their decisionmaking, five women on the Court would provide the kind of symbolic value to other women and to men that is essential in breaking down the intractable gender schemas that slow the progress of American women.

IV. THE SYMBOLIC AND INSTRUMENTALIST ARGUMENTS FOR PARITY

There is empirical evidence that women's presence in positions of leadership has a positive impact on women's advancement in society. Clearly the mere presence of a Sandra Day O'Connor on the Court had an effect on women's ability to see themselves as judges. A number of women have been encouraged to persevere despite barriers, because they now see women as partners in law firms, judges, senators, congresswomen, law faculty and in other powerful positions. In addition to encouraging more young women to aspire to positions of leadership, some scholars note that achieving a critical mass of women holds the promise of reducing gender bias and altering performance benchmarks. Political scientists Jennifer Lawless and Richard Fox have noted that "[p]olitical theorists point to symbolic representation and the role model effects that women's presence in positions of political power confers to women citizens."

The instrumentalist argument for parity is based on the evidence that having women on the bench leads to different outcomes in certain kinds of cases. The presence of female judges also neutralizes the gender bias of male judges in such cases. While the research on the impact of gender on case outcomes has been somewhat mixed, recent studies have demonstrated a statistically significant connection between women sitting on the bench and outcomes in cases that are of particular importance to women, such as Title VII cases.

* * *

Thus, both symbolic and instrumentalist arguments grounded in empirical evidence favor a mandatory parity provision on the Court. The presence of more women would have a demonstrably positive effect on the number of women in leadership positions as well as increasing substantive justice and reducing bias among other male justices. However, one might argue that the means proposed to reach such normatively desirable ends, parity provisions or quotas, are inherently anti-democratic because they prefer one group in society over another. The next section argues that such means are justified and are actually consistent with full civic membership for women in a democracy.

V. THE CONSTITUTIONAL AND DOCTRINAL BASES FOR PARITY

A mandatory provision for parity on the Court may be grounded in an expansive reading of the Nineteenth Amendment. Some scholars have argued that that Amendment guaranteed full political participation for women, not just the vote. Reva Siegel and Akhil Amar have argued that in fact the Nineteenth Amendment provides a constitutional foundation for a broad view of "equal citizenship in a democratic polity."

* * *

If one embraces this expansive interpretation of the Nineteenth Amendment, then a parity proposal for the Court is an effective tool to achieve the promise of full political equality for American women. Mandatory parity proposals are admittedly a form of affirmative action. In the case of the United States Supreme Court, affirmative action is an appropriate response given the notable lack of any progress in appointing more women to the Court over the past twenty-five years. Affirmative action programs have been one of the most important means to achieving gender equality in the areas of education and employment. In this country however, such initiatives have not been used to any significant degree in the political realm.

* * *

Parity provisions are solidly within the doctrinal framework of affirmative action, the mechanism used in the past forty years to achieve full participation by women in the workplace and in educational institutions. There is a well-developed jurisprudence approving the use of certain kinds of affirmative action to remedy past racial and gender discrimination, including most recently *Grutter v. Bollinger* and *Gratz v. Bollinger*. While recent cases have rejected the use of explicit quotas in higher education to achieve equality, many commentators have noted the fluid line from formal quotas, to point systems used by the University of Michigan in *Gratz,* to flexible systems like those used by the University of Michigan Law School and upheld by the Court in *Grutter*. In a recent article, Sylvia Lazos Vargas makes a persuasive argument "that *Grutter v. Bollinger* . . . [held] that it is a legitimate state objective for key democratic institutions, like a public university (or in the instant case a judicial body), to want to achieve discursive diversity." Lazos Vargas' observation is germane to the proposal for a mandatory parity provision for gender balance on the Court offered in this article. It is a legitimate goal of government to engage in action intended to enhance diversity in the dialogue that goes on in classrooms and also in judicial chambers. As Lazos Vargas argues, *Grutter* lays the groundwork for programs to enhance diversity based on their furtherance of the goal of fostering democratic principles through enhanced discourse. The mandatory parity proposal herein is grounded in just such a rationale.

Therefore, a mandatory parity provision can exist within a theoretical and doctrinal framework consistent with democratic values and constitutionally permissible mechanisms to remedy past discrimination. A political theory that embraces the dual and gendered nature of society, as well as an expansive interpretation of the Nineteenth Amendment and affirmative action jurisprudence, provide constitutional and doctrinal support for a mandatory parity provision for the Court.

VI. WHY NON-MANDATORY PARITY MECHANISMS ARE INSUFFICIENT

The difficulty with non-mandatory or aspirational parity proposals lies in the intractable nature of cognitive bias and its resulting gender schemas. Recent developments in social psychology demonstrate the powerful role cognitive bias plays in the slow advancement of women. This subtle but persistent barrier renders a mandatory provision a necessary tool in achieving gender equality. In light of the experience in other countries with non-mandatory parity provisions and the role of cognitive bias, mandatory measures may well be the only way to make progress.

For example, the 1996 South African Constitution includes an explicit provision for greater gender and racial diversity in the judiciary to restore legitimacy to a judicial system in which, under apartheid, ninety-seven percent of the judges had been white men. The Constitution recites the "need for the judiciary to reflect broadly the racial and gender composition of South Africa." It explicitly provides that diversity "be considered when judicial officers are appointed." Under the 1996 Constitution, the appointment power was transferred from the President and Minister of Justice to the Judicial Service Commission (JSC), chaired by the Chief Justice of South Africa and several other members. The JSC was to select candidates for judicial appointments with a specific concern for gender and racial diversity. Increased diversity was thought to be an essential component of a comprehensive plan to reestablish the legitimacy of the courts in a new post-apartheid South Africa.

Even with such unique constitutional provisions, one scholar has concluded there has not been a significant increase in the number of women judges in South Africa. Ten years after the new Constitution, only 12.4% of the judges in the superior courts were women. This is in large part due to residual patriarchal and sexist attitudes, as well as customary and religious law and "lackluster efforts" on the part of the JSC to appoint women judges. One might add that the JSC does not operate under a mandatory regime and that it is not a surprise that a voluntary, discretionary system has not yielded significant improvement in the face of continuing, entrenched sexism.

Such gender bias against women has been well documented in the social psychology literature and by political scientists. In this country, gender schemas have played a role in nominations to the Court. California Court of Appeals Justice Mildred Lillie was vetted and seriously considered by President Richard Nixon for a nomination to the Court. She would have been the first woman nominee to the Court. Just before he was to nominate her, the American Bar Association rated her as "unqualified" and Nixon decided against nominating Lillie. He eventually nominated a young administration official with no prior judicial experience, William Rehnquist, whom he had previously derided as a "clown." In a radio interview, Nixon staff member and White House Counsel John Dean noted: "And Justice Lillie had been selected by a very liberal democratic governor, but was known as a conservative on law enforcement issues, which Nixon liked. And she was a Catholic, so she was right on the abortion issue for Nixon . . . I think she would have made a great Justice . . . But what happened was the American Bar Association at that time was made up of all men and the old boys did not think that it was time for a woman to be on the high court."

Justice Lillie served for more than fifty-five years on the California Municipal, Superior, and Appellate Courts. She was still serving when she died at the age of eighty-seven in 2002. Lillie was enormously well respected by members of the bar. Her distinguished career as a jurist casts serious doubt on the genuine nature of the "unqualified" rating given by the ABA and raises the specter of gender bias as the true motive for the rating.

Commentators have noted that the "intellectual rigor card" is often used as the bludgeon for opponents to block nominees who do not fit into a traditional mold based on their race, gender or ethnicity. For example, when one of the most renowned Supreme Court justices, Louis Brandeis, was nominated in 1916, those who opposed his nomination (in large part due to religious bias since Brandeis was Jewish) cited his "unfitness" and lack of intellectual ability. The recent nomination of accomplished lawyer and White House Counsel Harriet Miers to the Court demonstrated the residual gender bias in the culture and the continued use of "the intellectual rigor card" as a weapon against nominees. Unlike Justice Lillie, the ABA panel did not actually rate Harriet Miers as "unqualified" prior to her withdrawal. However, the pundits certainly did with their savage invective.

* * *

The nomination of Harriet Miers and her subsequent withdrawal was a pivotal moment in American history. It illustrated the profound gender bias still at play in the nomination process and in society generally. As noted above, nominees are increasingly required to be "brilliant" graduates of an elite law school and sitting United States Circuit Courts of Appeal judges. Women who are brilliant are rarely characterized as such. Rather they are described as "hard-working," "good managers" or "well-organized." Those who are concerned about this trend can either challenge these kinds of de facto requirements or they can move for enactment of a parity provision. The latter is far more likely to bring change in the next generation.

Scholars have identified three general approaches to judicial selection: (1) enhancing diversity; (2) choosing the "best qualified" candidate; and (3) selecting candidates with a compatible judicial philosophy. The second approach, which is reflected in the new de facto requirements noted above, runs the risk of excluding women if the benchmarks for "best qualified" skew toward those attributes most often associated with men rather than women. These include intellectual acumen or brilliance in particular. As long as merit is equated with masculine traits like brilliance, it is less likely that the public will view women candidates as qualified nominees for the Court.

* * *

Some scholars have proposed fluid or non-mandatory mechanisms to achieve electoral equality without violating the principle of neutrality and embracing essentialism. However, these methods are not likely to be effective in the context of the United States Supreme Court. Unlike thousands of federal, state and local elective offices, there are only nine seats on the Court. Given the intractability of gender schemas and the few seats on the Court, waiting for the vagaries of the current nomination process to achieve parity may take another generation. As has been demonstrated in South Africa, non-mandatory or aspirational parity provisions are not likely to be effective in the face of an intractable barrier like gender bias.

VII. CONCLUSION

It is clear from the absence of specific criteria that the Framers envisioned a process of judicial selection for the Court that would be flexible. Presumably, they left the qualifications vague so that the process could be adapted to changing norms and times. Some early nominees did not have a formal legal education but rather had trained by apprenticeship. In subsequent years, some nominees did not graduate from "elite" law schools. Several distinguished nominees were not even judges. Clearly, the qualifications required for nominees have evolved over time to fit changing social structures and norms. Thus, introducing gender as a qualification at this point in our history would be consistent with the evolving nature of the nomination process. Such a requirement would reflect current knowledge about cognitive bias as an intractable barrier to women's advancement and the failure of the nomination process, as it currently operates, to yield more women justices on the Court.

A mandatory parity provision need not last forever. However, it should be retained until gender parity is established and it may be repealed by later generations once parity had been achieved. The historical value placed upon diversity, the symbolic and instrumentalist value of gender balance and a theory of the body politic that reflects its gendered nature all militate in favor of such a plan.

* * *

RENEE KNAKE, *TESTIMONY BEFORE THE COMMITTEE ON CODES OF CONDUCT AND COMMITTEE ON JUDICIAL CONDUCT AND DISABILITY*
PROPOSED CHANGES TO THE CODE OF CONDUCT ON SEXUAL HARASSMENT AND OTHER WORKPLACE MISCONDUCT (OCT. 30, 2018)

Knake is one of the authors of this casebook. You can read more about her background in the Introduction.

I would like to thank the Committee on Codes of Conduct and the Committee on Judicial Conduct and Disability for the opportunity to comment on the proposed changes to the federal Code of Conduct for U.S. Judges and the Rules for Judicial Conduct and Disability Proceedings regarding harassment and other inappropriate workplace behavior.

* * *

Support for the Proposed Changes to the Code of Conduct for U.S. Judges and the Rules for Judicial Conduct and Disability Proceedings

I am here today in support of the proposed changes to the Code of Conduct for U.S. Judges and the Rules for Judicial Conduct and Disability Proceedings. I am also here to offer recommendations that, if adopted, would greatly strengthen these proposals and their purposes.

I commend the Committees for their work. Your proposed reforms are a necessary first step. But, I believe you can and should go further. All professions and industries have experienced their own #MeToo reckoning regarding the mistreatment of women. No one should expect that the judiciary is immune. To give just one example that occurs to this day, when I contemplated applying for a judicial clerkship as a second year law student in 1998, I was warned to avoid a certain judge on the Ninth Circuit because he was known to mistreat female clerks. I wish the reforms we are considering today had been in place 20 years ago. No one should have to endure sexual harassment as a rite of passage in the legal profession. The Committees' careful and responsive work has the potential to spare such indignities, purge the federal judiciary of sexual misconduct, and thereby strengthen the rule of law.

Concerns and Recommendations

Judicial codes of conduct typically focus on fairness, impartiality and public confidence in the integrity of the judiciary. These are important, but the goals should be expanded. A workplace free from harassment will enhance the public's confidence in the integrity of the judiciary, serve as a model for the legal and other professions, and expand the pool of talented lawyers willing to devote their early years promoting excellent work product in the judicial branch, which is so vital to our rights and liberties. You are obviously well-familiar with the proposed changes, so I won't take the time to repeat them here. Instead, I want to focus on my concerns and provide recommendations.

If the ultimate objective here is to curb sexual harassment and misconduct, your proposed changes may fall short. Worse, they may prove unenforceable. I am especially concerned about judicial clerks who serve for one or two years before the clerkship becomes a stepping stone to higher-level clerkships, prestigious law practice, judicial office, or tenured professorships like the one that I hold. Unlike many places of employment, a judge's chambers is highly intimate. Judicial clerks are few in number and rely heavily upon the recommendation from their judge for the next step in their career path. In many ways, the relationship is more similar to that of a professor and a student than a traditional employment relationship. The pressure to endure harassment silently is fierce; indeed, a decision to report can ruin future prospects in the profession, even with the protections against retaliation and assurances of confidentiality contained in your proposed amendments to the Code and Rules. An unfavorable reference letter, or even the judge's refusal to write one, can compromise or destroy career aspirations. The proposed reporting process you are contemplating assumes that harassment inevitably will occur and places the burden upon the victim to address it. This process, alone, is unlikely to prevent the conduct your reforms aspire to remedy, especially in instances where harassment takes a subtle or insidious form.

We must appreciate why a victim may feel compelled to remain silent, and consider options that reduce adverse consequences to sounding an alarm. We should put in place enforceable rules that will promote a culture free of sexual harassment *in addition* to a process for uncovering prior bad conduct.

Here are my recommendations.

First, in addition to prohibiting "unwanted, offensive, or abusive sexual conduct, including sexual harassment or assault" as contemplated by the new Rule 4(a)(2), the Committee should consider a separate provision banning even consensual romantic or sexual relationships between judges and their clerks and other employees. A prohibition like this exists in many academic institutions today. The University of Houston, where I teach, prohibits "any consensual dating, intimate, romantic, and/or sexual relationship between an employee and an individual that the employee has responsibility to teach, instruct, supervise, advise, counsel, oversee, grade, coach, train, treat or evaluate in any way." This prohibition, intended to avoid "conflicts of interest, favoritism, and exploitation," also promotes a workplace culture free from sexual overtures. Such overtures may be viewed as consensual by the more powerful person and at the same time unwanted by the target who acquiesces only because of the power differential or because she soon will be moving on to another job. The prohibition need not remove all human autonomy. For example, Houston's policy contains an exception to the prohibition if granted by the Assistant Vice Chancellor/Vice President for Equal Opportunity. A provision like this for the federal judiciary would help curtail sexual overtures that may feel consensual on the part of the instigator but harassing on the part of the target. It also removes the potential for a "he said—she said" dynamic where a victim bears the burden of showing that sexual conduct is unwelcome.

Second, the Rules should mandate an annual, anonymous survey regarding sexual harassment and other misconduct. The survey should be administered by an independent third party, and sent to all former clerks, even if they previously declined to complete it. The results should be publicly available. A transparent survey of this nature would indicate that the judiciary values the reporting of misconduct and create an environment more favorable to reporting. It would also provide the judiciary information about the pervasiveness of harassment and other misconduct as well as the effectiveness of the reforms proposed here.

Third, we must also take care that the proposals, when adopted, can be enforced. The American Bar Association amended its Model Rule 8.4 in 2016 to include a provision banning "conduct that the lawyer knows or reasonably should know is harassment or discrimination on the basis of race, sex, religion, national origin, ethnicity, disability, age, sexual orientation, gender identity, marital status or socioeconomic status in conduct related to the practice of law." While Vermont quickly adopted a similar rule, several other states affirmatively rejected it. Indeed, the attorney general of Texas issued an opinion challenging its validity on first amendment grounds. As far as I am aware, no court has yet to rule upon such a challenge. I raise this issue not to say that similar provisions should not be included among your reforms, but as a caution. Your proposed reforms to the Code address sexual harassment but also "civility" (proposed revision to Canon 3.B.4) and "other inappropriate workplace behavior" (proposed revision to Canon 2.A). I recommend that the provisions on sexual misconduct be handled separately from the other behavior addressed.

I hope that the Committee will consider these recommendations. Thank you the opportunity to appear before you today. I would be pleased to answer any questions.

* * *

November 13, 2018

I write with a brief supplement to my testimony offered during the public hearing on October 30, 2018. As with my prior testimony, I offer this in my personal capacity and not on behalf of my employer or other organizations with which I am affiliated.

I am grateful for the opportunity to testify about much-needed reforms to address sexual harassment and other workplace misconduct in the federal judiciary. I was impressed by the thoughtfulness and deliberation evidenced by your Committees during the public hearing. I do believe that workplace sexual misconduct is more prevalent in the judiciary and legal profession than we may realize. Indeed, as just one example, after my testimony before your Committees, an employee of the Administrative Office of the U.S. Courts approached me to share her own story of workplace sexual assault which she reported but no investigation followed. My hope is that the reforms you implement will not only address reporting concerns like these but also create a culture where sexual misconduct does not occur at all.

* * *

ELIE MYSTAL, *INEFFECTUAL JUDICIAL RESPONSE TO #MeTOO WILL CONTINUE*

ABOVETHELAW.COM, APRIL 10, 2019

Mystal is the Executive Editor of Above the Law and a contributor at The Nation. He formerly practiced law at Debevoise & Plimpton after graduating from Harvard Law School.

I'm here at the National Association for Law Placement (NALP) annual conference in San Diego. For the uninitiated, NALP is the gathering where all the legal recruiters and law school career services people meet and discuss the future of getting people jobs.

Since the #MeToo era became a thing, I've looked at these people as the first line of defense for law students trying to combat workplace sexual harassment. It's hard to explain how powerless a second-year law student is, should their employer decide to turn their summer internship into an extended game of grab-ass. Career services back at the law school is one of the only places you can turn when you still need a job but also want to be treated with decency and respect.

At least there are a lot of law firms. Law clerks, people spending a year working for Article III judges, are arguably even more powerless. A judge is the king or queen of his or her chambers, and if they decide to mistreat you, there's almost nothing you can do. You can't easily "lateral" to another clerkship, mid-year. You can't get your life-tenured judge "fired." Your options are to basically take the abuse, in whatever form, for a year, or quit and risk blowing up your career before it really starts.

Career services aren't in a great position to help their law clerks, after they start their clerkship. But here at NALP, Ninth Circuit Judge Margaret McKeown was speaking on panel called "#MeToo in the Courthouse." McKeown can help. She's part of the "workgroup" Chief Justice John Roberts convened to address sexual harassment in the judiciary.

I've been critical of the workgroup in the past. Roberts thought it up in response to the Alex Kozinski scandal, and one way you can tell that the group has been ineffective at rooting out sexual misconduct in the judiciary is that Alex Kozinski is still the only federal judge who has been drummed off the bench for inappropriate behavior in the #MeToo era. You'd be a damn fool to think that Kozinski is the only Article III judge with a #MeToo problem. You'd have to be so stupid to think that I'm going to go in and assume nobody is stupid enough to think that.

Arguably McKeown's group is supposed to be rooting these bad judges out and putting together polices so that these people cannot continue to abuse their clerks. But after listening to her talk, it's clear that the judiciary is going to do functionally nothing to police itself in any real way. McKeown got through her whole talk without once using the word "accountability," nor did she propose anything that could be mistaken for accountability.

Instead, all the working group has are various theories intended to make reporting the behavior easier. She talked about how the Ninth Circuit has "revised" its confidentiality policy, making it clear that while judge's chambers are still sacrosanct, you can pierce the veil to report workplace harassment. She talked about new "informal" reporting options, for clerks who are arguably being harassed but don't want to make a literal federal case about it. And, of course, more "training." Not just for judges . . . but also for the law clerks. Yes, the working group on judicial sexual harassment has decided that law students need more training about how to identify their own abuse and which feckless governing body they should report it to.

The broad takeaway from McKeown's talk was to put the onus of identifying, reporting, and combating sexual harassment *on the law clerk,* who just happens to be the most powerless cog in the whole system. It's like if I put my six-year-old in charge of lawn maintenance, because he spends the most time outside.

* * *

McKeown closed by saying it was a "long-term process" to "change the culture" of chambers. But her talk illustrated that the real process hasn't even started yet. All the working group seems to be doing is asking law clerks to do the committee's work for them.

* * *

TERRY MOREHEAD DWORKIN, AARTI RAMASWAMI, AND CINDY SCHIPANI, *THE ROLE OF NETWORKS, MENTORSHIP, AND THE LAW IN OVERCOMING BARRIERS TO ORGANIZATIONAL LEADERSHIP FOR WOMEN WITH CHILDREN*

20 MICHIGAN JOURNAL OF GENDER & LAW 83 (2013)

Morehead Dworkin (far left) is a Scholar in Residence at Seattle University School of Law and the Jack R. Wentworth Professor Emerita, Kelley School of Business, Indiana University-Bloomington. Ramaswami (far right) is a Professor in the Management Department and the Deputy Dean of ESSEC Business School, Asia Pacific. Schipani (center) is the Merwin H. Waterman Collegiate Professor of Business Administration and Professor of Business Law at the University of Michigan Ross School of Business.

* * *

Having dependents is an important family status variable in the larger scheme of social differentiators that account for sex differences in career-related outcomes. In this study, we are interested in whether men or women benefit more from having access to networks when they have dependents. Prior studies have shown that mentoring and networking are major components of professional development that lead to career advancement. We are also interested in whether the outcome differs for those men and women who report having mentors.

This study is organized as follows. Part I discusses possible corrections through existing legal remedies. Part II follows with an overview of the important role of mentoring and networking for career advancement. Part III describes the results of our empirical study, finding that it is particularly important for women with dependents to have developmental opportunities that are sensitive to how they can benefit from joining networks. Part IV offers implications from the study together with recommendations for potential governmental interventions. Concluding remarks follow.

I.   Possible Corrections through Existing Legal Remedies

The broad gender disparities in business [discussed in earlier chapters of this casebook] are not unique to the United States. For example, only 2.5% of European company chairpersons are women, and the proportion of women on European company boards averages about 10%, with a high of 40% in Norway and a low of 1% in Portugal. By comparison, in the United States, 16.1% of board members of Fortune 500 companies were female in 2011. To overcome these disparities, many European countries have imposed quotas, which ensure women's participation in governmental and business organizations.

A.   Quotas: A European Solution

Norway, the first to adopt such a quota system, has influenced other European countries to adopt similar quotas. Belgium, Spain, the Netherlands, France, Iceland, and Italy have also recently adopted quotas. In addition, countries such as Australia and the United Kingdom encourage female representation through their corporate governance codes. Some international companies consider meeting the quota an opportunity to gain U.S. business and have actively recruited U.S. women to serve on their boards. [In 2013], there [were] 96 U.S. women on 136 boards in 12 countries.

The European Union considered a mandatory quota of 40%. It was, however, rejected and later replaced by a proposal to "smash the glass ceiling that keeps women out of top jobs" by setting a 40% goal. If adopted, larger companies would be required to favor women over equally qualified men. Companies would face sanctions not for failing to meet quotas, but rather for failing to favor women. They would, though, be required to disclose the identity of unsuccessful female candidates and why they were not chosen. Neither of these European systems would be legally sustainable in the United States, although the goal system comes close.

B.   Quotas, Goals, and Affirmative Action in the United States

The result-oriented European quota system relatively quickly diversifies representation and overcomes overt and covert prejudices and stereotyping. These advantages were understood in the United States decades ago. In the 1970s, however, the Supreme Court declared using quotas as a means to bring more Blacks into higher education unconstitutional. That decision, Regents of University of California v. Bakke, still stands. Bakke was controversial then, and the idea of racial and gender preference, also called affirmative action, remains so today.

* * *

When Title VII of the Civil Rights Act of 1964 was enacted, barring discrimination in private employment, affirmative action was only mentioned as a court-ordered remedy for intentional employment discrimination. Prior to Bakke, the United States Supreme Court stated, with regard to Title VII (which guarantees equal opportunity regardless of race, color, religion, sex, or national origin), that: "[d]iscriminatory preference for any group, minority or majority, is precisely and only what Congress has proscribed."

One year after Bakke, in United Steelworkers of America AFL-CIO v. Weber, a case decided under Title VII, the Court upheld voluntarily-adopted affirmative action in private employment. Because Title VII prohibited racial preference, the Court cited "the 'spirit' of the 1964 Civil Rights Act rather than its language prohibiting discrimination. It found that the purpose of the Act was to advance historically disadvantaged groups in employment; therefore voluntary affirmative action plans were permitted when they helped achieve this end."

The Court, relying on Weber and Bakke, upheld affirmative action for women (who are a majority in the voting population, but also traditionally discriminated against in employment) in Johnson v. Transportation Agency, Santa Clara County, California. The case involved a gender-based, voluntarily-adopted affirmative action plan under which the county employer promoted a woman over a man who had scored slightly higher on the exam taken for promotion. The Court held that an affirmative action plan that considered being female a plus factor was valid when there was a manifest imbalance reflecting women's underrepresentation. It noted that no positions were set aside for women and that no men were automatically excluded. Unlike the EU proposal, the plan did not require that a woman be selected.

The Court also affirmed the requirements for a legally defensible affirmative action plan. These include: 1) evidence of manifest imbalance or past discrimination; 2) an existing plan; 3) the plan exists only until the underrepresentation is corrected; 4) only qualified people may be selected;

5) no unnecessary trammeling of the interests of the majority; and 6) goals, not quotas.

During the late 1970s and the 1980s, several large organizations adopted plans. Some of these plans included mentoring programs. Soon thereafter, though, favoring one group over another to correct imbalance fell out of favor. In the late 1980s, under more conservative presidents, administrative agencies, and the Supreme Court, and reflecting the beginning of a split in public opinion, challenges to affirmative action met a more sympathetic ear and had greater success.

* * *

C. Pregnancy Discrimination Act

The Pregnancy Discrimination Act ("PDA") was specifically designed to provide women a level playing field in employment. Recognizing that Title VII was not preventing women from suffering discrimination on the basis of motherhood, pregnancy, and perceptions related thereto, Congress passed the PDA as an amendment to Title VII during the activism of the 1970s. The PDA prohibits "all forms of discrimination on the basis of pregnancy, such as discriminatory failures to hire and promote." Courts, however, routinely interpret the PDA restrictively.

Some courts treat pregnancy under the PDA as the equivalent of a disability, and one that is chosen because women have control over becoming pregnant. Because the disability is thought to be by choice, protection against discrimination is minimal. The law only requires that that pregnant employees be treated the same as other employees similar in their ability or inability to work. Thus, if an employer treats a similarly restricted employee poorly, it can treat the pregnant employee just as poorly. Some courts hold that the PDA "prohibit[s] only discriminatory animus against pregnant women." Thus, the PDA may not remedy sex-neutral policies even when these policies disproportionately affect pregnant women. A woman's ability to continue to work and give birth "seems to be in spite of, rather than because of, passage of the PDA." These restrictive interpretations "inculcate the cultural stereotypes and invidious treatment of women who have been, are, or may be affected by pregnancy or childbirth in their lifetime." The PDA is sufficiently vague so as to lead to wide discrepancies among court decisions regarding issues such as infertility and breastfeeding.

Discrimination on the basis of pregnancy operates at all levels of employment, including at the upper levels. Bass v. Chemical Banking Corp. provides one example. Bass sued her employer over the loss of a promotion opportunity. She alleged that her employer discriminated against her because she was the mother of young children. Instead, the promotion went to a woman without children. Her claim was dismissed because she failed to show that men with young children were treated more favorably than she. Men with young children, however, seldom suffer discrimination on that basis.

An example of how rare it is to have pregnant women in the top levels of organizations is the selection of Marissa Mayer as the CEO of Yahoo in July 2012. The same day that Yahoo announced that it was hiring her, Ms. Mayer announced that she and her husband were expecting their first child. The selection made Ms. Mayer the twentieth female CEO in a Fortune 500 company, a fact headline-worthy in itself, but also the first ever pregnant CEO in a Fortune 500 company. Unfortunately, her pregnancy generated more discussion than did her qualifications to lead Yahoo and her visions for the organization.

The widely acknowledged deficiencies of the PDA have prompted lawmakers to introduce the Pregnant Workers Fairness Act. This bill aimed to offer more protection to pregnant workers than does the PDA. Its goal is "to eliminate discrimination and promote women's health and economic security by ensuring reasonable workplace accommodations for workers whose ability to perform the functions of a job are limited by pregnancy, childbirth, or a related medical condition." For example, even if the pregnant worker cannot perform the same work as the non-pregnant worker, the employer would still be required to accommodate the pregnant woman to a certain degree. Lawmakers, however, failed to muster enough support for the bill and it recently died. Of course, judges could also interpret the language of the PDA in the manner intended by Congress when it passed the law. Construing the PDA in this way would also be consistent with the way the law is written.

D.   Family and Medical Leave Act (FMLA)

The Family and Medical Leave Act of 1993 (FMLA), another federal law attempting to accommodate work and family life, also varies in its effectiveness in addressing work-family conflicts faced by women with dependents. The FMLA allows unpaid, job-protected leave for up to twelve workweeks in a twelve-month period. It applies, however, only to employers with fifty or more employees. Covered employers must grant FMLA leave for the birth of a child and to care for the newborn child within one year of birth, adoption, or foster care. Additionally, the FMLA permits leave to care for the employee's spouse, child, or parent who has a serious health condition, among other reasons.

Because leave is unpaid, many workers cannot afford to take it, and many employees are excluded because of the fifty-employee requirement. In 2005, only 54% of employees were covered. Additionally, coverage is skewed toward higher paid employees. These limitations again put the United States far behind Europe and, indeed, much of the world . . . . Out of 184 nations, the United States is one of only six nations that do not provide paid maternity leave. Liberia, Papua New Guinea, Samoa, Sierra Leone, and Swaziland are the five other countries that do not provide paid maternity leave.

A few states have expanded the coverage beyond the federal law. Only one state, California, provides direct payment during family leave. Five states, California, New York, New Jersey, Rhode Island, and Hawaii, provide some payment during maternity leave in the form of temporary disability payments.

As the above discussion illustrates, the law does not adequately address the issue of gender inequality in the workplace, particularly regarding pregnant women. More information regarding gender discrimination needs to be obtained, and new approaches need to be considered. In this study, we suggest additional measures that can be taken, such as an increased focus on the role of mentoring and networking.

II. The Role of Mentoring and Networking

Mentoring is an "intense reciprocal interpersonal exchange between a senior experienced individual (the mentor) and a less experienced individual (the protégé), characterized by the type of guidance, counsel, and support provided by the mentor for the protégé's career and personal development." The positive association of mentoring with career outcomes for protégés makes it "a key employee development and talent management practice . . . ." Through these developmental interactions, "mentors enhance protégés' skills and aid their socialization to a new work (or non-work) setting."

Networking is an alternative, yet complementary, mechanism to mentoring that provides career and moral support, advice, and personal and interpersonal resources that aid in employees' career progression. It has been defined as the "process of gaining advice and moral support or using contacts for information in order to become more effective in the work world." Networking can be particularly helpful for those who did not have access to mentors early in their careers. Networking and mentoring, indeed, go hand in hand, both providing similar career benefits.

Women, and men and women with dependents, represent important sources of diversity at work, and networking and mentoring are mechanisms through which gender inequality in career attainment may be reduced. The "importance of mentors for employee career progress and organizational outcomes" necessitates an examination of the role that mentoring plays in a career enhancing strategy such as networking. The gender dynamics of interpersonal and developmental relationships, such as mentoring and networking, have received research attention.

Linehan and Scullion's qualitative study (completed in 2002) among 50 senior female managers "on the role of mentoring and networking in the career development of global female managers" suggests organizational processes hinder their career development. The findings showed "that female managers can miss out on global appointments because they lack mentors, role models, sponsorship, or access to appropriate networks—all of which are commonly available to their male counterparts." The female managers interviewed suggested "that men, as the dominant group, may want to maintain their dominance by excluding women from the informal interactions of mentoring and networking." If women had more access to networks and mentors, they could gain from the professional and organizational socialization that these relationships provide. Yet, the women in the sample reported encountering gender related barriers to their career progress. Gender differences in the work environment need to be considered in order to understand the causes and consequences of inequality and discrimination in the workplace.

Two comprehensive reviews and two mentoring handbooks suggest that mentoring theory, research, and its practical applications have made much progress over the past three decades. Despite this voluminous literature, few studies have examined the role of mentoring in network-related outcomes and, consequently, our current knowledge and insights about the interaction of demographics and mentoring on network outcomes appear limited. "This gap in mentoring research precludes our understanding of mentoring and leadership development," especially for women.

III. The Pathways Study

Our study, denoted the Pathways Study, explores two research questions: (1) how do gender and having dependents interact with network benefits and challenges?; and (2) how do gender and having dependents interact with network outcomes? That is, does having a mentor increase network benefits and lessen network challenges for men versus women with and without dependents?

The results of this study reinforce the value of mentoring for women's network outcomes, especially for those with dependents, and contribute to research on gender issues in career advancement. First, this study responds to calls for research on the role of mentoring and networking in women's careers. Further, we contribute to theory by heeding recent calls for research on the interaction of gender and family status as well as the moderators of the gender-network outcomes relationship. From a practical perspective, the study's findings would be particularly applicable to organizations and human resource managers interested in tapping diversity and high potential female talent. Finally, we analyze relevant legal issues in order to open and navigate the pathways for women with dependents to overcome organizational barriers.

A.   Theory and Research Questions

One could not overstate the importance of social capital for career advancement. As noted before, networking is one strategy for women to break through the glass ceiling. Taking the example of the legal profession, Higgins and Kay and Hagan emphasize the social capital perspective as being more appropriate for understanding disparities in career outcomes between men and women. They note that social capital includes social relations and connections between and among persons that bring one legitimacy, provide access to "privileged information about the firm and industry, and build networking capital beyond the firm . . . ."

Yet "women have historically lacked access to important organizational networks and contacts." Reasons for exclusion include "structural barriers, such as organizational form, institutionalization and genealogy of organizational leadership, domestic commitments and lack of child care," lack of role models and mentors, "rainmaking demands (bringing in more clients for the firm), long work hours, and part time work . . . ." Moreover, attitudinal barriers such as prejudice towards women, family, pregnancy, social hierarchy, sexual harassment, and sex-role socialization may lead to women being perceived as uncommitted and lacking in necessary abilities and skills for professional roles. Thus, organizational characteristics such as social structure and the societal and cultural constraints imposed on women may influence the occupational and professional participation and engagement of both men and women.

Although studies suggest that marital or family role commitment are unassociated with family-to-work interference and that gender, marital status, and number of children are unrelated to occupational commitment, biases against women, regardless of family status, in the profession persist. For example, Jenny M. Hoobler and her colleagues found that managers' perceptions of female subordinates' work-family conflict, whether conflict existed, influenced their perceptions of these women's person-organization fit, person-job fit, and performance. Lyness and Thompson "found that female executives were more likely than male executives to report lack of cultur[al] fit and . . . exclus[ion] from informal networks as barriers to their career advancement."

"Signaling theory . . . suggests that organizational decision makers have imperfect information about employees and rely on environmental cues such as employees' social relations to make personnel decisions." Being female with dependents may signal negative attributes that influence superiors' organizational decisions regarding women. Moreover, according to social role theory and the "doctrine of separate spheres," individuals view women as caregivers, and that signals their non-work demands, real or imagined, to organization members. Also, socially sanctioned gender-typical roles influence one's own and others' perceptions of and expectations about the two sexes. On the career front, on one hand, men, attributed masculine qualities of agency, competence, and success, are naturally associated with managerial roles or positions of power and responsibility. On the other hand, women stereotypically attributed feminine qualities of being supportive and nurturing, are less likely to be associated with managerial or high status roles, in turn making them less likely than men to benefit from a network.

Social norms valuing the "male bread-winner," or the idea that "men support the family," signal that men with dependents have a higher need of career support than women, especially those with dependents. This signaling may also suggest that investing in men's initiation and sustenance of networking relationships may be more beneficial. Indeed, research shows that because of differences in social roles and experiences of childrearing between men and women, the impact of childrearing or dependent care on social networks varies by gender. For example, Allison Munch and her colleagues examined "the impact of childrearing on the pattern of social contacts for men and women" by using cross-sectional data from "a probability sample of 1,050 Great Plains residents in 10 towns . . . ." They found "that social network size, contact volume, and composition vary with the age of the youngest child in a family." Childrearing reduced "women's network size and contact volume, while it alter[ed] the composition of men's networks." These results suggest that gender differences in social roles influence career-related outcomes by placing men and women in different social spheres. The influence of childbearing and childrearing to employees' career advancement is therefore crucial to understanding how gender differences in career outcomes may be maintained throughout one's life. Another study on childrearing and its relation to women's and men's networks suggested "that having young children at home decreases women's, but not men's, job-related contacts."

Organizational members may perceive women as having increased family responsibilities, and, therefore, not fitting for or not ready to be integrated into wider professional networks and roles. In this context, we suggest that for women with dependents, mentors can help increase the benefits of networks and decrease the network challenges they face with respect to attitudes toward gender, family, and social hierarchy. From a signaling theory perspective, when a woman has a mentor, signals may be sent to superiors, decision makers, and networks that the woman is indeed legitimate, capable, and fit for professional roles. Apart from signaling, mentors may provide their mentees career and psychosocial support. Career support helps protégés navigate "within the organization and advance [their] careers." This support includes "coaching, sponsoring, providing challenging assignments, protection from organizational politics or harmful individuals, and exposure and visibility to key players in the organization and industry." Psychosocial support, on the other hand, relates to more personal aspects of the relationship; through role modeling, acceptance and confirmation, friendship, and counseling, it aims to build the protégés' self-worth, feelings of competence, and personal and professional identity. In turn, these mentoring experiences can provide an initial link in the development of a network system for the individual. This raises the question whether women with dependents receive increased benefits from having a mentor, as compared to mentored men or mentored women without dependents. And would women with dependents who have a mentor be better able to overcome network challenges as compared to mentored men or mentored women without dependents?

B.   Survey Method

Data used in this study are part of a larger project on career pathways for women to obtain organizational leadership. The survey was administered, beginning in August 2007 and continuing into 2008, to graduates of leading business schools. In the U.S., surveys were sent to 11,291 male and 3,198 female Master of Business Administration (MBA) graduates, 173 female and 274 male Master of Accounting (MAcc) graduates, and 1,393 female and 2,875 male Bachelor of Business Administration (BBA) graduates of the Ross School of Business at the University of Michigan, and 1,643 MBA, MAcc, and BBA graduates of the Warrington College of Business at the University of Florida. Those earning MAcc and BBA degrees were sent surveys so long as at least three and ten years had passed since their graduation, respectively, to allow for sufficient experience to potentially rise in their organizations. In Europe, survey links were sent in a newsletter subscribed by 9,101 graduates of the Cass Business School of City University in London. In addition, a survey firm was hired to solicit additional responses from men and women outside the United States. The firm sent survey invitations to 10,370 men and women who were at least college graduates and were working full-time in Europe and Asia. All surveys were in English. Through the above methods, we received in total 1,516 usable surveys.

The majority of the sample consisted of U.S. respondents (59%); other countries represented in the sample with at least 10 respondents included the United Kingdom, Singapore, Hong Kong, Germany, India, Greece, France, and Thailand. The sample consisted of 69% males, 68% of the sample were between ages 30 and 49, 76.80% were in a committed relationship (married, civil union, or living with a partner), 2% had a two-year bachelor degree, 19.80% had a college four-year bachelor degree, 69.50% had a master degree, 3% had a doctoral degree, and 6% had a professional degree.

* * *

[The study results] suggest[ ] that women with dependents who also have mentors report having benefited from a network more than women with dependents who do not have mentors. Mentoring thus allows women with dependents to benefit most from networks compared to other groups. [The results also] suggest, however, that although mentored women with dependents report benefiting from a network more than when such women did not have mentors, returns diminish when considering overall network challenges or network challenges with respect to gender, family, and social hierarchy. The results suggest that mentoring is more helpful for women without dependents than for women with dependents to overcome network-related challenges. In contrast, for men with dependents, their network challenges are reduced when they have mentors compared to when they do not. Thus, although mentored women with dependents may have access to a beneficial network, they continue to face network-related challenges.

D. Limitations of the Study

As with any research endeavor, this study is not without limitations. We could not gather data directly from mentors about their own demographic characteristics (gender and dependents) and perceptions of women with dependents. Also, we did not go deeper into country differences. Cross-cultural differences in mentoring dynamics and outcomes may influence how mentoring interacts with demographic and context variables. Although we acknowledge that the dynamics of formal and informal mentoring may differ, we included both formal and informal mentoring cases as we did not have a theoretical reason to expect differences between formal and informal mentoring in the research questions and hypotheses examined. Moreover, fewer than 3% of respondents reported having formal mentors. Given that the focus of the study was all types of professional networks, we also did not distinguish between respondents' experiences with alumni networks, organizational networks, or professional associations. Our results are especially interesting because the majority of the sample members had graduate degrees from top schools around the world—yet, women in this sample who had dependents continued to have network challenges, despite having mentors. Nevertheless, one should exercise caution in generalizing the results from our study to employees without a similar educational profile. We also did not consider the number of dependents the study participants had, and treated those with one dependent the same as those with more than one dependent. In addition, our study only considered the network challenges as a bundle of different challenges, taking into account only the average scores, preventing us from having a more nuanced analysis of individual challenges. The data were collected through self-report surveys, and we also used single-item measures for some variables to ensure that the survey was not too long. Finally, the cross-sectional design of the study, where all data were gathered at the same time, does not allow us to make more definitive causal inferences as we did not have the research opportunity to gather longitudinal data.

IV. Implications from the Study

The results of the Pathways Study suggest that employers should be encouraged to provide mentoring for women to help open networking pathways for women to succeed in business. Our study shows that mentoring results in higher returns for women with children or other dependents, at least in terms of benefiting from a network. Women with dependents, however, continue to need organizational and social support to overcome network-related challenges so that they can make the most of their membership in such network. Fortunately, many companies have established mentoring programs for women and minorities in place. Our search of the websites of the Fortune 500 companies disclosed forty-two such plans. . . . Perhaps more investment needs to be made in the area of diversity training and sensitivity to the unique contingencies that impinge on the career paths chosen by women with dependents. Mentoring would be one plan to not only promote diversity in the workforce, but to also help employers overcome challenges minorities face with respect to career enhancing resources such as networks.

A. Recommended Governmental Interventions: OFCCP and EEOC

It is also possible for a government entity, such as the Office of Federal Contract Compliance Programs ("OFCCP") or Equal Employment Opportunity Commission ("EEOC"), to impose mentoring programs. The OFCCP might, through active monitoring of diversity, insist that government contractors adopt mentoring programs where gender diversity in management is lacking.

The EEOC recently strengthened its systemic litigation system, which could mean that employers will be defending more discrimination cases that involve many employees. Additionally, the EEOC may pursue litigation even when employees may not due to arbitration agreements. Furthermore, mentoring programs could be required as part of settlements to address the lack of advancement of women. Similarly, mentoring programs could be recommended as part of the remedy when companies have been found liable for gender discrimination. Moreover, mentoring programs have the potential to provide a more fair and equitable approach to advancement in organizations, while avoiding contention.

B. Recommended Governmental Interventions: The SEC

Another way the government could encourage companies to increase representation without forcing a quota is for the Securities & Exchange Commission (SEC) to make gender diversity a priority. This would help companies and society benefit from diversity.

The SEC already has the infrastructure in place to pursue this recommendation. For instance, it adopted a diversity disclosure requirement for proxy statements in 2010. Companies are required to state whether diversity was a factor in considering board candidates, how diversity was considered, and the effectiveness of its diversity policy if it had one. Diversity, however, is undefined. The SEC could now require companies to disclose whether they have a diversity policy and whether gender is a consideration. This disclosure would likely spur more companies to adopt gender diversity policies. It would be consistent with the stress on board independence and with the goal of maximizing shareholder wealth. It would also be consistent with the recommendations of the Congressional Glass Ceiling Commission, which looked at artificial barriers hindering advancement to mid- and senior-level positions. Its recommendations included demonstration of the CEO's commitment to diversity, inclusion of diversity in all strategic business plans, accountability of managers for progress, use of affirmative action as a tool for selection, promotion, and retention of qualified individuals, and implementation of mentorship programs to help women overcome barriers including lack of information, visibility, and resources. Once diversity is embraced, mentoring programs are likely to follow. Mentoring programs are one of the most accessible tools companies have used to help achieve diversity goals.

C.   Recommended Intervention of the Courts and Arbitrators

The authors have previously recommended that judges and arbitrators consider requiring firms to provide mentoring programs as part of the remedy ordered for violations of Title VII. Equitable relief is permitted under Title VII and mentoring may be particularly effective where there has been disparate treatment. A mentoring program coupled with appropriate changes in human resources practices may help women successfully navigate the pathways to positions of leadership.

V.   Conclusion

Various studies have suggested mentoring and networking as means to improve career outcomes, but past research has not examined how mentoring influences networking outcomes for men and women with and without dependents. The Pathways Study provides evidence that for women with dependents mentoring can improve the benefits women experience in their networks. Our results, however, also suggest that women with dependents, even with mentors, report higher network-related challenges than do mentored women without dependents. Mentoring helped reduce network-related challenges when women did not have dependents and when men had dependents. Although the good news is that mentoring does help women (at least those without dependents), women with dependents seem to especially need increased developmental investment. It may be that having dependents sends negative signals to senior decision makers and mentors, and continue to pose challenges.

Thus, organizations and mentors could do more to understand the career dynamics of and reduce the challenges faced by these women.

Past research also suggests that women who are married, with or without children or other dependents, have more difficulty gaining mentors. From our data, too, it is reasonable to conclude that it is precisely these women who need mentoring most. This may be because mentoring tends to boost confidence and provide career clarity and satisfaction. It may also be that a mentor can provide role modeling for women balancing work and family lives.

Perhaps with proper mentoring, more women with dependents will have the opportunity to achieve career success and to find pathways to positions of organizational leadership. And as delineated above, there are a number of ways the private sector, the government, the courts, and arbitrators could facilitate this goal.

* * *

MaryAnn Grover, *They Still Just Don't Get It: Lessons of the #MeToo Movement Through the Lens of Supreme Court Nominations*
22 Richmond Public Interest Law Review 123 (2019)

Grover authored this piece as a 3L student at the University of Richmond Law School while serving as Editor-in-Chief of the Richmond Public Interest Law Review.

Those who fear public speaking have no difficulty imaging the nightmare of standing before a group of twenty-one people, fully exposed. The pure terror of knowing you have no control over what happens next and the understanding that this might all be for nothing is likely not far from your mind. Yet, you stand there, fully exposed, waiting to be bombarded with questions, probed about the most traumatic experiences of your past. This nightmare was a reality for Professor Anita Hill and Dr. Christine Blasey Ford as they testified before the Senate Judiciary Committee accusing now-Justice Clarence Thomas and now-Justice Brett Kavanaugh, respectively, of sexual misconduct, just as it is a reality for each victim of sexual harassment or assault, if they confront their assaulter or seek to bring them to justice. The #MeToo Movement has encouraged many survivors of sexual violence to come forward to acknowledge their assault and name their assaulter. It remains to be seen, though, the full effect that the #MeToo Movement has had on those in positions of great power, like those nominated to the Supreme Court of the United States.

Article II of the United State Constitution grants the President the power to nominate "and by and with the advice and consent of the Senate . . . appoint . . . judges of the Supreme Court." This grant of power, to advise and consent—or not—is most importantly wielded in the Senate Judiciary Committee. Once the Senate Judiciary Committee favorably recommends a nominee, it is rare for the entire body to not approve the nominee. In 1991, the members of the Senate Judiciary Committee and those of the full body were accused of "just not getting it" when Professor Anita Hill levied charges of sexual harassment against Justice Clarence Thomas. In response to similar accusations by Dr. Christine Blasey Ford against Justice Brett Kavanaugh, Professor Hill authored an article in which she asserted that because of "years of hindsight, mounds of evidence of the prevalence and harm that sexual violence causes individuals[,]" and the #MeToo Movement, " 'not getting it' is not an option for our elected representatives."

With that assertion, Professor Hill raises questions about how much society has actually learned from her experience and the #MeToo Movement, why the lessons we have learned in the #MeToo Movement seem to fall short when it comes to Supreme Court nominations, and what impact that will have going forward. This article seeks to address those questions. In Part I, this article analyzes Professor Hill's experience stemming from her allegations against Justice Thomas and discusses what we should have learned from such an experience. In Part II, this article assesses the growth of the #MeToo Movement and what we thought we learned from the Movement. Part III of this article applies what we should have learned from Professor Anita Hill's experience and what we thought we learned from the #MeToo Movement to Dr. Ford's experience challenging the nomination of Justice Brett Kavanaugh. This section also explores the question of what we still have to learn and makes four recommendations as to how—drawing from Professor Hill's experience, the #MeToo Movement, and Dr. Ford's experience—society can move forward, respecting the experiences of survivors of sexual harassment and assault. These lessons include the need for definitive procedures in the handling of sexual misconduct claims against judicial nominees, the need to understand and respect that each survivor processes and reacts to their assault differently, the need for additional leadership opportunities for women whose experiences tend to allow them to better support survivors of sexual violence, and the realization that these lessons cannot be confined to vocal supporters but must be taught, even to dissenters, in order for these lessons to truly impact society's treatment of sexual violence and survivors of sexual violence.

I.   THE LESSONS OF PROFESSOR ANITA HILL

Anita Hill was a law professor at the University of Oklahoma when President George H.W. Bush nominated now-Justice Clarence Thomas to the Supreme Court of the United States on July 1, 1991. She had previously worked with Justice Thomas at the United States Department of Education and the Equal Employment Opportunity Commission (EEOC). It was at those agencies, one of which is tasked with investigating and charging claims of sexual harassment, that Professor Hill alleged that Justice Thomas sexually harassed her repeatedly. While sexual harassment was prohibited as sex discrimination under Title VII of the Civil Rights Act of 1964, "[e]vidence that sexual harassment was regarded as unimportant by the Senate abounded in the events leading up to the hearings concerning Professor Anita Hill's charges." In fact, upon hearing the accusations against Justice Thomas—that he described pornography and genitalia and repeatedly asked Professor Hill on dates—Senator Howard M. Metzenbaum (D-OH) stated, "[i]f that's sexual harassment, half the senators on Capitol Hill could be accused." Furthermore, even though Professor Hill submitted a statement detailing the harassment to the Senate Judiciary Committee on September 23, 1991, her statement was not shared with the remainder of the Senate until the existence of the statement was picked up by the press and public sentiment surrounding the statement forced the Senate Judiciary Committee to take Professor Hill's charges seriously.

This initial political misstep in the investigation of Professor Hill's charges was compounded by the Senate Judiciary Committee's widely-recognized mishandling of Professor Hill's hearing held on October 11, 1991. The hearing was marred by attacks on Professor Hill personally, her credibility, and her personal response to her harassment. The missteps of the Committee are detailed below, followed by a discussion of what society should have learned from such missteps.

A.   A Hearing Marred by Ignorance

An all-white male Senate Judiciary Committee, that had little understanding of sexual harassment or assault and its effects on survivors, conducted Professor Hill's hearing. Professor Hill was attacked for not having come forward sooner, for moving with Justice Thomas from the Department of Education to the EEOC after she thought she had put an end to the harassment, and for maintaining a professional relationship with Justice Thomas after the alleged harassment. The Senate Judiciary Committee failed to recognize, though, that Professor Hill did exactly what study after study says most women do when placed in such a vulnerable position: she sought to "find a way for her to avoid the harassment but keep her job." In fact, it would have been "unreasonable to have expected

Professor Hill to jeopardize her career by alienating Justice Thomas after leaving his employ."

Her hearing, or rather her "rigorous interrogation," was proof enough of what happens when a woman accuses a powerful man—soon to be one of the most powerful men in the country—of such misconduct. Throughout the hearing, Professor Hill was portrayed as a "woman scorned or as someone who had fantasized her sexual desirability." Senator Arlen Specter (RPA) went so far as to accuse Professor Hill of perjury and suggest that "the accusations were the result of Hill seeking revenge because Thomas didn't show enough sexual interest in her." Senators levied these personal attacks while Professor Hill was unable to present all of the evidence that supported her allegations. "[C]rucially, three women who wanted to corroborate Hill's testimony were not allowed to testify before Congress."

Ultimately, after not actually listening to Professor Hill's testimony and only being read "her edited words," Justice Thomas issued a forceful reply. He denied "each and every single allegation against" him and accused liberals on the Senate Judiciary Committee of "a high-tech lynching." The next Tuesday, October 15, 1991, Justice Thomas was confirmed to the United States Supreme Court by one of the narrowest margins in modern times, 52–48.

B. What We Should Have Learned

Prior to Dr. Christine Blasey Ford's testimony before the Senate Judiciary Committee, Professor Hill acknowledged, "[t]here is no way to redo 1991, but there are ways to do better." First among those ways, according to Professor Hill, is demonstrating appreciation for "both the seriousness of sexual harassment claims and the need for public confidence in the character of a nominee to the Supreme Court." The Senate Judiciary Committee failed in these areas in 1991. This failure and the subsequent confirmation of Justice Thomas sent a clear message to many women: "Who cared if we, like Anita Hill, spoke out about sexual harassment on the job? It wouldn't get us anywhere."

To many other women, though, Professor Hill gave them the courage they needed to speak up about sexual harassment in the workplace. In fact, between 1991 and 1993, sexual harassment civil lawsuits almost doubled. This helped shift society's perception of sexual harassment from "just the way it was" to a serious harm. By recognizing sexual harassment as a serious harm, society was able to "name experiences," like sexual violence, date rape, marital rape, and discrimination, and "to link these private moments of discomfort, pain, and terror to political and legal wrongs." In this way, the Thomas/Hill hearings should have taught society that actions should have consequences, even when those actions were taken by powerful men and seemingly rewarded by a group of powerful white men.

Furthermore, the hearing and the subsequent backlash at the treatment of Professor Hill should have taught society that women deserve to be heard and they will not be fully silenced. This was evident when, in 1992, an unprecedented number of women ran for and were elected to public office, in part because of outrage at the way Professor Hill was treated during her hearing. As a result of this election, 1992 was dubbed the "Year of the Woman." The "Year of the Woman" and the lessons society should have learned from Professor Hill's hearing, though, seemed to only last an instant, as the #MeToo Movement gained prominence only twenty-five years later and demonstrated how little society had actually evolved.

II. THE LESSONS OF THE #METOO MOVEMENT

On October 5, 2017, Jodi Kantor and Megan Twohey published the story that propelled a movement to the front of the nation's consciousness. It was on that day that the world first learned of nearly three decades of undisclosed sexual assault and harassment allegations against Harvey Weinstein. Throughout those three decades, "after being confronted with allegations including sexual harassment and unwanted physical contact, Mr. Weinstein . . . reached at least eight settlements with women." Ten days after the story broke, actress Alyssa Milano invited her Twitter followers to tweet #MeToo if they had ever experienced harassment or assault, and so began the national phenomenon. The #MeToo hashtag was created by Tarana Burke in 2007 to support survivors of sexual harassment and violence, but did not rise to national prominence until Milano's tweet in 2017. "Over the next few weeks, millions of women decided that sharing the hashtag was worth the ensuing sense of vulnerability, the inevitable skepticism, and, for many, the emotional and physical risk."

The #MeToo Movement and the lessons society has learned from it have not yet proven to have as short of a lifespan as those lessons society should have learned from Anita Hill's experience. Instead, the Movement has been championed by movers and shakers in Hollywood, on Capitol Hill, and throughout the world. Time Magazine even declared "The Silence Breakers" of the #MeToo Movement its Person of the Year for 2017. This is not to say, though, that society has learned all it can from this movement. The Movement continues to grow and transform. Below, this Article discusses the progress made since the Movement gained prominence in October 2017 and analyzes the lessons we thought we learned from the Movement that need to be reinforced in light of the Kavanaugh/Ford hearings.

A. The Movement's Impact

Between October 2017 and October 2018, "sexual harassment reports to the Equal Employment Opportunity Commission [went] up 12 percent, after years of remaining steady." This is a sign of what many have come to recognize as a refusal to tolerate such misconduct any further. However, it remains unclear how committed society is to this position, particularly in light of how contentious and partisan the Movement has become.

Regardless of the political implications of the Movement, though, it is impossible to deny its impact on many working-women. This impact is best demonstrated by a recent New York Times study that found that, since October 2017, "at least 200 prominent men have lost their jobs after public allegations of sexual harassment." Some of these men have also faced criminal charges for their sexual misconduct, and "nearly half of the men who have been replaced were succeeded by women." These women successfully created more #MeToo friendly workplaces throughout the country, as studies show that female leaders tend to "create more respectful work environments, where harassment is less likely to flourish and where women feel more comfortable reporting it." Furthermore, these women leaders are more likely to hire and promote other women and pay them equally, allowing these other women to likewise enter leadership positions.

The progress of the #MeToo Movement is not limited only to those able to take advantage of leadership opportunities when prominent men are removed from their positions. Instead, the #MeToo Movement has led to the creation of the TIME'S UP Legal Defense Fund, among other organizations, which provide funding and services to women who are seeking aid and legal services in the face of sexual harassment or misconduct. Furthermore, advances in the #MeToo Movement have created "an opportunity [for educators] to talk about serious and relevant issues like consent and sexual harassment" in the classroom. Thus, the #MeToo Movement began a culture shift, but, as the Kavanaugh hearings have demonstrated, that cultural shift has not completely taken hold in the highest echelons of society where it is most critical that it does.

* * *

III. THE LESSONS OF DR. CHRISTINE BLASEY FORD

Dr. Christine Blasey Ford is a psychology professor at Palo Alto University and a research psychologist at Stanford University School of Medicine. She was living in California and acting in this capacity when reporters appeared at her home and her job asking questions about a letter she had written to Senator Diane Feinstein (D-CA) detailing her sexual assault by Supreme Court nominee Brett Kavanaugh. Throughout the summer of 2018, Dr. Ford contacted the Washington Post, her United States Representative, and her Senator about her assault, but she requested confidentiality and refused to speak on the record, hoping to avoid being labeled a liar and experiencing the pain Professor Hill had suffered over twenty-five years earlier. "As the story snowballed, Ford said, she heard people repeating inaccuracies about her and, with the visits from reporters, felt her privacy being chipped away." Thus, because the publicity she was trying to avoid could no longer be evaded, Dr. Ford decided to come forward to tell her story. It was then, in an interview with the Washington Post, that she detailed how a drunk Kavanaugh pinned her to a bed and laughed while "grinding his body against her and clumsily attempting to pull off her one-piece bathing suit and the clothing she wore over it," as she tried to scream for help. Following Dr. Ford's allegations, two other women came forward to accuse Kavanaugh of sexual misconduct. While Dr. Ford was given an opportunity to be heard by the Senate Judiciary Committee, Deborah Ramirez and Julie Swetnick were denied an opportunity to testify.

A.   A Hearing Reminiscent of 1991

On September 26, 2018, Dr. Ford pledged to "tell the truth, the whole truth, nothing but the truth, so help [her] God" before testifying in front of the Senate Judiciary Committee. Leading up to her hearing, Dr. Ford repeatedly requested that the FBI investigate her claim, much like Professor Hill's claim was over twenty-five years ago; but her request was summarily denied as merely a delay tactic. This denial of a full investigation represented a shift in the mentality and strategy of the Senate Judiciary Committee from 1991 to 2018. No longer could members of the Senate Judiciary Committee level personal attacks against Dr. Ford, the #MeToo Movement made sure of that, but they could deny the full and fair investigation that Dr. Ford requested. Dr. Ford admitted that she did not have answers to questions about how she got to the party and where it took place, as she did not remember as much as she would like to. She requested an FBI investigation because of these gaps in her memory. But her request was denied, as she reassured the Committee that "the details about that night that bring me here today are ones I will never forget. They have been seared into my memory and have haunted me episodically as an adult."

Like Professor Hill, Dr. Ford's motives in coming forward when she did were the subject of great criticism, even as she detailed her fear of telling her parents that at age fifteen she went to a house party where she drank beer with boys. Her fear immediately following the assault is the same fear that silenced Professor Hill when she was sexually harassed, and it is the same fear that keeps many survivors from reporting their own assaults. Even that fear, though, was little compared to her "greatest fears" of what would happen when she actually accused Kavanaugh. In her written testimony, Dr. Ford testified,

> [m]y family and I have been the target of constant harassment and death threats. I have been called the most vile and hateful names imaginable . . . My family and I were forced to move out of our home. Since September 16, my family and I have been living in various secure locales.

This is not even to mention that she has "had to relive [her] trauma in front of the entire world, and [has] seen [her] life picked apart by people on television, in the media, and in [the Senate] who have never met [her] or spoken with [her]." Common experience and numerous studies demonstrate that Dr. Ford is not alone in these fears. Even those whose accusations do not occur on such a prominent stage fear similar repercussions. It is no wonder that victims often remain silent, particularly when they see Professor Hill and Dr. Ford take a stand only for Justice Thomas and Justice Kavanaugh to be confirmed shortly thereafter.

* * *

B.   What We Still Have to Learn

Even as Professor Hill admonished that " '[n]ot getting it' isn't an option for our elected representatives . . . our senators must get it right," it is clear that our senators did not get the Kavanaugh/Ford hearings right. That does not mean, though, that nothing was learned from the hearings. Instead, the Kavanaugh/Ford hearings highlighted four lessons that society must learn in order to "get it right" and fully effectuate the purposes of the #MeToo Movement. First, defined processes are necessary for vetting sexual harassment and assault claims that arise both during the confirmation process and in the workplace generally because such processes can serve as a check on the most powerful members of society. Second, in order to fully realize the purposes of the #MeToo Movement, society must recognize and respect that each survivor processes their assault differently. This understanding can be better internalized by utilizing the third lesson: because of their unique experiences, more women must be provided leadership opportunities. Finally, and perhaps most crucially, the Kavanaugh/Ford hearings have taught us that the #MeToo Movement cannot occur in a vacuum. Allies are necessary to the success of the movement. Below the contours of each lesson are discussed in turn.

* * *

3.   Women, Because of Their Unique Experiences, Must be Given More Leadership Opportunities

The recognition that survivors experience their assaults in their own way can be better realized by utilizing the third lesson of the #MeToo Movement: society must provide women more leadership opportunities. Regardless of whether women have personally experienced sexual misconduct, they at least understand the fear of it, and this understanding allows women to create more respectful environments where the goals of the #MeToo Movement can be better realized.

This need for women in leadership positions was made clear when Dr. Ford faced a Senate Judiciary Committee "dominated by white males, including all 11 of its Republicans." On the Democratic side of the Committee, Ranking Member Feinstein acknowledged that "[f]or any woman, sharing an experience involving sexual assault—particularly when it involves a politically connected man with influence, authority and power—is extraordinarily difficult." On the other hand, the all-white male Republican side of the Committee hired Rachel Mitchell, a female prosecutor who specialized in sexual assault cases, to question Dr. Ford. This served to highlight the Republicans as "a group of men unwilling to ask any questions of a vulnerable woman." Even when Dr. Ford expressed a desire for committee members to "engage directly" with her, the Republican committee members refused to do so. Only during Justice Kavanaugh's testimony did Senator Lindsey Graham (R-SC) interrupt Ms. Mitchell to deliver a furious rant in defense of Kavanaugh. "After Graham spoke, Mitchell was denied a single additional question" throughout the remainder of Kavanaugh's testimony. This difference in approaches taken to the Kavanaugh/Ford hearings by female committee members on one side the aisle compared to male committee members on the other side of the aisle demonstrates how critical it is to have women in leadership positions.

Study after study has shown the positive impact women in leadership have on their environments. By bringing their life experiences and perspectives to organizations, women "create more respectful work environments, where harassment is less likely to flourish and where women feel more comfortable reporting" harassment. This impact is not limited to the corporate world. In fact, "[i]n government, women have been shown to be more collaborative and bipartisan, and promote more policies supporting women, children and social welfare." By providing women more leadership opportunities throughout society, and particularly in institutions that have traditionally perpetuated a patriarchal focus, the goals of the #MeToo Movement can be better realized and accusations of sexual misconduct can be better vetted, while protecting survivors' needs.

* * *

It is time for society to take seriously the allegations of sexual misconduct, and to truly learn the lessons that the Thomas/Hill hearing, the #MeToo Movement, and the Kavanaugh/Ford hearings have tried to teach us. Those lessons have a staying power to which society can no longer turn a blind eye. In order to effectuate the lessons of these events and the #MeToo Movement, society must develop definitive procedures for handling claims of sexual misconduct; must recognize that all survivors process their assaults differently and respect those differences; must provide more leadership opportunities for women; and must bring everyone into the fold in a unified fight against sexual assault and sexual harassment. Until that occurs, I fear society will continue this trend, making the same mistakes over and over again.

Hannah Brenner, *A Title IX Conundrum: Are Campus Visitors Protected From Sexual Assault?*

104 Iowa Law Review 93 (2018)

Brenner is one of the authors of this casebook. You can read more about her background in the Introduction.

Title IX was designed to ensure equal access to education. Subsequent to the passage of this federal law, a series of U.S. Supreme Court cases defined the parameters of institutional liability. These cases complement the Department of Education's Office for Civil Rights' regulations that clarify the requirements Title IX imposes on schools. What remains unclear despite this legislative, judicial, and administrative guidance, however, is whether an individual must be a student or official member of a particular institution where the discrimination takes place to benefit from protection of the statute and ultimately have standing to sue a school for its alleged deliberate indifference under Title IX. At the core of this question is how to determine if someone belongs—are they an insider or outsider—for purposes of securing the protection of this federal law.

At a recent faculty talk, a respected colleague shared a story that illustrates the impact of the status differential at issue in these cases. He recalled a college party that took place at the liberal arts school he attended decades earlier. At the end of a drunken evening, a girl from a neighboring school, known to none of the partygoers before they met that evening, passed out on the couch. Unable to wake her, and afraid she might be at risk of serious harm, the students, for lack of alternatives, called a psychology professor (whose number they happened to have on hand) to help deal with the stranger who they feared was in peril. The professor inquired of the students who this girl was and what they wanted him to do; they reacted detachedly and with indifference, stating "she's not one of us." Fortunately for the young woman, the good professor's opinion differed. He replied to the students, "though that might at one point have been true . . . she belongs now; she is one of you," and then treated her reaction to mixing alcohol and Quaaludes with kind attention before dropping her off at home later that morning.

In this same way, individuals who are non-students at a given university sometimes find themselves in a setting where they may not technically "belong," at least insofar as being officially enrolled at the school. But because of the circumstances in which they find themselves— seeking help from a university physician, visiting a library, attending a performance on campus, delivering a guest lecture, participating in a sport recruiting event—their status inevitably shifts from outsider to insider. When this happens, are these individuals not entitled to the same protections and rights as others who might "belong" more officially to the institution? Is their presence on campus, even temporarily, not enough to trigger protection under Title IX? Because colleges and universities have become less insular and more open in a variety of contexts to a wide-range of individuals—some of whom lack official connection to the school—the question of institutional accountability and liability to this "outsider" class becomes increasingly relevant.

In the most obvious and narrow expression of their purpose, colleges and universities exist to educate their enrolled students. But this education is accomplished by engagement with those both within and outside of the institutions and their mission therefore deserves a more expansive definition.

* * *

If the promotion of safe campus communities is a priority, and the extension of the right to be free from discrimination in accessing the offerings of a university a goal of federal law, it seems irrelevant, discriminatory, and at odds with Title IX to distinguish among the "kind" of victim who is entitled to protection. After all, when sexual violence is allowed to proliferate on campus, the entire community of students, faculty, and staff is affected.

* * *

This Article seeks to add to the ongoing and complex Title IX conversation by exposing a novel, yet very real conundrum: *To whom* does Title IX apply? Should students who are officially enrolled in an institution be provided different protections than those who are not? Are non-students who interact within the university context simply left out of the spectrum of Title IX protections? And what sort of campus safety dynamic is created if we distinguish between victims when extending protections of the federal law?

* * *

III. SEXUAL VIOLENCE IN THE QUASI-CLOSED INSTITUTIONAL SETTING OF HIGHER EDUCATION

Sexual violence occurs across all sectors of society. It reaches into Congress, Hollywood, the legal profession, media, prisons, politics, the military, and of course, higher education. Its prevalence results in characterization of the world in which we live as a "rape culture." Perhaps never before have the voices of victims of sexual violence been so loud, powerful, and strong as they are now, against the backdrop of the movement widely known as #MeToo, in which victims have come forward in droves to share their stories publicly.

Some of these settings in which sexual violence occurs bear special characteristics that argue for classification as closed, or quasi-closed systems, which sets them apart from the broader community. This distinction matters because the context shapes the experiences of survivors of sexual violence as it relates to the reporting, investigation, and related adjudication of complaints.

IV. EXPOSING THE TITLE IX CONUNDRUM: WHOSE RIGHTS?

Each year, colleges and universities court star high school athletes, vying for their enrollment. Consider the case of K.T., a high school soccer recruit, who was invited to visit the campus of Culver-Stockton College ("College") in Canton, Missouri. Her visit was part of an "athletic activity" that was "sponsored and promoted by the school." While she was on campus, she was taken to a party at the Lambda Chi Alpha fraternity house, where she was sexually assaulted by a student who was enrolled at the college. Other individuals present at the time reported the incident to the school the same weekend the assault took place and K.T.'s family reported the incident to law enforcement a week later. The College did not commence an investigation and did not respond or attempt to take corrective action other than to cancel a meeting with K.T. and her parents once they learned of the nature of the requested meeting. K.T. filed a lawsuit against the school under Title IX relying on a theory of the school's deliberate indifference, but the case was dismissed based on her non-student status.

* * *

At first glance, the significance of this inquiry might be overlooked. After all, some of the same rights protected by Title IX can arguably be reached *vis-a-vis* tort law, criminal law, or by filing a grievance with the Office of Civil Rights ("OCR"). Individuals who are sexually victimized and lack an official connection to the education institution where the abuse occurred do in fact have other avenues of legal recourse, but these alternate avenues serve different goals and interests and have not always been entirely useful or productive for victims.

* * *

The tort law system also presents an avenue for victims of campus sexual violence to seek redress for the harms perpetrated against them by allowing for the pursuit of money damages from educational institutions and individual assailants; a tort-based approach is recommended by some scholars, but it can nonetheless prove challenging for a myriad of reasons, including limits on liability imposed by the intentional nature of torts and governmental immunity. And while there is also a Title IX grievance procedure available through the OCR, its focus is largely on compliance and eliminating future harms at the institution. This option by itself does not provide a sufficient remedy; while one outcome might be for the OCR to require a school to review its handling of a particular case, it is largely focused on institutional compliance with the mandates of Title IX. To be sure, "such a process does not provide the same deterrent effect that a civil suit for money damages provides." Therefore, Title IX and its private right of action remains a valuable tool that serves multiple ends: compensating victims when a school responds with deliberate indifference to acts sexual violence, and cultivating safer campus communities.

VI. RESOLVING THE TITLE IX CONUNDRUM

The conundrum of who exactly is entitled to protection under Title IX deserves serious consideration and demands clarification in law and policy, especially given the widespread prevalence and incidence of sexual violence on college campuses and the existence of Title IX as a viable tool to address this problem. It is an important threshold inquiry that must be resolved before courts can consider whether a school indeed acted with deliberate indifference to reports of sexual violence. There is little if any disagreement with the idea that the statute was designed to address discrimination on the basis of sex and thereby preserve access to education for those who are participating in the programs and activities of a university. Questions arise, however, related to the extent of Title IX's reach and the ways in which it applies. In this current inquiry, a very real conundrum exists as to exactly how far the statute extends and exactly who is entitled to its protections. Resolving this conundrum in the face of limited case law and legislative history proves challenging, especially given the incredible newness and novelty of even the question itself.

* * *

It seems inherently reasonable and within the letter of the Title IX statute to extend the federal law's protections to those who participate in a school's programs and activities, even if that participation is temporary. There are a number of theories that support such a conclusion: (1) statutory interpretation of Title IX; (2) analogous judicial opinions in other related contexts; and (3) constitutional equal protection concerns that arise from creating separate classes of victims.

* * *

VII. CONCLUSION

Assuming a victim of sexual violence believes that an institution acted with deliberate indifference in its response to her Title IX complaint, making the case that she has standing to file a lawsuit against the school becomes a critical threshold matter. The judicially defined standard for imposing liability in Title IX cases has largely been created from cases involving parties who are all members of a university community, as students, teachers, and staff. Therefore, it seems that a legal assumption has been made that only official members of a school have a right of action under the federal law and this assumption has not been subject to significant judicial scrutiny. The existing case law almost exclusively involves enrolled student or employees, and courts have not specifically been called on to address the rights of outsiders beyond the two cases discussed throughout this Article.

Colleges and universities may not be entirely "total institutions" in the way that Goffman and others might contemplate. That is, they are not so completely isolated as to label them entirely closed, and they in fact thrive on the constant influx of participants from the outside; thus, they are better conceptualized as quasi-closed systems. One of the features of a university that distinguishes it from other more traditional closed settings like prison is the practice of having non-system members regularly participate in its programs and activities. High school students routinely make campus visits as they decide which school to attend; community members attend lectures, book signings, and other cultural and sporting events; patients visit doctor's offices and medical treatment centers; and summer camps hold sessions on campuses where participants become an integral part of the community. This is but a narrow list of ways non-university members interface with members of the university community officially, albeit temporarily, on a daily basis.

Colleges and universities anticipate that those from the "outside" will inevitably, and necessarily, make their way in. Perhaps for this reason alone it makes good sense to resist the temptation to create different theories of liability for students and non-students and make available the protections of Title IX to those who participate in the programs and activities, broadly defined, of institutions of higher education.

* * *

CONCLUSION

■ ■ ■

One of our goals in writing this book has been to expose you to various theories of leadership and law while simultaneously encouraging you to explore intersections of gender, race, class, power and law. Another goal has been to identify post-feminism discrimination that the legal system does not yet address. We also have tried to inspire you with the stories of transformative leaders woven throughout the text. It is our hope that this book will serve as a building block in the foundation of your own pursuit of leadership and as a catalyst toward our collective effort to transform the world into one in which our leaders reflect the diversity of the public they serve.

APPENDIX

BIBLIOGRAPHY OF TRANSFORMATIVE LEADERS AUTOBIOGRAPHIES/ BIOGRAPHIES

■ ■ ■

This list of autobiographies and biographies represents but a fraction of the stories about transformative leaders. We hope it will serve as a starting place for inspiration and encourage you to add your own contributions.

GLORIA ALLRED, FIGHT BACK AND WIN: MY THIRTY-YEAR FIGHT AGAINST INJUSTICE—AND HOW YOU CAN WIN YOUR OWN BATTLES (2006).

PAUL ANDERSON, JANET RENO: DOING THE RIGHT THING (1994).

BARBARA BABCOCK, WOMAN LAWYER: THE TRIALS OF CLARA FOLTZ (2011).

JOAN BISKUPIC, SANDRA DAY O'CONNOR: HOW THE FIRST WOMAN ON THE SUPREME COURT BECAME ITS MOST INFLUENTIAL JUSTICE (2009).

JOHN CAMPBELL, THE IRON LADY: MARGARET THATCHER, FROM GROCER'S DAUGHTER TO PRIME MINISTER (2011).

MARCIA CLARK, WITHOUT A DOUBT (2016).

HILLARY RODHAM CLINTON, HARD CHOICES (2014).

HILLARY RODHAM CLINTON, WHAT HAPPENED (2017).

JANE SHERRON DE HART, RUTH BADER GINSBURG: A LIFE (2018).

ANGELA DAVIS, ANGELA DAVIS: AN AUTOBIOGRAPHY (1974).

WENDY DAVIS, FORGETTING TO BE AFRAID: A MEMOIR (2015).

SHIRIN EBADI, UNTIL WE ARE FREE: MY FIGHT FOR HUMAN RIGHTS IN IRAN (2016).

CLAUDIA POND EYLEY & DAN SALMON, HELEN CLARK: INSIDE STORIES (2015).

BETTY FRIEDAN, LIFE SO FAR: A MEMOIR (2001).

JANE M. FRIEDMAN, AMERICA'S FIRST WOMAN LAWYER: THE BIOGRAPHY OF MYRA BRADWELL (1993).

DIANE CAROL FUJINO, HEARTBEAT OF STRUGGLE: THE REVOLUTIONARY LIFE OF YURI KOCHIYAMA (2005).

MARY GABRIEL, NOTORIOUS VICTORIA: THE UNCENSORED LIFE OF VICTORIA WOODHULL—VISIONARY, SUFFRAGIST, AND FIRST WOMAN TO RUN FOR PRESIDENT (1998).

RUTH BADER GINSBURG, MY OWN WORDS (2016).

PENNY HARRINGTON, TRIUMPH OF SPIRIT: AN AUTOBIOGRAPHY (1999).

ANNA HAYES, WITHOUT PRECEDENT: THE LIFE OF SUSIE MARSHALL SHARP (2008).

ANITA HILL, SPEAKING TRUTH TO POWER (1997).

LINDA HIRSHMAN, SISTERS IN LAW: HOW SANDRA DAY O'CONNOR AND RUTH BADER GINSBURG WENT TO THE SUPREME COURT AND CHANGED THE WORLD (2016).

IRIN CARMON & SHANA KNIZHNIK, NOTORIOUS RBG: THE LIFE AND TIMES OF RUTH BADER GINSBURG (2015).

CORETTA S KING, MY LIFE, MY LOVE, MY LEGACY (2017).

QUEEN LILIUOKALANI AND DAVID FORBES, HAWAII'S STORY (2013).

RACHEL LLOYD, GIRLS LIKE US: FIGHTING FOR A WORLD WHERE GIRLS ARE NOT FOR SALE, AN ACTIVIST FINDS HER CALLING AND HEALS HERSELF (2011).

PATRICIA C. MCKISSACK & FREDRICK MCKISSACK, SOJOURNER TRUTH: AIN'T I A WOMAN (1994).

JACQUELINE A. MCLEOD, DAUGHTER OF THE EMPIRE STATE: THE LIFE OF JUDGE JANE BOLIN (2011).

MARY J MOSSMAN, THE FIRST WOMEN LAWYERS: A COMPARATIVE STUDY OF GENDER, LAW, AND THE LEGAL PROFESSIONS (2006).

DENVER NICKS, PRIVATE: BRADLEY MANNING, WIKILEAKS, AND THE BIGGEST EXPOSURE OF OFFICIAL SECRETS IN AMERICAN HISTORY (2012).

JILL NORGREN, BELVA LOCKWOOD: THE WOMAN WHO WOULD BE PRESIDENT (2007).

MICHELLE OBAMA, BECOMING. (2018).

ANN H. PETERSEN. TOO FAT, TOO SLUTTY, TOO LOUD: THE RISE AND REIGN OF THE UNRULY WOMAN (2017).

CONNIE RICE, POWER CONCEDES NOTHING: ONE WOMAN'S QUEST FOR SOCIAL JUSTICE IN AMERICA, FROM THE COURTROOM TO THE KILL ZONES (2012).

BETTY ROBERTS, WITH GRIT AND BY GRACE: BREAKING TRAILS IN POLITICS AND LAW, A MEMOIR (2008).

LIZ ROBERTS, FIRST LADY: FROM BOYHOOD TO WOMANHOOD: THE INCREDIBLE STORY OF NEW ZEALAND'S SEX-CHANGE PIONEER LIZ ROBERTS (2015).

MARY BETH ROGERS, BARBARA JORDON: AMERICAN HERO (1998).

SALLY KNAPP, ELEANOR ROOSEVELT: A BIOGRAPHY (2007).

ASSATA SHAKUR, ASSATA: AN AUTOBIOGRAPHY (2001).

JUDY SHEINDLIN, DON'T PEE ON MY LEG AND TELL ME IT'S RAINING: AMERICA'S TOUGHEST FAMILY COURT JUDGE SPEAKS OUT (1997).

CORNELIA SORABJI, INDIA CALLING: THE MEMORIES OF CORNELIA SORABJI, INDIA'S FIRST WOMAN BARRISTER (2001).

SONIA SOTOMAYOR, MY BELOVED WORLD (2013).

PETER SLEVIN, MICHELLE OBAMA: A LIFE (2015).

EVAN THOMAS, FIRST: SANDRA DAY O'CONNOR (2019).

LYNN TOLER, MY MOTHER'S RULES: A PRACTICAL GUIDE TO BECOMING AN EMOTIONAL GENIUS (2007).

MARY WALTON, A WOMAN'S CRUSADE: ALICE PAUL AND THE BATTLE FOR THE BALLOT (2010).

EVELYN WILLIAMS, INADMISSIBLE EVIDENCE: THE STORY OF THE AFRICAN-AMERICAN TRIAL LAWYER WHO DEFENDED THE BLACK LIBERATION ARMY (2000).

MALALA YOUSAFZAI, I AM MALALA: HOW ONE GIRL STOOD UP FOR EDUCATION AND CHANGED THE WORLD (2015).